GOOD COPS, BAD VERDICT

How Racial Politics Convicted Us of Murder

LARRY NEVERS

Published by LAN Publications

www.goodcopsbadverdict.com

Cover and internal graphic design by Tressa Foster

Cover photography by Alan Halstead and Richard Margittay

ISBN 978-1-4243-1878-0

Printed in the United States of America
10 9 8 7 6 5 4 3

For Nancy, my rock. And for Kelly, my heart and pride.
Both of you are the reason I made it through.

To
Yvonne

Thank you for
your support,

Harry Nevers

1

'NOT GUILTY, YOUR HONOR'

After leaving prison for the third and final time, I started having coffee every month or so with a group of active and retired police officers. Nothing formal, no agenda, just a few guys getting together at a diner. We order breakfast or lunch, tell war stories, talk sports and politics, and inquire about the health or lack of it among cops we've lost track of. In other words it's your typical coffee talk adjusted for profession. My companions would never be recognized on the street except by their friends, family and the people they've arrested. If I could say the same, I'd be just one of the boys.

My role at these sessions seems to be as the cop everybody else can point at and say: "There but for the grace of God, go I." I hear that a lot. I'm also told that what happened to me caused a lot of the heavy lifting to stop getting done out on the street. Not for lack of courage, or out of laziness, but because my case showed how a police officer can get an express ticket to prison for doing his job. I hear this not just from my coffee buddies, but first- and second-hand from police officers around the country. Better to avoid what I always regarded as real police work, I hear them say, because there's no telling when a situation will go bad and leave you vulnerable not just to some perp but to politicians and prosecutors.

Police brass and professors refer to my old plainclothes job as "proactive street patrol." That means making felony arrests not by waiting for a radio run, but by going out and introducing yourself to crimes in progress. "Good evening, you're committing a felony and you're under arrest." That often puts you in a tough spot. But I loved the job description. I took pride in serving and protecting and producing results. That was my motive for staying out on the street so long. My supervisors kept me out there because I stayed clean for two and a half decades and because even after all those years I was still the top "junkyard dog" in Detroit's Third Precinct. Some would say maybe I was tops in the entire city. You won't find "junkyard dog" in the Police Manual, but I'm proud a couple of my bosses used that term to describe me and various partners over the years. All it meant was that we were tenacious professionals who never milked one minute off the clock. We worked hard and got the job done.

At one of these monthly coffee sessions, a retired officer looked across the table and said: "Larry, whether you like it or not you're gonna die famous, for all the wrong reasons." That's something else I've heard more than once. Nobody has to tell me. The "famous" part is just a pain in the posterior. The "wrong reasons" part is a pain in the heart, the soul, the mind, the spirit – every important place it's possible to feel pain. I wasn't a brutal cop or a killer cop. I was a good cop. I wasn't a storm trooper in any White Occupation Army. I was an equal opportunity arrester. If you were dirty, I took you in whether you were black or white.

Working the street I was sworn at, spat on, punched and kicked more times than the number of cop movies you've seen. Knives and guns were pulled on me. I once found myself staring pointblank at the barrel of my own gun, aimed at my gut. I made more than 5,000 *felony* arrests. You'd need to rent a large hall to hold a party for all the police chiefs who never made a fifth as many felony arrests. Counting the villages and quiet suburbs where most Americans live, it's safe to say that the entire active force of your average police department never made 5,000 felony arrests in twenty-four years. How

many times did I interact directly with citizens in other ways
– making a misdemeanor arrest, interviewing street people
and witnesses, pulling over clean cars with dirty license plates
or dirty cars with clean license plates? Who knows? Maybe
50,000 times? More likely 100,000 times.

The point of those numbers is this: Nobody, unless they've
just been mugged, likes to interact with a police officer. Few
citizens I interacted with in the Third Precinct were church
deacons. Many would be hostile to Jesus Christ if he showed
up wearing a badge. Meanwhile, all it takes to initiate a citizen
complaint is to pick up the telephone. A citizen can formally
complain about anything from foul language to physical
harm. A suburbanite who thinks street cops should talk like
bank tellers can file a complaint of verbal abuse. A complaint
against your partner sometimes counts as a complaint against
you. Multiple complaints can be filed in the same incident.
Despite all that, only a handful of citizen complaints were
ever lodged against me. They were investigated. Not one was
upheld. That ought to tell you something. Anybody reading
this book just to find ways of shooting down my story probably
ought to start with that – my record. I was one of the most
decorated, hardest-working, most productive police officers
in what by some yardsticks is the most dangerous American
city. I've got nothing to hide. So be my guest. Dig away. What
you'll find is a police officer doing real police work.

What happened on Warren Avenue the night of November
5, 1992, was a nickel-and-dime arrest that went bad because
of crack cocaine. Top to bottom. No crack cocaine on the
street, and Malice Green would not have pulled up in front
of that dope house. No crack rocks clutched in his hand as
if they were diamonds, and I would not have been making
a felony arrest. No cocaine and alcohol in his system, and
he would not have resisted arrest the way he did – kicking,
putting his hand on my gun, swinging at me with something
metallic (turned out to be car keys) in his fist, and...most of
all...refusing arrest with such fanatic stubbornness that in my

exhaustion I began to wonder what the real deal was with this guy. No cocaine, and it would not have taken – even after I hit Malice Green on the head with my flashlight – at least three other cops arriving at the scene to subdue and handcuff him. No cocaine in his bloodstream, and he would not have died en route to a hospital. No cocaine, and the last felony subject I arrested would not have become the first to die in custody.

The kind of police officer I was, and cocaine's role in Malice Green's death, got swept away in a flood of racial hysteria. If hearing this white cop call it "racial hysteria" raises a red flag for you, don't go away mad. Hang around. Learn a few things about what happened in the hours and days and weeks after Malice Green's death. The hysteria began before dawn the next morning. It poured into the investigation – making me and my partner, Walter Budzyn, the only police officers in anyone's memory to walk the plank without a department board of review to determine whether we were making a proper arrest and had followed proper procedure in escalating the use of force. The hysteria poured through City Hall, where the honorable Coleman A. Young – Detroit's first black mayor – led the lynch mob. It poured into the media, where rumor – especially riot rumor – became news. It poured into the courtroom, where racial hysteria became a murder verdict. Then the hysteria became old news. Then it became history, where it's recorded not as hysteria but as righteous justice – except among those who somehow believe Walter and I got off easy. Anybody who can't see something wrong with that picture is, in my opinion, blind.

I was disgraced and portrayed around the world as a racist killer cop who almost caused my hometown to burn down. I was sent to prison three separate times. My family endured hardship and pain. If I seem too angry and bitter to fit what you know about the Malice Green case...well, please cut me a little slack and listen to my story. Not just on my behalf, but on behalf of every good and honest police officer who ever wore a badge. This all happened in Detroit, a place unlike any other place on Earth; but the truth of this story is important everywhere. It's time for a reality check on the arrest and death of Malice Green, and on how the criminal justice system responded to it.

A few things I am going to tell you can be known as fact only by me. I can't help that. Such things you will either believe, or not. But the overwhelming majority of things I am going to tell you can be checked out and verified – some by a little reporting, some by common sense, most just by looking at the public record. In the end your arithmetic will be simple. You will add up those things I tell you that are knowable, verifiable, provable – or are common-sense conclusions based on what anybody can know. Then you will stack all that up beside those few things I tell you that are knowable only by me. And then you will come up with your decision as a juror in the court of public opinion. The indisputable things I tell you will, all by themselves, defy every sound-bite version of the Malice Green incident and of what happened afterward.

Sometimes when I try to talk about this, the story gets lost because there are a thousand pieces to the puzzle. I keep wanting to spit them all out at once, or follow just one of them all the way down to the bottom line. Take, for instance, my insistence on calling the sound-bite version "racial hysteria." What else would you call it when a former state Supreme Court justice – a man who normally doesn't say anything about last night's ballgame without carefully choosing each word – stands in front of TV cameras and says "I understand bone fragments were found on Warren Avenue"? That's the kind of thing potential jurors – and potential rioters – were hearing in the hours after we arrested Malice Green. The fact is, Malice Green suffered not one fracture, let alone leaving body parts on the street. Any "bone chips" gathered up from Green's car turned out, after lab analysis, to be crack cocaine. In court, of course, prosecutors didn't try to say cocaine rocks were bone chips – they tried to imply that my partner and I planted the cocaine. But, of course, they couldn't imply we planted the cocaine found in Green's bloodstream. So first the prosecutors tried to ignore the cocaine evidence, against competent medical advice to the contrary. Then they went shopping to find a paid expert witness who would testify the cocaine didn't mean anything. "Justice" wasn't blind; it had tunnel vision.

In court as well as in the news media, puzzle pieces that didn't fit that scenario of racist cops run amok got scattered in the wind. The puzzle pieces broadcast day after day after day were carefully selected to paint a picture of brutal white cops beating a black citizen to death for no reason. Wrong picture. Bad puzzle-solving. Walter and I got railroaded not for what happened on Warren Avenue, but for every real and imagined white-cop misdeed in the last one hundred years. I give Walter credit for understanding this almost from the get-go. I didn't. I expected, right up to the jury verdict, that somehow sanity would prevail, that someone would step in and set the record straight. I admit my hopes had shrunk considerably as it came time for a verdict to be read. But I knew in my heart I was just doing my job the night Malice Green died. I also had full faith in the criminal justice system I served. And right there is one of the many ways I've changed since 1992.

Let me tell you right up front what might be the hardest thing for most of you to believe. It's a wish I have thought about many times. In the end, you will either believe this is my wish, or you won't. I want you to think about this all the way through to the last page. I want you to test it against everything you come to know about me and about my job and about what happened. And here is my wish: That the Detroit Police Department, which failed to provide my partner and me with a whole lot of things...I wish more than anything that the department had provided us with a dashboard video camera.

A videotape from Warren Avenue wouldn't be pretty. I never said anything about this was pretty. It was an arrest that fell apart when a guy who should have submitted – who was required by law to submit, just as I was required by law to make him submit – instead dug in his heels like no one I had ever arrested. Circumstances led me to do something I had never done during a very long career of doing real police work. Anyone who has crashed his head into his car's windshield, or seen a pool-hall fight, or been to a few boxing matches knows about blood vessels on the skull, and how much blood they will release as a result of trauma. So, yes, this imaginary videotape would be bloody. But you would also see how and why this arrest escalated to that point. You would see a felony suspect refusing to hand over evidence, then resisting arrest stubbornly – for a very long time, as arrests go. Resisting first with Walter Budzyn. Then with me. Then with other cops who arrived on the scene and struggled to handcuff him. And before the arriving cops pulled him away from me, you would see how I used my flashlight – and you would understand why there were no fractures, and no bone fragments on Warren Avenue. I am a big guy. A Mag light weighs two pounds. If I had been swinging that flashlight as you have been told, the number of times you have been told, Malice Green's skull would have been crushed like a pumpkin in the road. It didn't happen that way.

That much of my imaginary videotape can be reconstructed from the evidence. One thing that cannot be reconstructed from the evidence, because only I can know it, is that you would also see – after a couple minutes of bizarre struggle – Malice Green put his hand on the butt of my undrawn gun. And you would see that was the instant I used my flashlight on his head – the small end of it, forearm only, holding it by the bulb end. An EMS driver who arrived toward the end of our struggle testified that I hit Green with a blow like "a flick of the wrist." He was right.

Not pretty. But it is my strongest wish that this arrest had been captured on tape – a big-time irony when you consider the best-known of all videotaped arrests. In fact, if the Rodney King arrest had not been videotaped, you would never have heard of Malice Green and me. The Los Angeles riot was recent history in November 1992. That's why the instant buzz was "white cop plus Malice Green equals Detroit riot." Less than twenty-four hours after Malice Green died, and with no real idea of what happened on the street, Police Chief Stanley Knox suspended me and six other officers, summoned TV cameras and declared: "This is not Simi Valley. We will convict." How's that for due process? Two days later, NBC aired an interview in which Mayor Young declared that Walter and I were "murderers." Long before the investigation, such as it was, was completed and we were charged, every Detroit resident had "No justice, no peace" ringing in his ears for weeks.

While my partner and I attended a hearing to determine whether we should be sent to trial on the charges brought against us, my lawyer was summoned to police headquarters and handed a piece of paper. It said I had been fired "for committing second degree murder." That same day, the city announced it was writing a $5.1-million check to Malice Green's family – probably the biggest, quickest settlement of a civil suit against any government anywhere at any time. The chief judge of Detroit's criminal court, once named by Reader's Digest as one of America's five worst judges, declared there would be no change of venue – a nice touch considering I had not yet asked for one, or stated the reasons for deserving one…as if those reasons needed stating. At trial, the court gave jurors the Rodney King videotape – as featured in the movie *Malcolm X* – to watch in their spare time. That shows how much I believed in the criminal justice system. As stacked as the deck was, I still thought we could get a just verdict. And that's why, having learned otherwise, a cop who used a flashlight to subdue an arrest subject decided one day, in a prison cell, that he wished it all had been captured on camera.

Videotaped use of force, even when justified by

circumstances and police department General Orders, can be misinterpreted. But sitting in that prison cell, I was no longer naïve. Our trial wasn't about truth-seeking. Calming down the racial hysteria – much of it created by the same people who pressed the case against us – was the object of our trial. Unpretty as a real videotape would be, it would erase the scenario scripted by prosecutors. How creative could the prosecutors get? I did not, for example, see Walter Budzyn strike Malice Green on the head even once with his flashlight. I don't believe he did. I don't see how he could have. But by the time of Walter's second trial, when he was tried separately, the prosecution's script had Walter savagely beating his "victim." Meanwhile, at my own second trial somehow I became the one delivering all the blows. How far from the truth will a prosecutor wander to get a conviction? Unfortunately, my dashboard videotape doesn't exist any more than a prosecution videotape exists. But keep my wish in mind as I tell you what you would see. Keep focusing on the knowable, and on common sense. And make your own videotape.

These things happened more than a decade ago, but they'll never go away. Malice Green won't come back to life, and my life – and my family's lives – will never be the same. How can I not be angry and bitter? This gets in the way of something judges and juries and Court TV audiences and editorial writers always want to see in a convicted defendant – remorse. I will go to my grave believing I committed no crime while making my final felony arrest. So what was I supposed to say when the system found me guilty of major crimes? Truth is, courts and TV watchers and editorial writers didn't want to hear me express remorse. They wanted to hear me say, "I'm guilty." First, guilty of murder – then, after a federal judge threw out that kangaroo verdict and I was tried all over again, guilty of manslaughter. Was I supposed to lie and say I think I'm guilty? Sorry, no. I feel mountains of remorse, in numerous ways. That's different than believing I am a criminal, and that's what the system demanded to hear from me. One minute you're innocent until proven guilty – or at least supposed to be innocent until proven guilty. The next minute the prosecution wins a game played with a stacked deck. No, I don't feel guilt. I feel remorse. I meant it when I said: "Not guilty, Your Honor." I always will.

But remorse – this thing the system and most media people and many citizens thought they didn't see me show enough of? Let me count some of the ways I have always felt – and always will feel – remorse.

Malice Green was a nickel-and-dime drug user. People don't deserve to die for being nickel-and-dime drug users. Most drug users do die before their time. Their hearts stop working, or they overdose. Or – like a user who was riding in Malice Green's car that night – their drug associations lead them to die violently at the hands of another user or a seller or someone they are trying to rob of money to buy drugs. That's the normal course of events. After spending so many years trying to take guns and drugs off the streets, like bailing a sewer with a teaspoon, how could I *not* feel remorse over what crack cocaine did to the city where I grew up and lived? I even feel – not remorse, but what…sadness? – for every sorry junkie, assuming he hasn't yet worked his way up from selling his own possessions to selling his family's possessions to stealing and selling someone else's possessions, and worse.

I feel tremendous, haunting, genuine remorse that Malice Green died. I have no idea how many confrontations I had on the street that could have resulted in a dead citizen and a near-instantaneous ruling that fatal force was justified. A hundred, maybe. But such incidents didn't happen. People didn't die on my shift. Just two nights before Malice Green died, and only a couple blocks down the street, a white police officer confronted a black citizen in maybe the ultimate situation where a "racist rogue cop" would have killed a black man, and gotten away with it. But the black citizen was brought in without incident and without a scratch because it wasn't a racist rogue cop on the scene; it was me. And I was that same person two nights later when I confronted Malice Green. I feel remorse but not guilt about what happened during that confrontation because I believe my actions were justified. I know any number of good cops would have escalated force the same way I did. Besides, Malice Green would not have died if he wasn't doing cocaine. And still, I desperately wish it turned out differently. So as you read my story, understand in every paragraph that I do feel remorse.

An "arrest that went bad" is self-explanatory. If somebody dies, it went bad. That would be true if I shot someone dead as they aimed a gun at me and started squeezing the trigger. In cop talk, that would be a "good shooting." But it would still be an arrest that went bad. I think you understand that. Would Malice Green's arrest not go bad if I had it to do all over again? Well, if it happened twenty times at 10:30 p.m. November 5, 1992, I would do the same thing every time. If it happened all over again tonight, I would do all kinds of things differently. I would have some training in alternative self-defense and arrest techniques, instead of just being sent on the street – as I was all those years – with a gun and a flashlight and instructions to bring in the bad guys. I would have some pepper spray on my belt – something suburban departments had in 1992 but Detroit did not, despite Coleman Young's great skills in extracting money from Washington. Those things would help, but in all due respect I must say it would help a lot more if Malice Green himself had done things differently. I feel tremendous remorse that I didn't have that training or that pepper spray, and that I had never confronted such a sustained cocaine frenzy. I feel tremendous remorse that almost twenty-five years of good arrests didn't show me a way to make this arrest end well, and that Malice Green's drug habit led him to do what he did. I feel tremendous remorse that he is dead and that I am in a kind of living hell. But I don't feel guilty.

In August 2002, I took a ride around the Third Precinct on a Sunday morning. Clear skies, almost 80 degrees, quiet, laid-back, a few churchgoers and porch-sitters. That's not the way I used to see it from an unmarked patrol car. In winter, it would already be dark when our power shift began at supper time, and still dark the next morning when my partner and I rolled back onto the ramp at the precinct. This Sunday-morning tour was like an old man looking at the back of his own hand for the first time in ten years.

Every corner turned was a return to an old arrest or two. There's a lot of desolation and razor wire in the Third Precinct. Some of my old war stories involve isolated fast-food joints or beer stores that were the lone commercial signs of life in the worst sections. Now, even several of those are boarded up. I stopped and stared at the boards covering a side door to a shell of a building that was once a hamburger joint where I played an almost comical cat-and-mouse game with a masked armed robber who had locked employees in the back room.

I also stopped and stared at the towering railroad depot that once was one of Detroit's most imposing buildings. My father and his generation went off to war from there, and in its time this was the bustling equivalent of Metro Airport. Like a train chugging down to a halt, it had gradually – like so much of Detroit – become half-empty, then empty, then lifeless and crumbling. At first some investor floated dreams of salvaging it. My partners and I worked private security there off-duty for a while helping to keep the homeless and the junkies from stripping the huge public hall and the office tower that rose above it. The investor's dreams died along with his bankroll. Now, on this Sunday morning, I could look straight through every one of the hundreds of windows and into the sky out the other side, the view unobstructed by a single pane of glass. Way up toward the top somebody – sober, I hope but doubt – had managed to crawl out on a ledge and paint his name. Like thousands of Detroit buildings, and probably the biggest of all, the train depot looked to have no future except to be torn down when somebody gets around to it. As I toured the old precinct there had been talk of pumping government money in and remodeling the hulking depot into a new police headquarters. I'll believe it when I see it.

Here was the parking lot where two guys knocked me down and tried to rob and cut me. There was the sidewalk where a car thief tried to run me over in a stolen pickup truck. Here was another sidewalk where Walter Budzyn, chasing a car thief on foot, turned a corner and saw the perp standing, out of breath, as was Walter. In a comic but effective piece of quick thinking, Walter shouted: "Which way did he go?" Instead of running, the guy froze and pointed on down the street...allowing Walter to run up and handcuff him. It really happened that way.

On Porter Street, not far from abandoned Tiger Stadium, I stopped and surveyed what I call, to this day, "My Tree." It in fact became famous among Third Precinct street cops and their supervisors, and even among some officers in other precincts, as Larry Nevers's Tree. It didn't look special, just one of several that stand between curb and sidewalk along a block of industrial and commercial buildings. I don't even know what kind of tree it is. It's not very high – fifteen or twenty feet. The trunk slants out a bit from its base, allowing for an easy climb, and in the warm season it grows a full canopy of leaves. When the Tigers were playing at home, thousands of baseball fans would spread out into these old neighborhoods looking for a place to park the finest objects of a car thief's desire. Some of them, drinking too much beer, would urinate directly beneath me, unaware I was perched right above them in My Tree. Often enough, it was the car thieves themselves who stopped to pee while I waited for them to get deep enough into their felony for me and my partners to make a good arrest.

The instincts or intuition or whatever you want to call it that make a good street cop are partly born into you and partly learned on the job. I can't exactly sum it up, but it's a whole bunch of sixth senses. You get so you know almost in an instant that you are looking at a hot car, for example. And I was the champ at pulling our car up near a group of street people and telling my partner: "Get ready to chase the guy in the blue jacket! He's going to run!" They always ran. Well, almost always. One piece of it, of course, is knowing the territory. And here I am on a Sunday morning, ten years removed from this work, and I glance down a side street and see a guy making his way up onto a railroad grade. I can tell you he was going up there to get a better angle for hopping over the razor wire surrounding a nearby junkyard. And that once in there he would come back out with a battery, or some car part, that he could sell for a bottle or wine or a few rocks of crack. I guarantee it.

And so it went for much of this melancholy Sunday tour. You might not think it's possible to be melancholy about chasing car thieves and breaking up armed robberies and the like. It is possible. I loved my job and I miss it. If none of this had happened, I would still be long retired by now. And I would still miss it.

There was, of course, nothing melancholy about driving down a small side street, Twenty-Third, making a right turn onto Warren Avenue, and being instantly at the dope house just as I was that night ten years earlier. Nothing melancholy about looking at the mural painted on the dope house as a shrine to Malice Green, alleged victim of the White Occupation Army. The mural still covers the front wall and includes pictures of the two alleged terrorists, Nevers and Budzyn, "Starsky and Hutch." I'm not sure I can describe what I felt like as I looked at this place again. Definitely a crystal-clear, split-second flash of all the things I've told you so far, and more. Not just the anger and the remorse and the urge to spit out all the countless facts that I believe show I deserve vindication. Maybe a sense that this dope house and those circumstances and the racial politics of Detroit spelled inevitable doom for both a perp and a police officer.

I never expected to be famous. I was within a few months of retiring anonymously. There would have been a dinner, and some brass – maybe some of the same brass that began pursuing me the morning of November 6, 1992 – would sing my praises. Why not? I had enough citations and decorations and good cases to fill three or four careers. I had worked plainclothes in the Third for the last sixteen years, all that while in Coleman Young's police department. He had taken office demanding that guns and drugs be taken off the streets. That's what I did. In retrospect, that effort seems to have been futile, but I did it. So I was startled to discover that Coleman Young and the black power structure and the editorial writers couldn't believe somebody like me was still on the streets the night Malice Green died. What? Except for the color of my skin, I was Coleman Young's dream – somebody willing to wade in and do real police work in a city that couldn't get enough of it. After my gun and badge were taken away, I learned that a substantial number of the city's black citizens appreciated my work, and even understood – as much as anyone who wasn't there can understand – what happened on Warren Avenue. You didn't hear much from them publicly in my support. But then it took a while before you heard much public support from anybody. Lots of private support. Very little in public. It's as if the rogue racist white cop to end all famous rogue racist white cops was a role written especially for my dour Armenian face, and no one dared interrupt the movie.

Toward the end of my time in prison, I met a black guy who was an ex-Detroit police officer. He said he became a cop because of me, that I represented everything that was wrong with white cops, and that he felt he had to join the force to help set things straight. We met because, while off duty at a party, he shot a man to death. We wound up in the same prison. Of all the times I've confronted my lost anonymity, hearing that ex-cop's story might be the most startling. It's pretty much a daily thing in one way or another. I was sitting in a hotel lobby when a meeting broke up in a conference room across the hall. People flooded out and – as usually happens in a crowd – many stared at me, some in recognition and some trying to remember who they were recognizing. A few came over to ask politely where they knew me from. I was in a good mood and for a one-sentence answer told them I was a famous felon. The crowd turned out to be a judges' convention. What am I supposed to do? Ten thousand times start spitting out all the amazing true facts and say, "Look, I know you think you know who I am and what I did and what that means…but you're wrong…you don't understand at all." I don't think so. And then, of course, there is the very large number of black citizens who really believe the Malice Green incident was about rogue racist cops and who feel nothing but deep hatred when they see my face. I have no idea what to say to them. Well, actually, I do. It's this book. I hope some of you are reading it.

I never drank alcohol. I've always hated the taste. I quit smoking long before I got emphysema, and then lung cancer. I've kept one vice. I like to play blackjack, and maybe a little video poker. When my melancholy Sunday morning tour of the Third was finished, I spent an hour thinking about it in one of Detroit's downtown casinos. I had never set foot in one before, because my anonymity has been lost even when I'm a long ways away from Detroit. In the city, in a casino, I couldn't imagine how bad it might be. As it turned out, it wasn't bad. Maybe at mid-day Sunday, everybody was hung over and staring at their chips. As I was leaving, I got lost trying to find where to pick up my vehicle. The casino's greeter, a black man maybe thirty years old, didn't just point the way. He took me back up the escalator, through a game room, and into the parking structure. I thought maybe he was one of the many black citizens who understood and didn't buy into the sound bites. But on the way toward my car, he said: "I've seen a LOT of your movies. I can't wait to get home and tell my wife about this." I managed to negotiate this weird situation without telling him I was neither a movie star nor a soldier in a White Occupation Army. I mused about this. Mostly it made me wonder if the right course is to live out quietly whatever time I've got left, shut my mouth, let my family drift as far as possible back into anonymity, and hope people will wonder less and less often where they recognize me from.

But no, I don't think so. Neither does my family. I need to tell my story and get it out there. For me. And for all good, hard-working police officers.

2
INTO UNIFORM, AND
INTO PLAINCLOTHES

The last sixteen years of my police career I drove a booster car in the Third Precinct. You need to know what a booster car is, how I came to have that job, and how I did it. If you understand those things, you will understand the Malice Green case in ways a thousand sound bites could never tell you.

I joined the police department almost by accident, and the first couple of years were pretty dull stuff. But it didn't take me long to see where the real police work got done, and to seek out that assignment. When I finally got that job, I made it my life. Whenever someone asks what my assignment was, I give the same answer: "To make good felony arrests." That always struck me as the essence of police work. Somebody needs to write speeding tickets, and somebody needs to shuffle papers. You absolutely need uniformed patrolmen because somebody needs to answer radio runs, whether the complaining citizen's plight is real or imagined, major or – most often – minor...and because somebody needs to show the flag of law and order. But when it comes to making good felony arrests, and at the end of almost every shift feeling like you are making a difference, there is nothing like wearing plainclothes in an unmarked booster car.

The average citizen thinks of police officers as being either of two types he sees in movies and TV shows – uniformed patrolmen or homicide detectives. Or maybe a guy on a motorcycle with aviator sunglasses and a ticket pad. Some people would add narcotics officers and maybe the vice squad to the list. Narcotics and vice and homicide all work in plainclothes. Homicide detectives' cars are unmarked (and don't carry all the onboard paraphernalia like sirens, oscillating lights, or sometimes even radios). Narcotics vehicles also are unmarked, but most often they are confiscated property – from rusty pickups to luxury cars. Homicide, narcotics and vice all have specialties when it comes to arresting felons. It's a very strict division of labor. Not so for the plainclothes patrolmen working unmarked booster cars out of a precinct station. They prowl their streets all night every night, bringing in every kind of felon known to man and the state criminal code. They're not specialists. They're street cops.

Unmarked patrol cars are mostly free from slavery to routine radio runs. They monitor hotspots and investigate suspicious activity. A really good plainclothes cop comes in early, makes himself familiar with every felony committed in the precinct since his last shift, then hits the street armed with good knowledge of which bad guys are newly at large and in demand. Previous experience, methodical note-taking, and contacts on the street give a good plainclothes officer an idea of where to find his prey. Even on a slow night there is always that long hotsheet of stolen cars hanging from the dashboard. In for a dime, in for a dollar. Find a guy with a hot car, and you might well find a guy with an illegal gun. Find a guy with an illegal gun, and you might well find a guy who is pushing drugs. Find a guy with a hot car and an illegal gun who is pushing drugs and you might have exposed just the tip of his iceberg. And so the nightly hunt goes. To a professional plainclothes officer, catching felons in the act – before their crimes land on an incident report, and before they victimize another citizen – puts the "good" in "good felony arrest." Making the arrest by the book and sending the prosecutor a case that will stick goes without saying.

Every major city makes use of plainclothes patrolmen in unmarked cars. Most cities come up with a unique local name for such units. Generations ago in Detroit, car thieves were called "car boosters." Catching car thieves in the act, or recovering hot cars before they become scrap metal, is a routine part of a plainclothes officer's job – which is how, somewhere along the line, two plainclothes street cops in an unmarked car became known, in the Detroit department, as a "booster car." New York State Police call them "funny cars." The L.A. County Sheriff's Department calls them "ghost cars" or "slick cars." In Houston, they're "cool cars." In some locales they are "trouble cars." New York City calls its plainclothes cops the Street Crime Unit. Not real creative, but it does say precisely what booster cars are about.

Did that make me an "undercover" cop? No. In fact, describing unmarked cars and plainclothes patrolmen as working "undercover" is humorous if you stop to think about it. Yes, plainclothes street cops do a considerable amount of surveillance. A booster car bears no exterior signs that it is anything but a stripped-down four-door sedan, except for the blue flashers discreetly mounted in the grille. But successful surveillance comes from skill, not disguise. If a stripped, full-sized four-door sedan doesn't have a "TAXI" sign on the roof, it might as well have one saying "POLICE." A white guy driving such a car in a poor black neighborhood at midnight...well, you can call that undercover if you want. My partners and I must have put more than 50,000 miles on one '85 Plymouth, all inside a precinct of just over seven square miles. Then one fine day the department handed us a brand-new Chevy. Within two or three days, we'd be cruising past a corner and little kids would wave and shout: "Hi, PO-lice!" As for attire, plainclothes meant *really* plain. On a typical night I'd head out wearing a sweatshirt, jeans, and gym shoes. In winter I'd wear a car coat, and maybe galoshes. When we rolled onto the streets each night, we didn't look like we were headed to the masquerade ball. We certainly didn't look like the necktied detectives you see on TV. Maybe I'm just a blue-collar sort of guy. I never could associate a suit and tie with police work.

Truth is, since the bad guys very seldom are bad guys just once, a hard-working plainclothes cop gets to know up close and personal an amazingly high percentage of his precinct's junkies, hookers, armed robbers, car thieves, murderers and their associates. Not that I wasted hours of paperwork arresting hookers, who would be back on the street before the ink was dry. But if you are talking to a hooker, you are most often talking to someone who has intimate knowledge of where a felon was just hours, or minutes, earlier. A booster cop interacting with street people and junkies is more like the opposite of undercover. Ordinary citizens might not have known me; but if you were dirty and in the Third Precinct, there was a good chance you and I were on a first-name basis. If you were recently dirty, and had not yet paid whatever price the justice system decreed, you were not likely to talk with me of your own volition – but someone else…that hooker, maybe…might talk with me about where you were. Networking is productive in any line of work.

Good booster-car work is about self-initiative, about not sitting back and letting the work come to you. Best of all, the job description lets you do that. Leave the reactive work to the uniformed guys; even the good ones seldom can find a minute to break free of the radio runs. Leave stale crimes and endless desk work to the detectives. They dress better and after a promotion or two get quoted in the newspapers, but they're not street cops. Only the plainclothes patrolman is on the street every night as a generalist. A booster cop encounters most anything illegal. He builds respect and an arrest record by his wits and experience, finding a little variety on his plate, functioning as one-half of a two-man crew that – once out of that precinct garage – is pretty much on its own.

Driving a booster car turned out to be my dream job, but I didn't dream of being any kind of a cop when I was a kid growing up on Detroit's west side. In those days the department had special units known as "The Big Four" – three plainclothes cops and a uniformed driver – that showed up if trouble was brewing on a street corner. I'd see them cruise by and I'd think something like, "Damned glad I'm not causing any trouble!" The idea of riding in such a car, wearing a badge and carrying a gun, never occurred to me. In fact, I never touched a handgun until, at age twenty-eight, I became a cop.

Nothing at the heart of this story – police work, race, politics – meant a thing to me as I was growing up on Monica Street, midway across Detroit's west side. I learned how to play sports from other kids on the street. My father and I didn't really find our good times together until after I was an adult. I delivered the evening edition of the *Detroit Free Press* in the neighborhood, picked up a part-time job at a neighborhood candy store, and then at an adjoining print shop as soon as I was old enough. Ours was a happy enough household, even if my brother and I were as different as two kids could be. I wasn't much of a student, and my brother was sharp. He wound up as a dentist. In the end, we made an odd couple of brothers – one pursuing fillings and one pursuing felons.

Our block was as close to being a melting pot as you got in the '50s. Doctors still had neighborhood offices attached to their houses in those days, and the doc who lived on our corner was, obviously, the most affluent person on the block. His son, Jack Long, was one year older than me and a friend. Our block had Protestants and Catholics, Hungarians and Germans and, in the Nevers household, Armenians. Life seemed good enough; and if that was because we didn't know any better life, that was OK by me.

There were no black residents in the neighborhood, something else I never questioned. I had black classmates at McKenzie High School. Again, for a working-class member of the Class of '58, this was not an issue. We all tended to keep within a circle of friends drawn from our neighborhoods, but there was no racial animosity, no gangs, no black power, no white backlash, no real inkling of the fires to come in the late '60s. Down the road – when it came time to let my bride indulge all our borrowing power and put us in her dream house – I had good neighbors who happened to be black. Hard as it might be for the politically correct crowd to understand, there really are a few million of us old white men who came up judging neighbors on whether they cut their grass, period. If we became cops, we judged our partners on whether they would be there in a tough situation, period. And we judged the citizens we came into contact with according to whether they were breaking the law, period. At least that's the way I came up on Monica Street and at McKenzie High.

I also came up as the shyest guy on the block. Worse than that. Maybe the shyest guy on the west side. I got along well on my paper route and then my part-time jobs. I ran with the other guys, played ball in the streets and parks, went to the movies, hung out. But in high school I never dated. I could handle a Teamster yelling at me to sell more newspapers. But girls scared me to death. My mother – who worried that I might get out of high school before going on a date – got on my case about attending the senior prom. I was too shy to ask one of my classmates. So I invited Jack Long's sister, Ethel, the doctor's daughter. I don't know if Ethel understood what a bold step it was when I kissed her on the cheek. I borrowed my cousin Dick Hovsepian's '55 Olds convertible for that prom. I must have been impressed, because a year later I bought the car. Dick later changed his name to Howe. Dick was a latecomer when it came to anglicizing his name. Neversian had become Nevers two generations before I was born.

It didn't take long after graduation to find my bride – even if I didn't know it at the time. I met Nancy on a blind date that summer of '58. She hadn't graduated yet from Our Lady of Mercy High School, and I still had an eighteen-year-old's wanderlust. But we dated off and on for several years, had our adolescent ups and downs, and made a perfect, if unlikely, couple...she was as outgoing as I was quiet, and I enjoyed letting her do most of the talking. Nancy was also very popular, so I guess I was surprised at how determined she was that I was the guy for her. She was already a good-looking kid, but she went on a diet, got herself looking like Connie Stevens, and I was hooked. We made it official on September 15, 1962, at St. Mel's Catholic Church in Dearborn Heights. We honeymooned in the Poconos. Two days later we marked Nancy's twenty-first birthday. I was twenty-two. Thirty years later, Nancy began a long and difficult role as my strongest supporter, publicly and privately, in the aftermath of what happened at Warren Avenue and Twenty-Third Street.

I had given college a try, attending classes at the old Detroit Institute of Technology for a year and a half. I'd have to say my best "course" was intramural flag football. I've always been a hard worker, and good on details. Unfortunately, when it comes to reading, I labor over it like an engineer poring over a blueprint, or an actor learning his lines. I'm a quick learner in the real world but a slow reader in the paper world. Maybe intramural football was my best subject because I could run much faster than I could read. Give me a straightforward "bible" to study painstakingly and I'd make the honor roll. A few years after my half-hearted attempt at college, for example, I could recite entire passages from the Detroit Police Manual. But give me a big stack of books and say, "Mr. Nevers, we'd like you to skim these tonight," and I'd be likely to say, "You skim milk, not books." At any rate, I was a lot more interested in the real world than the classroom. I wanted to make a living and get on with life.

That neighborhood part-time job in a print shop turned out to be a false path I followed for quite a while. It led me to operating photostat cameras for a bigger print shop, then to another job buried inside the world's largest corporation, General Motors, then to another job at an ad agency. I really, really hated the work. Shut inside the same room every day, hanging up the material to be reproduced, clicking the shutter. Not my style. I liked to get out and move around, have an opportunity to show a little initiative. I'm sure somebody thought those photostats were important, but I couldn't imagine a duller way to spend a shift. These were not the best of times, for me or for Nancy. I was big-time bored. We did the all-American thing and spent too much money, even though Nancy had a job, too. We were childless, something we never thought much about. The next thing you knew I was twenty-eight years old and realizing that if I was going to have a career – a decent job that I could go to every day for thirty years or so without feeling like I was in prison – it was time to get moving. The idea that I would find exactly such a job, work it hard and well until I was an inch from retirement, and then wind up in a real prison…well, let's say it's not a possibility that occurred to me at the time.

The ad agency I worked for offered no security, virtually no benefits and – the final straw – started giving me more hours without more pay. In a move that made all kinds of sense in every way except the wallet, I walked. So now I needed a different job not only for my soul, but also for our livelihood. I found one in an unlikely way.

Ask yourself what the Motor City's sprawling blue-collar population did for recreation in the '50s and '60s. Nowadays, everybody – including me on occasion – plays golf. But back when I was coming up, the executives had their country clubs and the rest of us had our bowling alleys. Detroit was the bowling capital of the universe. Like any working-class kid in that time and place, I started bowling young, with neighborhood kids. Good game. Probably one of the things that kept me out of trouble. Off the streets and in the alleys, so to speak. And I kept bowling into adulthood, with my father and my uncle. Bowled my way right into the police department, in fact.

My cousin Dick had put together a Thursday night league at Redford Lanes. It was late 1967, only months after Detroit had a major riot in which forty-three people died, the Army and the National Guard were called out, and the city's fortunes would be changed forever. But I was a working stiff who liked to bowl, not a sociologist. If you grow up in a city and don't know any other life, then no matter how bad times get you expect that things will be straightened out and, one way or another, the city will still be there a few years down the road, more or less as the same place you've been living all your life. Not that I thought it through that way; but it must have been the way I was thinking by spring of '68 when, after learning from two police officers on my cousin's bowling team that there were openings for recruits at the Detroit Police Academy, I got a serious idea that: "Well, maybe this is the job for me."

The two bowling cops did everything they could to talk me out of it. It's a lousy job, they said. But most everybody bitches about their job, and people get into jobs they aren't suited for, and maybe I thought these were two guys bitching about a job they didn't like but a job that would be good for me. The pay wasn't spectacular, but job security would be first-rate. There'd be benefits. I wouldn't be locked up in a room all day with a photostat camera. And though I had never in my life dreamed about going out and bringing in the bad guys, that seemed like something important and worth doing.

On August 5, 1968, I began twelve weeks of training at the police academy, then located in Palmer Park in northern Detroit. We went on salary as soon as we started class, so even though I was just a student, I felt I truly was into my new job – the first paycheck I ever drew that wasn't somehow connected to my teenaged part-time jobs in the neighborhood. Events around me – assassinations, Vietnam, LBJ driven from office because of the war – might have been Earth-shaking; but I was focused and excited about finding a place in life. The local newspapers had been on strike for months, the Tigers were running away with the American League championship, and one year after the riot the old town was caught up in pennant fever. Things looked pretty good if you weren't looking very far.

Academy training was predictable. We studied the Detroit Police Manual inside and out. It told us everything from how to shine our shoes to how we were obligated to act in making an arrest – beginning with verbal orders and escalating on up to fatal force if necessary. For once, I was a good student.

The manual was clear, a bible amounting to a blueprint for my new career. We learned how to fire a revolver with some proficiency, and how to handcuff a suspect. We learned some basics of criminal law. We did a lot of calisthenics, and we ran. I had begun, even at twenty-eight, to get soft. The physical training was welcome, and I felt good about it. One day we had, as I recall, a half-hour demonstration of judo. That half-hour would be the only in-service "training" I ever received in non-lethal self-defense.

Forty of us were still around at graduation, all male, twenty-seven whites and thirteen blacks. At the ceremony, when I was selected to read the Code of Ethics to my fellow graduates and their families, I knew I was greener than the wooden seats at Tiger Stadium, and that the real learning lay ahead. But when they handed me a badge with the number 2034 on it, somehow I knew I finally had a job that would be a keeper, and that somewhere in the department I would find a place to excel. Good thing I felt that promise, because the beginnings of my new career were as unpromising as it gets.

I was assigned to the Fourth Precinct, dominated by an industrial strip downstream along the Detroit River, which forms the border with Canada. It was a sleepy precinct. I found myself walking a beat in Del Ray, an old Hungarian neighborhood struggling to stay alive in the shadow of steel-mill smokestacks on one side and the Fisher Body Fleetwood plant on the other. This went on into the dead of winter. I checked doors and encountered no one else dumb enough to be out for a stroll in sub-freezing weather. I never did figure out the wisdom of using police resources that way. I knew my assignment was temporary, so I didn't get discouraged and I looked forward to when I would be assigned to a car. This "temporary" assignment lasted most of a year, though, and if you had asked me what I learned about police work walking that beat, the only honest answer would have been: "Not much."

When they finally put me in a car, it was the afternoon shift,

4 p.m. to midnight, catching a ride in whatever car needed a body. The afternoon shift was the busiest, but the Fourth was relatively quiet even at night; and I was generally treated as excess baggage by "partners" I seldom saw two nights in a row. Not a whole lot of learning going on there, either. The path to real police work seemed to lie in getting assigned to a permanent crew, being rotated with the same guys from afternoons to midnights to days, and settling in with an experienced partner.

When a permanent assignment came, I found myself on midnights with an independent-minded, union-conscious bunch known throughout the city as "F Troop." I was still a rookie, and still self-conscious about the uniform and the way it called attention to me even in simple acts like entering a coffee shop. But I kept my uniform just right, shoes and leather belt shined to a gleam. On my first midnight roll call, a veteran member of F Troop came over, stepped on my shoes, scuffed them up, and said: "Now you look better." Can't say I appreciated that, but in truth I had a lot more respect for what the uniform stood for than I did for wearing it like a Marine in dress blues. In any case, about fifteen minutes into my F Troop experience I could tell I was a long way removed from the academy. My probation year wasn't up yet, so I wouldn't have said anything even if I had thought of something to say.

On that first night, I was paired in a scout car with a patrolman named Gary. Almost immediately out of the garage, he headed off to the waterfront, upriver from the heavy industry, and into an area lined with warehouses. Silently, I wondered what kind of felons we might encounter on my first ride in this somewhat unusual unit, and the first shift where I'd start at midnight and still be on the job at sunrise...a sight I'd see countless times in the next two decades. At twenty-eight I was older than most rookies, but I was excited. Real police work was by now just around the corner, I was sure.

What was around the corner turned out to be the Free Press

warehouse, a big building where the newspaper I delivered as a boy took in tons and tons of newsprint rolls to feed its hungry presses. Gary turned in alongside the building and toward the river. I figured it had to be burglars. Gary must have known something about break-ins here, and we were going to try catching them in the act! He drove within a few feet of the river, and parked our marked car in an area that was open but not visible from the street. He got out, still not saying a word. I looked around trying to size up our vantage point. Great view of a wall, some freight doors, and absolutely no sign of life. What do I do? Get out and follow? I stayed put.

Gary went around to the trunk, opened it, retrieved something, and climbed into the backseat. He had a blanket and a pillow. "Wake me up if we get a run," he said. Within a few minutes he was snoring. The sounds of F Troop. So much for getting on with the business of learning real police work.

I sat looking south into Canada and the lights of Windsor. Not what I had in mind. Almost immediately, another scout car pulled beside us, and then another. A little landslide off the riverbank would have done more damage to F Troop than Sitting Bull did to Custer's army.

The lack of activity from the other cars indicated no sergeant had come here to roust slacker patrolmen. For an hour, I sat and counted lights across the calm water. Thankfully, the radio finally barked a run. "Four-eight, make Springwells and Jefferson – an alarm ringing in the area."

I grabbed the mike and said: "Four-eight on the way." I turned and said to Gary in the back seat: "We've got a run, get up!" No response but the sound of F Troop. This time I yelled. Still no response. I heard a car door slam, and saw the dim outline of another patrolman beside a rear door of our scout car. It was too dark for me to see his face.

"BLAAM!" A muzzle flash illuminated the shotgun that had just been fired two feet from Gary's ear and into the water. He jumped up so fast his head hit the roof.

"We got a run," I told him. I kept all the laughter inside,

which – rookie or not – wasn't easy.

Gary cursed something about making paybacks, got behind the wheel, and we answered my first radio run with F Troop. Like most radio runs, it turned out to be nothing.

I spent several riverfront nights with other cops who drank beer and shot rats with .30-caliber rifles and 12-gauge shotguns. No beer for me. Except for a rare strawberry daiquiri at a wedding or such, I never drank and still don't. I don't like the bitter taste, an inbred trait I've always been grateful for. Wish I could say the same for cigarettes.

I kept my mouth shut about the malingering and became an accepted member of F Troop. The least professional cops on the shift had no idea that I was keeping my eye on a couple guys who played it straight, aiming to get assigned as a fill-in with them when their regular partners were off.

F Troop formed a league of a half-dozen four-man teams at the Oakwood Blue Jackets, a bowling alley in the precinct. Shifts changed once a month, and so did bowling time. Coming off midnights, we'd bowl at 9 a.m. When the F Troop league bowled at 12:30 a.m. following an afternoon shift, it conflicted with my old league where I still bowled with my father and uncle. One night the family team ran late, so I didn't make it over to the Blue Jackets. Two of the younger F Troop members – one of them from my bowling team – got pretty juiced, I was told, and went girl-hunting around 3 a.m. When they tried to awaken two young women who lived in an upper apartment just a few blocks from the precinct station, they were greeted with semiautomatic rifle fire. They died at the scene. As far as I know, no one was ever charged.

Looking back on my early days as a cop, it's amazing I never lost my focus and my belief that the department would one day put me in a real police job. Watching other officers catch sack time in a scout car and shoot river rats was just a brief and weird introduction to F Troop. But it would be a long four and a half years from the academy until I got my wish. I hung in, rolled with whatever assignment I was given, kept my mouth shut and tried – mostly without success – to get beyond drunk drivers, false alarms, domestic squabbles and the like, and on to the business of arresting felons and learning how to be a first-rate, productive cop. Why was I such a bulldog for making that leap? I had no youthful dreams of being a police officer, and no comic-book ideas about crime-fighting or crusading for truth, justice and the American way. My ambition was simple. I had found a workplace that appealed to me but I was stuck in a corner doing routine grunt work, surrounded mostly by guys who wanted to do as little as possible and just get by. Call me dumb, but I wanted to get in on the heavy lifting, take some self-respect home with me at the end of a shift, and be known among good cops as a good cop. If I had wound up in one of the car factories, I would have been the same way – trying to escape the assembly line's dreary repetition and onto a team where I could learn something and where self-initiative produced results.

My assignment to F Troop had put me on rotation with the same group of guys, but within that group I continued to pinball from car to car. Two-man scout cars had three-man crews – with the third officer riding that car only when one of the two partners was scheduled off, or sick. If the senior cop was off, his partner drove the car. For a rookie patrolman, that meant three things: if he rode his assigned car, he was always a passenger; he seldom rode with the car's senior officer; and nights when both partners were working, the young cop was shuttled off to another unit.

Occasionally, I worked "the cruiser," the car known in my youth as The Big Four – a black car with "Detroit Police" on its side but no roof light, ordinarily manned by some of the precinct's best officers. The driver wore a uniform and the other three wore plainclothes, usually shirt and tie. Each of the thirteen precincts put one cruiser on the street, reserving them for backup or highly volatile situations. Drawing a night on the cruiser carried a little prestige, even though I got these rare assignments only because a body was needed and my body was available. Nothing much ever occurred on nights I rode the cruiser, but I got a taste of working plainclothes. Except for the shirt and tie I liked it.

Each precinct also had its own "morality crew," a mini vice squad consisting of a sergeant and two or three officers working plainclothes. You can imagine their duties. Gambling, prostitution…anywhere human frailties wandered across the line into public nuisance or worse, usually at the misdemeanor level. It was the morality crew's job to keep a reasonable lid on "blind pigs," as illegal after-hours drinking spots are known in Detroit. A surprising amount of morality crew time was spent busting bars and liquor stores for selling to minors, or for selling hard liquor on Sunday…which is now legal. I was assigned to the morality crew a few times. Being a non-drinker, I was not very effective. Chalk up another plus for being a non-drinker, because a career on the morality crew definitely was not for me.

Most often, I would be assigned as fill-in on a scout car, in uniform, answering radio runs, writing tickets, learning which bakeries and diners to tap for a coffee and a bite, in what rotation. Meanwhile, I would see the two-man booster car on the street. Between radio traffic, observation and buzz around the precinct, I knew where the felony arrests were being made. As much as rookie cops might get bounced around, they didn't get bounced into riding a booster car, even for one night. I began to understand where I wanted to be. Nice work if you can get it. I had no idea how to get it.

After I had been third man on a scout car for a while, the senior man was promoted to sergeant and I became number two. This meant I was always going to get the same ride, either in the passenger seat or – if my partner, Willard Dhans, was off for the night – as the driver.

By now I was approaching thirty years old and still, in truth, pretty green. How green? One day I had to go to court on a misdemeanor case, a guy driving without a license. An hour or two later, Willard and I were traveling down Fort Street and there's the same guy – *driving a car.* When we gave him the pull-over signal, he took off. So here we were in hot pursuit of an unlicensed driver who had probably driven to court to pay his fine for being an unlicensed driver.

The guy raced a few blocks straight to his house and ran inside. This being hot pursuit, I ran in after him. Meanwhile, Willard, wise in his own ways, got on the radio for backup. I wound up face to face with the fleeing driver in his kitchen. I have no idea what was on his mind – and comical as the situation might seem, who knows...maybe he had done something a whole lot worse than drive without a license – but he picked up a carving fork and brandished it at me. A carving fork is not a shotgun, but – as all street cops know so well – an angry or drunk or stoned citizen is not a normal human being. He is energized, irrational and capable of anything. The cop, meanwhile, is *obligated* to put him in handcuffs. This is the unpredictable moment of truth in police work. Ordinary people are taught to walk away from confrontations. A cop can't walk away, can't say, "OK, maybe I'll come back and arrest you some other time." A cop can't stand and watch as his subject departs saying: "So long, I'd rather not get taken in today." Once initiated, the arrest process has to be completed. This is legal truth, and this is psychological truth. It is the basis of what happened two decades later on Warren Avenue.

And so I stood in a kitchen pondering resistance to arrest and threat of bodily harm – in the unlikely person of a man brandishing a carving fork. I unsnapped the strap from the handle of my revolver and said something like bad movie dialogue along the lines of: "C'mon, don't make me use this thing." My warning turned out to be irrelevant, because what the guy did was run into a bathroom and lock the door. I was pondering what to do next when a more experienced backup arrived. I told him the circumstances, and in one way or another demonstrated I had no idea what to do. The older cop looked part disgusted and part as if he had walked in on a grade-school class. Then he kicked open the bathroom door and arrested the subject without incident.

Willard was a great guy and a decent cop. Unlike my early experiences with F Troop, I was not embarrassed to ride with Willard, even though he was knee-deep in the culture of "just doing enough work to get by." Willard took occasional sack time, though his spot of choice was over on the grounds of one of the precinct's two salt mines. Anyone with a night scope and a sharp eye from the bridge over the Rouge River could have, on occasion, found a scout car lurking behind a huge stockpile of sodium chloride. But the fact was the Del Ray neighborhood in most hours of most nights didn't need much routine patrolling. Only a few blue-collar saloons and one decent dining spot, Joey's Stables, had survived amid the smokestacks, and more than half the street traffic was workers commuting to and from their jobs on Zug Island, a steel mill outpost in the Detroit River. Joey's was torn down years ago, but in those days it was a popular watering hole among any city notables who ventured into the industrial side of town.

If Willard, and our beat, couldn't teach me much about making felony arrests, we were second to none in the nuts and bolts of uniformed patrol duty, misdemeanor arrests – which mostly involved traffic stops. I got my first hints that I was blessed with good aptitude for detailed observation, the ability to pick up on small tics of behavior and circumstances. This is the street cop's radar. In future years, it would become second nature to me to detect, from a booster car, a gun or drugs being slipped under a seat – signaled by nothing more than the characteristic dip of a driver's or passenger's shoulder as we pulled in behind them. Or to scan every passing vehicle, mechanically and subconsciously, for a license plate that was cleaner or dirtier than the car itself. Or to automatically note a vehicle, midway through a Tigers game, carrying three or four young men at five miles an hour past unending rows of parked cars belonging to those inside the stadium. Such observational powers are not rocket science, but systematizing them and applying them relentlessly takes discipline and hard work. Good intuition, like a good eye for the basketball hoop, involves both practice and talent. Back in the days with Willard I was still on my learning permit, but Willard saw it coming when he told me I had a sixth sense for identifying somebody driving without a license. It sounds like full-moon theory, I know; but it was true.

I probably drew my revolver only a handful of times while wearing a uniform in the Fourth. I fired it once. One shot.

Willard and I had just started a shift at midnight. He rolled our car onto Fort Street and, to avoid a red light, cut through a gas station that had closed for the night. He went right between the pumps and the front door, and we both saw someone crouching inside, near the cigarette machine. I got out and ran toward the back. The suspect was also running, through the repair bay, and I lost sight of him. About a seven-foot wire fence formed a sort of corral at the back of the station, with old tires piled to the top. As I got back there, our man was climbing the tires into the alley. I yelled that we were police, and for him to stop, but over the fence he went, and started running down the alley.

Even at a moment like that, all those hours of memorizing the Police Manual were clear in my mind — foremost in my mind. At the time, the rules required use of whatever force necessary, up to and including fatal force, to prevent a suspect's escape in case of murder, rape, robbery, burglary or arson.

I positioned myself in the darkened alley, identified myself again as a cop, yelled at him to stop or I'd shoot. He didn't stop. I fired one shot into the near darkness. He kept running toward Dearborn Street. I didn't know whether he was armed, or with what, so I didn't want to chase directly after him into the dark. I ran back around the front and between some houses on Dearborn Street. Suddenly he's running toward me, on the sidewalk, and I went through the halt-or-I'll-shoot orders all over again. He dropped down on the sidewalk.

"I'm shot, man."

"No, you're not" – which I really thought was the case. But

when I went to handcuff him, his back was covered with blood. A bad wound, but he lived.

You have to follow the book. To do that, you have to distance yourself. Emotion doesn't follow the book. In the cold light of dawn, the burglar turned out to be fifteen years old. It also turned out he had at least thirteen prior contacts with police, and two years earlier – one year past eligibility for Little League – he had been arrested for removing a safe from the premises while committing a B&E. For all I knew at the time, he was a thirty-year-old armed with a machine gun. You follow the book and hope for the best. Nothing guarantees things will turn out that way. My sergeant put me in for a commendation.

When Dave Malinowski came to the precinct fresh from the academy and started filling in on scout cars, I discovered I was not alone. Dave and I had similar thoughts about police work. Willard, at my request, got Dave assigned as third man on our car. On nights Willard was off, Dave and I made quite a pair. Seldom has so much vigilance produced so few results. Two young uniformed cops in a marked car, eager between radio runs and traffic stops to arrest some felons, but not really knowing how or where to do it. Certainly not in what might have been Detroit's most crime-free precinct.

In the early '50s, a new suburban lifestyle had lured the first trickle of Detroiters into abandoning the city. The '67 riot opened the spigot. Most who stayed behind, of any color or ethnic background, were old or poor or both. By 1970, much of the city outside our sleepy blue-collar precinct was awash in muggings, holdups and every sort of street crime. In tough neighborhoods of any city, at any time, it's common to hear that "the criminals have taken over the streets." In Detroit at the time Dave Malinowski and I were wondering how to get a job bringing in felons, the criminals *had* taken over the streets, and *all* the neighborhoods were tough. It was just a matter of degree. Like the man said, you could look it up – 23,038 armed holdups in 1970, one for every sixty residents, sixty-three holdups a day. That's counting just the armed robberies that were reported to police.

At the edge of downtown along Woodward Avenue, once the city's showcase street, anyone so inclined could sit in a diner and watch retirees getting mugged when they ventured outside. A joke making the rounds said a guy pulled his car over on the Lodge Freeway to fix a flat front tire and was jacking the front end up when he felt the car lurch. He looked around the fender and saw someone else jacking up the rear of the car. "What the hell you doing?" the motorist asked. Came the reply: "Listen, man, you take those wheels and I'll take these, OK?" Such was the view from the street – crime and more crime.

Big social change was under way. The city was becoming majority black, racial issues meant big political chips to be cashed in, and the city would soon have its first black mayor. Ordinary people, and good cops, were not much interested in racial politics or sociology, but in whether you could walk down the street without becoming a felony victim. A collision between racial politics and street reality was inevitable, even if most of the crime was black-on-black. With so many whites on the run from the city, black power was about to become something more than a slogan. White cops – good white cops, bad white cops, indifferent white cops – became the prime target for angry slogans and political chip-cashing.

That was the climate in which Dave Malinowski and I patrolled the sleepy Fourth and schemed about how to get more involved with bringing in a few of the bad guys who, ironically, were in such ample supply almost everywhere else in the city. We shared another passion, softball. He was a hell of a shortstop, and I was just an adequate but speedy outfielder who could run an infield grounder into a hit. It turned out that Dave's skill on the diamond, and his recent graduation from the academy, led him quickly to the kind of police work we both were looking for.

In January 1971, the department formed the plainclothes STRESS unit, entirely devoted to attacking the street-crime rampage. The acronym stood for Stop the Robberies, Enjoy

Safe Streets. A STRESS cop's only mission would be to bring in felons. Some of the most experienced and best cops in the city were assigned to STRESS. But a disproportionate number of its ranks were brand-new police officers who would be unrecognized on the streets – both specifically and in terms of mannerisms. It also helped that certain facets of the initial STRESS strategy would require a kind of bravery that many more experienced officers would be reluctant to put in play. Not that older cops weren't brave; just that some kinds of bravery absolutely require youth. Only kids feel immortal. The STRESS operation that became a political football required officers to feel immortal – or at least to take chances with their own mortality, chances that few experienced cops could conceive of taking on a nightly basis. It's no accident that the history of combat is largely a history of youth.

Young Dave had played softball with several members of this new unit, and it didn't take long for his STRESS transfer request to be granted. I didn't know anyone in STRESS, and I had almost no history of making felony arrests, so I didn't think seriously of applying. Besides, I was developing a certain loyalty to my partner, Willard, and a sense that I owed him some more of my time. That's the way it went when occasionally I would see Dave when I'd go to court to testify, and he'd offer to put in a good word for me on a STRESS transfer. "Can't. I don't want to leave Willard," I'd answer.

One day in 1973, Willard turned down my dream job, a decision that set everything in motion. He was offered a booster car, which probably would mean that his partner – me – would go to the new assignment with him. It would mean full-time felony work in plainclothes, and permanent assignment to an 8 p.m. to 4 a.m. shift. I lobbied Willard, hard, to take the job. His wife lobbied just as hard against it.

Willard understood what this meant to me, and after taking a couple days before siding with his wife, he said: "I'm not going to take the booster car. If you want to try and get it, go ahead."

Next day, I approached the precinct executive lieutenant.

"I'd like to be considered for the booster car."

"How much time do you have on the job?"

"About four years."

"Come back and see me after you have seven years."

Next day, I called Dave and asked him to put in that good word, and requested transfer to STRESS.

Dave was a great shortstop, but I was just as good a quarterback and running back in flag football – both of which we had played together on Fourth Precinct teams and which he was now playing on STRESS teams. For several Sunday mornings, at Dave's invitation, I trekked over to Wayne State University and played football with Dave and his fellow STRESS officers. What's good for a shortstop is good for a quarterback. My transfer request came through. I was going to STRESS.

I wanted to make felony arrests, and I was about to get an opportunity. If you had told me that nineteen years later I would be charged with murder for making my felony arrest number 5,000-and-whatever, I would have asked what you were smoking. If you had told me that one day my lawyer would work hard to keep the word "STRESS" from even being spoken in a courtroom where I was the defendant, I would have asked which address on Mars you were from.

3
WHAT SAFE STREETS?

Just before 7:45 p.m. on April 26, 1973, wearing a pair of dress slacks, a good shirt and a nice sweater, I walked back into the same building where I had gotten my spit-and-polish introduction to the police department. It looked like the academy had been commandeered by winos, junkies, and street hustlers. Everybody wore faded jeans, mostly tattered. Hair and beards were Beatles-length. One guy's chest was criss-crossed with Pancho Villa ammo belts – and most men in the room, it would turn out, carried two guns or more somewhere on their person. Short-barreled shotguns lined one wall. There was a pool table, a couple of Ping-Pong tables and a few card tables. The academy had been moved several miles south. My new unit had taken over the old academy building in Palmer Park.

I scanned the fifty or so very plainclothes cops, looking for Dave Malinowski or one of the men I had been playing football with on Sunday mornings. Dave spotted me – something that did not exactly require a trained eye. He walked over and said: "Welcome to STRESS."

Several men entered the room dressed as obtrusively neat as myself, clean-shaven except for maybe a mustache. One yelled, "Roll call!" Instinctively, I looked around for a regimented line being formed. Instead, conversation stopped, but no one moved. Standing at ease, slouched in a chair, or leaning against a pool table, STRESS listened up for the nightly rundown. I had two overwhelming reactions. Culture shock. And, "I think I'm going to like this place."

I didn't realize, of course, that I was standing amid a chapter of Detroit history – and a big chunk of mythology. Even the elite unit's brightest, most experienced officers could not have foreseen that STRESS would be disbanded, decades would pass, they would become old men, and *still* the mere mention of STRESS would be like pumping oxygen on glowing coals. The word STRESS to this day will still push hot buttons in a jury box. This, despite the fact that STRESS existed only a little more than three years, and the decoy operations that made STRESS a racial/political rallying cry lasted barely more than a year. That part of STRESS, in fact, had been disbanded before I got there.

The department – aghast at what predictably happened after it let cops walk the streets in crime victims' shoes – had pulled the plug. The decoy operation, beyond question, had been effective. Soaring street-crime statistics reversed and fell sixteen percent. But decoy work played hell on the health of bad guys and cops alike. People died. Most STRESS cops were white; and all but one of the dead perpetrators were black. Black politicians started calling the decoy operation "genocide." Ordinary people – including many black citizens who had to walk Detroit's streets – had welcomed STRESS as a guerrilla unit in the war against crime. In the end, though, Detroit's unique street-crime decoys had to go. Put an armed cop in a vulnerable crime victim's place, let a felon threaten his intended victim's life, and some ugly statistics are going to result. Nobody could figure out how to deal with this very basic equation. Not the bad guys. Not the department's supervisors. Not the courts – where a man charged with murdering a STRESS officer won acquittal after arguing that STRESS's reputation led him to shoot first. Only the politicians could figure out what to make of it all: votes.

By the time of the Malice Green incident in 1992 – twenty years after the decoy operation was halted, nineteen years after STRESS was reorganized as the Felony Prevention Section, and eighteen years after the unit was disbanded altogether – the newspaper stories took great pains to identify me as "a former STRESS officer." Such is the power of STRESS mythology. They might as well have called me "a former Gestapo officer."

So you need to know a little about STRESS and the year I spent there, getting my first taste of making good felony arrests.

Before Detroit had STRESS, it had the Precinct Support Unit – unmarked cars carrying plainclothes cops and functioning much like booster cars except they were free to cross precinct boundaries, roaming citywide to focus on the hottest major crimes and crime spots. Nothing unusual about that. Most major cities have similar units.

There was really nothing unusual, either, in the decision to regroup and target the incredible surge in street assaults and robberies. John Nichols, the police commissioner (as Detroit then called its chief), was a tough cop from the old school, not exactly a great public speaker, but determined to do PR for law and order. He once portrayed himself in one of the worst cop movies ever made, *Detroit 9000*. And when he reorganized the Precinct Support Unit to go after the street criminals in January 1971, he came up with the folksy, sloganeering "Stop the Robberies, Enjoy Safe Streets." The public relations worked like a charm until the deaths started piling up. Where they piled up was in the part of STRESS that truly *was* unusual. If there ever has been another police operation in the country like the STRESS decoy operation, I don't know about it.

Experienced officers recruited to STRESS from the Precinct Support Unit and from the precincts accounted for most of the new outfit. They rolled from Palmer Park every night in unmarked cars to hunt various types of felons via planned surveillance, or good information to be followed up, or skilled observation of the passing criminal scene. Some crews, however, included at least one officer willing to offer himself up as a decoy. The point men in decoy operations tended to be young, assigned to that job fresh from the academy. When they hit the streets each night, their mission was to be what no cop wants to be – vulnerable. They dressed as women, or they carried an empty gas can down darkened street like a stranded motorist, or they sat waiting for a bus at the least desirable stops in town. If you want to catch a holdup man, you need a holdup. God knows Detroit had plenty of those to choose from. But catching holdup artists through a middle man, the civilian victim, is really inefficient when you stop to think about it. The holdup man is no longer at the scene by the time you interview the victim. Victims can make bad trial witnesses if you do find the bad guy. And occasionally, of course, the victim doesn't survive the holdup. What could possibly be more logical than putting a cop in the civilian victim's place?

You could not invent a more dangerous form of police work. For one thing, the goal was not to nail felons on loitering charges. You cannot say, "I think this guy plans to hold me up, so I am going to arrest him for armed robbery." An armed robbery charge requires an armed robbery – which meant a decoy had to put his life on the line as often as a baker makes doughnuts. For another thing, even though each decoy left Palmer Park as part of a three- or four-man crew, his backup partners might be near-useless in protecting him. An effective decoy had to be seen by the bad guys as, above all, alone. Muggers and holdup men don't target groups. Perps might attack in groups of two or three or four; but the typical victim is a solitary, isolated figure. At the moment of truth, the best-positioned backup would often be no help to a decoy. A passing bus, or an unforeseen piece of business between bad guy and "victim," could trash the most carefully planned scenario and escalate the danger even higher.

The STRESS decoys went to the heart of all the possibilities, and all the limitations, of using police officers to remove felons from the street. America has always loved movies where bad guys and lawmen come face to face. If the bad guy won't submit peacefully, movie audiences have no problem with doing whatever it takes to bring him in. In the real world, it's a different picture. People love to talk about crime in the abstract. It's like the relationship between a hamburger and somebody who hasn't worked with cattle. The burger shows up on his plate as a tasty, round quarter-pound object. It could just as well have grown on a hamburger tree. The connection, the reality of what the burger-joint customer is eating, doesn't register. Cops, like cattle ranchers, have better understanding of the raw material. So docs a citizen who has had a gun stuck in his face just once have a somewhat different view of law enforcement. The point is, felony arrests, like hamburgers, don't grow on trees. Arrests can't always be neat and tidy and twice removed from the crime that prompted the arrest in the first place. Cops are professionals. But even professionals, over the course of hundreds of face-to-face confrontations with armed felons, will wind up in a situation with a violent result.

Society gets uneasy when events on the street blur the line between law and order, when the bad guys – and the law itself – make the order-keepers use force. It's an easy line to toe in the abstract, but sometimes impossible in a street cop's real world. If a police officer has probable cause that a felony has occurred, or if a felony suspect resists arrest, he is empowered – indeed obligated – to apply the full force of the law as needed to arrest that suspect. If a cop observes a felony in progress, it's a total no-brainer. Even then, society gets uneasy about use of force. Most police officers seldom confront that situation. They are behind a desk or on routine duty. STRESS decoys faced extreme situations almost every night – not in the abstract, not second-hand, but up close and personally threatening. They put themselves into the very situations citizens were terrified of finding themselves. So the possibilities for bringing in felons were endless; so were the limitations.

The first person to die during a STRESS arrest was a robbery suspect, on May 11, 1971. By the end of the year, twelve citizens and one STRESS cop – shot while chasing an armed woman on foot – were killed. Two robbery suspects were shot to death along John R Street by a decoy who was mugged while walking with an empty gasoline can. A department board of review determined it to be a clean shooting, and the prosecutor found no reason to press any charge against the officer. But the officer was white, the dead felons were black – and were teenagers. Their ages, and the fact that the list of "STRESS deaths" the newspapers tabulated had reached ten, marked the quick end of any feel-good PR about the unit.

And then there was the involvement of the same officers in multiple shootings. That was inevitable – statistically, and because some cops are quicker to lay their bodies on the line than others. I wasn't yet in STRESS at the time, but common sense tells you that if a cop on that kind of assignment is involved in multiple shootings, there are two possible explanations: good police work, and bad police work. Public opinion doesn't make case-by-case analysis. Public opinion loves easy sound bites. Among the city's black leaders and politicians, the easy sound bite was to portray STRESS as a bunch of trigger-happy white cops out to commit genocide on the city's black youth. It was an unfair image. A number of very good cops in the unit were black. As for "trigger-happy," one black officer fired 139 rounds while assigned to STRESS. That's 129 more rounds than I fired in twenty-four years on the street, including my time in STRESS. And it's not the kind of thing you heard about as the STRESS genocide legend got milked for black votes.

The decoy operation, at any rate, became a nightmare for the department, and the part of STRESS that had captured all the public attention was quickly shut down. At the end of 1972, the newspapers' list of "STRESS deaths" showed just seven fatalities for the year. Three of them were police officers.

In March 1972, a Wayne County sheriff's deputy, Henry Henderson, was killed in a bizarre shootout. A STRESS crew working the Dexter-Chicago Boulevard area observed a man entering an apartment carrying a gun and a holster. When the three-man STRESS crew intruded on the card game inside, a gunfight broke out. A STRESS officer said he showed his badge through the door. The card players said they thought it was a gun. Each side said the other fired first. Henderson died. Two other off-duty deputies and a civilian friend were wounded. Attempted murder charges were brought against the three STRESS officers, all of whom were acquitted in a case of mistaken identity. All the STRESS officers and every card-playing deputy were black. One of the STRESS cops was Al Nettles, who went on to become a member of Coleman Young's security detail after Young rode into the mayoral Manoogian Mansion on an anti-STRESS platform. Not only was Nettles a good cop; his STRESS crew was a good crew. Bad things can happen in dangerous situations. Coleman Young, though, was very selective in his understanding of that fact – or at least his public stance about STRESS. The officer Young promoted to head the new mayoral security detail was yet another black ex-STRESS cop.

In December 1972, STRESS Officer Gerald Riley was off duty, standing in line at a bank when a holdup broke out. Riley tried to arrest the bad guy and was shot to death for his troubles. His young son was with him, and watched his father die.

Four days before Riley's death, a four-man STRESS crew tailed a car from a dope pad. When they pulled beside the car at a traffic light, occupants of the car opened fire and wounded all four STRESS officers. The three suspects fled. Two days after Christmas, while staked out in search of the three, STRESS Officer Robert Bradford was shot to death. His partner, Robert Dooley, was shot in the eye and three times in the back. He survived, paralyzed, and identified the trio as the shooters. Two suspects fled to Georgia, where they eventually died in a rooftop shootout with Atlanta police. The third, an eighteen-year-old named Hayward Brown, became the subject of an intense manhunt in Detroit. Cops chased every lead, every connection, raided apartments, kicked down doors. One civilian died after firing a shotgun blast at raiding police. Toward the end of the month, Hayward Brown was captured...but he is the one who was acquitted after arguing that fear of STRESS led him to shoot first. Like I said, bad guys are seldom bad guys just once. And, as happens often enough, Hayward Brown did not need interaction with police to die a violent death. He was shot dead twelve years later when he tried to rob occupants of a dope pad.

After Officer Bradford was shot, no "STRESS death" occurred until March 3, 1973. On that day, STRESS Officers Richard Worobec and Roger Brooks were appearing in a case before Recorder's Court Judge James Del Rio. This rather colorful judge was at one time – despite being friendly to criminal defendants – known to carry a gun on the bench. Brooks and Worobec had arrested two men and two women after finding them in possession of narcotics and three guns. Worobec was on the stand testifying. Brooks had completed his testimony, moved to a seat in the audience, and – because it was a very hot day – had taken off his flak vest and was sitting on it. At that point, defense attorney Gerald Dent removed a revolver from his briefcase.

When Brooks caught a glimpse of the revolver, he thought the gun was evidence in the trial. Then he saw, clearly, bullets in the cylinder. When Dent pointed the gun at his own head, Brooks thought the courtroom was about to get very messy. But Dent leveled the revolver elsewhere in the room and began shooting. Brooks could not be certain who or what Dent was firing at, but that's irrelevant. Roger – not only justifiably but by obligation – pulled his revolver and fired at Dent. So did the detective in charge of the case, who was seated at the prosecution table. Meanwhile, on the witness stand, Richard Worobec had no doubt who the target was. As Worobec dived to the floor, one of Dent's rounds passed through the witness-box partition. Worobec was carrying two weapons, drew both, and fired both. Dent became "STRESS death" number one of 1973.

Why Dent did what he did is unclear. The prevailing theory was "suicide by cop" to assure payment of his life insurance. Worobec suspects that Dent also intended to take out "this so-called scourge of the black community" – Worobec being the STRESS officer who shot the two muggers while decoying with a gas can.

If Judge Del Rio was carrying a gun that day, he didn't fire it. He dived for cover when the shooting started. Detroit being in so many ways like no other place on the planet, it's no surprise that Recorder's Court might have been like no other court on the planet. Some say my first trial, which occurred in that court, had a lot to do with the state Legislature ultimately disbanding the court. Black political figures to this day claim the court's disappearance was racially motivated.

Officer Worobec had come under fire, literally, at a young age. He was in his second year on the street as a patrolman when he survived a 1969 ambush by rolling under his scout car. His regular partner was off sick that night, and Mike Chapski, an officer Worobec barely knew, was assigned to the car. Chapski died in a burst of gunfire from paramilitary members of the Republic of New Africa as they emerged from a meeting at New Bethel Baptist Church, where the Rev. C.L. Franklin was pastor for years and where his daughter, Aretha Franklin, first sang in public. Worobec's wounds put him on disability for almost a year. When he returned, he remained on the job a total of thirty-five years before retiring. A dedicated cop.

No one could second-guess attorney Dent's shooting. An entire courtroom saw it. Worobec, accused like many white STRESS officers of participating in racist genocide, was once married to a black woman. Life and truth aren't as simple as sound bites.

The second "STRESS death" of 1973 did not occur until October. I was one of the shooters. By then, after just five months with STRESS, I had seen more and learned more about making felony arrests than I had seen and learned in four and a half years patrolling the sleepy Fourth. The decoy operations were gone, but STRESS was still a hard-working unit.

STRESS cars were four-man operations, but there were five men on a crew to cover for an officer's off nights – just as three men were assigned to a two-man precinct car. After that first roll call, I briefly filled in on various cars, but soon found a home on the car known as STRESS-5. Brooks and Worobec had earned promotions off STRESS-5, where I teamed up with Mike Hall, Woody Woodruff, Dave Siebert and my old friend from the Fourth, Dave Malinowski.

Seniority on any crew of police officers is measured by date of hire. In my case, that created an amusing situation. Mike Hall was senior officer on the crew, Woody was second, I was third, Dave Malinowski was fourth, and Dave Siebert was fifth. But if you measured it in any realistic way, I was the rookie. Even Dave Malinowski – with whom I had futilely chased felons when we both wore uniforms in the sleepy Fourth – was by now a seasoned STRESS cop. Dave Siebert, technically the least senior member of the crew, had been at STRESS since day one, straight out of the academy. There were twenty-five-year cops on the force who had not seen as much as Dave Siebert. Needless to say, I had come over here to learn. I stood in awe of my partners, and I wondered if I'd be able to keep up.

Almost from the instant I first rode in STRESS-5, my overriding focus as a police officer – dictated by both the realities of the street and the orders of my superiors – became to take guns and drugs out of circulation. Very few felonies did not involve guns or drugs. Most involved both. The logic of our mission was therefore impeccable. If you weren't providing backup or chasing a hot felony, you devoted most of your time and self-initiative to sniffing out guns and drugs. Best of all, you could quantify it. The elusive nightly goal for a crew was the hat trick – arresting, on one eight-hour shift, three different people for illegally possessing three different guns. The term "hat trick" was coined by Detroit hockey fans to indicate a three-goal night by a Red Wings player at the old Olympia Stadium. Mike Hall was so determined to score the hat trick that in some quarters his nickname became "Roadblock" – so designated for the number of cars we'd pull over looking for that elusive third gun. We confiscated an illegal gun every night, sometimes two. Our car led the whole unit. But we never scored a hat trick.

After leaving STRESS, driving a two-man precinct booster car, I scored the hat trick two or three times. On another occasion, with Mike Dameron as my booster-car partner, we made four separate gun arrests during a single shift. Aside from bragging rights, that helps illustrate a fact about plainclothes work... the two-man booster cars where I spent most of my career were more efficient than the supercharged four-man STRESS crews, as good as my STRESS partners were. Assuming, of course, that you're talking about two good booster cops. For one thing, working a booster crew you only have to learn the personalities of two other people; on a STRESS car you needed to get inside the minds of four other people. We are talking not just the subtleties of how people react in a tight situation, we are talking everyday decisions like where and when to stop for lunch. That could be brutal at times. Here you are prowling the streets of Detroit, maybe walking into a potentially violent situation around the next corner, and three guys in your car are pissed off because lunch is going to be Chinese instead of Italian. Honest.

Or take the softball thing. Malinowski, Woodruff and myself liked to play softball. If the STRESS team had a game scheduled during our shift, we went and played it – with full knowledge of our superiors. We put in our hours. We worked our asses off when we were in the car. But Mike Hall and Dave Siebert didn't want to lose one possible minute of chasing felons. They would drop us off at the diamond and go hit the streets alone for an hour or two. So depending on which four men were working that night, you might have a couple who weren't talking to each other because of a softball game. I was the designated communicator. Hall and Siebert would talk to me even when they were pissed at Malinowski and Woodruff. Perfectly human stuff, just as if we were shoe salesmen instead of cops. Only difference being that our job was a lot more dangerous.

Disagreements over softball and Chinese food notwithstanding, we were a good crew. I had wanted to be where the heavy lifting got done, and here I was, in an elite unit. You felt like you were accomplishing something, day in and day out. One day, two boys aged eight and six were kidnapped from in front of their Detroit home. A few days later, their bodies were found dumped in a field twenty miles outside the city near Metro Airport. Somehow human nature knows exactly when to use the word "heinous." This was a heinous crime. The whole town was outraged and wanted the killers brought in. Turns out there were three suspects, identified in their person and their location through a combination of citizen tips, work by homicide detectives, and networking by plainclothes cops. Our STRESS sergeant, Bill Shine, promised a weekend off to any crew that brought in one of the killers. Tracking leads, we ultimately wound up breaking into the apartment of a drug dealer named George "Texas Slim" Dudley who had been killed two weeks earlier. Our man was in bed with a woman, and some of Texas Slim's blood was still on the bed. Siebert put on the cuffs. Bill Shine kept sandbagging our promised weekend off, then finally gave us a few hours – on a rainy day.

On a Monday afternoon, October 1, 1973, we were sent to a stakeout at a Kentucky Fried Chicken restaurant on Wyoming near Seven Mile Road. Stakeouts are generally tedious and unproductive. This one seemed even more likely to be tedious and unproductive because it was broad daylight. We were called in because of a tip. I didn't know anything about the nature of the tip, only that we were going to the place because of word there might be a robbery.

Three of the STRESS-5 crew – Woody Woodruff, Dave Siebert and I – took up positions inside the restaurant. The STRESS-3 crew set up in the WY7 bowling alley across the street. We had been there less than an hour and were still trying to find better positions and vantage points when it all began to happen. Dave Siebert had climbed up a ladder, and I was crouching in the kitchen. Woody was somewhere back there with me. The place was empty of customers when I heard the door open. I could see behind the service counter, but I couldn't see who was standing on the customer side. When the assistant manager turned and started filling a chicken bag and a paper bucket with money, I knew this was not an ordinary takeout order. He looked in my direction, and nodded the obvious – that a holdup was under way. As soon as he put the money on the counter, I charged out of the kitchen.

To my considerable surprise, the person on the other side of the counter was a large young woman, armed with a pistol. I had about one-tenth of a second to ponder that before I yelled: "Police! Drop the gun!"

Instead, she grabbed the money and ran out the front door. Woody, Dave and I ran out the back door and down the alley toward a side street. We could hear STRESS-3 officers yelling at her to stop. When we came out of the alley, she ran in front of us, and past the driver door of her getaway car. A young man was behind the wheel – armed, as it would later turn out. "Let's get outa here! Let's go!" she yelled at the driver as she circled around to the passenger side, swung open the door, and aimed her gun at the STRESS-3 cops – one of whom fired one shot at her. I remember seeing a bullet tear into the dashboard. Meanwhile, Woody, in front of me, also fired one shot. Dave fired one shot. As I ran in the street past the open car door, she was turned to sit down, still brandishing the gun. I didn't know if she had been hit, and I also fired one shot as I ran by.

EMS was called immediately. She died at the scene, in the front seat of the green Chevy. Three hundred dollars spilled onto the floor from the KFC bag and bucket. She had been shot once in the arm and once in the chest. It was never determined which of us fired the fatal shot.

The driver had to be lifted out of the car. He wasn't wounded; he was a paraplegic – the result of being shot during an earlier holdup. The getaway car was equipped with hand-operated accelerator and brake pedals.

A week later about fifty protesters marched in front of police headquarters carrying the dead woman's baby daughter.

"We don't think felonies can be prevented by murdering the felons," one protester told a reporter.

Eventually, a suburban attorney sued the city on behalf of the holdup woman's family. The suit claimed that her gun – pointed first at the holdup victim and then at five cops from two different crews – had been planted. I was about to endure my first up-close experience with the deep pockets and weak spine of the city law department, and the kinds of mistakes that medical examiners can make. All of us were called in to discuss the case with a city attorney.

"Autopsy results indicate she was shot in the back," the attorney said. "We're going to settle this case out of court."

Excuse me? How many witnesses – civilian and police – does it take to make a good case? How could someone even suggest, under the circumstances, that we planted her gun? We did not – I emphasize did not – shoot her in the back. Even if one of us had, that would only have meant she was at that moment aiming her own gun at another cop in another direction. I was, for the first time I can recall, incredibly angry at my own department – and more so at City Hall lawyers who twisted good police work into an admission of guilt, in the form of a settlement check. They were more afraid of Wayne County juries than we were afraid of the bad guys.

Nothing, of course, carried as much power with a Wayne County jury as the mythology of STRESS. Whisper the word and collect a buck. In this case, a quarter million bucks. In 1992, after the Malice Green incident, this same lawyer became a walking advertisement for himself by telling any reporter who would listen that he couldn't believe the police department had allowed me on the streets after the KFC shooting.

Our STRESS crew's response to the holdup, in fact, followed the book. The perp shouldn't have held up a restaurant at gunpoint. She shouldn't have aimed her gun first at the store manager and then at five armed cops while ignoring commands to halt – and telling her getaway driver to pull away, with the assistance of devices made necessary by his own willingness to be a bad guy more than once. She shouldn't have died violently. Nobody should. But don't the bad guys bear responsibility for their actions? Isn't there some point where they make a violent end inevitable? Hadn't one STRESS cop already died while chasing an armed woman down the street?

My partners and I were outraged. The only place a good cop could look for backup was from another good cop. Certainly not from the city's law department.

One month after the KFC shooting, Coleman Young was elected to the first of his five four-year terms as mayor. The holdup, and our response to it, undoubtedly added a few votes to his victory over John Nichols – the white police commissioner who had founded STRESS. Young's most fervid campaign pledge was to abolish STRESS, to increase black presence in the police department, and to give more supervisory jobs to blacks. For once, a politician kept his word.

When Young took office, he made a classic speech in which he warned the bad guys to "hit the road to the other side of Eight Mile" – meaning across the city's border with its northern suburbs. He abolished STRESS. He launched a sweeping racial and gender diversification of the police department. By the beginning of his second term, he had appointed the city's first black police chief, William Hart. If the bad guys went north of Eight Mile, I never noticed it while driving a booster car in the Third. Diversification never meant much to me personally, except that my seniority was trampled on and other cops started getting citations for actions I never would have bothered writing up.

As for the new chief, Bill Hart, he was sent to prison in 1992 for embezzling something more than a million dollars from a secret department fund. Eventually he wound up in the same federal facility as Walter Budzyn and me. Walter – always a compassionate guy – would push Hart around in his wheelchair. I talked to Hart occasionally. He seemed like a nice guy. By reputation he had been a good cop in his own days on the street. There is no doubt in my mind whatsoever that he could have taken others down with him had he chosen to do so. Nor has there ever been any doubt in my mind about a very short leash reaching from Coleman Young to any of his police chiefs. Certainly not from Young to the man who was chief in the fall of 1992.

STRESS was an honest effort to rein in an incredible wave of street crime. It had its problems, but was never given a real chance – either in terms of time or leadership – to solve them. What would I, with the benefit of hindsight, have done differently? Not that I'm a managerial expert. But I did have a decent view from the ground up.

For starters, it's no accident there is not even a paragraph in this chapter about my STRESS training. All "training" was on-the-job. You got in a car and you rolled. I worked with some first-rate cops, but this is no way to run a unit, or a department. In fact, in twenty-four and a half years on the force, I did not spend one day in any kind of training program after leaving the academy – other than fingerprint and Breathalyzer classes I requested. Perhaps you find that incredible. Apparently, the prosecutors in the Malice Green case did, too, because they listened with a straight face as one of their witnesses, a ranking policewoman, testified as to the extensive training all Detroit officers receive in non-lethal self-defense. If my freedom hadn't been at stake, I would have laughed out loud.

Second, there is the matter of equipment. We had our bare hands and our guns, period. No pepper spray, no batons. If I formed a new STRESS unit today, it would have state-of-the-art equipment, as well as good training in how to use it.

Third, I think of that lieutenant who, when I asked to go on a booster car in the Fourth, told me to "come back after you have seven years on the job." I don't know what the magic number is, and a year on one assignment can be like five years on a different assignment. But if you are going to have an elite felony unit, its members should have some experience arresting felons.

And fourth, as an elite unit, the concept could have been

tightened up a bit; some protocols more firmly established. I was a by-the-book kind of guy. So were my partners. Management has to make sure that everybody is, all the time.

But those things are nothing more than fine-tuning. STRESS was not a bunch of white cowboys out preying on young black men. Not so far as I could see from a seat in STRESS-5, and not among the other STRESS officers I knew – which was most of them. The department was majority white. That wasn't our fault. In the very recent past, Detroit itself had been mostly white. My academy class was one-third black – in a department that not too many years earlier had been almost entirely white. By the time I arrived at STRESS, most of Detroit's citizens, and most of its felons, were black. That wasn't our fault either. One rogue cop surfaced in the STRESS ranks, and was prosecuted for planting a weapon during a fatal off-duty altercation. That could have happened in any unit.

By 1989, a young black city council candidate proposed bringing back STRESS, and claimed to have taken surveys among residents showing overwhelming support for the idea – even though the survey used the word "STRESS" and the word "undercover"…meaning decoys. The word "STRESS" without the word "white," it seems, did not touch so many hot buttons, except those of Mayor Young. When asked about the young politician's idea, the mayor said: "That decoy thing had to do with robbery, didn't have much to do with guns and murder and with dope. And those are the major problems facing the people of this city, not robbery."

Well, Young had that right. STRESS had dropped the decoys and moved on to guns and dope before I joined the unit and before Young got elected. Throughout Young's tenure, in neighborhoods that City Hall neglected, my main focus as a street cop was taking guns and dope off the street. That's what I was doing the night that, according to Coleman Young, I became a murderer.

The STRESS myth that Young capitalized on outlived him. Throughout my career in plainclothes, and even today, street people will say to a booster cop: "You guys are STRESS!" Meaning nothing except an officer in plainclothes. In fact, any dirty or rough police incident that might have occurred on the streets while STRESS existed was, rest assured, blamed on STRESS.

Some of the best coppers I ever worked with rode STRESS cars. They know that. Other police officers know that. People who appreciate the realities of crime, and don't live in the safe and tidy abstract world, know that. Coleman Young knew that when he raided STRESS for his bodyguard staff, even as he was shutting STRESS down.

Sometimes realities of police work just don't fit the political realities that will get you the most votes.

4

HOW TIGER STADIUM
FOUND ME A HOME

A few more than one hundred police officers got switched to new jobs when Coleman Young disbanded STRESS. A handful of young officers who had never known any police life except the fast-paced elite unit quit the force. Dave Siebert, while visiting California, took a liking to sunshine and decided to join the Los Angeles Police Department. Experienced cops had to start from scratch and endure the LAPD academy course alongside raw recruits. Midway through the paramilitary regime Dave had enough and quit – as did all other experienced out-of-state sun-seekers in his academy class. Dave came back to Michigan, sought to rejoin the Detroit department, but discovered a freeze had been imposed on hiring white officers, even experienced ones. Eventually, he became a private investigator. At least one young STRESS officer went off and became a lawyer. The overwhelming majority of STRESS cops took transfers, some back to uniform, some to other plainclothes bureaus, including narcotics. I was transferred to the Commissioner's Task Force on Burglaries.

It was a new unit, which before long became known as the Headquarters Surveillance Unit, targeting not just burglars but rapists, car thieves, murderers and armed robbers. The operating principle was that great truth of police work – and much of society's uneasiness with police work: Bad guys are seldom bad guys just once. In a nutshell, we tailed known felons and arrested them when they committed new crimes. This is the one police job I had where almost every day I practiced racial profiling from start of shift to end. Close, sustained undercover surveillance simply does not lend itself well to inter-racial match-ups. Ninety percent or more of my assigned targets were white.

The two years I spent on this job were enjoyable at times – genuine undercover work, using a variety of civilian vehicles with one officer per car playing tag team to avoid detection. It was rewarding when a surveillance finally paid off and you caught a felon in the act. I had a chance to work occasionally with the FBI, DEA, Treasury Department, Immigration and Naturalization Service, Border Patrol and the Bureau of Alcohol, Tobacco and Firearms. My partners and I never lost a case once we got to court. But the most boring of all police work is to sit in a car and watch another car that is parked a block away – for six, seven, eight, nine hours. I preferred retail felon-chasing, rather than a daily dose of programmed, targeted surveillance. With STRESS gone, though, the surveillance unit was a good place to land. After two years I got booted out, my second taste of Coleman Young's hell-bent determination to remake the police department in his own image. Word came down that room would be made for more black surveillance officers by transferring several of us according to reverse seniority. The most experienced cops' tickets out of the unit would be punched first. This was a direct violation of department personnel regulations. We grieved it via the union. But it took years to win the case, which by then was moot to me because I had found a home in booster-car work. You would need a very large box to contain all the valid reasons for white cops' animosity toward Coleman Young. The mutual disrespect was huge.

We were told to fill out transfer forms with our choice of precincts, and that the department would try to honor our requests. My first request, of course, would have been not to go back to uniform. Not an option. I listed the Sixteenth Precinct as one choice because it was near my home. I put down the Fourth Precinct as another choice, because I had begun my career there, knew most of the officers, and, most importantly, knew the turf.

When I was reassigned, in February 1976, naturally I was sent to the Second. As it turned out, I would spend the rest of my career in the Second Precinct – though its name would soon be changed to the Third.

This was the pits. Back in uniform, and in a high-crime precinct. Don't get me wrong about the second half of that equation. I liked to be assigned where and when a lot of work needed to be done. Over the years, when I could get my choice of nights off, I would always take Sunday – not only because it was family day, but also because Sunday normally was such a dull day on the job. So being in a high-crime area didn't bother me. But being in uniform meant I'd be tied to the radio, chasing domestic calls and bar fights. On top of that, the Second had lousy eating spots – unless you wanted to eat Mexican every night. There wasn't even a doughnut shop in the Second. On nights when we really needed a doughnut, we'd have to sneak across the line and share a coffee with a car from the Fourth.

The Second's station was practically underneath the Ambassador Bridge to Canada, just a few minutes from the Fourth's station at Fort Street and Green where I had served with F Troop. The Second spread out away from the river, across Michigan Avenue and Grand River Avenue. Seventy-five percent of residents were black, fifteen percent Hispanic, ten percent white. Crumbling neighborhoods included some of the oldest wood frame houses in the city. Two major relics of the precinct's better times, Tiger Stadium and Olympia Stadium, still served as home to the Tigers and the Red Wings – only now the vast majority of fans were driving many miles from the burbs to see the games. That spring of '76, wearing a uniform, I'd get my first opportunity as a cop to catch a couple innings on lunch hour. Both of these old sports palaces, it would soon turn out, played a role in my return to plainclothes.

For several months, I bounced from car to car like a rookie, but in truth I didn't mind. I needed to learn the turf, and I needed to learn the precinct's personnel. Better to be riding with strangers than to settle into permanent assignment with an incompatible partner. Compatibility between street-cop partners in many ways is similar but more complicated than compatibility with a spouse. For one thing, you spend a lot more waking hours with your cop partner than you do with your marriage partner. For another, if your work ethics and patterns don't mesh with your partner's, you will be very frustrated and unhappy and unproductive. For yet another, you need to know in your heart and mind that this guy will, when the time comes, go to extremes to save your life. A cop's relationship with his partner is the most overworked cliché in cop movies and TV shows. It's a cliché, but believe it. In a lot of those shows, it's the only true thing you'll see.

Nothing I observed bouncing from car to car made me eager to select a permanent partner. Most cops I worked with during those four or five months seemed interested in nothing but collecting a paycheck. They did exactly what was expected of them, nothing more, sometimes less. I knew supervision would try to accommodate me if I found a good partner, but mostly what I saw only made me wonder why these guys chose law enforcement as a profession. Meanwhile, tied to the radio, wearing a uniform and riding with strangers, I managed to make more than one hundred felony arrests – many of them "good" in the booster-car sense of self-initiative. That was, in fact, a better record than any of the Second's booster cars in the same period.

One night I had just begun the midnight shift, riding for the first time with a young guy named Mike Angeluski. It's 12:15 a.m. I look to my left and I see a guy outside a print shop, nobody else around. I tell Angeluski, "Hey, something's going on here. Let's go." We're in uniform in a marked car, so I park it up the street and we sneak our way back hiding behind parked cars, and sure enough here's this same guy looking in through an opening in a freight door. And just then another guy sticks his head out. So we pull our guns and run across the street and arrest both of them. That's worth something. Self-initiative. Just as we're transporting them, the radio puts out a B&E alarm, and we've already got the perps in the back seat. At the station, I tell the desk lieutenant maybe the sergeant ought to write us up. "Bullshit," he says. "That was a radio run." Lieutenant Robert Heise was just pulling my chain. Fantastic street cop, and an old boss from STRESS. Angeluski and I got a citation.

Almost as soon as I arrived at the Second, I had resubmitted my original transfer request, the same one I put in after getting bounced out of the surveillance unit. The request sat there, but sooner or later it would be honored. Apparently, somebody in the Second had noticed my work ethic, because the commander called me in for a discussion.

"Why do you want to leave the Second?"

"Because it's a cesspool, because I hate wearing a uniform, and if I have to wear it I might as well be somewhere nearer my house or a place where I know the guys."

"What would it take to keep you here?"

"Put me on a booster car."

"Can't be done. Not with layoffs. We've already got a couple guys with seniority who were bounced *off* a booster car."

"Sorry, then. I'll wait for my transfer to come through."

I understood his situation. Layoffs are layoffs and seniority is seniority. But by now I had been a cop for almost eight years. I knew where the action was and where I belonged, but I was back to being a uniformed patrolman catching rides mostly with cops who weren't much interested in being cops. Coleman Young was shrinking the department while diversifying it. Meanwhile, the bad guys had not exactly taken the mayor's advice and fled across Eight Mile Road. This was probably my lowest morale point as a police officer, until my final day on the job. Even those first months walking the beat in the frigid Fourth had been a time of anticipating better things to come. Now, all I could do was suck it up, come to work every day, be a professional and wait for a transfer. The one thing I could be glad of was that if I rode with a different rookie or burnout case every night...it would *still* be better than being locked up in a room with that photostat camera.

My young partner from the print-shop B&E seemed to have a rejuvenated attitude toward police work as a result of having a little self-initiative recognized by the brass. I noticed his attitude, and other signs of compatibility, so in June we became permanent scout-car partners.

One day in July, with our shift working afternoons from 4 p.m. to midnight, Angeluski called me at home and said, "We're supposed to wear plainclothes tonight."

"Why?"

"They've had more than a dozen stolen cars and B&Es reported in the last two night games at the stadium, and Heise wants to do something about it."

Lt. Heise had been put in charge of the uniformed Tiger Stadium detail, officers assigned from every precinct in the city to handle traffic before and after games, and to patrol inside the stadium while the game was in progress. Apparently, my old STRESS colleague had put in a word for me as someone whose surveillance experience might be useful. It was like setting your pet cat on the floor and rolling him a five-foot ball of catnip. The uniform stayed in the closet and I headed off to work a happy fella.

A plainclothes stadium detail made all kinds of sense in terms of police work – and it answered a high-profile PR need for the city. If the bad guys hadn't left the city, the mass of metro Detroit's affluent and even middle-class population had. All the movie theaters were in the burbs. All the shopping malls were in the burbs. With notable exceptions, the fine restaurants – and even the not-so-fine – were gravitating to the burbs. Even the *jobs* were increasingly in the burbs. The Lions had moved to the burbs, and the Pistons would soon follow. Take banks, newspapers, government and utilities out of downtown and there'd be nothing left. Office towers were mushrooming in suburbs like Southfield and Troy. Many residents of the fifth largest market in the United States had not ventured into the city for years. It was vital for Detroit not to have so much crime around the stadium that even sports-crazed fans wouldn't enter the Corktown neighborhood, just west of downtown, to see a ballgame.

That first night – without a chance to strategize a surveillance routine – Mike Angeluski and I arrested two men for breaking into a car, and three others for auto theft. Good felony arrests, caught in the act. We were onto something that I immediately hoped might be my ticket out of uniform. As it turned out, 1976 was not only the magic summer for Mark "The Bird" Fidrych at the corner of Michigan and Trumbull. It was the magic summer for Larry Nevers, too. The Bird made his magic by talking to baseballs. I made mine by intercepting felonies – something you don't get much chance to do while wearing a uniform.

I think My Tree is overdone whenever my cop friends talk about my nights on the stadium surveillance detail. I didn't spend *that* much time sitting up there. I think those guys just enjoy laughing at the image of me getting a leg up and straddling a branch with a sharp eye out for car boosters. But, hey, it was a good vantage point. And you tell me the last time you heard of a bad guy looking for cops in trees?

From the first day, of course, I dreaded what would happen when the Tigers left town. But as each road trip came up, Mike and I were left working plainclothes in the neighborhoods, one day at a time. Then I lived in dread of what would happen when the baseball season ended. But if we were productive at catching felons outside Tiger Stadium, I told the brass, then why not outside Olympia Stadium, too? So there we were, still working plainclothes – and setting up surveillance around Olympia for Red Wings games and musical events, and staying in the booster car on other nights as well. The magic of '76 for me was that, without it being formally announced, I had parlayed a crime problem for suburban sports fans into a booster-car job. With the Tigers in town, I worked the stadium area until the crowds cleared out, then finished the shift doing booster-car work elsewhere in the precinct. Most nights I policed the Second's neighborhoods, serving and protecting residents. Only rarely did I have to pull the uniform out of the closet again – election days, Freedom Day fireworks, an occasional state visit or other public event that required a major presence of uniformed cops. As years went by, putting on the uniform become so rare that I had to have it altered almost every time I wore it. But right to the very end, in '92, with Olympia gone to the wrecker's ball, when the Tigers were in town, booster cop Larry Nevers became Larry Nevers, tree-sitter and stadium surveillance guru.

So it was that I never took a transfer and for the next sixteen years worked plainclothes in those seven square miles. I'd have to say I succeeded in my initial goal of learning the local turf.

Over time, as laid-off cops were called back to work, I convinced my bosses to expand the plainclothes stadium detail from two to four and sometimes six officers. I had a chance to train some young guys in surveillance, and we all feasted on bad guys who came to the ballpark expecting to feast on sports fans. Before I left the department we made more than eight hundred felony arrests around Tiger Stadium alone, maintaining a conviction rate somewhere above ninety percent.

Nights working around the stadium were certainly different. A normal night on a booster car was spent cruising crime hotspots along the precinct's backstreets and main drags, finding trouble in its natural desolate habitat. On ballgame nights, as many as forty thousand people would descend into the old stadium neighborhood, cram themselves into a small space, and leave behind on the streets their second most valuable possession – plus whatever they might have locked inside it. Officers on my detail became absolute experts on what to look for, and where, as the bad guys came shopping for loot. If there was a night without action, I don't remember it. Maybe the ultimate unreal scene in this unreal setting would come on those occasions when some guy from the burbs would be watching a double play or taking his seventh-inning stretch while, unbeknownst to him, his vehicle was the object of a high-speed chase through Corktown. Somebody once asked me if Walter Budzyn was a risk-taker. "Absolutely not," I said – then laughed at the only exception I could think of. Working the stadium detail one night, Walter was racing his unmarked car through alleys and bumpy streets in pursuit of a car thief. The hood of Walter's car flew open, but he refused to let the guy go. Instead he hunkered down and kept up the chase while peering through the tiny slit of a space at the bottom of his windshield. The thief outran Walter, but not Walter's radio call. Intercepted. Caught. Arrested.

Police officers aren't lawyers, but good cops quickly become expert at legal niceties that, if not followed, can put all your good work in the tank. So it went with making a good arrest of a car booster. You see a guy walk up and shatter a car window, for example. Do you have a car thief? Well, no. You have a guy who broke a window – to say nothing of the fact that he might be (don't laugh) somebody who locked the keys out of his own car. But what if some guy breaks a window and sits down inside a car not his own...is he a car thief? Well, no...he's a trespasser, I guess. How about the matter of the trespasser starting the car's engine? Once upon a time, car thieves leaned under the dash to hot-wire the vehicle. Then they took to shattering the key lock with a hammer, inserting a screwdriver into the ignition, and starting it that way. Then came new ignition systems and a new method – shattering the left side of the steering column and grasping a rod that would crank the engine. Surely, if someone who breaks a window, sits in a car not his own and does one of these things to start a car, then you have a car thief? Well, no. The Wayne Country Prosecutor's Office assured us that to make a UDAA (unlawfully driving away an automobile) case, we'd have to see the perp actually *make the car move.*

Legislators and prosecutors and judges are supposed to understand law and order better than anybody, but like most of society they have that tendency to think in the abstract. The hamburgers and cattle thing again. In a car thief's dream like the streets around Tiger Stadium, the reality was that having to let the perp roll the car before nailing him for UDAA created a lot of high-speed chases. Think about it. Anyone with an IQ above room temperature knows that someone who breaks into a car and punches out the ignition is a car thief. Car thieves should get the full measure of punishment for being what they are. But at the point you know he is a car thief, you can't arrest him for car theft. So you let him roll the car, and if your timing isn't perfect, and you don't get him boxed in, he's off and running. Ain't the law grand? But, being professionals, we abided by the law. Once, in two weeks of ballgames, we did enough damage to five police cars that they had to be taken off the streets. The brass, as punishment, ordered us back into uniform. That lasted one night, during which a number of suburbanites had to call for rides home.

By the way, regarding highly specialized information I'm not likely to be able to use in an office job, I can tell you that when a car thief breaks a steering column to get at the ignition rod, it creates exactly one blink of the left turn signal. So if you're ever sitting up in a tree with a radio, wondering when to tell your partner that the perp is ready to roll, now you know. Of course, it's been more than a decade since I got taken off the street. Maybe new technology has bypassed that particular trick. I don't know.

Radio contact with your partners in any kind of surveillance is vital. Early on we'd have to go through a third party, at dispatch, and it was difficult to say the least. Then we got prep radios with our own channels on them, and that helped a lot. We could talk directly with each other. When it came to catching a car thief, our timing was usually pretty good in this business of letting him roll the car a few feet so as to support a UDAA arrest, then moving in and boxing him off.

One night, with the ballgame an hour or two old, I saw a pickup cruising a dark side street about five miles an hour. It turned out there were three guys in the cab and three in the pickup bed, but – as was typical – I couldn't make out that much detail. You get your cues from a vehicle's movements, often having no idea who is inside it. The pickup stopped next to a Camaro or Trans Am – prime car-theft targets. I was, of course, up a tree and in radio contact with our crew. One kid hopped out of the truck bed and stood lookout while one kid from the cab moved toward the car. I thought we were about to have a UDAA, but shortly after I heard glass breaking I saw someone running back with a radio or some other item. I called for our car to move in, and we stopped them before they had moved more than a few feet.

We had all these guys but one – the driver – lying on the grass to be handcuffed. I was afraid this guy was going to try driving away, so I moved to the open passenger door of the truck and ordered him – several times – to throw the keys out the window and come out my side. All he would do is sit and stare off into space. Finally, I reached in, grabbed his right arm, pulled him out to the ground and handcuffed him. Almost immediately, he told me he was a diabetic and needed an insulin shot. Whether he planned to fence a hot radio for an insulin shot, I don't know. But as soon as we got to the station and told the sergeant what we had, I also told him the kid said he needed an insulin shot. A scout car took him to a hospital. Some time after that the kid filed a complaint, soon followed by a lawsuit claiming I had punched him and broken his arm. I'll give the law department credit for at least checking with the hospital and ascertaining that the kid did not seek medical treatment for a broken arm – which seems like something you might do while at a hospital getting an insulin shot...if your arm is, in fact, broken. That's the end of any credit I give the law department, because rather than fight the case the city cut the kid a check for $5,000.

In City of Detroit parlance, that's a nuisance settlement. To me it's a hell of a lot more than a nuisance. It's a symbol of the city's disregard and disrespect for cops doing their jobs. Down the road, when the mayor and the news media portrayed me as the rogue and racist "Starsky," this phantom broken arm became important, like the KFC holdup settlement. No one who heard the sound bites understood the truth. Much was made of citizen complaints and these two lawsuits against me. You need to know how that works, and how this particular car thief fits the picture.

Citizen complaints, obviously, result from contacts between

cops and citizens. Police officers who don't make contact with citizens don't get complaints. So it's only the working street cops who figure into this at all. The brass – who pontificate for the TV cameras if a controversy erupts – don't get citizen complaints. At least, I never heard a desk complain. So we are talking about street cops only. And you have to understand that lazy cops make far fewer contacts with citizens than hard-working cops. And that cops who do a little real police work and spend their evenings interacting with felons are interfacing with a different sort of citizen. Such citizens, if they confront a good police officer, often have one valid complaint: "He arrested me!" That said, complaints can come from the most innocuous contacts. I once got a complaint from a woman I stopped for a traffic violation. It could not possibly have been more routine. She did not complain that I had stopped her for no reason, or that I threatened her, or physically abused her, or even used any inappropriate words. She complained that *my demeanor made her nervous.* Here you are disarming one person a night, on average, and an official complaint goes in your file because someone who runs a stop sign thinks you were a bad charm-school student.

Once upon a time, a "citizen complaint" meant that a citizen walked into a precinct and filled out a form. During the Coleman Young years, official complaints got dumbed down to the point where a guy could go home, tell his wife that he had been stopped by police, do a little ass-covering in the way he told his story, and *his wife could call in a complaint.* Furthermore, if one incident resulted in more than one person making a complaint – or the same person complaining about more than one alleged outrage during a single contact – each of those went into your file as a separate complaint. Still furthermore, any serious complaint against a cop went not only against him, but against his partner – regardless of his partner's involvement or non-involvement.

That's the background against which the news media, with plenty of help from the city, put out word that several citizen complaints had been filed against me during my twenty-four and a half years on the force. I've gathered up all that I can find, and after eliminating multiple complaints arising from the same incident, I make it to be a total of thirteen, none of them sustained. Of those thirteen, three involved use of force. Of those three, on two occasions it was my partner who allegedly misused force. That leaves one strong-arm complaint across my 8,943 days as a cop. That one case was the kid I pulled out of that pickup truck while working the stadium detail. As I recall, he was white.

At the top of my story, I guessed I made somewhere between 50,000 and 100,000 citizen contacts. Some suburban cop I've never met calculated, in a letter to the editor, that during my career I made at least 62,000. I have no idea. I do know my felony arrest record, which makes the estimate, if anything, an understatement. I don't see any way of reading my citizen complaint file except as something *favorable* to me. The fact that it was used as an indictment of my career tells you something about politicians, prosecutors, the media, and a gullible public that loves sound bites.

Most often I'd position the surveillance detail south of the stadium, across Michigan Avenue where thousands of fans crammed their cars onto the streets of Corktown or into mom-and-pop backyard parking lots. A fair number of fans also parked north of the stadium, across I-75, and made their way to the ballpark on a pedestrian overpass. One night, after a few incidents had been reported over there, I moved the detail across the freeway, putting one officer on the roof of the Teamsters Union hall six blocks from the stadium, leaving two unmarked cars with one officer apiece, and me on foot. We were all, of course, in radio contact.

I was wandering the area when our man on the roof radioed that two suspicious young men were standing across the street. Now, what is "suspicious" about standing on a street corner? These two guys were black. Was this racial profiling? I have no idea whether the first thing that crossed my man's mind was that these two guys were black. It would not be an audacious, racist thing to have crossed his mind, because the baseball crowd is about ninety-nine percent white. But what raised the scenario from two black guys standing on a street corner to two *suspicious* black guys standing on a street corner was that, for one thing, they seemed to be standing without a purpose ...not headed anywhere, not waiting for somebody, but with all the mannerisms of casing their surroundings. And, oh yeah, this was July and both were wearing leather gloves. The cop on the roof, the one who used the word "suspicious," was, by the way, black.

I headed in that direction, hoping to find a place where I could observe what these two were up to. I was moving around, seeking a clandestine spot, when our man on the roof radioed that the pair were walking toward me. I wasn't sure whether this was coincidence, or my efforts at concealment weren't working real well. I ducked into the Teamsters parking lot, still looking for something to hide behind. In doing so, I passed out of sight from the rooftop, and to my surprise found not a single car in the parking lot. I could see the pair on the sidewalk now, and I ducked behind a large light pole. Not real successful, because now they were walking right in my direction. I keyed my radio, which I carried in a brown paper bag, and said: "I'll be off the air for a while. They're walking right at me." I turned off the radio, stepped from behind the pole, and began walking away.

When I heard their steps picking up pace and running toward me, I turned to meet them. Both pounced, knocking me to the pavement. My brown paper bag looked a little silly sliding away across the parking lot. One guy sat on my stomach, punching me in the chest while the other tried to get my wallet out of my rear pants pocket. I kept squirming, trying to keep him from getting my wallet and at the same time trying to pull my gun. The second guy was getting a bit antsy because he couldn't extract my wallet. He yelled to his buddy: "Cut him! Cut him!"

I managed to get an arm free, draw my revolver, and moved from defense to offense. Suddenly the two perps moved as if on hot coals. "Police officer!" I yelled. Both took off running. I fired several shots while still lying on the pavement, but seemed not to have hit either robber. They were gone.

I retrieved my radio, notified my partners what had happened, gave them a very brief description of the pair, and said what direction they were headed.

One of my crew, Max Bandy, picked me up and we circled the neighborhood. After about fifteen minutes, I saw two guys coming out of a backyard a block or so from the Teamsters hall. Both were shirtless.

"That's them!" I told Max. We pulled alongside as they walked nonchalantly down the sidewalk. We got out, each of us approaching one of the suspects. Both protested and claimed ignorance of what we were talking about. Then one of them started complaining that, by the way, he had been shot. Sure enough, he had a bullet wound in the buttocks. He went to a hospital under guard. His friend went to the precinct lockup.

I found a knife and their shirts, one of them bloodstained, in the backyard they had emerged from. Precinct detectives did their job, submitting a warrant request to the Wayne County Prosecutor's Office, seeking to charge both with armed robbery. Charges weren't filed for two months. Meanwhile, of course, the two had been released. Maybe it took so long because the two perps said they were innocently walking through the parking lot, asked me for a cigarette, and I started shooting. Or maybe I'm just jaded. Years of dealing with Detroit prosecutors who treat cops with disrespect – even cops who have a lengthy record of good cases – will do that to you.

At any rate, two months had passed and both suspects had to be arrested all over again before I could have my day in court. I say "my" day in because, yes, I was a cop...but they did jump *me*, and I suspect that if I hadn't been an armed police officer I would have wound up in the hospital myself – or worse. If I had been an unarmed Teamsters official working late, what do you suppose would have happened when one perp yelled, "Cut him! Cut him!" That's speculation. My good armed-robbery arrest was a fact.

When I discovered that warrants had finally been issued,

I began actively looking for the two assailants. The one I shot had an address in the precinct, the other had given a phony name and address the night we brought them in. Before I could find either one of them, I got a call from the prosecutor's office asking whether I objected to a reduced charge of unarmed robbery for the suspect who had given his real name. Utterly frustrated, I told the prosecutor to be my guest. I never did find the guy with the phony address. Good reason – he was a guest of the state under his real name, having been convicted of armed robbery and rape. He was free on bond at the time he jumped me.

The prosecutor's office – once it knew the whereabouts of the guy in prison – was obligated to arraign him in a timely manner in the matter of his attack on me. Didn't happen. He skated without facing charges in my case. What the hell, I was just a cop.

Max Bandy, who helped me arrest the pair, was still a Detroit cop in 1998 when his son Shawn, twenty-three, wearing the uniform on the streets of Detroit, was shot to death by kidnap suspects who opened fire from the back of a van.

The sixteen years I worked plainclothes in the precinct weren't about the stadium surveillance detail and keeping the ballpark safe for suburbanites, or about getting mugged myself in the Teamsters parking lot. The stadium detail was more like a productive and useful side job that consumed a big chunk of many summer nights. I got a chance to train a few younger coppers. I got a chance to do a little surveillance that usually produced a good arrest quite quickly. I got a chance to do some work that mattered, sooner or later, to almost everyone in metro Detroit. Most of all, the stadium detail had been my ticket out of uniform and back into full-time work making good felony arrests. That's the main reason I never got tired of climbing trees.

5
THE
BOOSTER-CAR LIFE

On March 5, 1970, Nancy brought our daughter Kelly into the world. It's probably the best thing either of us has ever done. For our generation, we were a little slow at becoming parents. Even so, I wasn't ready for it. Remember, I was also slow at finding my life's profession. I became a cop at twenty-eight and a father at twenty-nine, so when I made the turn at thirty I was still learning how to be both. Kelly was, however, the most beautiful baby girl on the planet – of course. She instantly became the love of Nancy's life and mine, and remains so to this day. In her young life she has endured much and learned much. Sharp cookie, like her mom. And like her mom, she has been an inspiration for me throughout the hard times since November 5, 1992. Once Nancy and I were enjoying Kelly in our lives, we wished we had started earlier and had two or three kids. After the bad years began, Kelly probably wished the same.

Most everybody has a certain amount of trouble balancing a career and a family. For a plainclothes officer working the power shift every night…well, it's kind of embarrassing to talk about balance. Most days it was more like ships passing in the night, and then passing again in the morning. Except for the two years she stayed home after Kelly's birth, Nancy has always held a job. Kelly grew up thinking of adult life as a shift change. She became a nurse, so I guess it runs in the family.

Nancy and I both grew up in the city, but her parents moved to Dearborn Heights, a nearby suburb, before we married. By the time I joined the department in 1968, we had been living briefly in an apartment near her folks. The city at that time – and throughout my career – required employees to live in Detroit. This was no big deal to us, and it meant we could buy a nice little colonial for $18,000 on Archdale just east of the Southfield Freeway and north of Grand River Avenue. This is where Kelly learned to walk, where her regular playmate across the street was a black girl whose father was a good guy and a good mechanic. The surroundings were natural for me, because growing up on Monica Street, where I borrowed my cousin's convertible for the prom and pecked my friend's sister on the cheek, made me a Detroiter and a west-sider.

Nancy, like any good American wife, had her eye on something more like a dream house. She had the all-American hobby of dream-shopping for houses as she drove city streets. By 1976, when Kelly was six years old, Nancy seemed to be getting serious about her hobby, because if a house really caught her eye she would knock on the door and ask if the owner had considered selling.

Her dream-shopping zeroed in on the Rosedale Park neighborhood, which straddles Grand River Avenue west of the Southfield Freeway. This was one of the few Detroit neighborhoods that had held on to its upper-middle-class status. Like all Detroiters, Rosedale Park residents had to drive outside the city to find a department store – or even, with rare exceptions, a decent grocery store. Rosedale Park had that city-life edge – accountants and salesmen keeping a revolver handy in the bedroom, a lot of iron latticework on screen doors – but it was a *nice* neighborhood…a refuge for people who either wanted to live in the city, refusing to give in to the bad guys, or who had no choice but to live in the city, or who had grown up in the city and thought of it as their natural habitat. I guess I fit all those descriptions. But I wasn't sure I fit Rosedale Park financially speaking. These were nice houses, and cops – even hard-working cops who prowled the streets by night and made extra money testifying in court by day – were not exactly upper-income types.

Bretton Drive was one of the nicest streets in Rosedale Park, and one day while dream-shopping Nancy saw the house she had to have. Before long she was knocking on the door, inquiring if the owner had thought about selling. Well, yes. He was getting toward retirement time, and, yeah, if the deal was right he might sell. It was a beautiful colonial, and to tell you the truth – even with house payment calculations rushing through my brain – I fell in love with the place, too. Besides, the same house in an Oakland County suburb or one of the Grosse Pointes would cost twice as much. I actually had looked at Nancy's dream house, and started leaning toward her enthusiasm, before realizing I had stopped in front of that house dozens of times. Back in STRESS days, Dave Siebert had lived there for a while. We had car-pooled to work, and I would pick him up on Bretton Drive. Dave's father-in-law became the seller on our mortgage papers. We moved to Rosedale Park in February 1977.

Emanuel Steward, the boxing coach who made a legend out of the Kronk Gym and a champion out of Thomas Hearns, lived down the street. When Leon Spinks won the heavyweight championship, he bought a house across the street. The late Maryanne Mahaffey, a very liberal city councilwoman, lived on Bretton Drive. I was invited to visit her place a number of times when her burglar alarm went off. After I was arrested and TV crews swarmed Bretton Drive, she told the world that my kind of rogue, brutal policing would not be tolerated in Detroit. The black couple next door to the east – who enjoyed the tomatoes I grew in the backyard – refused to talk with reporters, and passed me an envelope containing three hundred dollars for my defense fund. The young black guy living next door to the west told the cameras I seemed like a nice enough guy.

We did a lot of work on that house, fixed it up, enjoyed the yard, took our turn cutting grass on the center strip where the city seldom did any mowing. It really *was* our dream place. That's despite things like Kelly getting mugged one night in our driveway, with the perp putting his hand over her mouth and ripping a gold chain off her neck. The robber was black. I was down in the ghetto at the time serving and protecting black residents of a more dangerous neighborhood. You're not supposed to think of things that way. Under the circumstances, it has become a little difficult for me to think of things any other way.

When I think of my police career, I always think of the daily routine starting and ending on Bretton Drive…although most days didn't really have a start and an end. The 7 p.m.-to-3 a.m. power shift consumed the night, and testifying in court consumed most of many days. I learned to sleep in shifts a couple of hours at a time, and the fact is I was suited to it. Except in weeks where I had to testify every single day, it never bothered me much at all.

A typical day might mean getting up after three or four hours' sleep, just as Nancy was ready to head out the door. If I was testifying that day, I'd need to be in court by 9 a.m. If it was Wayne County Circuit Court, it meant I needed to put on a necktie. Recorder's Court, the city's criminal court, was more informal. I couldn't give you a good estimate of how many times I testified in the many thousands of misdemeanor and felony arrests I made. Prosecutors – and how's this for irony? – loved to see me on a witness list. I did my job professionally, made good arrests, testified well. A Recorder's Court judge, knowing my experience on the stadium detail, once called me as an expert witness in somebody else's auto theft case. My days in court were sometimes a strange contrast to my nights on the street…brightly lit, surrounded by three-piece suits, very orderly – though the hallways, witness stands and audiences were well-populated by characters who would probably make your average suburbanite nervous.

One morning, I arrived to testify in Recorder's Court, stopping first at the basement Police Detail Room to sign in. As I walked back into the hallway, I found six gang members from my precinct sitting on a long bench. Whatever their case was, it had nothing to do with me, and I started walking past them toward the escalator. When we made eye contact, all six stood, turned, faced the wall and "assumed the position" – hands forward on the wall, back arched allowing an officer to make a search safely. They were serious. Like I said, booster-car work is not undercover work. All the bad guys knew me.

Either partner on an arrest could, of course, testify when a case got to trial. Usually we would split up court duties, to avoid working twenty-four hours a day and to share the extra income.

At the beginning of each fiscal year, your first 60 hours of court duty was paid at time and a half – but had to be taken not in cash, but as comp time. You could keep those 60 hours of comp time in the bank straight through to retirement if you wished. Most cops used it up on vacation. But many, including Walter Budzyn and me, built up quite a bank. Building up those days as a retirement bonus was a good idea, because suburban cops – who might go an entire career without making as many felony arrests as a Detroit officer in a booster car made in a month – were not only better paid and better equipped, but had pension benefits two or three times that of city cops. Literally. Some of the best suburban cops are "retired" Detroit officers writing traffic tickets and wondering why they had put up with mean streets so long for so little reward and so few thanks. Officers who rode with me got more court time than they would riding any other car in the precinct. Anyway, Walter and I thought we were being prudent about retirement planning. As it turned out, our bank of comp time got eaten up real quick for other reasons.

With a court appearance out of the way, I'd be back home at midday or mid-afternoon, grab an hour or two of sack time, get up and shower again, and get dressed in my "uniform" of jeans and sweatshirt. The only other items I needed before heading for work were my handcuffs, my revolver and my flashlight. The gun I carried ninety-five percent of the time was a Colt Python .357 magnum that Nancy had bought for me about a year after I started. It was the gun I carried the night Willard and I interrupted the gas station burglary. One night Willard and I were driving down Fort Street and saw a tire lying in the middle of the road. We stopped the car. I got out and tossed the tire off to the sidewalk. Maybe half an hour later, I touched my holster and discovered the Python was missing. I yelled at Willard to circle back, and there it was, lying in the middle of Fort Street. One day in downtown Detroit, I found myself staring back at the Colt from the wrong end. On my last night as a police officer, Malice Green reached for the same gun. In all my years of police work, I fired my weapon – either the Colt or a smaller, lighter .38 snub-nose I sometimes carried on surveillance – on only five occasions, ten rounds in all. Six of those rounds were fired when I was jumped outside the Teamsters hall. Your objective as a cop is never to use your gun. But like the man said, you don't leave home without it.

The power shift got its name because it overlapped the busy second half of the afternoon shift and the busy first half of the midnight shift. Furthermore, at midnight, while the afternoon shift hit the ramp returning to the station and the midnight shift prepared to roll, power-shift cars were likely to be the only cars on the street. That's why the power shift included marked scout cars as well as unmarked booster cars. Shifts were scheduled a month in advance. Most nights two booster cars were on the street, sometimes one. On a Sunday night in the dead of winter, there might not be any booster car scheduled at all.

Getting to work early every night wasn't some workaholic waste of time. You've probably had a job yourself where doing it right required prep work that couldn't be done on the clock. So it went with me. Nobody else in the precinct was as religious about it, or as organized about it, as I was. I couldn't see any other way to get the job done right. You don't just roll out the door and start collecting felons off the street. I might have been a bad reader when it came to school subjects I didn't care about. But when it came to something that interested me – which turned out to be police work – I was a bear for the printed word. It came at you from several directions.

I'd walk in the door at 6 or 6:15 p.m. and start devouring the teletype, incident reports and the stolen car hotsheet. The teletype circulated once a day. It contained a synopsis of the previous twenty-four hours' worth of major crimes across the city. Incident reports came from the precinct desk. All the incident reports from the day shift would be new to me, and there'd be a couple hours of reports from the front end of the afternoon shift – a few of which might land in the basket during my prep period. From these reports and the teletype I'd absorb fragments of information – a perp's license plate number, a last name, a street name, a description, a crime location, a similarity to an incident report from last week. The hotsheet was a long, columnized list of maybe 5,000 stolen-car license numbers. At first, we pin-tacked the hotsheet to our dashboard. Then the department complained because dashboards started to look like Swiss cheese. After that, we used Scotch tape. Working in Detroit, often as not we bought our own Scotch tape.

Before rolling out the garage door at 7 p.m., I'd keep my ears open while my eyes were studying. A perp might be getting booked, while his accomplice remained at large. A precinct detective might need someone picked up. Two detectives worked the same shift. If I caught one for a chat, that meant he also had come in early. I made it a point to review all their case files whenever I could. If street cops get sidetracked by too much paperwork (and they do), detectives are drowned in paperwork. It's their job to follow up on street cops' work, to get warrants, and to interact with prosecutors. By reviewing their files, I could find the latest cases where a warrant had been issued but the suspect hadn't yet been arrested, or where a suspect had failed to show up in court as directed.

All this prep activity, crammed into forty-five minutes or an hour, gave me an edge on other street cops before I even turned the ignition of my car.

Prep time sometimes proved valuable for other cops who found me in my "office," most often because of my crew's unique mug-shot library. If I had stopped to think what our mug library ultimately would amount to, I would have bought stock in Polaroid. It all began because of a first-class partner I had named Woody Horne.

Throughout my years in the precinct, I worked with many partners. A full crew would be three men permanently assigned to the two-man car. But there were times when I had only one steady partner, catching a third man as necessary either from another crew or by taking a uniformed officer into plainclothes for the night. In fact, there were periods when I was a permanent "crew" of one. The people who rode with me in that car ranged from seasoned plainclothes cops to rookies I trained. I had some partners I trusted with my life, and I rode with a few guys whose lack of skills or lack of courage meant that when I stepped out of the car I might just as well have been alone. Some of the very best times in that regard came in the years soon after the precinct was reorganized on August 15, 1980.

The city had thirteen precincts when I started, and had thirteen when I left the force – even though the numbers assigned go all the way up to Sixteen. That's a relic of changes and combined precincts over the years. For a year or two after the 1980 reorganization, there were only twelve precincts. The Second disappeared from the map when it was merged with the downtown precinct, the First. The new precinct was renamed the Third. Downtown remained part of the precinct for a while, then was split off again. So when I say I spent more than sixteen years driving a booster car in the same precinct, we are technically talking about the Second and the Third. Either way it was the same real estate, except for that brief period when downtown was a part of it.

When the First and Second were combined to form the Third, there was as you can imagine a lot of scrambling for assignments. No one was going to take my booster car away, because I had seniority and because I was so productive. A few of the Third's plainclothes cops wound up back in uniform as new guys from the old First, including Walter Budzyn and Max Bandy, brought their seniority over to the Third. Somewhere soon after the merger, I wound up with the best three-man crew, top to bottom, I ever had.

I met Mike Dameron when he was a patrolman who often got

assigned to the uniformed stadium detail. Detroit had a Scooter Patrol at the time – the brainchild of a chief named Johannes Spreen who was hired out of the New York department. You'll find more pedestrians on one block in Manhattan than you'll find in an entire precinct in Detroit, but that's another story. When you did get a crowd of pedestrians in Detroit, such as at a Tigers game, the scooters made some sense. Most scooter cops were content to show the flag and write misdemeanor tickets. Mike, though, would often show up in support of my plainclothes crew when we rounded up multiple felony suspects to take into custody, or otherwise could use a hand. He was a good street cop.

Woody Horne had been first man on his own booster-car crew in the old First. When he got to the new Third, he naturally wanted his own car again. That wasn't going to happen, even though with a bigger precinct we sometimes put three booster cars on the street. Woody's good reputation preceded him, and I wanted him on my car. He came, even though I had already enlisted Mike Dameron, whose seniority made Woody our car's third man. I don't know if Woody liked the idea of working with me, or did it because his only alternative was a return to uniform. But suddenly I had an outstanding crew. Woody and Mike were both dedicated, hard-working officers, and great human beings. If there is a booster-car heaven, I've already seen it.

Woody brought a Polaroid camera with him, along with the idea that we should photograph everybody we arrested. So began a unique and in the end massive piece of self-initiative. The collection of photos became so large that one day in 1990 I felt compelled to count them. At the time, the crew of Booster Car 3-31 had compiled a mug-shot file which included more than 7,000 faces. A mug-shot has two essential purposes: to jog a memory, or to help find a suspect who is nothing but a name on a piece of paper. I can't tell you how many times that mug file paid off for us. Or for other street cops and detectives – sometimes even from other precincts – who would wander over almost on a daily basis during my prep time and ask something like: "Hey, you got a picture of that guy you busted for holding up the liquor store on McGraw two years ago?" Of course we did. If we ever arrested the guy, we had his picture.

Which brings us to yet another common-sense footnote to the racial profiling issue. How did we organize this hefty mug-shot file? Alphabetically. But how else? By race. We had an alphabetical black file and an alphabetical white file. The black file was larger, so we put all the female mugs in the white file. Was this racial profiling? Of course it was. Anyone who wants to thumb through a couple thousand mug-shots of white guys while trying to identify a black guy is...well, really suited for government work.

So there you have the prep time routine of a hard-working, dedicated street cop. And when this hard-working, dedicated street cop was ready to roll at 7 p.m., where did I go? Usually we drove straight to a coney island restaurant, so named because in Detroit chili dogs are called coney islands. This trip straight to the chow line wasn't what it seems. Most people, I suppose, go to lunch four hours after punching the clock. A power-shift street cop doesn't go to lunch at 11 p.m., when things generally are heating up. He doesn't go to lunch when the afternoon and midnight shifts are passing in the night leaving the streets unpatrolled. And chances are he woke up from his post-courtroom nap just in time to get ready for work. So the first thing my partner and I would do most nights is grab a meal and compare notes, though still on the radio in case we were needed. If we took another break, it was usually near the end of the shift. The bottom line, cuisine-wise, is that I often didn't eat a bite at home. And I probably ate one hundred times the average citizen's consumption of coney island hot dogs, which probably accounted for the need to alter my uniform on those occasions I had to pull it out of the closet.

I wore out a lot of booster cars, which eventually got replaced. But for radio purposes, every one of my cars was known as 3-31 – the "3" designating the precinct and the "31" designating my crew. Booster cars were known as "30-series cars." The uniformed power-shift units were "80-series cars." You could identify any car on the radio by its number designation. Anyone working in the precinct knew that 3-31 was my car. Even scout cars had permanent crews, and anyone who knew precinct personnel was likely to know that 3-4 was a particular uniformed patrol crew. If my car called for backup more than three or four times during my years in the precinct, I can't recall it. Everyone knew that. That's why on November 5, 1992, all the cops in Three listened up real close as Walter Budzyn radioed that 3-31 wanted some help at Warren and Twenty-Third.

Marked patrol cars usually got a radio run almost the moment they rolled. Booster cars generally got radio runs only if it was a priority case, usually in progress. And dispatchers generally held back from the booster cars altogether at the top of the shift, because of our well-known lunch schedule. On April 24, 1981, I missed my coney island hot dog. Whatever health benefits I got from eliminating a little grease from my diet almost cost my life.

I was driving toward downtown, probably to the Lafayette Coney Island. I don't remember. The rest of it I remember vividly. Mike Dameron, my number two, was my partner. We knew each other's work habits and attitudes very well. The radio barked: "Need car in Number Three to make the Book-Cadillac Hotel. Man with a gun."

Whether to volunteer for a run was the passenger's decision. The MDT – mobile data terminal – was a recent addition to the car, a powerful tool. It was the passenger's job to punch in license plate numbers into the MDT and check whether a car was hot, and whether its owner had outstanding arrest warrants. The passenger also was the car's designated report-writer, and was responsible for keeping the car's activity log up to date. Traditionally, driver and passenger would switch after four hours, but that was entirely up to preferences of the crew. At any rate, whoever rode as passenger had to do all the paperwork and therefore got to decide whether to volunteer for a run. I knew what Mike's answer would be, but I asked anyway.

"Do you want to make it?"

"Sure," he said.

He picked up the microphone and radioed: "3-31 will take the Book-Cadillac run."

The dispatcher said: "3-31, you are busy."

We were only about a mile from the hotel, one of the saddest symbols of old downtown's decline. It was once the city's showcase hotel, the bridal-suite destination of well-heeled newlyweds from around Michigan, its ballroom the scene of politicians' inaugural parties, a watering hole and dining spot and sleeping place for high-powered visitors from around the world. By the time Mike Dameron and I caught the man-with-a-gun run, major sections of the building had descended to welfare-hotel status, operating as state-subsidized housing programs. Several floors also had been turned over to a shelter for battered women.

I turned our car into the hotel's entrance drive on Washington Boulevard, once a row of fine shops and restaurants and now a dreary strip inspiring old-timers to shake their heads and blather about what used to be. As I pulled up to the hotel entrance, I noticed a two-door Olds Cutlass off to one side. What struck me as odd was the seating arrangement of the two occupants – one man in the driver's seat and another seated directly behind him. As I stepped out of our car, I decided to have a discreet look at the Cutlass license plate just in case these guys were somehow involved in our 911 call. This particular example of a car thief's favorite target had no license plate at all. Ordinarily, of course, I would instantly be interviewing the two strangely arranged occupants. But we had a higher priority – getting inside the hotel, finding out who made the call, and why.

Just inside the door we were met by two men in suits, who identified themselves as hotel security.

"Did you see them?" one man asked.

"See who?"

"The guy in the Oldsmobile. He has a gun."

Mike and I ran outside just in time to see the Cutlass pulling away. We got back into our car and followed, expecting them to run, maybe resulting in a high-speed chase through downtown. Instead, the guy drove slowly, cautiously even. About a block and a half from the hotel we activated our emergency lights. The suspect came to an immediate stop.

Just as I opened my door, the rear passenger made a very sudden and characteristic move. He bent at the waist for a moment and just as suddenly was sitting bolt upright again. I had seen that move countless times. Without fail, the person in question had been concealing a gun, a knife, narcotics, narcotics paraphernalia, or alcohol.

I drew my Colt, holding it at my side, and approached the Cutlass. As I approached the driver's door, I could see blood was draining down the driver's head and onto his face. I didn't take time for an introductory question or two, but simply ordered him out of the car. Since the passenger was on the same side, I ordered him out the driver's door as well. They complied, as they did when I ordered them to "assume the position," with their hands on the roof of the car, feet spread and back. I put my gun back in its shoulder holster and began to pat down the rear passenger.

Mike went into the Olds and found a .38-caliber revolver on the driver's-side rear floorboard. The hammer was cocked.

Mike got out, standing on the other side of the car, threw his cuffs on the roof, and pointed his weapon at both suspects while I began to cuff the rear passenger, who, we later learned, was a man named Sevoid Lutes, age thirty- two. I had gotten one handcuff on his left wrist when he started protesting. "What's this for? What's this for? I didn't do nothing!"

He began squirming, trying to get away from my grasp. I pushed his handcuffed left arm farther up his back, trying to get him to calm down. "What's this for?" he kept shouting.

"Take it easy! Take it easy!" I shouted back.

My grasp wasn't good enough, because Lutes swung around, winding up a haymaker with his free right arm, and striking me in the head. We both went to the pavement. The following moments are less clear in my memory. He had stunned me.

Mike came around to help, but Lutes kicked Mike in the chest and sent him reeling. The handcuff on Lutes's left wrist now became a serious weapon to be avoided. Imagine swinging a dangling handcuff like a gladiator's chain. As fast as things were moving, I couldn't help but notice the two security guards from the hotel had moved up the street to watch. It would have been a nice little gesture if they had offered to help.

I felt my gun slipping out of its holster, and then lying beneath Lutes and me as we struggled on the pavement. If I ever have been focused in my life, I was focused on recovering that gun. Lutes got his hand on it first. I grabbed the cylinder with both hands to prevent it from turning. He kept sticking the barrel in my midsection, and I kept pushing it away.

"Shoot him, Mike! He's got my gun!"

"I can't!" With the perp and me locked in close mortal combat, it was impossible for Mike to get off a shot that wasn't just as likely to hit me as the bad guy.

The good news was that I had hold of my gun. The bad news was that I couldn't use my hands for any other purpose. At one point, he swung my gun toward Mike, but I deflected it away. The two hotel guards continued to watch from their ringside seat. Mike tried to maneuver for position. He couldn't pounce, because that might result in me being shot. The wrestling match seemed to last for hours. Maybe it was two minutes. Maybe less.

As I began to lose my breath, I began to lose my grip, and began to seriously believe I was going to die. The way this guy was struggling, with plenty of strength and stamina, I suspected he was high on some sort of narcotic. I held to my death grip on the gun's barrel and cylinder and tried to think of some way to go on offense. Instead I ran out of gas.

"I can't hold him any more!" I yelled. And I let go of my gun.

Lutes rose up, standing over me. I closed my eyes to avoid watching my own death. When no shot came, I looked up and our eyes met momentarily, and I thought: "This is it. Why doesn't Mike shoot him? What is taking so long." I suppose that thought lasted a split second. It seemed an eternity.

Lutes's motion, however, wasn't to aim the gun at me, but to turn toward Mike. He took one bullet from Mike in the midsection. Instead of falling, he merely bent at the waist. I knew Mike couldn't have missed because they were only five or six feet apart. I also knew Mike carried a .45-caliber weapon, and I didn't think anyone could still be standing with that kind of wound. I remained motionless and defenseless on the pavement, still exhausted, and thinking something like: Maybe if I don't move, the gunman won't notice me.

As Lutes, incredibly, raised back up he again pointed my gun at Mike. Ducking defensively, Mike got off two panic shots, which missed. I still believe this guy had to be doped up, because he began to run down the sidewalk back toward the hotel, my handcuffs dangling off his left wrist, my .357 in his right hand. Mike gave chase around a corner, yelling at Lutes to stop. He refused, and Mike fired one more shot, hitting him in the back. Lutes lay in a parking lot, where he died still clutching my gun.

While Mike was giving chase, I radioed for backup. I used Mike's cuffs to arrest the Cutlass driver – who had remained standing beside the car throughout the episode. I asked the responding officers to go around the corner and check on my partner because I had heard a shot.

For me, ghost-white and pondering a near-death experience, this was a scene where a bad guy had run amok. But procedurally, at that point it became a police shooting scene. My patrol sergeant arrived, also in plainclothes, and confiscated my gun from the dead perp, Mike's .45, and the .38 Mike had retrieved from the Cutlass. The sergeant stuck all three in his waistband and took us into the hotel to await further orders. I felt like I had been walking three days across the Mojave Desert. I would have given twenty bucks for a drink of water.

The sergeant walked into the hotel bar and asked for a glass of H2O. The bartender drew it and said: "That'll be one dollar." The sergeant paid, walked back into the lobby and held the glass out to me. Zoom! A hand came from nowhere, snatched the glass, and poured it down another parched throat – Mike's hand, Mike's throat. I went in search of a drinking fountain.

The process, and the people staring at us, gave every sense that we were being treated as criminals. What the hell was that about? Didn't these people realize Mike and I both had just almost lost our lives responding to *their* 911 call? The sergeant moved us to the hotel office, and someone apparently got things sorted out, because they sent up a tray of coffee. The sergeant's orders had been in error, anyway. He should have been told to take us down to Homicide, where we did eventually give our statements and answer questions. The Homicide sergeant who interviewed me was Roger Brooks, whom I had replaced when I joined a STRESS crew. I was still pale from the experience. "Maybe," he said, "you ought to consider a new line of work."

The investigation revealed that the driver of the Cutlass was an unwilling accomplice. Lutes had come uninvited to the driver's house with a scheme for taking Lutes's estranged wife out of the battered women's shelter. When the driver refused, Lutes pistol-whipped him. The perp ordered his unwilling accomplice and his girlfriend to take him to the Book-Cadillac, where Lutes ordered her to go inside and bring out the estranged wife. Instead, the girlfriend went in, notified security, and generated the 911 call. What would have happened to the estranged wife had she been taken out to the Cutlass is pure speculation, but Lutes's .38 and an educated guess don't paint a nice picture.

As is supposed to happen with all deaths in custody, a board of review was quickly convened for Mike and me. It was a clean, though fatal, arrest. Two years later, Mike and I received special citations for good police work – the only award I ever got from Michigan's then-governor, James Blanchard. Why the delay, and why from the governor instead of City Hall, I couldn't say. Maybe the old Book-Cadillac mystique attracted attention in Lansing. The hotel eventually was boarded up, but I've still got my citation.

6

THE STREET VALUE
OF RESPECT

Talk to anyone who is, or was, a street cop. In uniform or in plainclothes. Forty years ago or yesterday. Ask them about working the street, and the essence of the job. No matter their politics or religion or level of education or which football team they root for. Or their race. There's one thing they all will tell you.

You can't back down.

That's it. The universal truth of going out on the street and requesting a disorderly person to move along, or a suspect to submit to a search, or a felon to, please, sir, come along with me to the station. You have to be in command. Let the bad guy start thinking he's in command, or can assume command, and it's going to go bad. Guaranteed. Whether you are dealing with a garden-variety street person, or a dangerous habitual felon, he will know a soft touch when he sees one. He will sense any opportunity to reverse roles, to get in control. If you show fear or even hesitancy, he will smell it like a dog.

Not that I never felt fear. When you do, you put it in your pocket and forget about it because you know it's dangerous to do otherwise. If circumstances prevent you from forgetting about it, at least you keep it in your pocket, don't show it, and stay in command. I think I was courageous my share of times. Night in and night out it was less a matter of courage than simply a matter of not being cowardly. I had a job to do. It required me to stick my nose in places where noses get broken.

I took a professional approach to managing my emotions. I was pretty emotional in front of the Book-Cadillac with my own gun sticking in my gut. That was rare. Fear can get you killed. Anger can get you killed. I kept both in my pocket.

Only one thing on the street made me angry every time it happened. And I think it, too, is universal among police officers. That is, the gut-wrenching anger you feel at a perp who leads you on a high-speed chase. I have had suspects pull a weapon on me without making me angry. At least not the kind of anger that arises when some guy decides to run and goes through a red light at eighty miles an hour, and you don't even see a tap on his brake light. The potential for mayhem among innocent bystanders is as great as a bad guy opening fire in a crowded room. At every intersection and blown stop sign you only get angrier at the fleeing felon. Show me a police officer who has never gotten seriously angry at a high-speed runner, and I will show you a police officer who has never been in a high-speed chase. I have verbally abused runners after catching them. On a couple such occasions – after chasing someone who was clearly willing to murder anyone who got in the way of his car – anger got far enough out of my pocket that I became zealous in the handcuffing process.

So why chase these guys? Well, obviously you can't ban all chases. Where do you draw the line? Do you not chase habitual reckless and maybe drunk or high drivers who are on the street without a license…meaning they are a loaded cannon if you don't apprehend them? Do you not chase a burglar, who is a felon and might well be something more than a burglar? Do you not chase an armed robber? Do you not chase a murderer, on grounds he might kill six more people while driving through the next intersection? Do you chase up to sixty miles an hour? Eighty miles an hour? One hundred miles an hour? I don't know. I was a by-the-book cop, but I didn't write the book. If the manual said "Chase," I would chase. If it said "Don't chase," I wouldn't. I do know this – letting everyone go who puts a foot on the accelerator is a form of backing down. It's a real Catch-

22. And I think you can see why high-speed runners make a police officer angry.

I have never invented any kind of gizmo, but for years I tried to think of a solution to high-speed chases. I thought a mechanical governor of some kind, built into all new cars, might allow cops to punch a code into a transmitter and shut off the engine of any fleeing car. Surely that could be done. But if fifteen-year-old kids can hack into Pentagon computers, then the bad guys would figure a way to use such a device to stop innocent motorists and rob them, or worse. I even thought along James Bond lines – some kind of device you could fire from the grille of a police car, shooting out a wire or a rope with... what?...on the end. Suction cups? A harpoon? All such ideas must be a dead-end or somebody else would have solved the problem long ago. But high-speed chases make emotion intrude on what needs to be an emotionless job, and that was enough to make me do much pondering about how to sidestep that particular piece of police work.

"Emotionless" doesn't mean heartless. It doesn't mean you initiate citizen contact by getting on the muscle, not even verbally. It just means you don't let the bad guys get the upper hand. Not even in a simple, non-felonious situation. If you let a small-time pimp or pusher control a street interview and walk away from you, while various of his associates look on, it's as good as writing your ticket out of the precinct. You'll have lost respect on the street, and you won't be doing your fellow officers any favors. A good street cop must treat people with respect and at the same time demand respect in return. I treated the citizenry fairly; meanwhile, everyone on the street knew that if you were dirty, I was going to arrest you. "Dirty" didn't mean just a smudge. Our job was to make good felony arrests, not to roust drunks and people who double-parked. Every arrest means paperwork and an hour or two or three off the street back at the station. I made the paperwork count, worked a productive shift, and used common sense. Sometimes that meant not only making arrests by the book, but also using a little creativity while making no arrest at all.

One night I took a radio run on a report of someone with a gun. Six or eight people, family and neighbors, were partying on a front porch. Most were roaring drunk. Sitting there in plain sight was a loaded revolver. My partner and I worked the crowd for a minute, BS-ing with them and trying to get a feel for the situation. One guy gave me the eye and clearly had something to tell me. We found a quiet corner and talked. The older woman sitting at the end of the porch owned the gun. It was legal, and registered. I asked my informant – probably the one who called police – if he would get the registration papers for me. He did. The gun was indeed legit. I had no evidence it had been so much as brandished, let alone pointed at anyone, let alone fired. Still, alcohol and a loaded gun are not a real good combination. I had to do something, but I didn't want to arrest anyone. The front-porch good times were raucous enough that I was able to get the gun and slip into the house without the old woman noticing. I put it in her freezer. Next night when I came in to do my prep work, a sergeant came over and said some old lady had come in raising all kind of hell because I had stolen her gun. "Tell her," I said, "to look in her freezer." If she had written a sentence or two on a piece of paper, it would have been recorded as a citizen complaint.

If citizen contact brought me into conversation with a happy drunk who had not been driving outrageously but probably shouldn't be behind the wheel, I sometimes kept my booster car patrolling the street and did society a favor at the same time. I'd point out the nearest pay phone and tell the driver to call someone to come get him, and to bring an ignition key. Then I'd take his ignition key off the ring and drop it down the nearest sewer. I was designating drivers before anyone heard of designated drivers.

So you show a little heart and common sense, and you don't talk wise-assed until confronted by a wise-ass, don't escalate until escalated. When in Rome, and all that. There were nights when most citizens I talked to had accumulated more prior arrests than they had completed grades in school. Street-corner chat in the Third had a different texture than, say, two sociologists having a lunch discussion over a nice bottle of wine. Nonetheless, I could talk civilly to a three-time felon. Civility adjusted for street talk, of course. After all, I got to know most of these people pretty well. And although bad guys are seldom bad guys just once, you can always hope that a little interaction with police will keep the bad guys on their toes, hold repeat offenses to a minimum, and develop information leading you to those who are currently dirty. Like I said, networking is a powerful tool in any line of work.

One guy who was well-known in the Warren and Twenty-Third neighborhood was Robert Knox, no relation to Stanley Knox, the police chief who one day would vow that Detroit was "not Simi Valley." I arrested Robert Knox several times on drug-related offenses, including armed robbery. I probably talked to Robert Knox another twenty or thirty times without arresting him. With a guy like Robert Knox, you know that if he lives long enough, you are going to arrest him again. It's the cycle of crime among career criminals and junkies. Nothing those two sociologists come up with at lunch is going to change the reality of it. Meanwhile, when you make contact with such a person and he is not at large from a new crime, the two of you talk the talk. That's the kind of "civility" I mean.

I can't tell you exactly when Robert Knox gave me the nickname "Starsky," except it was not in an encounter that resulted in arrest. He probably made me smile the first time he said it, way back when Knox was a teenager and Mike Angeluski was my partner. It would have been that kind of conversation. Booster Car 3-31 stopped in Three's neighborhoods far more often than the pizza man, so it's not surprising that the cop in jeans and sweatshirt, who talked to everybody and wasn't to be messed with if you were dirty, got a nickname. I had a ton of them, in fact. Over in Mexicantown I was known as "Italiano" (how's that for erroneous racial profiling?). In one black neighborhood I was known as "Green Eyes." In the same neighborhood where some called me Starsky I was also known as "Frizzo." Don't ask. I can't explain it. Only a professor could explain how "Rizzo" gets fractured on the street. Ratso Rizzo? Frank Rizzo? Who knows?

Anyway, when Robert Knox was a teenager, all my hair was black. Years of coney island hot dogs and fighting gravity hadn't rearranged my face and belly. No casting director would have mistaken me for Paul Michael Glaser. But a little resemblance to the TV star was there, especially when I was standing beside a booster car. Young Robert Knox thought it was an amusing name to hang on me. Robert Knox got around, so the name "Starsky" got around, too. Among a select group of citizens, most of whom had long-term problem relationships with the Michigan Criminal Code, I became Starsky. Whoever was working with me – and many partners followed Mike Angeluski – became "Hutch." It could just as easily have been Freebie and the Bean or Butch and Sundance. But by the time the news media got done interviewing Robert Knox's friends on the street for instant analysis of my character, I would have settled for Frick and Frack. Or, for that matter, Frizzo. I never called Robert Knox by a nickname. Definitely not "Bob."

I suppose in polite society much of a street cop's interaction with sidewalk citizenry would be called "banter." Say "banter with an edge" and that would be about right. I met these people on their turf, talked their talk, gave them their due…but if they tried to sharpen that edgy banter in their favor, I stayed in control and didn't back down. Such banter at the corner of Warren and Twenty-Third – with Robert Knox involved, no less – wound up in news media sound bites with absolutely none of the context I am giving you here. Sound bites and prosecutors made "Starsky" look like a damning nickname. It wasn't.

From time to time, I worked with police officers who had trouble, lots of trouble, putting their emotions in their pocket so they could go about their job. Some of them, in fact, would back down even before the car door opened.

I worked with a white cop who was intimidated by black

suspects, to the point he avoided them. Meanwhile, he was a real cowboy with white suspects. It was a pattern. It was real. And I began to see it. My suspicions were confirmed one night on a routine felony arrest when he lit into a barrage of profanity that dumbfounded me, coming from this particular officer, and started pushing this white kid around. Working with such a cop in a precinct that is overwhelmingly black is not a good way to go. Skin color had nothing to do with the way I approached a subject. On occasion white perps and black perps alike put some anxiety, and even fear, in my pocket. I kept it there, out of sight. The Book-Cadillac incident is a rare example of where I failed.

I worked with a black cop who was so unenthusiastic about showing initiative that one night I confiscated an illegal gun from a driver, cuffed the suspect and returned him to our booster car...all without my partner setting foot on the street. I honestly believe this officer also had a problem arresting black citizens, though for other reasons than those of the aforementioned white partner. Be that as it may, on nights he and I worked together it was a case of: "Well, at least I have someone to eat lunch with."

You will read a thousand news stories about cops and race and not even find this perspective mentioned. Race shouldn't matter to a cop on the street. Not white arresting white, white arresting black, black arresting white, black arresting black. Only a very dim bulb might not speculate how all four of those combinations can, in some way, intrude in some contacts between citizens and cops. All I will speak for is my own contacts, and I will speak passionately. I was a walking, talking Detroit Police Manual. I had found, for once, a "book" I could study and, where it related to my work on the street, *memorize*. If you were a felon, I was happy to arrest you, by the book. If you were six-foot-three and two hundred and fifty solid pounds, it didn't matter whether you were black or white. When confronted by a big, strong guy I always began my thought processes the same way (and pardon my French):

"Oh, shit!" I liked to do my job well. If black folks thought I was happy to be making a good arrest, they were right. If white folks thought I was happy to be making a good arrest, they were also right. You can believe me or not. But I will tell you this: Ask around the Third, among people who knew my work, police officers and citizens alike, and they will tell you the same thing.

One of the very best partners I worked with was a young black officer named John Edwards. He was third man on the crew early in my booster-car days. When we pulled our car over to interview some unsavory citizens, John was the first one out the door. One April night in 1977, at 2 a.m., I saw a broken window in a drugstore at Grand Boulevard and Rosa Parks Avenue, and a trail of empty watch cases leading toward an alley. I knew that if my white face wandered back there, plainclothes would not be enough to cover my identity and any perps would run. I sent John back. He walked up to a black man crouched next to a garage. "What it is, brother?" John asked. The guy replied: "Be cool, blood. I just got some watches out of Cunningham's and there's cops all over." We recovered thirty-six watches, arrested the burglar, and got a commendation. John Edwards was a good cop. He moved on to a department in another state. Our loss.

I only wish the Detroit department was as color blind as I was. Really. Take the matter of citations and awards. If I say that in Coleman Young's police department productive old white cops like me started getting written up for citations far less often, while officers of color and the opposite gender got papered with citations…then maybe you think you hear racism and bitterness. Bitterness, yes. Racism, no. At least I don't think you would call the above statement racist if it were true. And you can look it up. Suddenly black rookies started getting citations for seeing a gun on the floorboard during a traffic stop. Do you know how many guns I took off the street? Good question. Can't give you a specific answer. But an honest guess is that I took at least 1,500 guns off the street.

That's conservative. Less than two a week. Remember the hat trick – three in one night? Or the night I got four? No cop in the history of law enforcement has received 1,500 citations. Female officers started getting citations for recovering a stolen car with somebody in it. How many times did I do that? Hell, I'm not even going to guess. We are talking about citations that I, and my best partners, would be embarrassed to accept. Meanwhile, it came to the point that we'd do an unusually good piece of police work, and no one took note.

If merit awards grew on trees in the Coleman Young police department, I sometimes wonder why Walter Budzyn – portrayed by his accusers and in the news media as a brutal racist – didn't get one for, after recovering a stolen Buick, washing the car before returning it to its owner. It seemed to Walter like the right thing to do. The Buick belonged to Rosa Parks.

The scraps of paper, and occasional medals, that cops get for doing good police work might seem to a civilian like so much ceremonial nonsense – merit badges for guys too old to be Boy Scouts. Sorry, no. Insurance salesmen and journalists and schoolteachers like to get awards, like to know their peers and superiors recognize a job well done. Why not police officers? No offense to anyone in your average job, but a police officer who is a slacker isn't just lazy – he's putting lives at risk. Citizens' lives and fellow coppers' lives. I was naïve enough to think that the more awards you got, the better cop you probably were. I still think that way.

Cops know good awards from phony awards. Dumb down the awards and you dumb down the department. I got a few commendations for nuts-and-bolts stuff, but not many. I never wanted to be put in for even a commendation unless my actions showed at least a little initiative. I earned a bundle of commendations. I earned twenty-six citations, which are supposed to represent very good police work and usually aren't given for responding to a radio run. I earned two departmental citations, which is a reasonably big deal, complete with a medal and a little ceremony. I earned two lifesaving medals. I never earned a medal of valor, the highest award in the department. Part of me now wants to say they're all just so much paper and ribbon, but a bigger part of me is proud to have them.

Mike Dameron and I got lifesaving medals for bringing some people out of a burning house. I think we got the medals because firemen got awards for the same incident, after arriving as Mike and I were making our second trip into the house. I should have gotten one for saving some guy who was trying to jump off the Ambassador Bridge. I grabbed his hand when he started to go.

I got another lifesaving award I'm most proud of even though it didn't involve any burning buildings or berserk gunmen. It came only from good booster-car street smarts and good cop instinct on a freezing February day. Driving down Hancock I saw a beer truck parked on McKinley. Just the trailer, with no tractor. No big deal. But it stopped me because it didn't belong there. I circled over, pulled up, and heard noises from inside. I called a fire rig with some bolt cutters. We broke in and freed the driver, bound and gagged and freezing to death.

Instinct probably isn't the right word – though I think officers with street smarts do have some makings of that the day they were born. Intuition is probably a better word, because of course your experiences teach you things...which become so basic and matter-of-fact you can't express them. I told you with a straight face, for instance, that I had an uncanny knack for knowing a person was going to run if a police officer stopped to say "Good evening." My partners will assure you it is true.

Working the stadium detail, it got so I was almost always right about whether a driver crawling down a side street was going to pass through, or if someone was going to jump out and steal a car. Or whether someone walking down the sidewalk during a game was really out for a stroll, or was about to commit a crime. Instinct? I don't know. But Willard was already talking about it when I was a rookie.

Be it instinct, or intuition learned from experience, street smarts are invaluable on a booster crew. But, in truth, ninety percent of being a good booster cop came from simply working my ass off. That was the simple secret ingredient to my method. Various friends in other lines of work tell me it's effective just about anywhere. Set goals, work hard, see results. I called it making my scratch every night, "scratch" being at least one good felony arrest. Most of the time I made my scratch. Any time I had a partner who wanted to work as hard as I did, we probably batted .800. Though, as in baseball, you did have your little streaks. The best month my car ever had, we made sixty felony arrests. That's in twenty nights of work. That's why they called me a "junkyard dog."

We'd vary our route through the Third every night so no one knew when we'd show up. Just as individuals seem like they are standing in line to commit new crimes, certain locations become the scene of crime after crime. Active dope pads were an automatic. During prep time, I might discover an incident report revealing that a guy named PeeWee snatched a purse at Grand River and McGraw. Well, I know PeeWee. I have his picture from the last time I arrested him. PeeWee didn't flee to California with the $30 in that purse. He bought a couple of rocks, and he hasn't gone far. So we make Grand River and McGraw an area to be visited several times during the shift. Maybe we haven't made one of the junkyards lately, so we drive under the nearby railroad viaduct, or even up on the tracks, looking for a parked car – meaning some thieves are inside the junkyard shopping. Maybe, as on most nights, there is a fresh warrant on some perp who lives or hangs in the precinct, so he gets added to *our* shopping list. Maybe we'll volunteer on a promising radio run. We look for suspicious and furtive activity inside every car that passes. We look at the cars themselves for punched-out trunk locks and dangling plates. I'm calling out plate numbers, and my partner is checking the hot-sheet and punching numbers into the MDT. If my partner is busy with paperwork, or on the radio, I sometimes even punch in a number myself while driving. Even on a dull night, we might use the MDT fifty times.

I mentioned putting ignition keys down the sewer. That was a sometime thing. Putting drugs down the sewer happened all the time. You could start a Midwest drug cartel with all the dope I put down sewers, a little bit at a time. I rarely wrote misdemeanor tickets. Possessing small amounts of marijuana was a misdemeanor. Into the sewer. Possessing cocaine or heroin in any amount was a felony under state law, but common practice was not to clog the system with cases involving small amounts. Into the sewer. Why take the booster car off the street for an hour or two of useless paperwork?

Junkies had their own sewers: their stomachs. I once pulled a guy over on a hot summer day. As I approached his car, I could see several glassine envelopes on the seat beside him. Hmmmmmmmmmm and click – the sound of his power windows going up and his doors locking. I stood there, two feet from his face, while he swallowed the envelopes' contents. Then he powered down his window and did the "Good evening, officer" thing. Another time I left the house without my handcuffs. Mike Dameron and I arrested two guys in possession of enough dope for a good arrest. We made do with Mike's cuffs, putting the two perps in the back seat, one's left wrist cuffed to the other's right wrist. Since they were not cuffed behind their backs, as the Manual requires, Mike rode in the back seat with them. Mike had stuck the dope on the passenger sun visor. We were in the precinct garage, and Mike had just stepped from the car, when one guy came flying over the front seat, dragging his friend with him, grabbed the dope from the visor, and – even as we struggled with him – swallowed it. The only case we had was for the emergency room at a nearby hospital.

If you see an endless pattern here of guns and drugs, you're right. From the day I arrived at STRESS, my work life centered on removing guns and drugs from the street. I'm not sure how many kinds of felons I never arrested – forgers come to mind. I got most of the rest. Murderers, rapists, burglars, armed robbers, car thieves. But in my time on the street, I soon came to chuckle whenever I heard the phrase "drug-related crime." It was just another way of saying "most crime." Usually committed with a gun.

Picture this scenario. Guy has a job, starts doing drugs. Gets to the point where he's doing crappy work and missing days on the job. Maybe he gets fired for that, or maybe he flunks a drug screen. Now he has lost his income, but not his habit. So first he drains the household cash. If his girlfriend or wife or mother isn't flush enough to keep him supplied with drugs, the jewelry and appliances start disappearing. His wife or girlfriend or mother aren't going to turn him in – well, seldom – so he has managed to become an addicted sponge without appearing on an incident report. At some point, though, he can't hurt his family and friends anymore financially, because he has them drained. If his girlfriend is willing, he might start running her on the street as a prostitute. If not, he turns to larceny or armed robbery. Or all of the above, which then become "drug-related crimes." At least in my book.

Corny cliché? You bet. But if it wasn't true, you could take half the police cars off the street. You definitely wouldn't have had Booster 3-31 at the corner of Warren and Twenty-Third around 10:30 p.m. on November 5, 1992.

I want to think all those years of pulling in guns and drugs like a vacuum cleaner were worthwhile. I don't know. Maybe those two sociologists can decide over lunch. All I know is that I arrested people who were breaking the law, and I brought them in by the book. I kept my fear and anger in my pocket, and didn't let the bad guys take control. I worked hard, and if police medals counted, I could be buried in Arlington National Cemetery. As for race, if my nightly scratch for a year consisted of white guys, all it would mean to me is that all my new mug-shots would go in the same pile.

There is a lot of economy of motion in a good booster car. My car was productive, proactive and professional.

Much as I hated paperwork, I added one invaluable piece of bookkeeping to the job. I maintained a run book. This was hand-written information that didn't disappear into the bureaucracy...facts and observations I or my partner entered throughout the evening – names, ages and addresses of witnesses and suspects; descriptions of cars; evidence confiscated; phone numbers...little notations of a night on the street that often proved invaluable weeks or months later. I used hard-cover ledger books like the ones accountants used before computers came along, filling each page with notes written during or immediately after a contact or an incident. The run book stayed with the car on my days off. When a run book was full, I took it home. I've still got them all. The last entries in my last run book were written by Walter Budzyn. They include Malice Green's date of birth, the clinic Walter went to for treatment of a leg scrape he got while struggling with Green, and "cocaine, 4 rocks."

7

'NO AMOUNT OF FORCE IS TOO GREAT'

Police officers usually refer to the Detroit Police Manual by its formal name, "General Orders." Mostly I've been calling it the Manual here for two reasons. One, "manual" is descriptive for someone who isn't a cop or maybe lives in another part of the country where the officer's bible has a different name. And two, "the Manual" really describes my relationship with those pages. Supervisors, and even partners, come and go – sometimes daily. Every street situation can become unique in a split second. But regardless of who is giving you orders tonight and regardless of who is riding beside you tonight and regardless of what happens out there tonight, you can't go wrong if you know and follow your bible – particularly the nitty-gritty passages. Or so I thought.

General Orders is like a football playbook fattened up. It's thick, and it's looseleaf so you can plug in updates and additions. You get a copy while you're a rookie at the academy and you keep it throughout your career. It tells you hundreds of useless things – like exactly how to wear your uniform and whether to salute the mayor. Even today I can recite a few of these useless things. All the important things I could not only recite…I lived by them.

General Orders was the kind of reading material that made sense to me. It laid things out in a straightforward way, and it had real-world meaning. Like how to do your job right, and the basics of how to make good arrests that would become good prosecutions. When I told you my classmates chose me to read the Code of Ethics at academy graduation I didn't mean to imply that I was some kind of philosopher. Just the opposite. I was no philosopher then, and over the years the deepest I got into philosophy was pondering a gizmo that would help eliminate high-speed chases. I let the police officer's bible do the philosophizing for me, which made me the perfect choice to recite the Code of Ethics. I might not be much of a reader, but General Orders were one set of written words I would pore over like scripture and would follow out the window.

Police officers have impact on criminal behavior just by putting in an appearance and showing the flag for law and order. Seeing a scout car means something to traffic speeders and genuine bad guys alike, and it means something to good citizens who live in high-crime areas. Interacting with the citizenry raises the impact of police presence another notch. The things cops say on the street carry more weight, even with career criminals, than the things civilians say. The badge means something to everybody. Whether it's respect or fear or hatred or however an individual might respond, when a police officer says "move along" or "let me see what's in your hand," it means something different than if a bar owner or a bouncer or a bystander says it. There's a lot of power associated with a badge and a gun. A police officer is empowered to make an arrest, and he is empowered to use force if necessary to do that. Ordinarily, this is enough to get done what you need to get done on the street without using force, let alone escalating force. It's not quite as simple as "ask and ye shall receive," but citizens of all stripes generally follow a police officer's orders. Sometimes reluctantly, sometimes with verbal resistance, less often with minimal physical resistance, still less often with serious physical resistance, even less often with a serious threat to an officer's life. Every one of those citizen responses to an officer's verbal commands carries with it an appropriate, escalating counter-response from the officer. It's all right there in General Orders.

The book on police escalation of force is abundantly clear, from issuing verbal commands, to applying minimal physical restraint, to using stronger physical force, to using fatal force. Under General Orders, none of this is an option. An officer must overcome resistance. An officer *must* make an arrest for a felony committed in his presence. He *must* use whatever force necessary to do so. Department regulations require that once subdued, subjects *must* be handcuffed. Specifically, they must be handcuffed behind the back. All efforts *must* be made to recover evidence of a felony. Mark all those orders well. An officer following the book in a felony arrest has no choice but to overcome stubborn resistance and cuff the suspect. That's common sense. More important, it's the Manual. It's the law.

You might wonder if a street cop like me actually made mental reference to the fine print of General Orders while out on the street. Answer: Yes, the Manual was not a sticky-note reminder pasted on my forehead...it was more like a neon billboard. Remember the round I fired after breaking up that gas-station burglary while I was an inexperienced patrolman in the Fourth Precinct? It was by the book. Felon fleeing a burglary. The book said shooting was a proper response to the crime, so I shot. I got a commendation for that arrest. Would I have shot if it happened twenty years later? Probably not. Things change, including the Manual. Contrary to the views of some, I changed too. Experience will do that to you. So if Malice Green had been fleeing a burglary, I wouldn't have shot at him – not unless I perceived him as a dangerous threat, to me or to citizens.

The power that comes with a badge and gun is not something I ever took lightly. The same goes for ninety-nine percent of the police officers I knew and worked with. I enjoyed – no I *loved* – playing mind games to outsmart the bad guys and bring them in with minimal trouble. The banter between "Starsky" and the street people was a big part of that. Communication is important, and we communicated. I hated a situation that went south and required use of force. I did everything possible to avoid that. I was not, for example, a shooter. I've already given you my numbers in that regard. One clip in the semiautomatic handguns carried by most younger officers today holds as many rounds as I fired in twenty-four years. In the decade after Detroit police brass saw to it that I wound up in prison, a number of younger trigger-happy Detroit cops shot citizens in situations where neither I nor any of my partners would have fired one round. As with much of my story, the ironies are often spectacular. Take the case of two gang-squad cops who killed a Cuban immigrant on Vernor Highway.

Vernor is a "highway" in name only. It's a congested street that runs through Detroit's Hispanic neighborhood and southwest into the downriver industrial section. The Third Precinct station is on Vernor, not far off Michigan Avenue, at the northeast end of Mexicantown. A handful of neighborhood restaurants are a popular destination for suburbanites willing to explore the city, and there are signs of good citizens trying to make the neighborhood work. But even Mexicantown, a bright spot compared to most of the Third, has a serious crime problem. On the fringes, it's real serious. If anything, it was more serious – especially drug traffic and related crimes – back when I worked the streets.

When Fidel Castro emptied his prisons and exported a supply of felons to the U.S., a number of them filtered into Detroit and the Vernor neighborhood. Narcotics officers will tell you the Mariel "immigrants" were especially valued as mules for the drug trade because if one showed up to take a delivery in, say, Chicago, he had a unique way of proving he wasn't an undercover cop. Or at least I'm not aware of any police officer submitting to the lip tattoo that Castro's wardens used to identify prisoners. Walter Budzyn, driving his own booster car in the Third before he became my partner, took special interest in this scene. He kept regular contact with immigration officers and sort of made drug and immigration crimes his on-the-job hobby – and off the clock, for that matter. It didn't do

Walter any good in our unspoken competition to drive the precinct's most productive booster car, but Walter knew a lot about that particular underside of that neighborhood.

In April 1993, while Walter and I were awaiting trial in the Malice Green case, two gang-squad officers panicked on Vernor Highway while interfacing with a Cuban street person named Jose Iturralde. The report they filed said Iturralde refused to take his hands out of his pockets, the cops thought he had a gun, and one officer fired, killing Iturralde. It turned out Iturralde was unarmed, and that not one but both cops had shot him. Unlike what happened to Walter and me, these two officers were assigned to a board of review – in other words brought inside to work desk duties while the department investigated. That's normal procedure. They were not charged with a crime until July, and then only when the demands of Hispanic leaders led to a charge of second-degree murder. Both were acquitted at trial. Walter and I, by contrast, were suspended without pay in less than twenty-four hours, given no board of review, labeled "murderers" by the mayor, and subjected to Stanley Knox's "we will convict" promise.

When I look at something like the Iturralde case and note that both officers were black, and that their gang-squad boss at the time would later become chief, and that black jurors acquitted the two officers...then some people say that's racial sour grapes and whining on my part. I don't think so. When I say there is no way I or Walter Budzyn would have shot this guy... that if I shot every subject who refused a command to take his hands out of his pockets there would have been bodies halfway to Toledo...it's not self-serving speculation. Months before the late Jose Iturralde interfaced with the two gang-squad cops, he was confronted by two other cops, also on Vernor Highway. This time he *did* have a gun. The gun was confiscated without incident. The two cops who confiscated it were Walter Budzyn and me, happening to work a shift together back before we became partners. That particular incident is one of many that never made their way into the hundreds of newspapers stories about Malice Green, or the handful of stories that got written about the Iturralde case.

More than a few police officers and lawyers have remarked to me that if I had shot Malice Green, we never would have been charged with a crime. That might be true. Certainly escalation of force by drawing my handgun would have been far more appropriate in Malice Green's arrest than in many police shootings that have dogged the department in recent years. *Far* more appropriate. But a police officer following the Manual doesn't draw his gun unless he feels it is necessary, and he doesn't fire unless he intends to kill. I didn't think it was necessary to draw my gun in arresting Malice Green, and I certainly wasn't trying to kill anybody. Old-time, hands-on coppers like me didn't back off from trouble, but didn't start shooting without reason. I'm not trying to say every cop who ever shot an unarmed perp is trigger-happy. Things happen quick out there. A newspaper reporter has a thousand times longer to write a paragraph than a cop has to make a decision about whether to shoot. I'm just saying I was on the street a *long* time, and I got up-close with a remarkable number of felons, and when it came to applying force necessary to effect a difficult arrest, by the book…I was not a shooter. My final arrest was a difficult one to say the least, but it never occurred to me for an instant to draw my gun. To keep it out of Malice Green's hands, yes; that became a real serious concern. But to draw it myself, no. I escalated force. But using fatal force never crossed my mind. As a matter of fact, I don't believe I did use fatal force, even though a man died.

Malice Green and Amadou Diallo were the nation's two most publicized death-during-arrest cases in recent decades. Both Green and Diallo were black men. Both were confronted by white officers working plainclothes patrol. Both cases led to criminal charges and nationally televised trials. Both cases involved street cops making an honest attempt to do difficult and dangerous jobs. The similarities pretty much end there. Diallo was struck by nineteen of forty-one shots fired by four New York City officers as he stood in the vestibule of his Bronx apartment building. The young New York cops – who rode a four-man booster car but *together* didn't have as much street experience as I did the night Malice Green died – were looking for a rapist when they apparently mistook Diallo reaching for his wallet as a move for a gun. There was confusion, miscommunication, and in just a few seconds four times as many shots were fired as I fired in twenty-four years on the street. Diallo died.

I've thought more than once about certain differences between the two cases.

- The New York cops lived in the suburbs while patrolling a city that offers every kind of neighborhood. I lived in the city I patrolled, a crime-ridden shell of its former self.
- Diallo committed no crime. Green possessed crack cocaine outside a dope house and refused to give it up.
- Diallo did not resist arrest. Green resisted arrest – an additional, serious crime. In fact, by my count, Green could have been charged with seven crimes as various as using the dope he possessed, carrying a knife with a blade longer than three inches, and assaulting a police officer.
- Diallo was shot, a conscious application of fatal force. Green was not shot, and no sane person believes I intended to kill him.
- Mayor Rudolph Giuliani took a clear innocent-till-proven-guilty stance regarding his four cops. Mayor Young, without showing any interest in determining the facts, declared Walter and me to be "murderers."
- The New York cops were granted a change in venue for their trial. We were denied a change of venue.
- The New York cops were found innocent of all four charges brought against them, right down to reckless endangerment. Walter and I were found guilty of second-degree murder.

I can't assure you beyond any doubt that I would not have fired if I had been in the Bronx that night. You never know for certain about such things unless you were present for the split-second when it happens. But I can make an educated guess, and my very strong guess is that I would not have fired. Maybe my gun wouldn't even have left its holster during that walk-up from the booster car to Diallo's doorstep, which is not to condemn the young officers. The lead cop in the case wasn't a shooter. He had fired his weapon only once before in the line of duty. These four cops went onto the street with their training and equipment and experience, which is all any police officer has at his disposal, and that is the package that responded to the situation. Because the Diallo shooting happened in 1998 and because the officers were young, they undoubtedly had a bundle of more up-to-date training than I did. I feel for them. Of course, I feel for the Diallo family, too. Who doesn't? But my vantage point is that of a police officer, and the knowledge of how something done by the book can go horribly bad in an instant. The book these days, by the way, says that once you are committed to firing your gun, you keep firing.

So much for guns and how I used mine.

A police officer can, of course, use force – and can escalate force – without drawing his gun. The modern street cop's arsenal includes pepper spray, the "baton," individual self-defense techniques such as "pressure points" and group techniques such as "swarming." What you saw in the Rodney King video was a group of police officers using both swarming technique and batons – pretty much by the book, actually, despite what it looks like on tape. But I won't get off-track and go there. Besides, the only "swarming" that ever happened out of my booster car was if it took both my partner and I to make a subject submit to arrest. Two cops do not make a swarm, and I wasn't issued a baton, or pepper spray, and taught how to use them. That half-hour demonstration of judo back at the academy was the extent of my exotic self-defense training. I wouldn't know a pressure point from needlepoint.

One thing I was issued when I started walking the Del Ray beat in '68 was a nightstick, the kind that cops twirled in ancient black-and-white movies. As a rookie on street patrol, I became adept at that myself. Twirling is the only thing I ever used my nightstick for – that and occasionally to tap on a light pole as accompaniment to my solitary beat-walking. Soon after making my way off foot patrol and into a scout car, I stopped carrying a nightstick. You had your gun and you had your hands. Mostly you had a gift of gab, and a willingness not only to confront the bad guys but talk to them in their language. You could escalate the words by threatening use of physical force.

Somewhere early in my career, police officers started carrying Kel lights – long flashlights that weighed about two pounds and could obviously serve as a weapon, and for that reason no doubt served often enough as a deterrent. The one I carried was about a foot long, powered by three D-sized batteries. You can buy them in sizes up to eight batteries. It's unusual for a police officer to enter a situation with a drawn gun; it's routine to enter with a flashlight in your hand. But weaponry was not the reason we carried these lights. It wasn't even for their deterrent value. It was simple. We carried Kel lights to see with, and they became a vital piece of equipment for that reason alone. I'm sure their illumination power saved a few lives over the years, cops' and citizens' lives alike, simply by letting you see the situation you were dealing with. Street cops work in dark places and peer into darkened cars. It's good for everyone not to be flying blind. The Kel light, and later the Mag light (made from aircraft magnesium alloy, and rechargeable), lit up a corner of the night spectacularly. I can remember when we first got the things, and someone would drop by the house, and I would take them down to the basement to demonstrate just how powerful that beam was. The department didn't furnish them, by the way. We had to buy our own.

As for using a flashlight as a weapon, I can recall exactly three times of note. One night I used my light to smash a woman on the elbow. She was holding a gun. One night I used my light to rap the head of a young man seated in a car who, after assuring me he was unarmed, could be seen to have a revolver on his ankle. I struck both of these people harder than I struck Malice Green on the head. In fact, before I struck Malice Green on the head, I struck his clenched fist much harder. Several times. He sustained no fractures on his hand or fingers. But that is getting ahead of the story.

In the course of somewhere between 50,000 and 100,000 interactions with the citizenry, those are the only times I can remember using my flashlight that earnestly. You do remember such things. Anyone who has trouble believing me can go try to find anyone – cop or perp – who convincingly says otherwise. Ironically, you might find as much use of the Mag light as a weapon by Emergency Medical Service personnel as you would by police officers. EMS techs are unarmed. They get in some tight situations. They carry Mag lights. I say "ironically" because of the role EMS personnel wound up playing in our prosecution.

When it comes to escalation of force, common sense tells you the same overriding message that General Orders tells you and the same thing your supervisors tell you. An older generation of lieutenants peppered every roll call with a warning that could be fairly summed up as: "Don't take any shit out there." Meaning, "Be courteous. Respect the dignity of all. But if you are attacked, if a citizen resists arrest, let there be no doubt who is going to win that confrontation." Is that so surprising, or illogical, or unfair, or bad? The language might change, the culture might change, techniques might change – but the bottom line remains the same. The whole idea of policing the streets comes down to respect for, and adherence to, the law…in the person of the police officer who in the end must step in if the law is broken. If that police officer is threatened or attacked, the whole system is under attack. If he does not prevail, a lot more is at stake than a police officer's dignity. Or, for that matter, his life.

That's philosophy, I suppose, but it's practical philosophy, and even I could talk that kind of philosophy for many pages. Better to give you the exact words from the street cop's bible. Here's what General Orders has to say:

Detroit Police Manual General Orders
Volume III, Chapter 1, Section 13

The state requires the officer to perform this duty regardless of hazard. No amount of force is too great in making an arrest if it is necessary to overcome obstinate and dangerous resistance. The officer must remember that the officer is responsible for a prisoner and required to do what is necessary to secure the prisoner. The officer must use discretion, and if the officer performs this duty in a wise and careful manner, the officer will be justified. The officer is a representative of the law to whose lawful demands all must submit. The officer is charged with the duty and armed with the power to compel submission. Officers are required to use force deemed necessary to effect an arrest...up to and including deadly force.

Volume III, Chapter 1, Section 8.5

There must be a submission to the arrest by the arrested person. This may be a forced submission. Whether the arrested person submits voluntarily or resists all the way to jail or court, the element of custody or control is gained.

Anyone who can't see "obstinate and dangerous resistance" in a cocaine-induced frenzy has a serious vision problem. But that, too, is getting ahead of the story.

8
48 HOURS

Billy Polk was such a typical perp. So typical he was special. Billy was a bad guy more than once. The things I arrested him for escalated in seriousness. He accused cops of brutality and, for a minute at least, got the system to take his charges seriously. Finally, one day – having been sent in his direction because I networked with a citizen standing near a dead body – I arrested Billy as he stood with a shotgun in his hand. It was the kind of arrest that's likely to win you some sort of award. But two days later my career was over, and the lynch mob was gathering. I guess you could say Billy, and his type, got the last laugh.

Jimmy Dukes was a friend and fellow booster cop. One day, Jimmy was filling in for my regular partner at the time. Jimmy and I had shared a few hair-raising experiences, working the same car or responding to the same incident. On this day, my first encounter with Billy Polk, it seemed Jimmy and I were dealing with nothing more than a reckless driver.

The Twenty Grand Motel on Warren once had a lounge that was a showcase for Detroit's many world-class musical acts, even before Motown Records was launched. Later, the Supremes played the Twenty Grand in their early days. But as I pulled out of the motel parking lot on this day, the Twenty Grand had become nothing but a worn-down haven for transients, prostitutes and drug dealers. Almost all inner-city motels had, in fact, gone in that direction. Legitimate travelers avoided them, and the bad guys filled the vacuum. Aside from its obvious use for hookers, a motel room gave pushers a place to operate away from a known address, and a chance to move around. The bad guys' women are often not only a source of revenue, they often get stuck holding an illegal gun or other evidence…and the perps know a woman will be body searched only if a female officer is available to do it. Walter Budzyn and I once arrested a man and a woman in a motel near Henry Ford Hospital. After waiting for a female cop to arrive and make a search, we were given an amazing catalogue of evidence removed from her private parts, including dope, a pipe to smoke it with, and several hundred dollars.

Jimmy and I hadn't encountered anything that criminally exotic in this visit to the Twenty Grand. It was a hot spot where I had made several arrests in the past, but I don't remember details of why we were in the parking lot on this day. As I prepared to pull out, I saw an Oldsmobile going west on Warren about forty-five or fifty miles an hour. Ordinarily I wouldn't care about a penny ante speeder. But this was one of those winter days when streets became a skating rink, and anyone who doesn't absolutely have to get somewhere shouldn't even be driving. This Olds was moving as recklessly as a car going ninety on a July afternoon. At Fourteenth Street the driver didn't even slow for a red light. I knew he wouldn't be able to stop for the light at Grand River, a major intersection two blocks away. I hoped the light would be green when he got there.

The light was red, but the Olds managed to luck its way through the intersection. I already had turned on the oscillating lights in the booster car's grille, and Jimmy had flipped on the siren. On the other side of Grand River, the Olds's driver hit his brakes and spun out, striking a light pole and a mailbox, and winding up facing east in the middle of the next intersection. I pulled up, driver's door to driver's door. I got my first look at Billy Polk as I yelled at him to pull over to the curb. He looked at me, expressionless, and started driving again – only now he was eastbound. I wheeled our car around, cringing at the idea of a chase on these streets…but with plenty of evidence that this guy was every bit as likely to broadside an innocent motorist whether we chased him or not.

Much to my relief, he didn't go far – just a short way back to Grand River, where he skidded into the parking lot of a Top Hat hamburger joint. Billy stopped the Olds in the middle of the lot, stepped out, and started walking away as if Jimmy Dukes and I – who had followed him into the lot – didn't exist. I yelled at him to stop, and he kept walking. I ran up behind him, cautiously on the ice, and grabbed his jacket collar. One or both of us lost footing and down we went. The odor of alcohol was obvious as Jimmy and I struggled to handcuff him. This was the extent of our physical contact with Billy Polk.

We took him to the precinct to process him for driving with a suspended license and what we were quite sure would be a drunk-driving charge. His only complaint at the time was that one stem of his eyeglasses had been broken during the struggle. He made no other complaint to the officer in charge.

The plan, of course, was to have him blow into a Breathalyzer device and measure the alcohol content of his bloodstream. A reading of .05 percent means "impaired." Anything above .10 percent means "legally drunk." No qualified Breathalyzer operator was working in the precinct that shift, so we had to transport young Billy over to the Thirteenth, along with all our paperwork. Already I was beginning to regret loss of time that could be spent felon-hunting.

Jimmy Dukes and I presented Billy to the desk officer at the Thirteenth, a black lieutenant I had worked with when he was in the Second, an affirmative-action beneficiary who would have been all over my case if Billy had complained of abuse – especially since this arrest had been made in a different precinct. Billy made no such complaints.

Billy, despite the time lapse, blew .18 on the Breathalyzer. We finished our paperwork and headed back to the Third. Three hours wasted on a drunk driver. "Oh well, we'll get 'em tomorrow night."

The next time Billy Polk passed through my life I arrested

him for the nickel-and-dime burglary of a church. It wasn't nickel-and-dime to the pastor, of course. I can't remember if the justice system did much of anything to Billy for that transgression, but I do remember the pastor being justifiably angry after showing up for a hearing that no one bothered to notify him had been canceled.

In the summer of 1992, Billy took Jimmy Dukes, me and the city to court, alleging police brutality and civil rights violations. In his lawsuit, there seemed to be no part of Billy Polk's body, spirit or hopes for a good life that were not crushed by two brutal cops in the parking lot of the Top Hat hamburger joint. Most of the damage, according to the allegations, came from a phantom haymaker allegedly swung by Jimmy Dukes. This particular aspect of Billy Polk's fantasy interested me for two reasons. Jimmy Dukes maybe weighed one hundred forty pounds, with his gear on. And Jimmy Dukes is black.

The civil trial played hell with my life – though for once it was good to see the city defending itself instead of shelling out even a nuisance settlement of a few thousand dollars. Or, I should say, the city hired a private attorney. Maybe the city's own army of attorneys was too busy caving in and working out settlements. At any rate, the lawyer required us to be in his office between 7 and 7:30 every morning for two weeks, and I continued to work the power shift at night. The jury included men and women, black and white. In return for fulfilling their duty as citizens, jurors were treated to classic performances by Billy Polk and his lawyer.

Billy came to court every day in the same clothes and walking with the help of a cane. He would arise and stand upright at the plaintiff's table while court was in session, looking all around, and then would sit down again. If a witness or the city's attorney doubted the veracity of Billy's allegations he would moan and make creative but unintelligible sounds. Several times a day he would disrupt testimony and ask for a drink of water or a bathroom break. The judge always obliged.

Billy's attorney had found a medical doctor who was

tailor-made for soap-opera fantasy. Jimmy Dukes's phantom punch, it seemed, had caused eye damage, ear damage, arm damage and leg damage. Worse, Billy's attorney told us in his introduction and summation, Billy had been so traumatized and left in so much pain that he found himself seeking relief in alcohol, marijuana, prescription drugs, heroin, and cocaine. A once-promising life had gone in the toilet because of the two brutal defendant cops. Jimmy Dukes and I knew there might be substance in Billy's bloodstream, but not in his story. I wondered if the jury would see it that way. Jimmy and I wished jurors could have seen Billy in the hallway, as we did several times during the two-week trial, not hobbling on his cane but twirling it like a riverboat gambler on a roll. The attorney, of course, had told the jury Billy could not walk without it.

I reminded our attorney that I had arrested Billy for a church break-in *after* the drunk-driving arrest. While fleeing energetically, on foot, he dropped his loot and vaulted over a fence – without benefit of a cane for assistance. Amazing agility for such a permanently disabled perp. Other officers who watched him go over the fence testified at our trial.

Maybe the jury would have swallowed the tale anyway, except for Billy Polk himself. As the trial neared its end, Billy asked for one of his bathroom breaks, which was granted. The jury watched as he strolled down the aisle, forgetting his cane. It took only about a half-hour for Jimmy Dukes and me to be found innocent. No civil-rights monetary settlement for Billy Polk. At least one juror said afterward they stayed in the jury room that long only to make a good impression.

Billy's grievous injuries at the hands of Jimmy Dukes's phantom punch were, of course, cited in the news media coverage of the Malice Green case as proof of my brutal nature. Billy, the KFC shooting – which allowed my accusers to work in the word "STRESS" – and my alleged mishandling of the diabetic car thief outside the stadium pretty much summarized the most "brutal" incidents of "Starsky's" infamous reign of street terror. If you find that hard to believe, you could look it up. So could the reporters and commentators if they really wanted to get at the truth.

Billy Polk crossed my path for a final time on November 3, 1992, the day I found him holding a shotgun.

Election Day meant one of those rare, dread returns to uniform and to a marked car. As always, I was uncomfortable in both the uniform and the marked cruiser. But in Detroit, serving and protecting included a tradition of uniformed police securing the citizenry's ballots at the end of the day. I had no choice. The only good thing about it, from my perspective, was that it became a paid holiday, which meant time and a half. The election shift started around 6 p.m., and ended when all the ballot materials from the precinct's fifty or so polling places were transported safe and secure for inclusion in the citywide count. The polls closed at 8 p.m., so in the first couple hours – other than making a drive past our assigned polling places – we were free to take care of other business or grab a meal.

I had a new partner and first man on my crew – my old "competitor," Walter Budzyn. I had been working without a permanent partner for a while. Walter was also experiencing personnel turnover on his car. We had known each other a dozen years, since he came over in the 1980 precinct merger. He worked on the stadium detail many nights. We were the two most experienced booster cops in the precinct. It made sense, finally, to solve our mutual partner uncertainties by riding together. Walter gave up his car and came over to mine. I can't confirm the exact date it happened, but shift changes normally occurred on the first day of the month. That means to my mind that election night was almost certainly our third night together as regular partners. Some people remember it as five to ten days. Whatever. Point is, the myth of the longtime "rogue" Nevers and Budzyn team known as Starsky and Hutch, a tale the media and Court TV couldn't get enough of, was pure B.S.

Walter was a compassionate sort. I told you about washing Rosa Parks's Buick. When it came time for the news media to add up all of "Hutch's" official misdeeds, one of them was a reprimand for leaving the precinct without authorization. The facts? An old couple's car had been stolen outside Tiger Stadium. They lived across the river in Canada, had no way back home, and were terrified at being stuck in Detroit. Walter put them in his car and drove them across the Ambassador Bridge, which you could hit with a softball thrown from the Third station. Not only did he break department protocol, he created an international incident. And, of course, made an old Canadian couple very happy.

Walter and I really had been competitors in many ways all those years, me on Booster Car 3-31 and Walter on Car 3-30. Truth is, I was the proactive one. My crew always made more arrests than Walter's. It wasn't even close. But Walter was a good cop. Quiet. A workaholic who often could be found around the precinct even on off days. He was in charge of maintaining all the booster-car radios. You'd find him back in the shop, checking batteries, or fiddling with some radio part that was foreign to me. Walter wasn't afraid to get out of the car and onto the street; he had particularly good knowledge of the Hispanic neighborhoods, and he never malingered. Besides that, with Walter on the car I knew my crew would always be carrying the best prep radios in the precinct. I was glad he'd be my new regular partner in 3-31.

On November 3, though, we weren't riding 3-31. We were two old cops in uniform riding a marked scout car with the special designation of 3-Election-5. Midway through killing the time from 6 to 8 p.m., we heard the dispatcher radio: "Volunteer car in Number Three to make 1432 Twenty-Fourth Street. A woman with a knife." No one responded, meaning all the cars in Three were already busy on runs. The dispatcher came back. "Still need a car in Number Three to make 1432 Twenty-Fourth. We are now getting this address as a shooting."

We were about a half-mile away. I turned to Walter and said: "You wanna make it?"

"Let's go," he said, notifying the dispatcher: "3-Election-5 will make 1432 Twenty-Fourth."

The dispatcher acknowledged as I turned north onto Twenty-Fourth from Hancock Street. I could see six or eight men and women standing on the sidewalk in mid-block. As we pulled up, they began shouting, "He's in there! He's in there! Call EMS! Call EMS!"

Walter hit the door first. A woman stopped me for a second and whispered: "Billy did it."

"Billy Polk?"

She nodded her head.

I ran up the porch in through the open front door. Walter was standing over the body of a middle-aged black man covered with blood and suffering gunshot wounds to the upper chest. Walter notified Emergency Medical Service and our supervisor as we stepped back outside.

"Let's go get the shooter," I said. "I know where he lives" – a piece of information that came from the same woman who had whispered Billy's name as we arrived on the scene.

Our volunteer backup, another election car, pulled up. We asked them to secure the scene while we went after Billy Polk.

We didn't have far to go. Billy lived maybe a half-dozen houses down the street. I told Walter to cover the rear as I approached the front door. It opened with an easy push, startling me a bit. I peered in, with my Colt drawn and held down at my side. Billy stood with his mother in the middle of the room. He was clutching a 12-gauge shotgun.

I was in full uniform, so there was no question I was a police officer, even if Billy happened to be too stoned or wired to recognize me.

I yelled: "Drop the gun, Billy!"

I had raised my revolver and aimed it at the guy with the phony limp who had testified in court that this particular member of the White Occupation Army had brutalized him and left him a cripple. Billy was in a position to shoot me, and I was in a position to shoot him.

I yelled, again in the most forceful voice I could muster,

"Drop the gun, Billy! Don't make me shoot you!"

A split second of hesitation seemed like a long time. Then the shotgun bounced as it hit the floor. I ordered Billy to the prone position. Walter had heard all the yelling, came into the room and handcuffed Billy. We walked him outside.

Billy was bleeding profusely from a cut apparently sustained during whatever events led to the fatal shooting, by whomever, of the dead man, who turned out to be his stepfather. Instead of taking Billy to jail, we first took him to a hospital.

If a bad guy who had been fingered as a shooting suspect held a shotgun as you entered a confined space, and you talked him out of firing it, you were probably looking at a departmental citation – even if you were an old white dinosaur in Coleman Young's police department. I hadn't had a departmental citation lately, and I confess it no doubt crossed my mind that night some time after returns showed Bill Clinton had been elected president for the first time.

Only once in twenty-four years had someone died after I fired my gun, and the odds in that case were five-to-one against my bullet being the fatal one. Given that I was running while I fired, I sincerely doubt it. Fatal force was not something I was interested in applying. Even to someone who had tried to make a big cash score by lying about me in court and wrecking my career. If I had shot Billy Polk, it unquestionably would have been reviewed and adjudged as a righteous shooting – but I would have been assigned to a board of review pending the investigation. In which case, I would not have been on the streets two nights later, two blocks away from Billy's house, checking activity outside a dope pad operated by a gentleman named Ralph Fletcher.

I knew Fletcher's clientele as well as – or better than – I knew Billy Polk, for the same felonious reasons. In fact, among the small crowd I would find gathered outside Fletcher's dope pad on the Thursday after election night, only one person was someone I did not know from Adam. That, of course, would be Malice Green. It is no wonder that gossip and the criminal justice system alike scrambled to find a reason I would mindlessly beat Malice Green to death. It was something I had no history of doing, something I had no reason for doing. It was, in fact, something I did not do.

They called me a racist murderer, but I had no motive and no abusive history. That was inconvenient for them, but amid the racial hysteria it didn't matter. No reporter among the scores of reporters and hundreds of news stories about Malice Green even once mentioned what happened less than forty-eight hours earlier and two blocks away when I brought in Billy Polk. If ever a supposedly racist white cop had motive and opportunity to murder a black citizen, can you think of a more classic example? It didn't happen, for the obvious reasons. I wasn't a white racist cop. I escalated force appropriately, to the point of telling Billy I would shoot if he didn't drop his gun and submit. He did. End of story. The Malice Green story could have ended the same way, if only the junk I spent so many nights trying to get off the street wasn't in Green's hand and in his bloodstream.

Eventually, a fellow cop nominated me as precinct Officer of the Year for my actions in the Billy Polk arrest. I had meanwhile been charged with murdering Malice Green. The Officer of the Year nomination disappeared like a rock trying to float in water. I know a warrant was issued for Billy Polk, but he never was taken to court. Maybe he acted in self-defense. Maybe he didn't do it. Maybe prosecutors who didn't want to be bothered with prosecuting two punks who jumped me outside the Teamsters Hall didn't want the Billy Polk case to see the light of day while they were trying to sell the world on me being a different sort of police officer. I have no idea. I only know this is the first time you ever heard of Billy Polk.

9

WHAT HAPPENED OUT THERE

The 1992 presidential election, which for me meant putting on a uniform and taking a shotgun away from Billy Polk, was on Tuesday. On Wednesday, Walter and I went back to plainclothes and the booster car. That night and next, for reasons I've forgotten, we worked the 4 p.m. to midnight shift instead of the power shift. Usually that happened when uniformed patrol was short-handed. Wednesday night was quiet except for a car-jacking and a concealed weapons arrest. Thursday night, November 5, Walter's world and mine changed forever inside the cramped quarters of Malice Green's Mercury Topaz.

On Thursday, as always, I began my shift by checking the teletype and incident reports. Then, while Walter gathered up our hand-held radios, I went out to the brown 1990 Chevy four-door known as 3-31 and logged onto the mobile data terminal. You have to remember, my police career stretches back to the days when if you wanted to communicate with the station you had to find a call box on a street corner, open it with your key, and pick up the phone. When the MDT first came on the scene, it took some getting used to, but it soon became a felon-chaser's biggest edge. Its capacity seemed endless. Driver's license information, vehicle registrations, even criminal histories...all were there. If the system wasn't running slow, you could get at this stuff in a matter of seconds. Radio runs and their status were displayed on the video screen.

Forget call boxes. The MDT was light years ahead of even the days when a cop could radio an information request from his car to a clerk who had to search hard-copy files for answers.

I wanted to look up the status of a red Tempo four-door reported stolen the night before. The victim had flagged down Walter and me at Warren and McKinley and told us he was car-jacked at gunpoint. We put him in the back seat and spent about half an hour cruising the neighborhood looking in vain for the Tempo, then dropped the victim at a phone booth and went to the station to file our report.

We didn't know it at the time, but the car-jacking report was a hoax. Months later, as the "victim" testified in our murder trial, we discovered the Tempo owner had surrendered his car to settle a debt. Phony car-theft reports were not unusual in Detroit. Addicts frequently gave up their vehicles in return for drugs, or "rented them out" for a few rocks of cocaine. When a "rental car" didn't come back, the owner often reported it stolen. But as we began our shift on November 5, 1992, I thought the red Tempo was not only a "good" theft, but had been taken at gunpoint. I entered the Tempo's plate number in the MDT and discovered it was still listed as hot. I was eager to get out and go looking for it, and the gunman who supposedly stole it.

Walter got in the car and informed me we had to go downtown to police headquarters and give statements in a departmental matter. Neither of us was involved except as witnesses placing two people in the same place at the same time. As usual with paperwork or any other distraction, I wasn't thrilled to see the booster car losing valuable time on the street. I finished my statement in a matter of minutes, but Walter's took a long time, maybe two hours. I waited around, fidgeted, drank coffee and turned on my prep radio so I could hear what was happening in the Third. A scout car asked for our location. "Busy at headquarters," the dispatcher said. I keyed in and asked dispatch to have the uniformed crew get on an open channel so I could talk with them directly. The scout car and I talked on channel five as I sat waiting for Walter.

"3-31 to 3-7, go ahead," I said.

"3-7 here. We found that stolen Tempo you've been looking for. It's parked on Twenty-Fourth, north of Hancock, unoccupied."

Scout 3-7 went on to tell me they were going to set up a surveillance of the Tempo, and that Walter and I should let them know when we got back to the neighborhood. Karl Gunther and Bob Lessnau were young uniformed officers who had learned their job well. I had a lot of respect for them. Some weeks they had made as many, or more, good arrests as Walter was making in his Booster Car 3-30. Tonight, despite being in uniform in a marked car, Karl and Bob had managed to establish an undetected surveillance on the Tempo.

When Walter and I returned to the neighborhood, we went back on channel five with 3-7 and told them we would cover the perimeter in case someone showed up and got into the Tempo. When dispatch gave 3-7 a radio run, Scout 3-10 radioed that they would take over the surveillance until 3-7 returned. I was happy. I'd much rather be doing something else.

For a couple of hours, "something else" was not much. My run book shows a few citizen contacts, including two men fighting in the lobby of a building, a couple suspicious cars pulled over, a B&E alarm on the John C. Lodge Freeway service drive. And, of course, we ran the usual flurry of plate numbers through the MDT while cruising the streets. See a suspicious car, run the plate. If it comes back clean, forget about it...*literally, forget about it*...and don't bother to read the details. When dispatch called the second scout car away from the Tempo surveillance, we decided to go over there and accept the surveillance tedium ourselves. On the way, dispatch gave us a run as well. "3-31, make 5624 Trumbull. Alarm on a dwelling." We acknowledged and headed in that direction. The red Tempo would have to sit unwatched for a while.

When we got to the address, the alarm – like most – turned out to be false, tripped by the owner. We were about to head back and take up the matter of the red Tempo when dispatch asked for a volunteer car to make a run on a man with a gun. We were right around the corner, so I made a quick turn. A young black male was running between buildings, headed in our direction. I stopped the car and waited for him to emerge.

"Come over here," I shouted.

As he walked toward me, he appeared over-concerned about the front of his waistband. I was standing beside my car door when I asked him to lift his jacket. Stuck in his waistband was a dark 9 mm. semi-automatic pistol. I grabbed the gun, which immediately revealed itself by its heft – but not its appearance – to be a plastic toy replica. I gave the kid several reasons that carrying such a realistic "gun" could be hazardous to his health, took his name and address, tossed the toy on 3-31's dashboard, and sent him on his way. At 10:30 p.m., I entered the kid's name, Damon Davis, in the run book. He said he was fourteen years old. That meant I had started keeping my run books two years before this kid was born. With a little effort, I could go through my collection of run books and track down by date and time countless thousands of incidents on the street. Damon Davis's name was the last run-book entry I would ever make. Meanwhile, of course, I had the red Tempo on my mind.

I headed 3-31 back toward the Twenty-Fourth Street and Hancock area to see if the Tempo was still there. As we approached Warren heading south on Twenty-Third – just a few blocks from where the Tempo had been parked – a small red four-door came across the intersection in front of us, westbound on Warren. I knew the Tempo was no longer being watched, and I figured this might be it, that someone had driven it off. My interest was further piqued by a glimpse of bullet holes in the passing red car's right front fender. I made a quick turn onto Warren, intending to speed into position behind the red car. Instead, I came instantly within a few car lengths because the driver was pulling abruptly to the curb in front of a dope house separated from the intersection only by a vacant lot.

The front of the building was an abandoned and gutted beauty shop. The entrance to Ralph Fletcher's dope pad was at the rear, reached by a walkway running next to the vacant lot. The pad was a filthy hole where hookers and junkies gathered to drink beer and use dope. Fletcher, known on the street as Fletch Man, charged his guests a couple bucks for the privilege. I was well aware of all this as we pulled in behind the red four-door. Two raids on the place by narcotics officers meant booster cars were *obligated* to follow up and keep tabs of activity there. I had been inside Fletcher's pad several times myself, once after arresting two armed-robbery suspects outside. The man and woman had emerged from Fletcher's place at 2:45 a.m carrying a baby, a concealed pistol and proceeds from the robbery. I asked if they wanted to leave the baby with anyone. The pair suggested the child's grandmother and said she was inside the dope pad. Sure enough, I found Granny in Fletch Man's place, and left the baby with her. It wasn't like the baby hadn't already spent plenty of time there. And she was with family.

As the red car halted, I pulled 3-31 near the curb in the standard stance – maybe two feet behind the subject car, with the booster car's grille centered on the other car's left tail light. At a glance, I realized this was not a red Tempo but a red Topaz, Mercury's version of the Ford product: same car, different nameplate. The Topaz's right rear passenger door flew open and – bingo! – Robert Knox flew out, heading into the darkness down the walkway beside the dope pad. I said, "There he goes!" Walter, a veteran of countless similar situations, hit the ground only a few strides behind Knox. I opened my door and stepped onto the street.

The Topaz's front passenger door opened and Ralph Fletcher emerged onto the sidewalk carrying an open jumbo beer. The driver stepped out and moved around the car to join Fletcher. I had never seen the driver before.

As Knox and Walter ran down the walkway between the dope pad and the vacant lot, they raced past three people coming the other way. I recognized all three as they came onto the sidewalk from the shadows – Theresa "Redbone" Pace, Robert "Joe" Hollins, and Emanuel "Ricky" Brown. I had arrested Brown on several occasions. I knew all three to be drug users. It seemed best for me to stay on the street keeping an eye on the party of five that gathered beside the booster car, rather than joining chase with Walter.

The street people were drawn in close enough that conversation across the booster car's hood was easy. We jawed about nothing in particular. At some point, I asked the stranger – who was driving the bullet-holed car and whose passenger had fled instantly – to produce his driver's license. This was so routine it was like breathing. If the stranger had complied, we would have run his name on the MDT. If the name had come back with no outstanding warrants, that probably would have been the end of Malice Green's encounter with law enforcement that evening. Green mumbled something, I thought, about his driver's license being in his car. Those were, to the best of my recollection, the only semi-intelligible words I heard Malice Green utter that night. From my perspective, he walked a few feet to his front passenger door, opened it, and sat down sideways with his feet on the sidewalk. Standing on the other side of the booster car, I couldn't see what he was doing.

This didn't bother me because, meanwhile, Walter had brought the fleeing Robert Knox back to join the group, and had patted him down. Walter recalls Green walking behind him and over toward the Topaz. Walter also asked Green for his license. Walter said Green already had his wallet and license in hand, apparently from when I made the same request. But Green kept going toward his car. Walter naturally wondered if Green sought to hide something in the Topaz (the two magic words again – guns and drugs) or, for that matter, get a weapon. I was paying no attention and trading typical street chat with this very typical cast of street characters.

"There's nothing going on here, Starsky," Hollins said, using the nickname Knox had given me some years before.

"When you're around, Joe, there's always something going on," I replied.

I had placed a foot comfortably inside the open door and on the raised edge of the floorboard. The gathering now included three men I had arrested in cases ranging from dope possession to armed robbery, one prostitute and one street person both of whom I had interviewed more than once, and one stranger – Malice Green. After our 4 p.m. start, the night was near ending as a second consecutive quiet shift. Especially so since Robert Knox had gotten just enough of a head-start on Walter to dispose of whatever – a gun or drugs or both – had inspired him to bolt into the darkness. Nothing was ever recovered back there. Probably it wound up with one of several people Walter found lurking behind the building. That's speculation, of course. But I can imagine no reason for Knox to run except to ditch something incriminating. At any rate, Walter – in what was a routine move for a good booster cop – chased Robert Knox back there, brought him out to the sidewalk, and now went over to the Topaz where I thought Green was getting his driver's license.

The chatter continued across the hood of my car as I stood on the street side. Then Hollins said: "What's with your partner? You better get over there and help him."

I shifted my eyes left to the Topaz. Walter had disappeared inside it. I ran around my car door, sidestepped between 3-31 and the Topaz, and approached the open Topaz passenger door. The stranger and Walter were sprawled inside in some sort of struggle. Walter seemed to be at least partially on top of Malice Green, though in the thousands of times I have reconstructed the next few minutes in my mind, I have never been able to see that image clearly. No doubt I couldn't see it very clearly at the time. We were about fifty feet from the nearest street light, and there was no bulb in the dome light of Green's car. The space between seats and dashboard of a Topaz is a tiny area for a struggle to be taking place. In some flashes I recollect of the following moments, it seems Walter is as much underneath

Malice Green as on top of him. Undoubtedly, their position changed several times. What is certain is that a struggle was in progress, and Walter was trying to control Green. From the get-go, it was clear that Malice Green was stubbornly refusing to yield, to submit, to surrender. Why?

"He's got dope in his hand!" Walter yelled.

How much could have flashed through my mind in and around that instant? A partner in trouble. Obvious probable cause to believe we were arresting a felon. General Orders *requiring* an officer to make a felony suspect submit, and to complete the arrest. Two decades of removing drugs from the street. The junkies standing behind me. And a thought I remember well, one that grew throughout the following few minutes. "What the hell is this guy hiding? What's with him? What has he done besides possess some dope? What kind of warrants are out on him? Has he killed somebody? *Why is he resisting like this?*" Escalation of force to some level was inevitable, and in fact already had begun. You ask for the dope and he doesn't hand it over, so you take it from him. Or at least you try.

The arrest of Malice Green began as a proposition I had faced...how many times? Take the junk away from the guy and bring him in. What began as routine should have continued as routine. Is it my fault, or Walter's fault, that it quickly stepped beyond routine? I don't think so. I followed the book, but the book took me places I had never gone before. The reason was Malice Green himself. If I had ten bucks for every time I confronted a citizen who resisted arrest, I could take Nancy on a very nice, very long vacation. I've been threatened with guns and with knives, and I've taken a punch. Several times I've had guys just stand there and tell me I'd have to shoot them. I've confiscated enough dope to make the entire population of Detroit high for a week. But I never encountered anyone with such maniacal, senseless, endless refusal to unhand evidence. Malice Green was not only in possession of drugs; he was possessed by drugs. I didn't know this at the instant I went to

Walter's aid, of course. This was my *real world* "take the victim as you find him," to cite a legal doctrine that would help seal my fate.

I leaned into the open passenger door from the curb and grabbed Green's wrist. His fist was tightly clenched.

"Open your hand! Open your hand!" I yelled, repeatedly. He kicked upward with his knees, pushing me against the doorpost and causing me to lose my grip on his wrist. I regained position and again got hold of his wrist and again yelled for him to open his fist. He refused. Finally, I was able to pry open just a baby finger, and a rock of crack cocaine fell out. Pieces of Malice Green's precious junk might better be called pebbles than rocks. They are maybe one-quarter the size of your average baby fingernail. One rock equaled five or ten bucks worth of high.

"Can I have that?" I heard Robert Knox ask behind me. I told him to back off.

My Mag flashlight is twelve inches long, two pounds of black aluminum and rechargeable battery. Before this night on Warren, I had hit a citizen with my flashlight only the two times I told you about earlier. The incident with a woman happened when I was in STRESS, after we had gotten her and a guy out of a car. I was paying attention to the guy when Dave Malinowski yelled, "She's got a gun!" It fell to the ground when I wheeled and smacked her on the elbow. The kid I rapped on the head was reaching to pull a gun from his boot while exiting a car. That's it. Period. But I had a Kel light, and later the Mag light, in hand during countless confrontations. It was a good, non-lethal deterrent and confidence-booster. You can't pull a punch when firing a bullet. A bullet will kill, no matter how softly you squeeze the trigger. The first time I hit Malice Green, on his clenched fist, I didn't particularly pull any punches. Everything about the struggle that was taking place centered on Green's clenched fist and his precious junk. Just as his entire being seemed focused on keeping that evidence away from us, it seemed clear to me that the struggle would end once we took it.

"Give it up!" I shouted. "Give it up!" And, grasping his wrist, I began striking his clenched fist. He again brought up his knees, and I lost my grip. I was already getting winded. My emphysema hadn't been diagnosed yet, but it was there. I was fifty-two years old and not exactly in great shape. Green's senseless will to continue resisting arrest, and the impossibly tight quarters inside his car, were – to say the least – making this a problem arrest. In weeks to come, everyone from prosecutors to politicians to editorial writers tried to paint a picture of two frenzied cops brutalizing a citizen. They got it part right. There was a frenzy. But the frenzy came from cocaine, not from Walter Budzyn and me. The frenzy prevented Walter from handcuffing Green and prevented me from getting hold of the evidence. Verbal commands had been useless. The struggle inside the car had been useless. Even a Mag light applied to Green's fist had been useless. Green had managed to create a stalemate of the worst kind, squared off against two cops obligated to end it.

My state of mind was not rage but that of anyone in any job who, when a simple task turns into an endless nightmare, rolls his eyes and says, aloud or to himself, "Oh, shit!" I truly hated altercations. Hundreds of times I had used trickery and fast talk to get a suspect into handcuffs. There was no way either method would work with this guy. He never said a word, just clutched his precious crack, squirmed, and kicked. Details of the struggle between Green and Walter inside the car were something I couldn't see, but Walter was not beating Green with his flashlight. I would have been able to see that kind of motion. Besides, crammed into that space, in a struggle, there is no way Walter could have swung a light. Meanwhile, for all Walter or I knew, Green might have had a gun beneath the car seat (he didn't) or a knife in his pocket (he did).

A routine arrest had escalated into something that definitely was not going to be easy. I didn't want any of the five bystanders jumping me from behind. I turned, faced them and told them to go. "Y'all can leave now," is the way at least one of them quoted me in testimony. I saw Knox and Fletcher head back up the walkway next to the dope pad, Brown crossing the vacant lot toward Twenty-Third Street, and Pace and Hollins moving toward Hollins's pickup truck parked on Twenty-Third.

As I turned back to the Topaz, where the struggle continued, Walter shouted: "He's trying to get out the other door!"

I ran around the Topaz, found the driver's door ajar, and swung it all the way open. Green's upper body tumbled out, one arm swinging free, the other pinned inside the car. I still had no idea exactly how Walter was positioned, but clearly he was on, or had hold of, Green's lower body. Otherwise, Green would have come completely out of the car. His head hung halfway to the pavement, his free fist still clenched like a vice.

I dropped to my knees facing mostly east, toward the rear of the Topaz, with my rear end against the open door. Once again I became as intent on prying that fist open as Green was intent on keeping it closed. But before I could grab his wrist again, Green swung his fist beneath the car and brought it back as an open hand. There now had to be, I was sure, at least a few rocks of crack cocaine littering the pavement of Warren Avenue. For an instant, I thought Malice Green, at last, was ready to call it a night. Several of the witnesses would later claim Green had a piece of paper in his hand. I never saw a piece of paper. Walter never saw a piece of paper. No piece of paper was ever found. For that matter, speaking of footnotes, no one to my knowledge ever got curious enough to find out why the Topaz had bullet holes in it. Nothing about Green's presence at the dope house, or his doped-up condition, or his actions seemed to be of much interest to investigators or the press. All anyone cared about was how and why I used my Mag light. And they got that wrong.

We were in a bizarre position for things to take a turn for the worse – Green hanging out of the car, his lower body pinned inside…me kneeling beside him. He reached and put his open hand squarely on the handle of my revolver. I felt a tug. "Let go!" I yelled. "Let go!"

I wore the Colt in a cross-draw position at my waist. After the incident in front of the Book-Cadillac Hotel, I always wore my gun in a snap-shut holster so it would never again fall out during a struggle. I reached with my left hand and grasped behind the trigger and over the strap to keep Green from getting the gun. He kept pulling upward on the handle. "Stop it! Stop it!" I yelled. And with my right hand – holding my flashlight toward the bell end and propelling it only with my forearm – I hit Malice Green on the top of the head. The way he was hanging from the car face-up, if I had lifted my arm and struck blows from above my shoulder I would have struck him on the forehead. I didn't. My upper arm remained stationary, and I snapped the small end of the flashlight against the top of his head. Three times, maybe four times.

Sometime just before or just after Green grabbed the handle of my gun, Walter used his prep radio to call for help. By now, I was getting seriously winded. Help seemed like a fine idea. I held onto the left sleeve of Green's jacket and hoped help was moments away.

I glanced down Warren and saw an EMS ambulance headed toward us westbound, aimed in the same direction as Green's car and Booster 3-31. I signaled the med techs with my flashlight – not the kind of thing, I think you would agree, somebody does if they are murdering a citizen and trying to cover it up. The EMS crew slowed, passed, and came to a stop just beyond the front of the Topaz. My back was toward them, but I heard their doors slam, and heard them walking toward me. As they stood a few feet away, I told them I had hit Green with my flashlight so they wouldn't think I had come upon a car accident or somebody else's altercation.

The tissue below the scalp is loaded with capillaries. Hit a man on the top of the head with a metallic object and he will bleed profusely even if his injuries are minor. Malice Green was bleeding profusely, though the wounds were hidden beneath his hair. I was more than ready for some backup to pull this man from his car, cuff him, and let the EMS crew do its thing.

Instead, Malice Green began squirming again, trying to break loose, and now both arms were free outside the car. His right fist was clenched. Instead of cocaine rocks, something metallic was protruding from between the fingers of his fist, and he began swinging at me. Once again I found myself yelling at him to "Drop it!" – utterly dumbfounded that Green would continue to resist. I jerked my upper body backward to avoid his swings, and – using exactly the same motion I had used previously – struck him maybe three times on the top of the head. The nearest EMS tech was the one who would later demonstrate in court and describe the blows as "flicks of the wrist."

Green stopped swinging and I stopped hitting him. Amazingly, he still would not submit. I retained my grip on the sleeve of his jacket, and he seemed to want to get at something around or under the driver's seat, pulling me toward the car. I was fatigued. I was dumbfounded. I still wondered what the hell this guy was really about, because his actions made no sense whatsoever, not logically and not in anything I had ever experienced in years of dealing with senseless actions on the street.

I think Scout car 3-7 was the second to arrive in response to Walter's radio call. Two patrolmen from the neighboring Fourth were the first. They stood around with their hands in their pockets doing nothing to help. When they wrote reports later, they would say they didn't arrive until it was all over. But they were standing around when Bob Lessnau exited 3-7, ran up, grabbed Green by the shoulders and pulled him out onto the street, away from Walter and me. "Watch his hands! Watch his hands!" I shouted repeatedly.

Our shift supervisor, a black sergeant named Freddie Douglas, arrived in a scout car about the same time as Lessnau and Karl Gunther's car 3-7. Scout 3-10 arrived shortly thereafter.

My part in the arrest was over when Lessnau pulled up. "Take it easy, Larry! Take it easy!" Douglas said as I leaned against 3-31, panting for breath. Down the line, prosecutors would plant in jurors' minds the idea that Freddie Douglas was yelling at me to stop swinging my flashlight at Malice Green's head. Freddie will tell you otherwise. "I didn't see anything but good police work," he said a decade later when contacted for this book.

Now three uniformed cops – Lessnau, along with Karl Gunther and Skip Kijek, who had been the last to arrive driving Scout Car 3-10 – were trying to subdue Green, who *still* kept his fist clenched, on the pavement of Warren Avenue. The metallic object grasped in that fist turned out to be car keys. One or more uniformed officers again struck flashlight blows on Green's hand. Still he grasped the keys, and still he twisted and turned, making the obligatory handcuffing process very difficult. Freddie Douglas shouted at Green, "Just open your hand! Let go of the damned keys!"

When Green finally complied, the uniformed cops rolled him over on his stomach and applied one handcuff. All three officers together could not pry his other arm from underneath him. They flipped him over again and discovered he had grasped a finger on a belt loop or pants pocket and refused to let go. The officers pried that finger loose and cuffed both hands behind his back, as regulations require. One officer searched Green's pockets and found an eight-inch knife folded in half. A second EMS crew had arrived after Green was removed from my car. All four EMS techs began treating him at the scene.

If Malice Green ever said anything to Walter or me except what I interpreted as indication that his driver's license was in his car, I didn't hear it. Walter also heard him say nothing. I would guess elapsed time from the moment I ran to help Walter until Bob Lessnau pulled Green from the car was five minutes. I don't know. It seemed at least that long.

The confrontation had been between Malice Green and two booster cops, but in truth Walter and I were separated by space and circumstances and we had no real handle on what kind of troubles each of us was encountering. First, it was just Walter and Green struggling inside the car. Then I joined in from the passenger side of the car. Then I circled to the driver side, as I just described. Methodical Walter, although sprawled inside the car and in one way or another partially pinning Green's lower body, assumed I had things under control – and, in fact, quickly made a second radio call telling backup not to go all-out, for fear of someone crashing a scout car in a needless rush. It was, however, so rare for 3-31 to ask for backup that 3-7 and 3-10 were already flying, hard, to get to Warren and Twenty-Third. Meanwhile, the prep radio got knocked from Walter's hand and Walter, the radio specialist, became paranoid about retrieving it inside the darkened car. It is not a good thing for a police radio to get lost at a scene and picked up by street people, something that had recently happened to another crew. So between that, and looking for more crack cocaine, Walter was busy grasping around the floor well of the Topaz during some crucial moments. In the end, this would be disbelieved. Believe it. I figured Walter was doing whatever he had to be doing, and he figured the same about me. That's what happens when a routine procedure escalates into something else under quick, bizarre circumstances. Somewhere, sometime, I'm sure some airplane pilot went over a checklist as he crashed into the ground. I guess that's one way of looking at Walter's actions as I struggled with Green.

I was regaining my breath and leaning against 3-31. A paramedic bag was lying on the street within Green's reach as the uniformed officers struggled to cuff him. I walked over and kicked it away. I had blood on my hands, on my jacket and on my flashlight. At some point, Walter asked one of the EMS crews for peroxide so his partner could clean himself up and clean his equipment. Later, that request for peroxide would be portrayed as an effort to destroy blood evidence. It was not a cover-up. It was a simple hygiene issue. I cleaned up in front of God, four EMS drivers, four carloads of cops, and a band of street people who had reassembled at the scene sometime after I asked Robert Knox and the others to clear out. No one destroys evidence in front of twenty or more witnesses. As far as visual evidence on the scene, the peroxide had one ironic effect. Put some blood on a flat surface. Then pour peroxide on it. Watch the blood grow in volume.

More to the point as I cleaned up after disengaging from the arrest, it flat-out never occurred to me that Malice Green might die. If I intended to kill a man with a two-pound flashlight, I certainly could have. I didn't intend for Malice Green to die. I wasn't even intending to inflict serious physical harm. Serious hurt, yes. Hurt – with a normal person – will bring resistance to an end. With Malice Green, it did not. So I hit him multiple times, in two sequences. First when he grabbed my gun, and then when he swung at me with keys in his fist. I know how hard I hit him. It wasn't hard enough to kill him unless there was something inside his own body that would make these blows fatal. The "unless" didn't occur to me at the time. Is it a good idea to hit someone on the head with a flashlight? Of course not. It's not a good idea to shoot someone, either. "Not a good idea" has a way of being trumped by circumstances. The circumstances are that before I ever struck Malice Green on the head he was deep into a struggle with my partner and me, and then he grabbed hold of my gun. Was he going to get my gun, like Sevoid Lutes did outside the Book Cadillac Hotel? Who knows? I do know that I didn't like that idea, that I was getting short of breath, and Green showed no signs of relenting. I had never been trained in any alternative way of bringing this thing to an end with my hands (and I'm not at all sure any alternative way would have worked). We weren't issued pepper spray (which I'm not real sure would have worked, either). Where is the big surprise that I struck him?

Green was transported to Detroit Receiving Hospital on the first EMS unit to arrive. It turns out to have been the *wrong* EMS unit, and the wrong crew – one of many things I did not know at the time, and one of several troublesome things about the EMS role. That's a major *understatement*, as you will see.

Freddie Douglas ordered Skip Kijek's partner, Paul Gotelaere – who had directed traffic while Green was being subdued – to ride in the ambulance. Kijek followed in their scout car. Sergeant Douglas ordered us to stay put pending a report on Green's condition. It was standard procedure for officers who injured a citizen during an arrest to remain at the scene until the citizen's condition is known. We did.

Walter ran the Topaz's plates on the MDT and made notes in our run book – Green's name and birthdate, the knife found in his pocket, the location at Warren and Twenty-Third.

After a prolonged struggle for evidence of a felony, I wanted that evidence. I think it was Karl Gunther who helped me push Green's Topaz forward so I could find the rocks that I assumed Green had thrown under the car. The two patrolmen from the Fourth would later say they helped in that search. I don't remember that. Maybe they did. All I remember is them standing there while I struggled with Green. We looked for little off-white chunks amid the asphalt and engine oil and dirt and debris of Warren Avenue. We didn't find any cocaine. Did we miss it? Did Green throw something else under the car? Was he dope-crazed enough to fight over a clenched fist that had nothing in it when he swung it beneath the car? I'll never know. Walter found four rocks on the floorboard. I had personal knowledge of one – the rock I pried from beneath his little finger, and which Robert Knox asked for.

Knox, in fact, was again standing next to 3-31 as I sat in the driver's seat after Green was taken away. Knox must have come back out from Fletcher's pad, joining a group of curiosity-seekers. Also standing there was Mickey Williams, a guy I had arrested as a suspect in cases involving murder, drug possession and armed robbery. I knew Mickey was wanted on several misdemeanor warrants. Mickey knew I knew that. We both knew that when you have a clientele of repeat felons, you seldom waste time with misdemeanors. Mickey was about six-foot-two, two hundred and seventy-five pounds, and was known as the neighborhood enforcer. He was not all that far from twice the size of Malice Green. Mickey had never resisted being arrested by me. I was very happy for that. I remained in a sort of low-grade state of amazement that Green could have resisted arrest so much, so long, so many ways, so silently.

What happened next between Mickey and me only shows, in my mind at least, how certain I was that Malice Green would have some blood cleaned up, some stitches taken, and would be all right. I might have been a cynical, street-smart cop, but I was not someone who would make a joke out of killing a man for the first time in my life.

The conversation flowed in much the same vein as when Walter and I first pulled up to the dope house.

"What did my boy do?" Mickey asked, referring to Malice Green.

"He pulled a gun on me," I said. "Wanna see it?"

"Yeah."

"Catch!" I picked up the toy plastic gun from the dash, reached out the window, and tossed it over the roof to Mickey Williams. "You probably can use it in your business."

Williams caught the gun and immediately realized it was a toy. He grabbed Robert Knox in a mock headlock, aimed the "gun" at him, and pulled the trigger. All the street people were laughing.

Realizing how this would look if some cop came rolling up without knowledge of the situation and cast of characters, I said, "OK, I need it back for evidence." Mickey complied, and I tossed the toy gun back on the dashboard. That's the last time I ever saw it, but not the last time I heard about it.

Most of the street people disappeared again into the night.

The prolonged crime scene scenario brought other cars to Warren and Twenty-Third. I can't catalogue them all. A female lieutenant I knew from the Fourth came over to 3-31 at one point and we talked. I don't remember much of the conversation, except that I asked her whether she had seen anything in the way of charges resulting from Billy Polk's arrest two nights earlier.

About half an hour after EMS left the scene, Kijek and

Gotelaere radioed that Malice Green was dead.

My instant reaction was that I didn't understand. I knew I hadn't done anything wrong. I *knew* Green would not die. Three or four forearm snaps when he tried to take my gun. Two or three forearm snaps when he swung at me with what turned out to be keys in his fist. He was still struggling after Bobby Lessnau dragged him away. *How could he be dead?*

I reacted with an emotion that is the opposite of emotion – shock. Something else had to have killed this man. Intuition told me Green's death went hand in hand with his zombie-like resistance. In the months and years ahead, I would learn much about what happens when a coked-up body becomes subject to stress, especially the stress of struggling with an authority figure who is trying to take away precious junk. At the time, all I knew is what I had observed during a struggle a half-hour earlier. Months later, experts would fill in the blanks for me, for a jury, and for anyone who would listen. No one seemed willing to listen. Of all the things no one would listen to, this one is the most baffling. When I was in prison, the president of the national pathologists' association would tell *Sixty Minutes'* Ed Bradley, flat-out, that cocaine – not me – had killed Malice Green. But as we sat in 3-31 along Warren Avenue, Freddie Douglas came over to inform me that this was now a homicide scene. I was more confused than anything. There is no greater confusion than feeling remorse when you know you haven't done anything wrong, but know that *something* went wrong, somehow. People didn't die when I arrested them. But Malice Green did.

From the moment the dope house was declared a homicide scene, it was like gravity started pulling Walter and me down into a very large and very deep pit. Protocol required Freddie Douglas to report Green's death to Homicide and to headquarters via telephone, rather than radio. He drove off to find a phone, leaving a vice sergeant from Four in charge of the scene. I don't know what this vice crew was doing there. They arrived after everything was over, departmental curiosity-seekers. I think they were the very first cops to suggest Walter and I were the bad guys. They would soon have lots of company at the highest levels.

Walter and I plunged ahead doing police work, like a soldier with an arm shot off but manning his post in shock. I went down the walkway and into Fletcher's pad. Your standard dope house comes with a fortified door, or at least a good lock. This door lacked even a handle. Push, and you were in. You could call it a kitchen, I guess – though the main clue was a waterless sink filled with garbage. Whenever the place had electricity, it was from a jumper cable used to steal power from a utility line. The place stunk of burned or wet or rotting wood and human waste. Every window was either boarded up or covered with opaque plastic to retain some warmth from kerosene heaters. Discarded needles and plastic pouches littered what were once a living room and bedroom, separated by a hanging bedsheet used as a doorway. If you wanted to make a drug arrest here, you'd have to search for today's evidence amid piles of yesterday's rotting evidence. Down the road, the prosecutors would be applying verbal cosmetics to the place and presenting it to jurors as Ralph Fletcher's "home."

Street cops were legally able to enter an abandoned building without a warrant if it was illegally occupied and the scene of illegal activities. Each time I had visited this place, I had asked Fletcher to produce rent receipts or utility bills, anything to prove he was legally occupying the premises. He never produced anything.

"Fletcher!" I yelled as I moved through the kitchen. He stepped out of the bedroom.

"Where's Knox?"

"I'm right here," Robert said as he stepped out behind Fletcher.

"Both of you come outside with me."

Walter entered their names, birthdates and addresses in our run book, underneath Emanuel Brown's. Maybe Brown had rejoined the sidewalk throng earlier. I can't remember. I could name Theresa Pace and Joe Hollins in my report. Walter and I were on autopilot, doing what a street cop does on a homicide scene to help the detectives. We didn't accept that we were the "suspects" in this investigation.

"You guys leave your car here and ride to Homicide with me," Sergeant Douglas told us. "Bring your flashlights."

It was near midnight. No one spoke during the ten-minute trip to headquarters. We walked past the First (downtown) Precinct desk and took the elevator up to the Homicide Section. I had taken this ride hundreds of times en route to the Narcotics Section, which shared the fifth floor with Homicide – which I also had occasion to visit.

Walter and I were put in separate offices. Gotelaere, Kijek, Gunther, Lessnau and Sergeant Douglas – the five officers who came to our assistance – were put elsewhere within view of the four EMS techs…Albino Martinez, Mythium Lewis, Lee Hardy and Scott Walsh. Next day the four EMS techs would be asked to identify all of us in a lineup.

Procedure requires all witnesses in a homicide case to be taken to headquarters for questioning. As Green's drug-using friends were led in, they also were given a good look at the five assisting officers.

Skip Kijek, about to be caught in the vice, had been present at the scene only because despite having gotten permission to leave work and attend a union board meeting, he had decided to work the shift on the street. Freddie Douglas was there only because Randy Martin, the sergeant scheduled to work the shift, had attended an all-day seminar on AIDS. (We already knew, of course, one thing you did in the wake of the AIDS scare; that is, whenever you are exposed to blood on the job, you find a bottle of peroxide and get rid of the blood.) I suppose in reconstructing any event you can find many shoulda-wouldas that drew everybody to that place at that time. Would even Walter and I have been there if the red Tempo hadn't been reported as car-jacked? *Highly* unlikely.

Our shift's regular union rep, a patrolman named Don

Taylor, didn't work that night and had attended the board meeting. Kijek was a steward, and he is the one who phoned the union attorneys and told them some officers needed counsel at Homicide. Sometime after midnight, Officer Rhonda Gambrell, a black woman and the union rep for another shift, showed up for a while. I really don't remember whether Kijek or Gambrell, or neither or both, urged me to write down everything that happened. I didn't need any urging. Writing a report was the end result of anything noteworthy that happened on the street. I had written thousands of PCRs – preliminary complaint reports – over the years. My writing was never any good, but the content was right. It goes without saying that what happened at Warren and Twenty-Third called for a PCR. So I started to write one, even without being asked.

Maybe halfway through writing my report, our union-appointed attorney, Fred Walker, entered the room.

"What are you writing?" he asked.

"My report of the incident," I said.

Fred Walker began reading what I had put down on paper.

"Tear this up," Fred said.

Years later, a retired homicide sergeant I respect a very great deal called this the most troublesome and harmful part of our case. It was routine during his years in Homicide, he said, for statements to be taken in any cops-involved case of any type. That statement, after all, is a big chunk of an investigation's starting point. The drill was for the officer involved to write a statement. The officer's lawyer could review the statement before submitting it. But there would be *some* kind of statement. If nothing else, the officer would state, "Yes, I was on duty at such and such a place at the time such and such occurred." *Something* to indicate cooperation with investigators. I wanted to write it all down, in the longest PCR of my life. Fred Walker said no. He was the lawyer. I complied and tore up what I had started to write. Down the road at my second trial, Fred would be called as a witness and would testify that, yes, I did tell him that night that Malice Green had tried to grab my gun. Whether a jury, eight years after the fact, would have put more weight on a statement dated in 1992 is something I'll never know.

Fred today says he would not have advised me any differently if he had it to do all over again. He had played a role in many officer-involved cases, probably the least of which was Walter's trial board for driving the old couple back over the bridge to Canada after their car was stolen. Fred had never seen anything like what he found at Homicide shortly after the clock turned to November 6, 1992. The place was crawling with grim-faced supervisors. Seven different street cops had been brought in and sequestered here and there, and clearly were targets. Besides, the investigators didn't want a statement from me. That's something I didn't know until years later.

"They weren't asking for a statement," Fred Walker said recently. "Perhaps even if they had, I probably would have said 'no.' They were going to do what they were going to do and didn't give a damn what Larry had to say. Nothing was going to alter the charges."

Kijek, who was both a detainee and a union rep, recalls the decision on asking for a statement as a midstream change on the part of Homicide. Somebody, Kijek recalls, decided around the time Walker arrived that no statements would be taken. I don't know. Ask the brass. All I know is that I was eager to give a statement, my lawyer said no, and a real good and experienced homicide officer tells me this was super harmful to my case. Whatever. In any event, it's pretty clear that these investigators didn't want a statement from me, and even before we were processed at Homicide that night somebody had decided to make this not an investigation but a slam dunk.

If a statement is evidence, how about cocaine? Before seeing me, Fred Walker had talked with Walter Budzyn. "Walter had a little bit of cocaine that he had taken from Malice Green," Walker recalls. "I had never seen crack cocaine before. Walter wanted to submit it as evidence. They had said, 'You just hang onto it and we'll deal with it later.' I went and got somebody and then they took it." And that's how Homicide got its hands on the stuff that started the whole incident – that and the coke that was in Green's bloodstream.

I remember a Homicide officer, Sergeant Lee Caudill, reading us our rights. I guess Walter and I had been brought together for this. I don't remember. The tension was getting high enough I'm not even sure whether I entirely realized my surroundings at the time. I recall Caudill asking, in Fred Walker's presence: "Do you wish to make a statement?"

"They do not," Fred Walker said.

Caudill left the room.

The unreality of it all was overwhelming. Rights were being read to me, instead of me reading rights to the bad guys. Headquarters was headquarters, not the Third Precinct. But these were familiar enough surroundings. I was no stranger to the section and most of the detectives. I had been here many times. I knew most by name. They knew me to be a hard-working street cop. Surely, the investigation would be fair. Confusion ruled my mind. Part of me was confident. But anxiety had begun to suck oxygen from my lungs.

The bedrock of my confident side was the process known as the board of review. It's a departmental panel of three command-level officers appointed to investigate an incident, interview the policemen involved, and determine whether they properly followed regulations and procedures. It's a time-honored mechanism, a street cop's ultimate incentive for following the book. Do your job according to the rules, and a board of review will say so. If a board of review certifies to a prosecutor that an officer acted within General Orders, it becomes a different ballgame. A board's finding is not admissible in court, and is not binding, but it can have a profound effect on prosecutors – even prosecutors who are eager to nail a cop. I had issued a lawful order to Malice Green, with obvious probable cause that a felony had been committed. The suspect defied my repeated orders. He physically resisted not one officer, but both Walter and me – and resisted more police officers later. I used necessary escalating force to subdue Green and retrieve evidence. I pried at his clenched fist before striking it with my flashlight. I did not strike Malice Green on the head until he grabbed the handle of my revolver. Surely a board of review would end the nightmare.

We sat for nearly five hours.

Sgt. Caudill came back and said we could go home. They confiscated my jacket and my flashlight, which would henceforth be known as "the murder weapon." They took my jacket because Malice Green's blood was on it.

A TV camera videotaped us from outside the police garage as we walked to Freddie Douglas's car. He drove us back to the Third. I was too drained to go inside and talk with anyone. I asked Douglas to turn in my prep radio for me. I trudged through the parking lot to my personal car, a seven-year-old Mark VII that was my one pride and joy when it came to mechanical toys. It was now 5:30 or 6 a.m.

As I drove the short twelve miles to the house I turned off the Mark V's radio. I just wanted silence and sleep. Instead of going inside, I parked and waited for Nancy to leave for work. I knew she would be supportive, but I wanted total solitude with my thoughts. I lay down on the couch, fully clothed, and replayed the night's events a thousand times in my mind. Finally I dozed off.

10

THE STAGE IS
SET FOR HYSTERIA

A nd so ends the first part of my story – who I was as a police officer, and what happened on Warren Avenue. I hope you had that imaginary video camera rolling, because you'll need to keep those pictures in mind as you try to make sense of what happened *after* November 5, 1992. To me, it makes no sense. I think you'll agree, even if you don't agree with me about everything. Even if you aren't willing to accept anyone's account of those things only I can know. Even if you aren't the type inclined to side with those who carry a badge and a gun. But let me sum up a few points to remember before you read details about the hysteria, the trampling of due process, and the railroading. A thick smokescreen of racial politics made common sense invisible to a lot of people as I lived through these events. A lot of that smoke is still floating in the air. So think of this chapter as taking a deep breath before plunging through the smokescreen.

I did what I had to do that night on Warren Avenue. By what I *"had"* to do, I mean a number of things. I mean my partner was in distress and in danger. I mean I stepped in when the wrong side of the law was withholding evidence and trying to gain control of a rightful arrest situation. I mean I followed the book as I know it, just as I did all those years in which I was commended, not prosecuted, for doing my job. I mean my actions were a response to Malice Green's own actions, not some kind of unprovoked attack on a passing "motorist."

I mean the incident did indeed go on for some time as arrests go – not as a "prolonged beating," but as a struggle to subdue a felon who refused to be subdued. I mean everything I knew about my obligation to make Malice Green submit, and how to get it done, came entirely from my days at the academy back in 1968 and from twenty-four years of street experience. I mean every decision I made during the arrest of Malice Green was made in real time, not with the luxury of sitting at a desk or a court bench and pondering the situation. I mean that when Malice Green put his hand on my gun I was already becoming exhausted – as I was when Sevoid Lutes stood over me in front of the Book-Cadillac Hotel taking aim at me with that very same gun – and there was no way I was going to let him get it. I mean I did what this police officer, with this experience and this training and this equipment, had to do in that *unique* set of circumstances. I suppose in his own doped-up way, and in his habit of resisting arrest, you could say Malice Green did what *he* had to do – despite police officers' commands, and even the shouts of his junkie friends to give it up. I suppose you could say the outcome was therefore inevitable. I cannot tell you how sorry I am about that. Both for him and for me.

We could argue about whether those unique circumstances and General Orders empowered me to strike Malice Green hard enough to kill him. But we don't need to argue about that, not if common sense has anything to do with judging this case. I will go to my own grave knowing I did not strike Malice Green with lethal force. I've said that here before. I'll say it again, because it seems like a fairly basic issue in an alleged "brutal beating death." Of course, you cannot take my word about that issue, though I like to think my service record counts for *something* in terms of credibility. But we don't have to argue about that, either. You can let the medical evidence guide your bottom-line opinion about what caused Malice Green's death. I did not intend serious harm, let alone death, to this stranger – any more than I did two nights earlier to Billy Polk, who I knew all too well. Nobody but the craziest of the crazies thinks

I did. Looking at it from a 180-degree different perspective, the most cynical old coppers will tell you no booster crew is going to damage an arrest subject who means time testifying in court, because court time means income.

It's been said a thousand times, and probably a million people believe it, that I was in an unexplainable out-of-control rage that night. On the street and on the Internet, that assumption was so strong that laughable stories were invented to account for my supposed rage – jealousy over a hooker, involvement in the drug trade, drunkenness (on the part of someone who doesn't drink), enthusiastic racial brutality (by someone who had *thousands* of opportunities to exercise racial brutality and never did). Where does this stuff come from? From four places, as far as I can see. Black racist stereotyping of white cops. Political whoring. Knee-jerk fear of a riot in Detroit – fear expressed by the same people who did everything they could to suggest there was reason to riot, the facts be damned. And total lack of common sense. If I had been in an out-of-control rage, swinging haymakers with a two-pound Mag light, you wouldn't need a pathologist to determine cause of death. That's why the street buzz wildly misstated Malice Green's injuries. Street buzz might not be real smart, but it knows what kind of damage would be produced by out-of-control rage and a Mag light. That scenario couldn't be true without fractures, so the hysteria invented fractures.

Lest I hog the stage, don't forget that the street buzz had two cops in an uncontrollable rage, Starsky *and* Hutch. This despite the fact that Walter and I were not exactly in close communication during the struggle, and despite the fact that I do not believe Walter struck Green even once with his flashlight. And then there were the uniformed officers who came along and also had to struggle with Green to get him handcuffed. They were also alleged to be in a brutal, senseless rage. It's ridiculous. Green simply would not give up and end the struggle.

Speaking of rage and fear, let me tell you something about how difficult it can be to get at the truth in the criminal justice system, where lawyers play word games not to seek truth but to seek victory. It's a no-brainer that I was going to be asked on the witness stand whether I feared for my life. "Yes or no, Mr. Nevers, did you fear for your life?" Yes or no? You're kidding. "Yes" would mean I was afraid. I wasn't afraid. Anybody who is afraid in that kind of situation has no business being a street cop. But "no" would mean I didn't think I was in danger and had no grounds for protecting myself. The really honest answer would be: "When he put his hand on my gun I knew – or at least thought I knew – that by striking him on the head I'd keep him from getting my gun. If he got my gun, you bet I'd be afraid. So I stopped him from getting it." Honest and reasonable, I think. But not exactly the way a lawyer would advise you to explain yourself to a jury.

I admit I've got an all-or-nothing take on this case. I don't think I did anything wrong whatsoever under the circumstances. I'm adamant about that. Maybe being paraded, like a war prisoner, through every living room that has cable TV and being certified as a dirty cop, a racist cop and a brutal cop has something to do with that. Maybe looking in the eyes of people who literally wished I would receive capital punishment for arresting Malice Green has something to do with that. But I do believe it.

One first-class police officer I respect a great deal is Roger Brooks, the same officer whose place I took on a STRESS crew and the same officer who was sitting on his flak jacket in Recorder's Court when a defense lawyer opened his briefcase, pulled out a gun and started shooting. Roger worked many police jobs with distinction. He was one of the best – who, by the way, after retirement from the Detroit force went to work as a "meter maid" in an affluent suburb to earn a decent pension. Roger is a smart and well-spoken guy. He was also the homicide sergeant who interviewed me after the Book-Cadillac incident. A couple years ago a writer asked Roger whether Walter Budzyn and I were over charged in the Green case. Roger said, "Grossly over charged. The most the prosecution might have had here was a very, very weak manslaughter case. Besides, we don't prosecute the good guys for winning a fight the bad guys started, do we?" A lot of intelligent and knowledgeable people see it that way, and I appreciate the sentiment – even though I disagree about there being any case to be brought at all, even one that didn't merit a conviction.

How can I see it that way? After all, the whole country watched me put my head in my hands and weep when twelve citizens found me guilty of murder, right? The news media to this day still refer to "the police beating death" of "motorist" Malice Green, right? It's in the history books that way. This viewpoint of mine is something really far out, right? Wishful thinking, cop talk, rationalization, something nobody but Larry Nevers and his friends could possibly believe? All I can say to that is: "Never underestimate the power of news media to choose a horse and ride it until it drops." Put something in print and in sound bites often enough and long enough and it becomes the unmistakable truth as far as public opinion goes. That would explain why one remarkable news story on this subject went pretty much in one public ear and out the other.

For readers who don't know southeastern Michigan, I need to explain that metropolitan Detroit consists of three counties. Detroit itself lies in Wayne County, and the city's northern border lies along the southern border of two other counties – Oakland and Macomb. Oakland is one of the nation's most affluent counties, with upscale cities like Birmingham and Bloomfield Hills. Oakland County has a significant black population, being the destination of choice for those middle-class and upper-class minorities who, like most of the white population, fled Detroit's crime and decay. Macomb is a historically blue-collar county, the place where Ronald Reagan learned he could attract Democratic votes – but in recent times Macomb, too, has replaced farmland in the north of the county with affluent subdivisions. Except for lines on a map, all three counties would be considered part of the same city, with suburbs stacked wall-to-wall northward from Detroit. If someone from Oakland or Macomb county is asked in Boston where they're from, they say "Detroit."

As far as the criminal justice system is concerned, however, three counties mean three different prosecuting attorney's offices. If Malice Green had died a half-dozen miles to the north, the case would have been reviewed by the men serving as prosecuting attorney in those counties at the time – Richard Thompson in Oakland County or Carl Marlinga in Macomb County. Bringing this up would be idle speculation about what would have happened in the other two-thirds of the Tri-County Area, except for one thing: Two years after we were convicted and sent to prison, while Walter and I were battling for a second chance via the appeals process, both Thompson and Marlinga went public.

Marlinga expressed the obvious – that our trial wasn't fair, that we hadn't intended to kill anyone, that this was "not a bad arrest, but an arrest that went bad." He cited the role of cocaine in Green's death. He called for a new trial, something the Wayne County prosecutor fought against successfully for a very long time. Marlinga's message was clear: He was troubled by the way Walter and I were railroaded, and finally felt he had to speak out. "Everybody is whistling past the graveyard, not wanting to create any controversy," he told the Detroit Free Press. "It's politically dangerous to say anything…at some point you just have to throw caution to the wind and do what's right and throw race and politics aside." Clearly, we would have gotten a fair investigation and course of action from Carl Marlinga. Whether he then would have charged us with any crime at all is speculation – though other Macomb County cases involving difficult arrests suggest to me that he would not. The Free Press, by the way, ran the Marlinga story on Page 4B.

Oakland County Prosecutor Richard Thompson went a step further. He said flat-out that he would not have brought charges of any kind.

In case you're wondering, neither Thompson nor Marlinga had a habit of trashing the Wayne County prosecutor in public. In fact, you'd have to look long and hard to find even one example of any prosecutor – around here, at least – challenging his next-door counterpart for imprisoning someone. My own attorneys couldn't remember any prosecutor making the kind of public statement made by either Marlinga or Thompson.

Thompson, no longer in public office and at this writing with the Thomas More Law Center, an Ann Arbor-based public-interest law firm, was interviewed for this book. He said of the Green case: "I believe there was a total miscarriage of justice. This was basically nothing more than a lynch mob. There was so much press and so many inaccurate statements highlighted in the press that it was impossible for them to get a fair trial."

Beyond that, Thompson said: "I would not have brought any charges against them regardless of the uproar, based on the evidence, based on the medical examiner's reports, based on the entire situation as it occurred. I think there was no crime committed. You have to make decisions. I prosecuted Jack Kevorkian, even though I knew the overwhelming sentiment was against prosecution there. You take an oath of office to do your job, and people then vote you out of office if they don't like what you did. But you can sleep at night."

It's fair to say that in Detroit itself any prosecutor who sent any two white cops to prison would not have to worry about getting votes in the next election. The same could be said for any Detroit politician who played the race card in the Malice Green case. I do wonder how they sleep at night.

It was all over – though the shouting never did end – before Thompson and Marlinga spoke out about the case. By then the storyline was cast in stone, most people were tired of it, and I'm not sure how many people even noticed the remarkable things these two prosecutors had to say about "the police beating death of motorist Malice Green." Thompson and Marlinga were two guys who understood the circumstances Walter and I faced on the street, and what it means for things to go bad when a cop is just doing his job.

The rest of my story depicts the flood that swept Walter and me down the sewer. You already know where it ends, but I think your eyes will be opened all along the way. Keep reviewing your imaginary videotape as you read what happened next. As for your honest questions about whether your imaginary videotape is accurate, I defy anyone to tell you I have not given an accurate account of my twenty-four years as a police officer, and my sixteen years in a booster car up until the night Malice Green died. And in the rest of this book I will show you how the opposing version of Malice Green's death is riddled with lies, deceit, political expediency, inconsistencies, revised testimony, denial of due process, characterizations that have no basis in my record – all driven, above all, by a racial stereotype that Walter and I were storm troopers in a White Occupation Army. I can also tell you some very interesting things about cocaine highs and how they affect the arrest process, and about what really killed Malice Green. In short, I can show you that Walter and I were destined for conviction no matter what happened on the street that night. At the corner of Warren and Twenty-Third, race had nothing to do with what happened. In court, and in the media, everything that happened was all about race.

In the real world, the dope house Malice Green was visiting the night he died would stay in business, uninterrupted, for at least another decade. During the writing of this book, at least two newspaper reporters were told, "Hey, don't you think it's interesting that the site of the most famous arrest in Detroit history is still a dope house?" No such story was ever written. Meanwhile, in the police Narcotics Section an unwritten rule advised officers not to mess with dope activity at Warren and Twenty-Third. Too much controversy, what with the "shrine" to Malice Green and all that. On November 5, 1992, I couldn't avoid dope activity at that address. I was obligated – by my job description and by my own insistence on being a hard-working street cop – to patrol that address, to be aware of what was going on there, and to halt any criminal activity I saw. Even that most basic fact got lost in the smokescreen. The fact is, Stanley Knox himself had issued a departmental directive ordering all patrol officers to give "special attention" to narcotics locations.

11

'THIS IS NOT SIMI VALLEY. WE WILL CONVICT.'

After I finally got to sleep sometime into the daylight hours of Friday, November 6, the phone woke me up around noon.

"They want you down to the precinct at 3 p.m.," a desk sergeant said. "They'll probably want your badge and your gun."

Malice Green wanted my gun, too. This time I would have to let it go.

They say everything looks crystal-clear in the cold light of dawn. Not for me. Not the dawn after Malice Green's death. Everything was a deep fog. Disbelief, shock, not understanding what had happened, or what was now happening. Not even *knowing* that certain things were happening. If I had known these things, the fog would just have been deeper.

Before I fell asleep on the couch, my own department's leadership had set a steamroller moving against seven officers, particularly Walter and me. By the time the phone woke me up our fate was a done deal, a fact I wouldn't realize for a very long time.

Stanley Knox put the steamroller in motion. Stanley Knox became police chief after Bill Hart's embezzlement problems cost him the job. Knox's wife was a command-level police officer. Every police officer I knew believed she would have made a better chief than her husband. That's not much of a compliment because Stanley Knox's greatest talent was wearing a dress uniform well, so at least he looked like he belonged in the job. That impression disappeared when he opened his mouth to give an order. No one who knew Detroit politics or Stanley Knox or Mayor Coleman Young would, in my opinion, have any doubt why Knox was calling for our heads privately by sun-up and publicly by sundown. Amazingly quick judgment for a guy who just a few hours earlier had been unreachable by phone or radio when Homicide officers were summoned to Warren Avenue. Knox's job was not to judge, not even to investigate. A good chief's job was to assure public and press that a fair and complete investigation was under way, stand back, and make certain it happened. Knox made sure it did not happen. He made an instant judgment and, almost as quick, took it public.

Knox began his Friday by summoning a group that included his own top brass, Internal Affairs, and the police legal section to a meeting in his office. I've heard third-hand stories of "I've got to have these guys' asses" being said in that meeting, at a time when any real investigation would barely be under way. I can't confirm that, of course. But there is no question that Knox's meeting tainted the investigation and the fix was in. Knox had already reached conclusions he would utter in an incredible press conference later in the day. At the morning meeting, he told the assembled brass that due process for us seven cops was going in the tank. He didn't use those words, of course. What he said – clearly, and forcefully – was that there would be no board of review involved in this investigation. No special panel of command-level officers would call witnesses, including me, and determine whether police officers on the street had followed General Orders in escalating force.

Knox's denial of a board of review was absolutely unprecedented. Every investigation of a fatal incident involving police officers is supposed to involve three cooperating but separate units: the Homicide Section, Internal Affairs, and a specially appointed board of review comprising one commander and two inspectors. Officers involved in such an incident are routinely taken off the street and "assigned to the board of review." The board of review acts as a sort of coordinator and is supposed to report to the chief. That's in the sense of *reporting* to the chief, not in the sense of being the chief's lackey. Every cop who gets in a jam counts on a fair hearing before a board of review. Not a free pass, but a fair hearing free of politics and grandstanding. Boards of review do nail police officers to the wall if they're guilty of a crime. A board of review can't convict and can't acquit. But it can find facts and make recommendations to prosecutors. It is supposed to make sure the overall investigation is objective. In a death-in-custody case, a board is supposed to be convened quickly and proceed judiciously. In the Malice Green case a board was named at 8 the next morning, but Stanley Knox instantly made sure that board never did a thing. No witnesses heard, no coordination, no oversight, nothing.

This board of review panel, despite trying, couldn't even find out what was going on in the Homicide investigation. The commander chairing the phantom board, a black commander named Charles Henry, would eventually win a substantial lawsuit against the city in which he contended his career had been shattered partly by his attempts to get the board convened and involved in the investigation.

At the Friday morning meeting, Commander Clinton Donaldson, head of Internal Affairs, argued strenuously against squelching the board of review. Knox's order was so bizarre that in the end Donaldson would refuse to sign off on the investigation. Not because he had somehow decided a few hours after Green's death that we were innocent – or guilty, for that matter – but because that's not the way due process works, and not the way an investigation is supposed to work. I'm sure Donaldson would have gladly "gotten our asses" if that's where the investigation led him. But years later, Donaldson, also a black man, told a writer: "We may never know what happened out there." You're supposed to know what happened out there before you charge somebody with murder and send them to prison.

This crucial backroom maneuvering occurred while I slept fitfully on the couch.

Some people in the department were eagerly going after us in less important ways. Home addresses and phone numbers and even photos magically made their way to the press. A second phone call soon after I awakened was from a newspaper reporter. What I told him, or at least what appeared in the paper, was: "I must have done something wrong. A guy died." I don't even remember what I said. The other quote the reporter used was: "If I can ever sleep again I'm just going to wake up and say this is a dream, it didn't happen, it didn't happen. Nobody knows what it's like out there."

I have no reason to think the reporter misquoted me. What he quoted me as saying is very close to what I was thinking, if it's possible to think in that deep a fog. My job on the street was to gain control of the situation. That's what I did. But Malice Green died. There was no easy explanation for his death. Let me rephrase that. There was an easy explanation. I hit Malice Green on the head and he died. That's the easy explanation. My fog was all about the easy explanation, and remorse, and shocked confusion because I knew I had not beaten a man to death...but I did hit him on the head...not hard enough to kill him...but he was dead. We must have done something wrong; but we didn't do anything wrong. That's the heart of the heavy fog that refused to lift all day and through the weekend. I wasn't thinking about less easy explanations. I was thinking about a Topaz and a dope house and the impossible news – sent back while I was tossing a toy gun at Mickey Williams and asking a lieutenant for news on Billy Polk – that Malice Green had died.

The idea that after twenty-four years on the street and a few months from retirement I would beat a man to death for no reason during a nickel-and-dime dope arrest made no sense, and I couldn't imagine that others would not see that it made no sense. A real investigation is supposed to get past easy explanations that make no sense. Even if the police brass tossed due process out the window and rushed to judgment, there was one other key piece of the investigation outside the department – the key piece of this investigation – where things that didn't make sense were supposed to be explained. Scientifically. Impartially. With no regard for anything but the truth. No racial politics. No easy explanations. That would, of course, be the medical examiner's office. And while I slept, the ME's office is where getting at the truth took the biggest hit of all.

Malice Green's body was autopsied Friday morning by a deputy medical examiner named Kalil Jiraki. His job was to determine what killed Malice Green. Several years later, Jiraki would write in an unpublished book manuscript: "The determinations that medical examiners make based on autopsies stem from experience relevant to the locale of the office, and the community that it serves." In other words – my words – the cause of death of a black man arrested by a white police officer in Detroit is one thing, the cause of death of a white man arrested by a white police officer somewhere in the sticks is something else. Over the next several years, an army of pathologists would examine and comment on the Malice Green case and a half-dozen would testify. Jiraki was the least experienced of them all, by far. The chief pathologist of a neighboring county, a guy Detroit prosecutors often called in on tough cases, would testify at my trial that Jiraki's autopsy of Malice Green was incompetent. Jiraki had an agenda. He had more holes in his vision than a blind pilot flying at night. I need to prove all that to you, of course; and I will do that in the most important chapter of this book, devoted entirely to medical evidence, cocaine, and how prosecutors did everything in their power to ignore and suppress exactly why Malice Green died. It's amazing stuff that will leave you wondering how much of a fairy tale it is that the legal system is about a quest for truth. For now, just be aware that by early Friday afternoon my fate and Walter Budzyn's were a done deal, in both the police chief's office and in the medical examiner's office. I didn't know that. I was struggling to understand why a man was dead and I was about to surrender my badge.

About the only thing I can remember regarding the couple of hours before driving to the precinct is getting a call from one of my old partners. Actually, I didn't even remember that. Years later, he reminded me of the call, and told me he had cried when he heard I was at the center of the firestorm sweeping through the department and, with the news media's help, through the city. I may have talked to my sister-in-law, who heard a news report on TV. I really don't know. I didn't call anybody. No one. No friend, no lawyer, not even Nancy – who more than anybody I wanted to somehow keep out of this. It's incredible, come to think of it, how many hours passed into a situation that would drastically change her life before she had any idea what was happening.

Everybody has traumatic events in their lives. Usually, these events pop up and get you in an instant – a car accident or phone call telling you about a death in the family, or being called into an office and told you've lost your job, whatever. Other times these events are scheduled in advance – like, say, lung-cancer surgery. My confrontation with Malice Green and his death was the former kind of event. A routine night patrolling the Third, the precinct where more Detroit cops had died in the line of duty than any other. One minute your partner is chasing a junkie into the night and a few minutes later you are a homicide suspect. Now barely a dozen hours later, I was facing the kind of traumatic event that's scheduled in advance. I knew that at 3 p.m. I would have to do something that symbolized a train-wreck of an ending to an honorable career. It would be the first of many long walks I took over the next few years. The routine of my life was about to be turned backwards. All those years of instant, unpredictable events on the street; now it was going to be hearings and trials and jury verdicts, all scheduled neatly on the calendar. Maybe that's why I had loved working the street. We've all got things big and small to dread. But on the street they were never scheduled ahead of time.

The Third Precinct station was a dump, but there were

worse. Driving down Vernor, if you didn't see marked cruisers in the parking lot out back you might think the one-story brick building was some kind of office for a nearby trucking company. I had parked my car and walked into this building thousands of times, to the point where I paid no more attention to my surroundings and movements than you pay attention to the next breath you take. I would be inside and reading the teletype and overnight reports without even being aware of taking the steps from my car. This time I was painfully aware of every step. I came in through the garage and made a right turn, stealing a glance at the desk to see if anyone would look at me. No one did. The public version of what happened out there – cops losing control, senselessly beating to death a man the press would a thousand times call "motorist Malice Green" – had already taken hold, even among some of those people who knew me and should have said: "Wait a minute. This doesn't track. What's the rest of the story?" All the vague thoughts about just how much trouble I was in started to become less vague.

I sat down alone in an office and waited. Then Nancy showed up. My brother's wife had called her at work and told her what was on the news. Nancy drove straight to the precinct, found me, and we sat and talked. Both of us cried. The emotional part of the fog, instead of lifting, poured out of me and covered everything.

A precinct sergeant, Dennis Fulton, drove both of us downtown to headquarters. Nancy waited in Homicide while I was taken to an office and handed a half-sheet piece of paper that said I was being suspended for conduct unbecoming an officer. The suspension would be without pay. In normal times, I can't imagine sitting in the same room with Dennis Fulton and not talking, let alone riding with him in a car and not talking. But if we talked on this day, I don't remember a word. I can't even remember exactly who handed me the suspension notice. Dennis's signature is on it. I knew what I was being told, of course. But the speed in which this all was happening meant more than I could possibly have understood. It was not yet twenty-four hours since I started the shift that ended with Malice Green's death.

I've got this fantasy where I see a cop in trouble for something that happened on the street, and the mayor and the police chief solemnly promise a full investigation, and the cop is moved off the street and assigned to a board of review, and investigators and prosecutors do a professional job of finding out what happened, and if it's a high-profile case then City Hall and the department keep their cool with the media and put the criminal justice system to work in an even-handed way… and the officer is, in truth, presumed innocent until proven guilty. Actually, it's not a fantasy because in the last decade I've watched it happen that way in other cases and other places. Considering some of the things that happened in the Malice Green case, the piece of paper I was given on Friday afternoon might not seem like much. But it was huge. If Knox's meeting that morning was the invisible start of the railroading, that suspension notice is where it hit radar.

According to department regulations, two things are supposed to happen before an officer is suspended without pay. First, a criminal warrant must be issued against him. Second, the board of police commissioners needs to vote approval of the action. No warrant had been issued against me, no approval voted by any board. This is a long, long way from being this case's most glaring example of the cart being put ten miles in front of the horse. But it was the first to happen in broad daylight. The train was in motion, and everything that drives the news media and public opinion was on board. I was illegally stripped of my job and my income and branded as a wrongdoer. It's not the loss of pay that's important here; it's the loss of due process at even the most basic level, and about the presumption of guilt. That same suspension notice got slid across a desk to seven different officers: me, Walter Budzyn, Bobby Lessnau, Skip Kijek, Karl Gunther and Paul Gotelaere – plus Sergeant Freddie Douglas, whose inclusion made it a salt-and-pepper case. Anyone present for the arrest of Malice Green was suspended without pay, except the two patrolmen from Four who were first to respond to Walter's radio call for help, then stood around and watched.

Seven cops was a convenient number. If you took a random poll asking how many police officers appear on the Rodney King videotape, the average answer might be "seven." The King videotape had been wallpapered across TV screens earlier in 1992 as verdicts came down from a courtroom in Simi Valley, California, where a jury found all police officers in the case not guilty. Less than two hours passed from reading the King verdict to the start of the Los Angeles riot in which fifty-four people died. The hot summer of the 1967 Detroit riot was twenty-five years in the past, even older history than my career as a police officer. But it was very much on somebody's mind, even on a cold November morning, when Knox started the ball rolling against us. No street disturbances of any kind had occurred the night before on Warren Avenue or anywhere else in the city. But for the next six months hardly a day would go by in Detroit without the "no justice, no peace" flag getting raised in the media. It became an unspoken part of the case against us. Find them guilty or face the consequences. Stanley Knox was way ahead of that curve on Friday, November 6. The first evening news broadcast since Malice Green's death had not yet been aired, but the seven of us were signed, sealed and delivered. Stanley Knox might have been slow, but he was quick.

At headquarters, I was relieved of my police I.D and Badge Number 2034. In a department that large, badge numbers need to be recycled, but I have no idea whether another cop is carrying Badge 2034 these days or not.

The symbolic surrender of the tools marking you as a police officer amounts to relinquishing city-owned property. So they didn't take the gun I was carrying, because it was my own gun. The next week someone would come out to the house and pick up my handcuffs, uniform and a stainless-steel .38-caliber snubnose revolver that had never been fired. A few years earlier the department had gotten a shipment of them, and I did the necessary paperwork to trade in the .38 issued to me at the academy in '68. When the department confiscated its revolver, it was still brand-new. I had continued to carry the Colt Python Nancy gave me so many years before, the one I dropped on Fort Street while tossing a tire off the road and the one that was turned against me in front of the Book-Cadillac Hotel. Detroit cops, uniformed or plainclothes, are required to carry a gun at all times, on duty or off. The idea is to increase the chance of police presence if – as happened more times than you could count in Detroit – a holdup or other unpleasantness occurred at a place where a police officer was buying groceries or having a beer or just driving down the street. So here I sat on Friday afternoon, surrendering my badge but carrying a gun.

At 3:45 p.m., while I was downtown at headquarters, roll call was held in the neighboring Fourth precinct. I didn't learn about what happened until three months later, when one officer present at the roll call sent a letter to my lawyer. One disappointment with the way many fellow officers and my union responded to our situation is that only one cop had the guts to speak up about what happened at Four's roll call.

Lieutenant Walter Shoulders, acting commander of the precinct I called "the Sleepy Fourth" when I walked a beat there fresh out of the academy, addressed the roll call. Sixteen cops listened to his rant: Lieutenant Rainelle Logan (the one I had chatted with about Billy Polk as Walter and I sat in the booster car on Warren), two sergeants and thirteen patrolmen – including John Doty and Robert Kane, the two stand-arounds who were the first to arrive at the scene on Warren.

The report sent to my lawyer listed the names of all present, and stated:

> *"He (Shoulders) informed us that the night before, 11-5-92, a number of police officers, two white officers known as Starsky and Hutch belonging to the Third Precinct, beat a black man to death with their flashlights for refusing to get out of his*

*vehicle. As they beat the black male a supervisor
also from the Third Precinct just sat there and
watched. The officers beat him so bad that he died
on the way to the hospital. Inspector Shoulders
then states, 'If I was the supervisor at the scene, the
man they beat wouldn't have been the only one
dying on the way to the hospital. They murdered
that man, and the citizens of Detroit have a right
to be upset.'*

*"I and others that were present during these
statements believe Inspector Shoulders was
informing us that he personally would have
killed the Police Officers involved at the Malice
Green incident. He, a professional police
supervisor, would have elected himself judge, jury
and executioner of Police Officers prior to an
investigation or knowledge of the events leading
up to the death of Malice Green. He also implied
that he as well as the Chief of Police had already
investigated the incident and that the Officers
brutally murdered Malice Green for no apparent
reason other than that he was black."*

Nobody has to play the race card in Detroit. It's always on
the table. This time it went: "We're tossing due process out the
window – and just in case that bothers somebody, Malice Green
was the victim of a racist attack." At a curbside populated by
black citizens I had arrested numerous times without incident,
and just around the corner from where I had arrested Billy
Polk two nights earlier, I selected the only person present I had
never seen before and I "murdered him only because he was
black" – the first time I had done such a thing in twenty-four
years of nightly opportunity to do so. You have to understand
that when the race card is in play, that kind of twisted logic
gets taken seriously, no questions asked. White cop plus black
citizen equals racist confrontation. Period. In the two years

before the Malice Green incident, two young black citizens were fatally shot in the back by police officers. The first dead man was fleeing a raid. The second was lying on the ground for a search. The first cop was acquitted of all charges brought against him; the second was convicted of reckless shooting, a misdemeanor. Neither incident raised any kind of stir in the community, because the officers who shot the two subjects in the back were black – just as both cops who shot the Cuban immigrant Jose Iturralde when he refused to take his hand out of his pocket were black. But less than twenty-four hours after Malice Green's death, after a struggle in which no shots were fired, the buzz was that Detroit would burn to the ground unless the "killer cops" were "brought to justice."

The twisted arithmetic was good enough to satisfy Lieutenant Walter Shoulders. At that, his black-racist tirade was hours behind Stanley Knox's high-echelon "roll call" that morning. Meanwhile, Walter Budzyn was also surrendering his badge on the last day of his spectacularly short tenure as my partner. I'm sure Walter was surprised to learn he was known in Four as "Hutch." In a couple of days Walter would be known as Hutch around the world. After we learned of that roll call in Four, Nancy wrote a letter to Shoulders and filed a written citizen's complaint against him. For a while, she called downtown for a response every couple weeks, then gave up. She never did get a reply.

Nancy and I caught our ride from headquarters back to the Third and then drove home in separate cars. By the time we got to Bretton Drive late in the afternoon, it was crammed with TV rigs and reporters. We parked on the next street and made our way into our dream house through a neighbor's backyard, just in time to get our first look at the media nightmare. We missed live coverage of Stanley Knox's 4 p.m. press conference, the first major installment of a news story that would dominate Detroit newspapers and TV for eight months. Tape of Knox's performance and interviews with everyone from street people to civic leaders filled the 6 o'clock news almost end to end.

While we watched TV inside the house, out on the street reporters milled around interviewing our neighbors.

Sometime soon my lawyer would advise me that for sanity's sake, I shouldn't watch or read any media coverage. For the most part I would follow that advice. The afternoon of November 6 I hadn't learned that lesson yet.

You have to understand that as I sat down to watch TV the only things I knew about Friday's events were those things I directly participated in. I didn't know anything about Walter Shoulders's roll call. I didn't know anything about Knox's morning meeting. I didn't know anything about Jiraki's autopsy. Because of Fred Walker's legal advice, I hadn't even interacted with Homicide detectives. I had no idea what the investigation was doing or where it was going, or what the department and the criminal justice system had in mind for us – except that it was obviously not good. I was expecting the union to step in and make sure everything was fair. I expected a board of review to do that anyway. I was haunted by Malice Green's death, but not by guilt in a criminal sense. I couldn't see how I had committed any crime. I had no intent. I was doing my duty. I believed I had used necessary force. I expected that eventually the system would come to that same conclusion. I really did believe that. I never said I wasn't naïve.

Stanley Knox came on the screen flanked by all the department brass. White shirts and lettuce-brimmed hats everywhere. Standing to one side was James Bannon, No.2 in the department, who probably would have been well into tenure as police chief if Coleman Young hadn't made naming a black chief a top priority. Bannon was the only high-profile white cop in Detroit who commanded a certain amount of respect from almost everybody – white police officers, black police officers, politicians of any color, editorial writers. He was, in fact, especially good with the media. If the media tended not to believe anything a police officer had to say, they tended to believe everything Bannon had to say. He had come up through the ranks, developed a reputation as a cop's cop, got himself a sociology degree from Wayne State University. Interesting guy. He even had a hand in creating STRESS, though he backed off from the idea after it became a hot potato. Naïve me felt just a little reassurance when I saw Bannon standing next to Knox in the press conference re-run. To me Jim Bannon stood for fairness and even-handedness.

Stanley Knox stepped to the microphones emotional, near tearful, and provided the following sound bites:

"This incident is disgraceful and a total embarrassment. To receive a blow like this actually brought tears to my eyes. I have no idea why they would do something like that. There was no excuse for it."

Knox said he didn't know whether the events on Warren Avenue were racially motivated but couldn't rule it out. Then, asked whether he saw a parallel between Rodney King and Malice Green, he said: "I think we all do."

And, twenty-four hours after I began my shift by checking to see if the red Tempo was still hot from Wednesday night's car-jacking, Stanley Knox said: "This is not Simi Valley. We will convict."

There is clear, and then there is clear. You can't be any more clear than Stanley Knox was. The verdict was "guilty."

A reporter cornered Jim Bannon, who said, "They didn't have to beat the guy to death with their flashlights."

No point in trying to tell you what was going on in my mind. I couldn't. But right there is probably where eighteen hours of fog-shrouded remorse about Malice Green's death began focusing entirely on thoughts about my own defense in a whole different arena. There was a light at the end of the tunnel, but it was on the nose of a freight train, and it was coming straight at me.

Flip TV channels Friday evening and all you saw was street people talking about Walter and me, and "civic leaders" talking about Walter and me. Even if they didn't know anything about Walter and me, and didn't know anything about what happened on Warren Avenue, they all had lots to say. And the TV stations gave them all the time in the world to say it. Why not? My own boss was leading the charge.

His Honor Coleman Young in these later years of his reign was a recluse much of the time, either in the Manoogian Mansion or on unannounced trips to someplace warm. On Friday afternoon, when I would have hoped to see a mayor step to the plate and calmly assure that a full investigation was under way and justice would be served in due course, Mayor Young let Stanley Knox be the point man for the TV cameras. Young issued a statement for the talking heads to read. He was "shocked and sickened at what I have learned regarding the incident... I have worked too long and too hard to build a community-based police department to have something like this happen. So long as I am mayor, we will not tolerate any mistreatment of the citizens of this city by the police department." There would be, Young said, a full and complete investigation.

The street people and the rest floated before my eyes in video and sound bites.

Fletch Man himself, proprietor of the dope pad (which so many times would be referred to as Ralph Fletcher's "home"), offered his insights about "Starsky and Hutch." No matter where you turned, in fact, you heard "Starsky and Hutch."

An alleged witness identified as Timis Brown told the cameras, "They beat him for an hour."

My neighbor on Bretton Drive, Councilwoman Maryann Mahaffey, said it was "an execution on the spot."

Malice Green's family was brought to a TV station to watch the press conference and to be interviewed immediately afterward. The family said Green was a quiet man who "was never involved in anything illegal...maybe a traffic violation."

Numerous reporters and anchormen echoed the theme that "motorist Malice Green" had never been in trouble with the law. Like many untruths publicized in the first hours of the story, this one got etched into stone and repeated so many times for so many months that a lazy viewer or reader might think Green was on a AAA day trip and got ambushed by Walter and me.

Dr. Bader Cassin, chief medical examiner for Wayne County, who had passed that morning's autopsy like a hot potato to assistant Kalil Jiraki, declared cause of death to be "blunt force trauma." Even as he told that to the cameras he privately had serious misgivings about cause of death. He was not, however, saying so in public.

Every so often some reporter would assure viewers that, so far, the streets of Detroit were calm. The media obviously did not have a whole lot to do with that. Neither did the city's leaders, though praise already was rolling in for their good work in making sure rioters hadn't taken to the streets. Their "good work," of course, was to put seven police officers' heads on sticks, with Walter's and mine on most prominent display. Suddenly every resident of southeastern Michigan had a vested interest in Starsky and Hutch being taken down. And as the no justice, no peace hysteria got fed its first big jolt of oxygen I had to somehow, for just the second time since pulling up behind Malice Green's car, try to answer the body's call for sleep.

12

POISON IN THE AIR, AND IN PRINT

Over the weekend, the only good things that happened were contacts with people who saw past what was burning up the airwaves. Old partners called. A few people dropped by. Looking back, I couldn't give you anything near a complete list of who showed up, or called, and when. They blend in memory across the first few days, and even weeks, of the storm. I know that Jimmy Dukes, who helped me arrest Billy Polk in the icy Top Hat parking lot, was one of those who phoned to offer support. I had two early visitors who stand out in my mind. Ron Martin had been a STRESS cop, in fact was involved in the infamous mistaken-identity shootout between STRESS officers and sheriff's deputies. Kevin Clark was a vice officer on my shift. Kevin dropped over twice, and brought his young son with him both times. Jimmy, Ron and Kevin were black cops who obviously knew that race – which to the public was what this case was all about – had nothing to do with it. Jimmy, Ron and Kevin worked the same streets I did. And they knew my character as a police officer.

Saturday was lineup day. Walter, Lessnau, Kijek, Gunther, Gotelaere, Douglas and I made our separate ways down to headquarters to be identified by witnesses. The seven of us would, in ways and to an extent you would not imagine, remain separate all down the long road ahead. Each of us was staring down the barrel of a gun, and we reacted in our own ways. We barely acknowledged each other on lineup day, much less had any secret session to synchronize our recollection of what had happened. That's just how the psychology of it sorted out. I can't tell you why. In the end, Walter and I would live together in the same prison cell for four years and still rarely talk to each other about that night, and then only to mention news about his appeal or mine. From the beginning, it was like seven guys who happened to have the same bad dream. Street cops keep their bad dreams to themselves. When I put this book together, I made contact with some of these guys for the first time in many years.

The Detroit Police Officers Association, my union, provided the lawyers. Fred Walker worked at the time with John Goldpaugh's firm, which did a lot of DPOA work. Somewhere in the first days, it was decided that Walker would represent Walter and Goldpaugh would represent me. I can't remember exactly when that was decided. But we had legal counsel present for the lineups. I must have at least said hello, but I don't remember it. The lawyers were there just to monitor the process.

What I remember is a tiny, hot, windowless room. I have claustrophobia that's real and intense. All seven of us were stored in that little locker room for hours as the lineups dragged on. We had almost nothing to say to each other except to talk about our crummy quarters, and how ridiculous it was to be identified by people who had been paraded past us two nights earlier as we sat in Homicide. To say nothing of how ridiculous it was for the street people to be asked to identify me and Walter – or even a couple of the uniformed cops. It was like asking someone to identify his own mother. Besides which, our pictures and even some videotape already were in the news media. But we were led out individually, in turn, many times. All seven officers were not lined up for all eight witnesses. I suppose Walter and I did all of them.

As the witnesses finished and went down the elevator and onto Beaubien Street, the TV cameras were waiting. It was obvious that some witnesses were enjoying their celebrity and their role in getting the cops. Ralph Fletcher was one of my favorites. I knew Fletcher better than I knew the guy where I took my dry cleaning. The struggle outside Fletcher's dope pad had occurred less than forty-eight hours earlier. Walter and I were not someone Fletcher saw that night through binoculars. He was standing next to the car when it started, and we interviewed him after it was over. We had even gone into his dope pad, gathering information for the reports we were then advised not to write. Besides, Walter and I had become overnight the two most notorious "rogue cops" in North America. But on Saturday, at police headquarters, Ralph Fletcher could not pick Walter Budzyn out of a lineup. This didn't stop Fletch Man from going down to the street and announcing for the TV cameras that he had "identified Starsky and Hutch." Fletcher would be a principal prosecution witness as to who did what during "the beating death of Malice Green."

Back home on Bretton Drive, I watched as the hearsay media "case" against us kept rolling across the screen all weekend and onward. It was like a contest to see how many people could be found who didn't know anything but were willing to talk about it, or how many people with motive to nail Walter and me could be found and allowed to lie on camera. They all got to speak their piece, and then the cameras would run off to find their next interview.

One of Saturday's featured citizens on the TV news was a man named Benjamin McCoy. He showed up on several channels alleging that about a month earlier he was walking to get some food, and ran from some uniformed officers. The infamous Starsky and Hutch came on the scene, McCoy said, beat him up and planted four rocks of crack cocaine on him. On one channel McCoy said he had filed a citizen's complaint, which he happened to have handy for display. Two things about that citizen's complaint: the TV news report was the first time I ever heard of it, and it was the last time I ever heard of it.

Let me say this about Bennie McCoy. I had arrested his brother at least twice, both times in 1990 – once for cocaine possession and once for leaving the scene of an injury accident. I don't know the disposition of either case. I suppose one might see those two arrests alone as a reason for Mr. McCoy to bear a grudge. But that's the tip of the iceberg.

Remember the morning I was testifying in Recorder's Court and happened to walk past six gang members who saw me and automatically "assumed the position" against the wall even though my arrival in that hallway had nothing to do with them? Bennie McCoy was not one of those six. Let's just say that he knew them very well, and that all were on the radar of any cop seeking to reduce drug traffic north of Tiger Stadium and west of Trumbull Avenue.

The incident that McCoy embellished for the TV cameras occurred one afternoon on Michigan Avenue just east of Fourteenth. A black patrolman named Wade Rayford was working uniform and wound up, with his partner, chasing McCoy on foot. I knew Rayford and liked him. He had spent some time in plainclothes, mostly riding with Walt but a few times in my car. While chasing McCoy, he got on his prep radio and broadcast that he was in pursuit of a perp for cocaine possession. There could be no drug-dealing charge in the offing, because when Rayford and his partner saw McCoy go out into Michigan Avenue and approach a passing car, the run and chase began before anything changed hands. McCoy ran across an I-75 overpass and disappeared. Several cars, including mine, responded. Some responding uniformed officers found McCoy in a vacant lot. When I arrived and walked up they already had McCoy handcuffed, sitting on the ground, and Rayford – who had struggled with McCoy on the ground – had confiscated some cocaine. I was delighted to see this result, because, although I had arrested his brother and several of his associates, I had never arrested McCoy.

McCoy was sitting there running his mouth, blathering that he hadn't done anything and every cop on the scene would be hearing from his lawyer. There was a substantial police presence on hand, including the sergeant who the day before

Bennie McCoy's moment of fame on TV would drive me downtown to surrender my badge. It seemed like everybody was afraid even to touch this guy and escort him to a scout car. Perhaps it's my imagination, but I associate this stalemate with a certain post-Rodney King directive from Stanley Knox – which you'll hear more about later. At any rate, I kept waiting for the arresting officers to take McCoy in, or for Sergeant Fulton to order somebody to do it. McCoy, meanwhile, kept blathering about police brutality and filing a complaint. Finally I had heard enough. I lifted him to his feet and started walking him to a scout car – during which time he only started yelling faster and louder. At one point he relaxed his legs and I had to drag him. I finally got him into a car and closed the door. That was the extent of my contact with Benjamin McCoy on the day, TV viewers were told, he was brutalized by Starsky and Hutch and planted with evidence. I don't even remember whether Walter was there. It was in the daytime, so maybe baseball season wasn't over and Walter was working the Stadium Detail with me for an afternoon game.

I arrested more than five thousand Benjamin McCoys in my career. As a matter of fact, on this day Bennie was not one of them. The arrest was all over when I got there, so I didn't even put his name in the run book. But now it began to seem like every person I ever escorted to a police car was magnetized by TV cameras. If any news reporter made even half an effort to get to the bottom of these tales, I never saw it. That certainly wasn't necessary in the case of the fourteen-year-old who made it on camera – and onto the air – to report that one night he was walking his dog at 10:30 when Walter and I told him to go home. The brutality is obvious. Pardon my cynicism.

"Starsky" took the bulk of these media hits, but Walter didn't fare much better. None of the sound bites ever reported about Walt recovering and cleaning up and returning Rosa Parks's stolen Buick. But on Saturday, an enterprising TV reporter did find a neighbor who said on camera, with a straight face, that Walt wore three guns while mowing the lawn. One small lie to help feed the legend of "Hutch."

We weren't faring any better in the print media. On weekends the two daily newspapers, the Free Press and the News, publish a joint edition. The Free Press reports the news in the Saturday edition, the News on Sundays. Because Malice Green died late Thursday night, Friday was the papers' first real chance to do any reporting, and the Saturday morning paper was their first real chance to print it. Here is how Free Press reporters wrote the top of their lead news story on Saturday:

> *The specter of police brutality that faded two decades ago in Detroit roared back to the present Friday after an angry crew of police officers beat, kicked and bludgeoned a man to death.*
>
> *City leaders were tearful, outraged and fearful of an outbreak of neighborhood violence in response.*

The third paragraph quoted from Mayor Young's statement.

The fourth paragraph quoted Stanley Knox's sound bites.

The fifth paragraph said we were suspended without pay and criminal warrants would be sought against some or all of us.

The sixth paragraph quoted me as saying: "I must have done something wrong. A guy died."

The seventh paragraph said that police officers "bludgeoned [Malice Green] with steel flashlights, fists and feet for reasons no police officials could explain."

I give them an "E" for efficiency. They got an indictment and a trial and a verdict onto the same piece of paper, with not a word from the defense.

We had been signed, sealed and delivered Friday morning in Knox's office and in the medical examiner's office. Signed, sealed and delivered again Friday afternoon and Friday night on television. On Saturday, looking for a little balance to show up in the print media – still hoping for somebody to say: "Wait a minute! This doesn't add up!" – we were instead signed, sealed and delivered once again. The newspaper story didn't even question what happened. It read as if the reporters had been there Thursday night on Warren taking notes. Reporters who by nature don't believe much of anything cops or mayors tell them were quite willing to swallow the official version of this story without chewing one bite.

Defense lawyers say you should never try your case in the media. Yeah, but what about when the other side is not only arguing its case in the media, but it's the only story in town? Thirty-six hours after Malice Green's death the public, and every potential juror, was in Day Two of getting bombarded by the myth of Starsky and Hutch. And now the newspapers were reporting the prosecution version of the story, top to bottom, as fact. Actually, it wasn't yet the prosecution version of the story. The police investigation was barely under way. This case moved lightning fast, but no one had even been charged with a crime yet. And, apparently, the only story left to tell was whether seven cops, and two in particular, would be strung up high enough to prevent a riot. From Day One, it was a bunch of people pouring gasoline on hot coals and congratulating themselves that no fire started.

I've got three beefs with what the media did to us before we wound up in court.

The first and most obvious one is that the media let anybody – I mean *anybody* – say almost anything about us, and then printed it or broadcast it without checking it out. It was endless.

Sometimes they circulated the most damning, flame-fanning lies without even identifying where the lies came from. When the Detroit News got its chance at the story on Sunday, it included an astounding paragraph.

Nevers asked the paramedics to see how Green was doing, bystanders said. After briefly examining the man, a paramedic said he wouldn't survive. Nevers sent the ambulance away. Douglas called for a second ambulance, which arrived shortly.

Never mind that every single word of the paragraph is a lie. Never mind that no one in Homicide was remotely saying anything of the kind then, or ever. Never mind that I *summoned* that first EMS wagon to stop at the scene. Never mind that it's impossible to dream up a more damning picture than a killer cop who tells an ambulance to drive away and leave his "victim" to die. How many readers stopped to ask: Where is this tale coming from? The best the News could do was to say "bystanders." The News not only put a hysterical tale in print, but gave it credibility by saying more than one "bystander" saw this happen. Who, pray tell, were these bystanders? Was one of them Robert Knox, who started the confrontation by running from Green's car, and who knew me well enough to be the one who nicknamed me "Starsky" because way back then I looked like Paul Michael Glaser? Was it Mickey Williams, who *after* the EMS rig left took the toy gun I tossed at him and jokingly pointed it at Knox's head? Was it Fletch Man, the dope pad proprietor who couldn't identify Walter Budzyn in a lineup? No, it wasn't. So what "bystanders" was the News talking to? Even as months passed, the people who gathered on Warren Avenue that night never would be identified in the media as who they really were: overwhelmingly a group of dope-house customers who had been arrested previously by the cop they were fingering. The four EMS techs were "bystanders," but they need their own chapter. And even the pathological liar in that group didn't claim I sent an ambulance away from a dying man.

So that's my first beef, whether it was a small lie like Walter Budzyn arming himself to the teeth to cut his grass or big lies like me preventing EMS from getting Malice Green to a hospital. You could fill a small book with the wildest claims about us that got on the air or into print with nobody taking the time to verify them, or ask whether they were fair, or even to consider the source.

My second beef is that the media let black community leaders and politicians take control of the story. It was like the police officers' skin color made pursuit of the facts the sole property of the NAACP. Late in 1993, while Walter and I were sitting in prison, the FBI office in Detroit sponsored a panel discussion on whether media coverage of the Green case was balanced. Don't ask me how such a meeting came to be. I have no idea. But the Detroit News ran a story on it, and the last two paragraphs of the story got it exactly right as far as I'm concerned. I was dumbfounded to read it when it was sent to me.

WJLB was the most powerful black-oriented radio station in town. Joann Watson, an NAACP officer and one of our most aggressive and loudest accusers, had a morning talk show on the station. Other on-air personalities spread rumors about what happened on Warren. But when it was all over, the news director of WJLB, one Mildred Gaddis, told this panel discussion as she was quoted in the Detroit News: "It seems the white media is so afraid to be called racist, that they allowed themselves to be used. To portray Malice Green as a martyr is sickening."

There was a lot of that martyrdom thing going around. Aside from the mayor, the most powerful black leaders in Detroit – and therefore the most powerful leaders in the city – are the preachers at the largest and most powerful churches. The most powerful of all was the Rev. Charles G. Adams, pastor of Hartford Memorial Baptist Church. Rev. Adams delivered the eulogy at Malice Green's funeral. It's fair to say that the non-stop racial rhetoric that followed Green's death was summed up for the 1,500 mourners who, according to the News, filled Adams's church. His words, the News said, "brought mourners to their feet time after time." The headline on page one was 'THEY DIDN'T HAVE TO KILL HIM.'

Let me remind you that I arrested Malice Green for possessing crack cocaine, not for being black, and that he was not a passive arrest subject. And now let me quote one of the passages that brought mourners to their feet and Rev. Adams's words to the front page of both Detroit newspapers and onto every TV screen in town.

"They crushed W.E.B. DuBois," Rev. Adams said. "They exiled Marcus Garvey. They compromised Booker T. Washington. They excoriated Malcolm X. They murdered Medgar Evers. They persecuted Paul Robeson. They expelled Adam Clayton Powell Jr.

"They slandered Harold Washington. They smeared George Crockett. They slew Martin Luther King Jr. They excommunicated Father Stallings. They discredited Marion Barry. They incarcerated Nelson Mandela. They killed Steve Bilko. They bludgeoned Rodney King.

"And THEY killed Malice Green."

If you're not from Detroit, you might not recognize the name George Crockett. He was a black judge, the father of George Crockett III, the judge who eventually would be assigned to preside over our trial. It would be racist, of course, to think that a different "they" might have difficulty giving a fair trial to some white cops who at this point had not even been charged with a crime. We were two of "them," identifiable by skin color and uniform, and that was enough.

In the Free Press, the headline across the top of page one was: 'RACISM KILLED…GREEN.' By the Free Press count, there were 2,000 mourners at the church. The lead paragraph said:

"America's malignant racism killed Malice Green, and unless that disease is eradicated, everyone in this country is threatened," the Rev. Charles Adams said Thursday at the funeral for the man killed by Detroit police.

And then:

"Racism killed Malice Green," Adams thundered as the congregation at Hartford Memorial Baptist Church voiced agreement. "And if racism is not destroyed, nobody in America can be safe. For if they got him at night, they'll get you in the morning," he said to applause.

Putting this story on page one was an automatic. The nightly news was an automatic. Signed, sealed, delivered and judged as racist killers. Take them down, or *they* will get *you* in the morning. It was news because it reflected community opinion. Non-stop, wall-to-wall community opinion that was largely based on opinion reported as news.

I don't mean to desecrate the memorial service for the man who died on my shift. The words speak for themselves. It is difficult to imagine louder words, or a lynch mob hearing anything more outrageous from its leaders. With such words coming from the pulpit, it was obvious we didn't have a prayer of getting a fair trial in Detroit.

The media's opinion writers didn't question the Rev. Adams in that regard. In fact, for the most part the media were right on board with him.

In retrospect, though, it looks like the newspapers sometimes were embarrassed by the railroading, even if they participated in it. You be the judge of this one, for instance. Remember Stanley Knox's quote on Day One: "This is not Simi Valley. We *will* convict"? Whether you are inclined to think I am a monster or a misjudged man, if you were a news editor what would you have done with that quote? It's a pretty remarkable statement either way you look at it, right? I think I have all the newspaper clips. Knox's televised quote doesn't seem to appear in any of them, let alone in a headline. Maybe it did. It must have. Maybe it was buried on Page 4B, like the comments of neighboring prosecutors in our favor. At any rate, I didn't find Knox's most outrageous televised statement in my clip file.

And then there was Knox's boss, Coleman Alexander Young, a lawyer by training. The mayor emerged on national television on Monday evening, November 9. I'm not sure exactly when the interview was taped. Speaking to NBC's "Dateline" with the investigation just under way and a week before we were charged, Young said: "A young man who was under arrest was literally murdered by police." Again, as a news editor fighting for truth, justice and the American way, what do you think you would do with that quote? It was buried deep. Again not even a headline. Editorial cartoonists, on the other hand, don't work by committee and often get to the heart of things. In the Detroit News, cartoonist Larry Wright drew the mayor building a gallows and shouting to reporters: "Get away! I won't allow you folks to try this case in the media!" In the Detroit News, Bill Day drew Coleman Young reading a newspaper with the banner headline: YOUNG: POLICE GUILTY OF MURDER. The cartoon shows Young fuming: "There goes the *@#@ irresponsible media again."

I said I had three beefs with the media. Actually, I can't count my beefs with the media, but I'm trying to sort them out. What I had in mind for number three is sort of a combination of the first two. Maybe I'd call it "active participation in the hysteria."

Some of that is unavoidable. I suppose when Dennis Archer, former state Supreme Court justice and then a leading contender to succeed Young in the Manoogian Mansion (which he did), stepped out from one of the many church meetings about this case, it was inevitable that a microphone would get stuck in his face. When Archer said: "We understand bone fragments were found on Warren Avenue," it was inevitable that it would get on TV. But what does that quote say about what was being said in that meeting, and about what was being said on the street? Considering that what was found was not bone fragments but crack cocaine? Considering that there were no broken bones, let alone "bone fragments"? What does it mean that this story – like countless other inflammatory tales – was never corrected? And that the damage that each story did to the truth – and to the jury pool – could not be repaired anyway? What does it mean that the false tale originated *from within the Homicide investigation?*

But forget bone fragments. Let me tell you about Victor.

This story appeared in the Free Press on November 16, under the headline GREEN'S FRIEND APPARENTLY BEATEN IN '72:

Twenty years ago, Malice Green witnessed the beating of a friend by one of the police officers who this month was suspended over Green's beating death, according to an NAACP official and a family member.

The incident apparently occurred in the same neighbor-hood where Green, 35, was fatally beaten Nov. 5, Joann Watson, executive director of the Detroit branch of the NAACP, said Sunday.

Watson said the NAACP is investigating the 1972 incident and has interviewed a witness and others familiar with it. Here's what allegedly happened, based on her interviews:

Green and two teenaged friends were riding motor bikes when two police officers ordered them to halt. Green and one friend stopped, but the other teenager was frightened and fled, even though they had done nothing wrong.

The officers chased the youth and rammed the police car into his bike, knocking him to the ground. The officers then beat the youth while Green and the other friend watched.

The youth's family filed a complaint against the officers, Watson said.

She declined to name the officers or the friends. There was no Detroit police confirmation of the incident.

"There were no criminal charges to the best of my knowledge," said Watson, who provided some details of the NAACP investigation during a public forum Sunday in Detroit.

Both of Green's friends, now in their mid-30s, attended Green's funeral, she said. The one who allegedly was beaten "is frail and still limping," Watson said.

Watson said that one of the officers involved is among the seven suspended without pay in Green's death. Green's sister, Monica, said the family knew of the beating, but she also declined to name the police officer or the friends.

Is this story a bombshell, or not? The story ran above a photo of a rally outside the Third Precinct station. Protesters carried a banner that read: JAIL THE KILLER COPS. One of the "killer cops," according to the story Joann Watson got placed in the Free Press, had such an extensive and long history of violence against black civilians that one of his victims stretching back twenty years was a friend of Malice Green. And Malice Green had witnessed this maiming – by the same "killer cop" who beat him to death twenty years later. And the twenty-year-old maiming was so bad that Green's friend was still limping when he attended Green's funeral.

Pretty spectacular stuff. Hollywood made a movie held together by inventing a white cop to stalk the boxer Reuben Carter from childhood. That white cop in the movie "Hurricane" was one hundred percent fictional. And if the white cop in the above story was supposed to be me, he was also fictional. In 1972, I was wearing a uniform in the Fourth Precinct. And if I had used my scout car to run down a fifteen-year-old kid and then beat him up, I think I would remember that. I also don't think a cop of that nature would stay on the job for two decades in Coleman Young's police department.

Like so many stories in the Malice Green case, this amazing tale materialized out of nowhere and into print, without verification, then went away without any follow-up. The Free Press ran it on the front of the second section. Maybe the paper didn't really believe the story, or else it would have run on page one. If so, that's not much comfort. As far as the buzz in the city where I would face trial, I have to assume readers took it to be a true story. I never saw it surface again in print. No follow-up on the supposed NAACP "investigation," or from the board of police commissioners, which also told the Free Press it would look into it. But there's more.

We haven't got there yet, but you know that in the end I was tried twice and sent to prison three times in the matter of Malice Green's death. As I sat in court awaiting sentencing at my second trial, Malice Green's sister addressed the judge.

And just before he gave me the longest sentence he could possibly give, Malice Green's sister addressed the court, turned and looked at me, and said I was the cop who ran down Malice's young friend while Malice looked on. She gave the young friend's name, Victor. You might say it was a dramatic courtroom moment. But not a single newspaper or TV station or radio station reported the story of Victor when it came up at my sentencing – let alone go find out if it was true. I am telling you it is not true. After they led me away, it would have been nice to see someone in the media do their obvious job and track that story down. After all, it was a win-win situation for any reporter who pursued it – a page one story whether it was true or false. It's almost like every reporter covering the story didn't want to run the risk of finding something that would give the lie to a script that was already in re-runs.

On Monday, November 9 – the same day Coleman Young told the nation we were "murderers" – Green's family sued the city for $61 million. Even if you are not a lawyer, you have some understanding of how much time and difficulty are involved in gathering the most basic information necessary to include in any civil lawsuit, let alone a suit for $61 million. The Greens' fourteen-page lawsuit had so much information in it that Doty and Kane, the two stand-arounds from the Fourth Precinct, were included as defendants. Even the media did not know, at that point, about Doty and Kane's existence. Their names set off a momentary feeding frenzy among reporters. Someone in the police department obviously was very, very friendly to the Green family lawyers. The suit named the city, Stanley Knox, the seven suspended cops, and Doty and Kane. It said Green's death was "unjustified, an excessive use of force and abuse of power, and murder."

We had not yet been charged with anything. In fact, Malice Green's funeral had not yet been held. If the odds of a fair trial for Walter and me seemed 100-to-1 against, the family's lawsuit looked like a lock. It turned out to be so much of a lock, you'd have to be blind not to see that the fix was in.

13

TUNNEL VISION IN HOMICIDE

The day after Malice Green's death, Lieutenant William Presley and Sergeant Danny Maynard were deer hunting upstate in the center of Michigan's Lower Peninsula. It being a Friday, the two Homicide officers chose the all-you-can-eat fish dinner when they came in from the woods to the sleepy village of McBride. Hunting had put Presley and Maynard totally out of touch with their jobs in the Special Assignment Squad. The first they heard of Malice Green came from TV news as they dined in the McBride Tavern. By the time they returned to work Monday morning in Detroit, the investigation already was traveling down roads they had never seen before. "The only thing I didn't like about this," Presley said in an interview ten years later, "was when you do a police (officer-involved) investigation you let the chips fall where they may, and let the facts speak for themselves. They weren't trying to do that. It was like they started out assuming there was a crime, murder, and then tried to prove it. To me the way this thing was going, they only wanted statements that were going to hang them."

"Them," of course, was Walter and me.

"I was the lieutenant in charge of SAS," Presley said, "and I wasn't even allowed in the room."

The Special Assignment Squad is a Homicide unit that investigates cases involving police officers. Not being allowed in the room means closed doors. The "they" behind the closed doors were Commander Gerald Stewart and his right-hand man, Lieutenant Tommy Alston. These two micro-managed the Homicide investigation. Forget the standard job description of OIC – "officer in charge," as the officer running any Homicide case is called in all paperwork and legal proceedings. The acting chief of Homicide, Alston, and his superior, Stewart, took control of the smallest details. Everything about the way this case was handled came from the top, hands-on, from Knox squelching a board of review to Stewart and Alston interrogating the hooker who became a star prosecution witness. The way they managed the version of events as told by Theresa "Red Bone" Pace pretty much sums up a hell-bent effort by the brass to make the Malice Green case add up to murder by cop.

Pace at the time was a drug-using prostitute who frequented Ralph Fletcher's dope pad on Warren Avenue. She was standing on the sidewalk with her boyfriend Joe Hollins, Fletch Man, Robert Knox and Emanuel "Ricky" Brown when Walter Budzyn first went after the cocaine in Malice Green's hand. Like most all the Third's street people, Pace knew me by sight. I had never arrested her, which couldn't be said of at least two of her sidewalk companions – and I think all four. She was the only white civilian at the scene. Both those factors would make her an attractive witness against two white police officers accused of assaulting a black man – assuming she didn't say the wrong things. Junkie testimony is junkie testimony, and you obviously have to make allowances for that. You listen and you try to make some sense of it and stack it up against other evidence. Common sense tells you that when such a witness says something that isn't good for her friends, she probably didn't make it up. That's why I think you'll agree that when Homicide brass got Theresa Pace to change two crucial points in her statement, it was not exactly a quest for truth.

Around noon Friday, November 6, Theresa Pace gave a nine-page statement to Homicide Sergeant Ron Sanders. He was known as a good investigator, a good interviewer, and a thorough statement-taker. Pace's account of what she saw the previous night included some wildly false statements about Walter and what she supposedly saw Walter do to her friend Malice Green. But, meanwhile, she also had some things to say about Green's actions, things you don't make up about a friend.

Pace told Sanders: "Starsky's partner was shining a flashlight down on Malice. Then Malice got this rock [of cocaine]. I saw this cause I was standing right on the sidewalk looking. Anyway, Malice was going fumbling in the glovebox and I saw him close his fist up the right hand. Starsky's partner said 'Let me have what's in your hand.' And Malice jumped back and wouldn't open his hand. So Starsky's partner reached down and tried to grab Malice's hand and Malice started kicking and fighting with Starsky's partner."

Later Sanders asked: "Did you actually see the rock of cocaine in Malice's hand before the struggle?"

Pace said: "Yes I did."

Sanders asked: "Did you see anything else in Malice's hand at the time he was clenching his fist with the rock of cocaine?"

Pace said: "No."

And: "Me and Joe kept saying to Malice, 'Give him the rock, give him the rock,' because we knew that Starsky's partner was going to beat the shit out of him if he didn't."

Sanders asked: "What do you mean you knew Starsky's partner was going to beat the shit out of him?"

Pace said: "Because I've seen him get upset before and he's real aggressive."

Now, a couple things about what Theresa Pace told Sergeant Sanders.

Nothing in Walter's record backs up what Pace said about him. You could interview every cop in the Detroit department, and you would not find an ounce of evidence to support that picture of Walt. He and I were not close friends, not before November 5 and not afterward. We had been competitors, each driving our own booster car until a matter of days before

November 5. We were still brand-new regular partners that night. It would look good for me to tell you that bad things happened to Malice Green while he struggled with Walter Budzyn. But I am telling you I do not believe Walter ever struck Green with his flashlight, not on the head or anywhere else. Pace said she saw Walter swinging his Mag light over his head and she "heard" three or four blows. That's nonsense. Walter went after the cocaine, got dragged into that little Topaz, and was struggling with Green in tight quarters. What happened with Walter inside that car was all about retrieving evidence, keeping Green from taking Walter's gun (or pulling a weapon that might be hidden inside the car), and recovering from a really bizarre situation Walter got himself into.

Regarding Malice Green, keep in mind Pace is talking about her good friend. And the key parts of what she told Ron Sanders are pretty much the same things I told you. Green started it all by kicking and by refusing to let go of his precious junk. I heard Pace yelling at him to give it up. Robert Knox also saw a rock of crack. He testified at our preliminary examination that after I went over to Green's car and recovered a rock I told him: "Here, you can have it," and that he said, "No, give me a beer." I don't recall the dialogue that way. I remember him asking for the crack. Either way, Knox saw the cocaine, and any exchange we had was just more street banter during what absolutely would have gone on to be a nickel-and-dime dope arrest if Malice Green just would have let it end that way.

Ron Sanders was not a member of the Special Assignment Squad. He was in Homicide Squad Six. On Friday, the morning after Green's death, he was assigned to round up some of the street people and bring them downtown. "They tried to hide on us," Sanders recalled ten years later. "We went to their house and got 'em. I was straight with her, and I believe what she told me was straight." Taking Pace's original statement was, to the best of Sanders's recollection, his last involvement with the Green case. "I didn't want anything to do with it because it was a political hot potato. I stayed away from it as much as I could."

On Monday morning, Lieutenant Presley and Sergeant Maynard returned to SAS from their hunting trip. Pace was brought down to headquarters again and taken into a closed room with Commander Stewart and Lieutenant Alston. Maynard was standing near a filing cabinet outside SAS when Sergeant Vern Humes emerged from the room where Pace had been re-interrogated, walked up to Maynard and said something astounding. Maynard recalls that Humes "kind of whispered: 'Man, they want me to throw out that first statement.'" Maynard immediately called Presley over and repeated, in Humes's presence, what he had just heard.

Presley recalls it clearly, saying: "They didn't like what was in there" (in Pace's first statement). "They led her down a different path." All three – Presley, Maynard and Humes – were standing by the file cabinet when Presley said: "We aren't throwing away any statements."

After that somebody, apparently Humes, wrote a new witness statement form and Pace signed it. No police officer of any rank signed the line indicating who took the new statement. Whether the statement writer forgot to sign (unusual, but it happens), or for whatever reason didn't want to be a part of it, I don't know. But the new statement was less than one page long, neatly handwritten, and not the kind of thing you'd take lightly and forget to sign. Stewart and/or Alston had talked Pace through her new version of events and ordered it written up. The two most important items from Pace's first statement had miraculously changed. The new statement read:

> *Question: "Did you actually see Malice Green fighting with Starsky's partner?"*
> *Answer: "I never saw Malice's arms, but his legs were kicking and based on his legs kicking I figured Malice was fighting back since the police officer was beating Malice for so long I figured Malice was fighting back."*

Question: "How come you couldn't see Malice's arms?"
Answer: "Because the police officer was on top of him and from where I was standing I could only see Malice's legs coming out of the car."

Keep in mind a couple things. Pace is talking about Walter Budzyn and the beginning of our struggle with Green. ". . . the police officer was beating Malice for *so long*"? Ridiculous. Beyond ridiculous. Somewhere, sometime, for some reason, Theresa Pace had developed a hatred for Walter – or maybe she was mistaking him for someone else. In Pace's eyes, compassionate Walter was Mad Dog Walter. But even from her warped point of view, and with events fresh in her mind, she had said the next morning that her friend Malice Green was "kicking and fighting" to hang onto some crack cocaine she clearly saw. Suddenly, on Monday, Pace said Green was just defending himself from a prolonged beating by Walter.

And more . . .

Question: "How do you know Malice had a rock of cocaine in his hand?"
Answer: "I saw what looked like a baggie so I figured it was cocaine."
Question: "Did you ever see any cocaine in the baggie?"
Answer: "No."
Question: "Are you sure it was a baggie in Malice's hand?"
Answer: "I can't say for sure."

Stewart and Alston had run the table. Green was no longer "kicking and fighting." And Pace no longer sees a rock, she sees a baggie. Besides that, she doesn't see a rock in the baggie. And, just for good measure, *she isn't even sure she saw a baggie.*

The above quotes are the entire Theresa Pace "second statement," except for two questions. The final question was whether she wanted to say anything else. "No." The first question noted that she had made a statement on Friday and "I," whoever the unsigned "I" was, wanted to ask some more questions. "OK," Pace replied. Needless to say, the new statement doesn't reflect anybody asking whether Pace had also changed her mind about Walter "beating Malice for so long."

I believe that if Vern Humes hadn't made Danny Maynard and Bill Presley aware of what was going on, the second statement would have contained no reference to the first statement – and the first statement would, in fact, have disappeared. Presley – who like Maynard and most other principals of the investigation has since retired from the police department – says he doesn't know that "anybody would go that far." Call me cynical. Down the line, Humes would testify under oath that his exchange with Maynard and Presley never occurred. I have no idea whether Humes felt intimidated, or was just recognizing where his bread was buttered. Maynard – an experienced and respected detective – says: "I know I didn't lie." I believe him, and I believe Presley. And I wonder how anyone who knows anything about the politics and street hysteria surrounding this case from the top down, and who reads Pace's second statement, could help but smell the rot.

After getting Pace's version of events adjusted to fit the murder-by-cop scenario, she, of course, became money in the bank for the prosecution. Months later, as our trial approached, Homicide – on orders from the prosecutor's office – put Pace in a safe deposit box, the headquarters lockup, for thirty-three days. She was not trustworthy enough to risk her disappearing into her drug habit and other activities. But somehow she was trustworthy enough to vouch for little details like whether her friend Malice Green resisted arrest and whether he possessed cocaine. Pace's quarters in the lockup were arranged after she complained that at the county jail she couldn't smoke. At headquarters she could smoke, and could come downstairs, hang out and use the phone in Homicide. While there, the Wayne County Prosecutor's Office wrote her three "witness fee" checks totaling $595. By this time, Sergeant Bill Rice had moved over to SAS and had been named officer in charge of the case. I assume he was assigned to go over to the prosecutor's office and pick up Pace's walking-around money, which probably accounts for the slip-up in one of the checks being made out to "Theresa Rice." Two of the checks were cashed at the Motor City Tobacco and Candy Co. after being endorsed to the "Detroit Police Homicide Flower Fund." Whatever. If Theresa Pace lacked $595 worth of cigarettes and soap while in the prosecutor's safe deposit box for a month, it wasn't the prosecutor's fault.

By my count the per diem fee for Pace's time on the witness stand doesn't approach $595. Depending on whom you talk to, it's unusual or rare or unheard of for a witness to get that cash in advance. And then there's the matter of whether Pace even got the money. During her testimony, she told the court that only about $100 of the "witness fees" made its way to her, that it wasn't her signature on the checks, and that she hadn't given anyone permission to sign her name. Sergeant Rice testified that he signed Pace's name with her permission, cashed the checks, and gave her all the money. That leaves only two possible conclusions: Somebody in Homicide picked up a few illegal bucks in return for entertaining Theresa Pace in the lockup, or the witness who changed her mind about Malice Green's resistance to arrest and his possession of cocaine was incapable of telling the truth about the allowance she got for being such a cooperative witness.

Another key witness you will hear more about later was an EMS technician named Lee Hardy, who rode in the second emergency wagon to arrive on Warren Avenue. Of all the witnesses to our struggle with Malice Green, Lee Hardy was probably in a position to see less than anyone. Yet he claimed to have seen *more* than anyone. The discrediting of Lee Hardy's version of events is so total that even his own supervisors and the judge who sent me to prison did not believe him – but that didn't stop Hardy's testimony from having a lot to do with my conviction. More on that later. For now, regarding the early days of the Homicide investigation, just know that Bill Presley, the top officer in SAS, took a look at the evidence that was coming in and told Lieutenant Alston there were serious problems with Lee Hardy's statement. In other words, Presley didn't believe it. Presley told Alston he thought Hardy ought to be interviewed again. In response, Alston told Presley that "because I was so busy hunting Bambi up north I hadn't been there to see Hardy's facial expressions." So Hardy, unlike Theresa Pace, was not re-interviewed. A non-credible witness's first statement stayed in the investigation package, while Pace was re-interrogated to get rid of Malice Green's inconvenient "kicking and fighting" and refusal to unhand cocaine.

Sergeant Ken Day was an SAS officer sent to the scene the night of Green's death and was in fact the original OIC assigned to the case. The report he signed at 7 a.m. Friday looks honest enough as a preliminary report. But it helps explain a good deal about the media frenzy that was unleashed that very day, and it raises a serious question about the people in charge of city government and the police department. His preliminary report concludes ("compl." is the "complainant," Malice Green):

"At scene Sgt. Douglas related the following: Officers involved were investigating compl. for possible narcotics dealing and upon their asking for I.D. he began fighting with them and one of the officers struck him with a flashlight in an attempt to subdue him. During our survey we came up with witness Ralph Fletcher who tells a somewhat different story. According to him, he had been with compl. when approached by the police, and the attack was unprovoked. Once in the office we were notified that 4 EMS techs had witnessed the incident and that in their opinion it was unprovoked. We had them come into the office and obtained statements. As of this writing the case is still being actively investigated and no opinion can be rendered."

There's a lot in that short paragraph. You already know that "unprovoked" could not be further from the truth. You know something about Fletch Man and his place of business, and you know that twenty-four hours after Sergeant Day signed the above report, Ralph Fletcher looked at a lineup and could not identify the cop who made this "unprovoked" attack five feet in front of him. You know that no one from EMS was present when the incident began, and thus could not possibly have any idea whether it was "unprovoked." You know EMS tech Lee Hardy's statement was so off the wall that the head of SAS wanted, but was ordered not to get, a new statement from him. As for Day's final observation that "no opinion can be rendered," keep in mind this was Friday morning. He was typing those words around the same moment Stanley Knox gathered his troops to declare there would be no board of review, and was gathering his thoughts for the afternoon press conference in which, near tears, he convicted us.

This kind of thing was going on while someone in Homicide was leaking rumor and worse to the news media, as if the media needed encouragement. Walter, for example, had requested medical treatment the night of the incident because he suffered a scrape on his leg while struggling with Green. He didn't claim that Green shot him or knifed him, just that he got an abrasion during the struggle – no big surprise considering that Walter's legs to this day are discolored and sensitive from Agent Orange, something he picked up in Vietnam. But his injury on Warren Avenue, according to one Homicide leak that appeared in the newspapers, was "self-inflicted." One Homicide investigator is the unverifiably but constantly rumored source of so many off-the-wall news stories that if half the reports about this officer's leaking are true, then this officer alone made an enormous contribution to convicting us in the press. That would include the tale of "bone fragments on Warren Avenue," which turned out to be rocks of cocaine.

Danny Maynard, who is white, recalls delivering subpoenas to some of the street witnesses and being chewed out by Alston because Alston wanted the subpoenas delivered by a black officer. Like Presley, Maynard feels that despite being in SAS, he was given the mushroom treatment on the case while Alston and Stewart micro-managed it. One thing he wasn't left out of was being asked to check the LEIN machine for outstanding arrest warrants against the civilian witnesses. All of them had outstanding warrants. Every outstanding case was set aside for up to a year, until after our trial, to make the junkies look better as witnesses. The warrants disappeared even before our preliminary examination. "I never heard of anything like that," Maynard says. Whether the various cases against the junkies ever were pursued, I don't know.

Like Chief Stanley Knox and His Honor Coleman Young, the people running Homicide seemed real interested in believing what the street people and junkies had to say. Meanwhile, they didn't believe a word from any of us who were there wearing a badge. Let me rephrase that. They didn't much care what we had to say. Keep in mind that our lawyer on the night Green died told me to tear up the statement I was writing…but he didn't have to tell me that, because Homicide had decided it didn't even want statements. They had a dead man with head wounds, blood on the street, the word of people like Ralph Fletcher and Theresa Pace and Lee Hardy. They had no detailed account from the officers involved about what happened. Sorting out this kind of situation is supposed to take time. But to Knox and Young and anyone who did their bidding there was nothing confusing about it. Not when the cops are white and you can peddle a rumor quicker than you can say "Rodney King." In less than twenty-four hours, seven cops were suspended without pay and the media were buzzing with riot talk. By the time of Theresa Pace's second statement on Monday, the mayor had declared us to be "murderers" – just in case Alston and Stewart had any doubts about what the investigation was supposed to produce.

Let me make clear that Bill Presley and Danny Maynard did not do interviews for this book because they want to tell the world they concluded I did nothing wrong that night. As SAS investigators, they worked objectively on dozens of cases involving police officers. Their job was not to pass judgment but to gather evidence and, as both of them say, "let the chips fall where they may" – meaning a fair trial of fairly gathered facts fairly presented to a fair prosecutor and then, if warranted, fairly argued before a fair jury. Other than a board of review, that's all I ever asked for – or had a right to ask for – at any step of the way...from Knox, from Young, from the media, from Homicide, from the criminal justice system. Presley and Maynard deserve a lot of respect for seeing it that way, too. If in their unspoken judgments either of them speculated that I over-reacted to the situation on the street, that I "lost it" and didn't make the best of a bad situation but was in no way a murderer, then they wouldn't be alone. That's a common enough, and easy enough, take on the incident. I don't see it that way. But who besides me could know the truth of it? The only thing I was losing during the struggle was my breath and my strength, and my confidence that I wouldn't lose control of the situation. I wasn't exhausted from trying to beat Green to death, but from trying to retrieve evidence, subdue him, control him, and handcuff him. Just like it says in General Orders. There is a fair way for other people to reach an opinion about what they cannot know for a fact; and then there is a railroading.

If the Malice Green arrest happened a thousand different times with a thousand different police officers, the one universal truth of police work – "You can't back down" – would have come into play every single time. When an arrest subject is trying to turn the tables on you...and there is a struggle...and the struggle becomes prolonged...and he is a young man high on drugs and you are fifty-two years old, out of shape, and have undiagnosed emphysema...and he puts his hand on your gun ...then there is going to be violence. If any police officer who ever set foot on the street – even Stanley Knox – can look you in the eye and disagree with that, I would be amazed. Maybe someone trained and equipped differently than Walter and me would have found a way to subdue Green without violence. I don't know. Maybe there would have been a different outcome if it weren't true that the only thing every witness agreed to was that as other officers arrived and pulled Green away, I was slumped and gasping for breath. I don't know. But any cop who has done real police work knows what I am saying here.

You don't need to be an experienced Homicide investigator to approach the knowable facts of this case by asking: "What was it like for these two cops when things hit the fan on Warren Avenue? What kind of cops were they? We all know the bad guys are always repeaters; how do Budzyn and Nevers stack up in that regard? Who are the witnesses against them? How do they stack up?" Instead, the investigation got launched with tunnel vision. Regardless of what anyone thinks about the rightness or wrongness of my actions, it's absolutely incredible that the news media hit the ground running with the idea that it all happened "for no reason." What makes that absolutely incredible is that the news media got their "information" from the Homicide Section – from police officers who knew better. "For no reason," of course, was code for: "There was a reason. It happened because Malice Green was a black man and Larry Nevers is white." Anyone who ever worked with me – *any* one of dozens of officers, white and black – will tell you that is not true. Don't you think that's a fairly basic piece of what became the biggest "racial" story in the country? Nobody paid any attention. They just congratulated themselves that the "racist cops" got burned and the city didn't.

A few weeks after Malice Green's death, Danny Maynard was assigned to an officer-involved case in which a patrolman was shot in the head during a foot chase outside a bar. There were many witnesses, and many of them were drunk. It looked obvious to Maynard that the wounded officer – whose head wound was not fatal – had been struck by his own ricocheting bullet after firing on the run. Just one witness said the wounded officer, who was black, was shot by another officer, who was white.

"Alston wanted me to get a search warrant for his (the wounded cop's) partner," Maynard recalls. "One drunk woman claimed she saw the white officer take a shot. I said, 'Tommy, this bullet was all deformed. I think it hit the pavement. The white officer said he didn't fire. It doesn't make any sense. One witness out of how many – two dozen? I'd have to lie to get a search warrant and I'm not going to do it.' He (Alston) got another officer to go for a search warrant. The lab report came back a day or two later saying the bullet came from the wounded officer's own gun. But I had told Alston I wouldn't lie, and he got upset."

That was the end of Maynard's SAS career. He was transferred out. The reason given was that Maynard was a union steward, and that was a conflict of interest. As with Theresa Pace's second statement, Bill Presley remembers it well.

"Danny had been the steward for six or seven years without anybody seeing a conflict of interest. That's because there wasn't any. For one thing, Danny did his job well. For another thing, he was a steward in the Lieutenants and Sergeants Association, not the Police Officers Association."

Presley, the lieutenant in charge of SAS – angered by Maynard's transfer and frustrated by getting the mushroom treatment on the case – told his bosses they might as well transfer him, too. And they did. "They wanted the white guys out of there," Presley says.

That left one white cop in SAS, Lee Caudill, the sergeant who read us our rights the night of the incident. Every other Homicide investigator mentioned here, SAS or not, up to and including Stewart and Alston, is black. That includes Ron Sanders, the sergeant who took Theresa Pace's first statement and then stayed as far away from the case as possible because "it was a political hot potato."

I initiated contact with Presley and Maynard for this book because of the way they handled themselves during the case and because they have important things to say about it, with Ron Sanders because I wondered what he thought of Pace's second statement (he didn't recall that she had made one), and with Lee Caudill because though his involvement in the case was minimal, he was there that first night.

Caudill, now retired and living in another state, has a somewhat different take on the case. Despite being the last white officer in SAS after Maynard and Presley were transferred, Caudill says he didn't see any racial bias within Homicide. Not even when he, too, was transferred out soon after our arraignment. "I personally didn't feel I was moved around because of racial reasons. Nobody said, 'You're an asshole and we're making this move'," he recalls. Caudill worked with Tommy Alston for years and respects him. Caudill says he was not surprised that Gerald Stewart micro-managed the case. "Homicide was Stewart's life."

Like Maynard and Presley, Caudill was an SAS officer who prided himself in playing cop-involved cases straight down the middle. His only involvement with the Green case was to read us our rights and take evidence the night of the incident, and later to accompany us to our arraignment. Despite defending the integrity of the Homicide investigation, he had some interesting things to say about what happened to us.

"It was to me so unfair what happened down the road," he says. "I think they were a victim of time, place and politics. Did somebody do anything evil or wrong in the investigation and prosecution? No. I listened to the testimony, to (the medical evidence), to the requirements you must meet to get to second-degree murder. I could maybe see manslaughter – or less – emerging at some point...assuming you bought into what the prosecutors were saying: that for no really good reason they beat this guy with flashlights. I saw too many officer-involved cases that didn't lead this far."

Asked whether you would never have heard of me or Walter Budzyn if one of us had shot Malice Green, Caudill said: "That's probably true."

Asked if – regardless of what he thought of the Homicide investigation and regardless of what he thought of the lead prosecutor's behavior in the case ("just doing his job in the adversarial system") – the L.A. riot and the political frenzy in Detroit had determined the fate of two white cops, Caudill answered with a question: "How unlucky can you be?"

Presley summarized our luck by saying: "Some cases you know the verdict even before it goes to trial. They fired the citizens up enough that these guys were going to be found guilty no matter what." Beyond that, to Maynard and Presley there was no doubt the investigation itself was steered on a sea of racial politics. Though Caudill didn't see it that way, he said of the incident with Pace's second statement: "I wouldn't doubt for a second that if Danny and Bill said it happened, then it happened."

Presley, Maynard and Caudill – SAS officers one and all – were limited to minor roles in the investigation, but they were present and couldn't be totally ignored. Maynard kept close track of what he saw. One thing he saw was a meeting at the prosecutor's office the week after Green's death. Maynard and Caudill were present, as were Alston and Stewart. At one point, the Wayne County medical examiner, Bader Cassin, tried to fill in the blanks of his botched management of Green's autopsy. Cassin told assistant prosecutors Douglas Baker and Kym Worthy that the presence of cocaine in Green's system was something the prosecution would have to address. Caudill was asked to leave the room. Maynard recalls Cassin saying: "I'm not so sure that had those injuries been on someone else they would have been fatal." And Worthy saying: "It [the cocaine] doesn't matter. They beat him to death." Worthy, who wore green fingernail polish in court during our trial, never lost her facts-be-damned focus. Ignoring the cocaine was like ignoring a missing wing while investigating an airplane crash.

Caudill says of that meeting at the prosecutor's office: "I was asked to leave. I did. They asked me to go out and stay with a witness. I was convinced they didn't trust me. I didn't feel they had any reason to distrust me. I hadn't seen anything at this point that made me believe they were steering the case."

Despite his minimal role, Caudill would, of course, be a prosecution witness. And he says that when he took the stand, "Worthy came after me in a way I've never been questioned before by a prosecutor. I knew they felt I was somehow going to testify in a way they didn't want me to. There were no secrets. I remember telling Baker that. They thought I was in some way going to help the defense. Before testifying in a case, I always talked with prosecutors about what the testimony was going to be. None of that happened in this case."

Caudill was angered when Worthy came after him with irrelevant, insinuating questions about his impending retirement. "Afterward I asked Baker what the hell is going on. This is not the way I've ever been talked to on the witness stand. At my retirement party, Worthy came up and apologized."

Ten years later, Caudill made a philosophic comment on the criminal justice system: "All of this comes down to what our own personal beliefs are. The legal end of this is so far removed from what our personal beliefs are. The courtroom is a different world. It's very difficult to move the street into the courtroom." And he said something I have been saying, as you know, ever since the thought occurred to me in a prison cell. "If we had a good videotape of that night," Caudill said, "who knows what would have come out? At least it would have been accurate. What the camera showed could not have been any worse, but it could have been better. If what happened is what the first jury believed happened, the tape would show it."

My videotape is imaginary. So is the prosecution's. And now you see why a real tape became my fondest wish. For starters, they could massage testimony from a Theresa Pace and they could endorse the wildly imaginative tale of a Lee Hardy and they could pretend the cocaine was meaningless…but the instant the tape started rolling it would crush the biggest lie of all: that these things happened "for no reason."

14

THE HEARING
I NEVER GOT

When a street cop gets in trouble for something that happened during an arrest, most often in his defense you're going to hear: "He was just a police officer doing his job." There's a reason for that. The job is after all dangerous and stressful, a low-paid job in which working stiffs are required to make life-and-death decisions just like a heart surgeon. Well, not "just like." Surgeons have an idea what they will be dealing with when they walk into an operating room. A surgeon doesn't have to worry about the patient grabbing a scalpel and stabbing him. Citizens expect a street cop to put his own life on the line, and can summon a police officer to do so just by dialing a three-digit phone number. Driving a booster car you don't wait for the call. Meanwhile, if anything goes bad out there, *the police officer* becomes the suspect. That's the truth of the job, no matter where you serve and protect, or how well you do it. In some locales, just wearing a badge makes you a suspect. Those are the facts, so before you say it's a cliché and a cop-out to talk about "just a police officer doing his job," you've got to work those facts into account.

Surgeons and police officers sometimes screw up on the job and sometimes somebody dies. Sometimes somebody dies even when doctors and cops do the right thing. Sometimes bad things happen because a surgeon or a police officer winds up in a situation he has never encountered before and is not prepared for. If something goes bad on the operating table, the doctor's own profession reviews what happened. This review occurs before anybody starts shouting that the surgeon didn't follow proper procedure. In fact, you probably haven't heard anybody brand a surgeon as a murderer the morning after losing a patient, certainly not if the patient was fighting him on the operating table.

No doubt, the doctor/cop comparison is a stretch in some ways. But in some ways it's right on the mark. In fact, the arrest that went bad on Warren Avenue was supposed to be reviewed by a panel of senior police professionals, just as a panel of surgeons might review a surgery that went bad. Walter and I never got our board of review because Coleman Young's police chief refused to let that happen.

I can't overemphasize how important this was to me…to both of us. I'm not sure I've ever discussed my story even for two minutes without mentioning the phantom board of review. Some people think I make too much of this. Those people aren't police officers. They don't understand what it means to have a hearing before a panel of command-level police professionals who fully understand, or should, the realities of difficult arrests and the obligations set forth in General Orders. Some people think I wouldn't have won a favorable ruling. I don't see it that way. I know for sure that whatever an unbiased board might find, it would not be that I murdered a motorist in an unprovoked attack. Some people think any board of review would have been stacked against me. Maybe so. But I've always thought most police officers who earn promotion are, unlike political appointees, intelligent and experienced and professional. Two out of three for sure, and that's what I would need from a three-member board of review.

I've never accused Stanley Knox of being the brightest bulb in the department. But I don't think Knox suppressed a board of review just because he was in a hurry to find us guilty by sun-up. I think he was smart enough to be scared as hell that a board of review might get somewhere near the truth, and the truth wouldn't line up with shouts from the lynch mob.

If a board chaired by a black commander ruled that we were "just police officers doing their jobs," it would cause some very serious problems for Chief Knox when he told the world: "This is not Simi Valley; we *will* convict." Even if a board found that we should have done some things differently but had escalated force amid resistance and obstinate refusal to submit, the lynch mob party line would have been in trouble.

No other fatal officer-involved case in department history, or at least in the memory of anyone alive, left the involved officers strung up without benefit of a board of review. Not one. It's ironic that police officers accused of violating procedures as defined in General Orders were denied this most basic element of due process – which is itself defined in General Orders. I think the fact that the news media raised no alarm about this tells you something.

Think about it. I spent two decades bringing in felons to a legal system that made me wait for a car to *move* before I could make a good car-theft arrest, even if the perp had already smashed the window of a vehicle belonging to someone else and had started the engine by breaking into the ignition system. A careful junkie could avoid a felony dope possession charge by carrying just enough crack for his next high – even if he bought his next high by stealing money or property. A street cop has to jump through a maze of such legal hoops to make a good felony arrest. Having made a good arrest, he must read the perp his rights. Due process and rights of a suspect pretty much define a street cop's day at the office. But when the system came after me, *my own department* trashed my most basic rights as a police officer.

So, no, I don't think I overdo it when I find it impossible to talk about the Malice Green incident without mentioning the phantom board of review. The easiest way of showing doubters that I am not blowing smoke about its importance is to tell you about Charles Henry.

Even though no board of review was allowed to take part in the Malice Green investigation, a board was automatically appointed. Chief Knox pretended it didn't exist. Charles Henry, a black man who joined the department three years before I did and rose to the rank of commander, was named board of review chairman. It would be a couple years before I – and anyone in the public who cared – discovered the most basic details about the politics that squelched departmental due process. In the end, Commander Henry would be awarded a million dollars for his share of the grief. By the time we get to the end of this book, you'll be wondering if anybody involved in this case, except Walter and me, *didn't* become a millionaire. But I've got to tell you the Charles Henry story now so you can understand what happened to the board of review.

I explained to you how an officer-involved fatality is supposed to be pursued in separate but coordinated investigations by Homicide, Internal Affairs and a board of review. And how the board of review has no legal powers, but its findings carry great weight regarding whether the involved officers followed proper procedures on the street. And how Knox, the morning after the incident, told his assembled top brass that the Malice Green board of review would not be allowed to do its job and interview witnesses – most particularly, the officers involved. And how at least one person present at the meeting, Commander Clinton Donaldson of Internal Affairs, forcefully objected to that decision. Details of how this situation played out in Commander Henry's eyes eventually emerged in a lawsuit he filed under the Whistle Blower Act.

Mayor Coleman Young surrendered his twenty-year hold on the Manoogian Mansion just months after we were tried and convicted. A new police chief, Isaiah McKinnon, was appointed by the new mayor, Dennis Archer. Meanwhile, Bob Lessnau – the officer who pulled Malice Green away and led the uniformed cops' efforts to put him in handcuffs – had been acquitted of assault while standing trial with Walter and me...and had filed a civil suit against the city. One of Bobby's complaints, of course, was that he – like the rest of us – never got a hearing before the board of review. Commander Henry was called to testify in Lessnau's trial. "I had no alternative but to tell the truth," Henry told a newspaper reporter.

A great deal of the truth can be found in an inter-office memo Henry wrote to Chief McKinnon on March 7, 1994, while Walter and I were sharing a prison cell. In the memo, Henry is looking back at the Homicide investigation that began with Knox's morning-after meeting. The "then chief" that Henry talks about is Knox, and "the writer" – in standard police lingo – is Henry himself. You just finished reading about the "Special Assignment Squad," and what Bill Presley, the SAS lieutenant, thought about the investigation. Following are key excerpts from Henry's memo. The excerpts are extensive because it's all amazing stuff. Everything in italics is verbatim from Henry's memo.

Upon notification of the convening of Board of Review #92-07-449, writer as Chairperson, contacted the Homicide Section Special Assignment Squad to apprise the Officer in Charge regarding the composition of the Board and to establish the Board's superintending control and coordination of the investigation as mandated by the General Procedures, Volume III...The Officer in Charge advised writer that the investigation regarding the death of Malice Green was progressing, and that a number of witnesses had been interviewed and there would be some investigation reports available in the near future. Writer then inquired as to when the involved officers and witnesses would be available for interview by the Board. The writer was advised per direction of the then Chief of Police, that no entity including the Board of Review would be allowed to interview witnesses or become involved in the investigation being conducted by the Special Assignment Squad. The writer at that time believed this to be a temporary order because of the notoriety, sensitivity and widespread media attention surrounding the investigation.

Writer advised the other members of the Board about the then Chief's order. The Board did receive some reports and documents regarding the investigation. However without the authority as outlined in department procedures regarding Boards of Review, it was impossible to determine the adequacy or objectiveness of the investigation.

Members of the Board became very concerned about the apparent conflicting orders of the then Chief of Police and moreover the ability of the Board to comply with mandates outlined in the General Procedures after learning through the media about department actions regarding the investigation.

The writer as Chairperson, contacted the then Chief's office for clarification. I was advised that a meeting of all entities involved in the investigation was scheduled for the near future.

On November 24, 1992, a meeting was convened in Commander Clinton Donaldson's office on the third floor of Police Headquarters. Attending that meeting were all members of the Board of Review, Commander Donaldson and Inspector Harold Scott of Internal Controls Division, and Inspectors Michael Falvo and Iris Worthington of the Labor Relations Division. Discussion was held regarding the direction of the investigation in light of all the notoriety it was receiving. Board members expressed concerns about the conflicting orders it had received. The Board expressed an inability to complete its work unless department procedures were followed. Allowing the Board to interview witnesses, officers and investigators involved in the investigation.

The writer recommended that in the alternative, the Chief of Police had the authority to reassign the Board of Review to the entity or entities now conducting the investigation or whomever he deemed appropriate. Commander Donaldson indicated he would meet with the Chief and convey the Board's concerns and recommendations.

The Department took a number of subsequent actions in regards to the investigation. The Board had no prior knowledge or input in any of the actions. Those actions include the following:

1. Securing criminal warrants for Sergeant Douglas, Police Officers Budzyn, Nevers and Lessnau.

2. Dismissal of Sergeant Douglas, Police Officers Budzyn, Nevers and Lessnau.

3. Suspension from duty of Police Officers Gunther, Gotelaere and Kijek.

The Board was notified by Commander Donaldson of a second meeting regarding the investigation to be held on January 20, 1993. Present at that meeting were members of the Board, Commander Donaldson, Inspectors Michael Falvo, Iris Worthington, Harold Scott, Gerald Stewart and Lieutenant Tommy Alston.

Inspector Falvo stated he had been meeting with the Chief of Police regarding the investigation and had made certain recommendations and received specific directions, some of which are as follows:

1. Inspector Falvo recommended dismissal of the Sergeant and three Officers after the Union insisted on a timely hearing as outlined in the labor agreement.

2. The Internal Affairs Section is charged with the investigation of those officers at the scene of Malice Green's death, but not criminally charged thus far.

3. Inspector Falvo will make recommendations to dismiss or reinstate the three suspended officers based on the results of the Internal Affairs investigation.

4. That a date of February 27, 1993, was recommended for Chief's hearings to charge and dismiss the three suspended officers.

(I am boldfacing the following paragraph because it is one of my favorites.)

Inspector Stewart and Lieutenant Alston voiced concern and caution that the Internal Affairs invest-igation not taint the Homicide Section investigation by re-interviewing witnesses.

Members of the Board again raised concerns and questions about the role of the Board of Review in the investigation. Members reiterated that every aspect of the investigation and every decision thereof was being carried out independently of the Board of Review.

Inspector Falvo had no direction from the Chief for the Board. Commander Donaldson stated he had talked with the Chief on more than one occasion regarding the role of the Board of Review and had made recommendations to the Chief thereof. However, the Chief would not recant his previous direction relative to the Board's involvement, nor would he give directions in the alternative.

The writer as Chairperson of the Board concluded that the then Chief of Police must have had sufficient reason he did not care to divulge for excluding the Board of Review. Further that he had the authority to do so.

The Board had no further involvement in the investigation nor did it receive further direction or instructions.

If you are a civilian, you probably have seen enough cop shows and movies to raise an eyebrow when reading that Internal Affairs was ordered not to re-interview witnesses for fear of "tainting" an investigation of police officers. Nothing was allowed to cast doubt on the party line, just as Bill Presley's desire to re-interview the EMS tech Lee Hardy was squelched by his bosses in Homicide. The investigation was "tainted," all right – by being kept in Alston and Stewart's hip pocket. The board of review not only did not "establish the Board's superintending control and coordination of the investigation as mandated by the General Procedures" – the board of review did not, in any meaningful way, even exist.

How can I not get angry just reviewing this stuff? I like to think you can understand my anger about that, and other things, and not use my anger against me in reaching your own opinion about this case.

When Commander Henry testified in Bobby Lessnau's civil suit, his testimony reflected the above memo. Donaldson, the

Internal Affairs commander, testified in a later lawsuit brought by the other suspended cops. For Henry's troubles, Chief McKinnon asked him to either take a demotion to lieutenant or to resign. Henry left. And then he, too, sued. A jury in Wayne County Circuit Court awarded him a judgment of $1,080,000.

I have always said I was "just a cop doing his job." That's exactly the proposition that a board of review investigates. Board members don't look at ways to bring a criminal case, major or minor, against an officer – and don't look, for that matter, at ways to find legal loopholes that will defend him. They look at what happened on the street and weigh that against what the academy and General Orders and the state tell a police officer he is obligated to do in that situation. If the case involves escalation of force, board members interview witnesses and reach a conclusion based on both their years of experience and their intimate knowledge of what "The Book" says about police procedures. Sometimes a board of review will come down hard on a street cop in trouble. Sometimes a board of review will determine that he was "just a cop doing his job." In the latter case, if a prosecutor wants to ignore a board of review's finding, he can do so. The board's finding cannot be introduced in court, but it will be sitting there on the record for one and all to see. It will impact news coverage, and it will impact how well an overzealous prosecutor will sleep at night. It is supposed to impact things like suspensions and firings. And in our case the board simply didn't exist.

In preparing this book, I talked to two retired Detroit police inspectors, dedicated and honest cops who sat on dozens of boards of review and who would not have been afraid to make a negative ruling in my case, look me in the eye, and say: "Sorry, Larry, but that's the way I see it." Both were professionals, meaning they wouldn't tell me how they, or any honest board member, would have ruled in the Malice Green case. How could they? Stanley Knox made sure it's only a hypothetical question. There were no board sessions, no command-level officers sitting across the table asking police officers and other witnesses for a picture of how it all came down on the street. That's different from courtroom lawyers dancing around rules of evidence, letting themselves testify by innuendo, seeking not truth but victory with word games and dog-and-pony tricks for a jury. Yeah, I know, a trial is supposed to be the crown jewel of the criminal justice system I served for so many years. But, like I said, my viewpoint on that has changed a bit.

One inspector, who sat on at least twenty boards of review, told me that some commanders would beg off the assignment and manage to reach retirement without participating in even one such investigation. "You can make enemies while sitting on a board of review," he said.

Both inspectors expressed outrage that the Malice Green board of review was not allowed to do what it was supposed to do. Both inspectors regard the prosecution and trial of Walter and me as a political circus. Both went far enough to say – based on what they can tell from following news coverage of the case, and their years of experience with difficult arrests – that an unbiased board *might* have found that we escalated force entirely according to proper procedure, and that I was "just a cop doing his job." There are other possible findings that would be less favorable to me, but far short of what Coleman Young, Stanley Knox and Detroit's criminal justice system had in mind. We'll never know what Charles Henry and his two colleagues would have found. It appears that Commander Henry made some enemies without even taking testimony or rendering a decision of any kind.

To understand any investigation of police officers you have to know about the "Garrity Rule." If you are a cop, you already know, and you just call it "Garrity." When police officers come under investigation, Garrity becomes standard operating procedure. If an officer is called to a Garrity hearing, he is ordered to answer questions upon pain of dismissal. Anything he says under Garrity cannot be used against him in a criminal trial – only in departmental discipline. This does *not* mean criminal charges cannot be brought against him. It does *not*

mean he cannot be asked to testify in court. It only means
that his Garrity statement cannot be introduced as evidence
in a criminal trial. If a statement made under Garrity produces
information that criminal investigators did not know, they are
free to gather that same information from other sources or
from evidence and use it in any criminal proceeding. Garrity,
in short, allows investigators to get a quick handle on what
happened in an incident without putting an officer in danger
of being fired, or otherwise disciplined, for exercising his right
to remain silent in the face of a possible criminal charge. Once
an officer has been "Garrity-ized" that officer is *required* to
answer questions. Garrity is the mirror opposite of Miranda
rights. Reading someone his Miranda rights tells him that
anything he says *will* be used against him in a criminal case,
and reminds him he has a right to remain silent.

Garrity interviews in the investigation of police officers are
as common as scrambled eggs in a diner. Internal Affairs and
Homicide investigators conduct Garrity interviews. Boards of
review *always* question officers under Garrity. Let me qualify
that. In interviews for this book, every command level officer
and every lawyer was asked if they ever heard of a board of
review being conducted under Miranda rather than Garrity.
The answer was always "no," accompanied by a look that said:
"What a strange question." In 1995, I didn't know much about
that sort of thing, but being in prison I had time on my hands
to pursue my anger about never being given a board of review
hearing. So I wrote a letter from prison to Jim Bannon, by then
retired from his job as executive deputy chief.

Bannon, you will recall, stood at Knox's side during the
next-day press conference in which we were signed, sealed and
delivered to the lynch mob. Even after that performance, Bannon
seemed like the right guy to answer my question. His reply raises
more questions than it answers about how the department sealed
off the Malice Green investigation, and no doubt met Coleman
Young's goal of not leaving even a hint that might lead the public
to say: "Wait a minute! This doesn't add up!"

As a retiree in 1995, Bannon had no files handy so he based his return letter on his personal diary. He started by saying I had correctly quoted General Orders on convening a board of review. He said he was informed of the Malice Green incident shortly after midnight, and that at 8 o'clock the next morning he reviewed preliminary reports and ordered a lieutenant to notify a commander and two inspectors that they were next on the list and would sit on the board investigating the Green case. This is the way it is supposed to go – quick movement by a board to determine whether officers involved had followed proper arrest procedures. As you know, that determination never happened. Eleven days later, with the board still sitting on its hands, criminal warrants were issued against me, Walter, Bobby Lessnau and Freddie Douglas. Bannon wrote that two days later:

> *"On November 18, 1992, a discussion was had between myself, Chief Knox and Commander Clinton Donaldson about proceeding with the board of review in light of the prosecuting attorney's action of the 16th. Donaldson believed the board should proceed. I disagreed with him based on the department's experience in the Algiers Motel incident. In that case a board of review mistakenly questioned one of the officers under a Garrity warning rather than under Miranda, thus making the statement inadmissible."*

A couple of things about that paragraph. First, why am I not surprised that Jim Bannon managed to drag in the most infamous incident arising out of the 1967 Detroit riot, when police officers shot three young blacks at the Algiers Motel – even though Bannon knew full well that there was nothing racial about the Malice Green case except the accident of skin color? Second, the Garrity Rule resulted from a U.S. Supreme Court ruling the same year as the Algiers Motel case. Third, I have not been able to find anyone who ever heard of any board of review since then that did not proceed under the Garrity Rule. In other words, I have no idea what Bannon's paragraph means.

Donaldson, the Internal Affairs commander, wanted to do

Garrity interviews from the get-go with uniformed officers who showed up on Warren Avenue and had only minimal involvement in Malice Green's arrest. Instead, those officers were suspended – except for the two stand-arounds from the Fourth – just like Walter and Freddie Douglas and Bobby Lessnau and me. Donaldson's idea, of course – and this would be standard procedure – was that if the other five patrolmen were "Garrity-ized" they would be compelled to describe anything incriminating they saw that night. Eventually, five officers were interviewed under Garrity, but only *after* the rest of us had been charged with crimes. Those five Garrity-hearing transcripts are out there. Read them and you will find nothing to support the prosecution. In fact, the only consistent witness testimony in the Malice Green case is the testimony of the police officers – four different sets of partners from four different cars, plus a sergeant who arrived in his own car.

Bannon then wrote:

"The ultimate decision as to whether to proceed with the board in your case was left up to Prosecutor O'Hair and Inspector Gerald Stewart of the Homicide Section. Prosecutor O'Hair, Deputy Chief Younger and Inspector Stewart all agreed that the board should not proceed due to the danger of contaminating the pending court case. The board (of review) was so informed by Deputy Chief Younger."

These guys had no right to do this. It had never been done before. To my knowledge, it has never been done since. You can backtrack from Commander Henry's account, as board of review chairman, and see where decisions were made while he was itching to put the board to work doing its job. You can backtrack from the meetings Bannon mentions all the way to Knox's "roll call" the morning after the incident. And I have no doubt you could backtrack from almost anywhere and wind up at the Manoogian Mansion and Mayor Coleman Young.

Bannon went on to say that the board of review's failure to interview any of us who were charged with crimes in Malice

Green's arrest was "due in part to the refusal of the attorneys for the officers to allow their clients to be interviewed under Miranda." My attorney at the time, and in my first trial, says he would have – of course – refused to let me face a board of review under Miranda. Nobody does. More important, my attorney says he was never asked.

This is departmental stuff. This is not the criminal courts. But due process within a disciplinary investigation is absolutely vital, as any police officer knows, to a cop getting a fair shake – particularly in a case where the street has him tried and convicted from day one. Stifling departmental due process made our lynching in many respects an inside job. A prosecutor is free to ignore what a board of review might find. But with a board of review bypassed entirely, a prosecutor is free to use his imagination. As Walter and I, unlike any other two cops in Detroit history, would soon discover.

There is one further piece of departmental due process, which for Walter and me was even more of a joke. That is the "chief's hearing," in which evidence of wrongdoing is handed to the chief and he makes a disciplinary ruling – ranging from suspension right up to dismissal. Standard procedure, if the alleged wrongdoing results in a criminal charge, is for the chief's hearing to be held after the case has been resolved. If an officer wishes to appeal a judgment from a chief's hearing, he may demand a trial board – which, like the chief's hearing, has the power to fire him. In the case of a conviction for a major crime, a chief's hearing and a trial board would, of course, be meaningless. Anyone convicted of a major crime is gone from the force. With Walter and me none of this applied. Like everything else in the Green case, it was hush and rush. A chief's hearing was scheduled early on, and our lawyers told us not even to bother attending. We were in court for our preliminary examination on criminal charges, waiting to see whether we would, in fact, be ordered to stand trial, when Chief Knox handed our lawyers the pieces of paper saying we had been fired "for committing second-degree murder."

15
COCAINE AND COMMON SENSE

Sometimes you find big clues in small places, even when the truth you seek is complicated. My tossing that toy gun to Mickey Williams after Malice Green was taken to the hospital is one such small place. I knew how hard I had struck Green. The idea that he would die did not enter my mind. When EMS took Green away, I bantered with the street people, tossed the toy gun around, asked the lieutenant from Four if she had heard anything about the Billy Polk case, and no doubt I groused to myself about paperwork I'd have to do because a guy refused arrest and wound up with a bloodied head. I remind you of all this because these are not the actions, and not the thoughts, of someone who has just beaten a man to death – let alone a cop with my record, my experience, my approach to working the streets, and my attitude toward human life. The news that Green had died was the most unexpected thing I saw or heard in decades of dealing, every night, with the unexpected. I could not understand it. That is not medical science. But it is common sense and the truth, and it is a very long way from how the prosecution spun the forensic evidence.

Cause of death is something forensic pathologists decide. It is expert opinion. You might call it uncommon sense. Sometimes expert opinion about cause of death is like calling a meteorologist during a cloudburst to verify that it's rain you see on the sidewalk. A guy steps in front of a train and dies, for example. There is no room for varying opinions about what caused his death, even if you paid someone to have a different opinion, or even if you had an agenda with the guy who stepped in front of the train. Call in a hundred pathologists and they'll all say exactly the same thing. In the case of Malice Green, cause of death was a lot more complicated. Call in a hundred pathologists and expert opinion is not unanimous, and even the majority opinion differs in the details. Reaching your own intelligent opinion about why Malice Green died requires knowing which experts said what, counting noses, and holding expert opinion and common sense up to the light side by side. It was the prosecution, not me, who avoided the light and even tried to hide the idea of cocaine playing any role whatsoever in Green's death. They had to do so. There's no other way their version of what happened on Warren Avenue makes any sense. For them, cause of death was not complicated but simple: two white cops.

An unusual number of pathologists have looked at the Malice Green case. Prosecutors came up with two who saw no significance to the cocaine in Green's bloodstream. One prosecution expert was no expert at all and had his own agenda. His own boss disagreed with him, and the most experienced pathologist in his office disagreed even more strongly. The second prosecution expert was infinitely more qualified but, in my opinion, had his own serious agenda problems – something you can judge for yourself. Of the many pathologists who have testified on this case or analyzed it, these two are the only *two* who, like the prosecutors, did not want to hear any talk about cocaine. No way could anyone who surveyed the experts find fairness, or a quest for truth, in the prosecution's ignore-the-cocaine scenario. The credible, overwhelming majority of expert opinion on the matter of what caused Malice Green's body to shut down leads straight to cocaine. Beyond that, it's worth remembering that if Green had not been doing cocaine there would have been no confrontation, no relentless resistance... and no blows to the head. Incredibly, the prosecutors refused even to accept that simple truth in their case theory. What they sold to jurors was that two police officers suddenly, after a combined forty-four years on the street, just up and committed murder by beating a man to death for no reason – after summoning witnesses to watch it happen.

The truth about cocaine in the death of Malice Green follows a trail from the Wayne County morgue to the prosecutor's office to courtroom testimony to a story aired on *Sixty Minutes* to a pathologists' conference in New York, skipping across the long chronology of my story. I'm not a pathologist and neither, probably, are you. But there are lots of pathologists to hear from. The trail begins in the first few hours after Green's death, when the politics of the case reached even into the county morgue and became the politics of cocaine.

The old morgue, on the edge of Greektown and not far from police headquarters, was a cramped, understaffed, underfunded place with a history of management controversy. On Friday morning, November 6, 1992, less than twelve hours after Green's death, the Wayne County medical examiner, Dr. Bader Cassin, did not have a valid medical license – having neglected to submit his renewal application. This is only a footnote, revealed later. It's not the reason the highest-profile case anybody in the morgue would ever touch wound up in the hands of a young assistant M.E. named Kalil Jiraki. Jiraki had been board-certified as a forensic pathologist just eight months earlier. Jiraki wound up doing the Green autopsy the way two factory hands might toss a hot potato while working on a busy assembly line. After Walter and I were sent to prison, Jiraki would be fired and Cassin would be rumored in the press to have been fired, but instead would resign. They were the two principal players when Green's body arrived at the morgue from Detroit Receiving Hospital.

Because several staffers were absent, either to attend a professional conference or on vacation, Jiraki had been working extra days and long hours. The morgue is a busy place. Jiraki himself was scheduled to leave town the next day on vacation. With numerous bodies on hand, and four autopsies to be done, Jiraki expected Cassin to step in and perform the Green autopsy. Instead, Cassin – despite being the head man and the person who would have to field questions from the media – tossed the case back to Jiraki. This left Jiraki darting from body to body in the autopsy room, no doubt tired from his workload, and looking forward to his vacation trip scheduled to begin in a matter of hours. Medical students passed in and out of the room. Jiraki had other company, including a morgue photographer and visitations from Homicide investigator Monica Childs.

Two years after Walter and I went to prison, Childs would become locally famous for bringing down Gerald Stewart's replacement as head of Homicide, a woman named Joan Ghougoian. Childs blew the whistle on Ghougoian for allegedly making improper promises to murder suspects in return for confessions. Ghougoian was replaced by Bill Rice. You will remember Rice as the sergeant who signed Theresa Pace's "witness fee" checks. Anyway, at the time of the Ghougoian case, a Detroit News profile said of Childs: "Her attitude, she said, comes from being raised by a mother who was heavily into the civil rights movement and by growing up in a city that in her young eyes appeared to be patrolled mostly by white men who treated black people with no respect. 'I became the police' Childs said, 'because I hated the police.'" According to Kalil Jiraki's account, while Malice Green's body awaited and underwent autopsy, Monica Childs passed in and out of the room and made clear what Jiraki was dealing with and what Homicide wanted to hear. Jiraki was one of my greatest adversaries in the criminal case, so I have no reason to doubt the account he wrote, after our conviction, of the autopsy room scene. At trial, Jiraki had been much less clear – evasive, even – about Childs's presence. Nonetheless, Childs's testimony contradicted Jiraki's – just as Homicide Sergeant Vern Humes would deny telling Bill Presley and Danny Maynard that he had been instructed to get rid of Theresa Pace's first statement.

Jiraki wrote an unpublished book manuscript about the Green case. The manuscript was circulated to, among others, a few of his colleagues and Janet Wilson, a Free Press reporter, who wrote a lengthy story based on it. A couple of the best parts, however, didn't appear in the newspaper story – at least not the best parts of the manuscript that made its way to me, typeset in galley proofs. I would have bought Jiraki's book, but despite being advertised for a couple of years as an upcoming title from an obscure online publisher, it was never released for sale. I don't know exactly why. At this writing, *Medical Examiner Under Fire: The Malice Green Police Brutality Trial* still shows up as number 1,267,697 on the Amazon.com bestseller list even though you can't buy it from Amazon and to my knowledge no copies have been sold. Besides referencing the Free Press story based on his manuscript, I am going to claim "fair use" and quote a few key passages of Jiraki's rant that the Free Press didn't use.

I mentioned earlier this paragraph from Jiraki's very first page:

"The determinations that medical examiners make based on autopsies stem from experience relevant to the locality of the office, and the community it serves," Jiraki wrote. "The outcome is a synopsis of views: both the ones prevalent in the area and those held by the police and the legal system. Thus the forensic office blends smoothly with the legal and social systems that it serves."

Now, I'm just an old cop, and I had to read that passage six times to nail down my understanding of it, but I think I have it right: Jiraki is saying that cause of death in Detroit, Michigan, might be different than cause of death in Cheboygan, Michigan. Or that white cop plus black citizen equals blunt-force trauma. Jiraki has said a lot – in his manuscript and elsewhere – to confirm my interpretation.

In his account of the Green autopsy, Jiraki says repeatedly that Green's death was presented to him from the beginning as

229

"a police beating case." He says this was not indicated externally on Green's body because of his long hair – leading Jiraki to ponder whether Cassin had declined to do the autopsy himself on grounds it was a natural death, or a drug-related death. With Green's body in a hallway waiting to be brought into the autopsy room, Jiraki says he encountered "Detective" Childs, who "told me briefly that (Green) had been beaten by a police flashlight." While describing the autopsy itself, Jiraki writes: "Meanwhile, Monica Childs kept walking in and out of the autopsy room, asking if we were done, and if I knew the cause of death…Every time she came in, she would give me more information and she would ask me whether the injuries were consistent with a flashlight beating. She then brought me the flashlights used in this case." Childs would deny, under oath, that she brought in the flashlights before Jiraki was finished, as he says she did. But it's clear that Jiraki was hearing from various sources – while he did his work and before reaching his conclusion – a "synopsis of views: both the ones prevalent in the area and those held by the police and the legal system."

As Jiraki went about his work, he also talked things over with the morgue photographer, who Jiraki writes "(told) me that these police officers involved had a history of roughing up people in the neighborhood and that there were a lot of complaints against them.…I asked him if the officers involved were white, and he said that they were, so I said: 'I get the picture, say no more.'"

By the time Jiraki attended the daily 3 p.m. staff meeting, he told his colleagues that Green's death "was a police-beating case using flashlights, but Dr. Cassin seemed not to believe what I was saying; he felt that there was more to the case than that. I had a hard time believing it myself, especially since the case of Rodney King in Los Angeles, and the major riots accompanying that case, were still fresh in everyone's mind."

No kidding. In Knox's office earlier that morning. In the media later in the day and for months to come. And in the medical examiner's office. Nobody could look at this case from day one without seeing Rodney King and without fearing riots. Anyone who didn't understand the real scene on Warren, and the content of Malice Green's bloodstream, would never see anything but Rodney King in the face of Malice Green. Kalil Jiraki did his part to keep it that way.

Monica Childs phoned soon after the staff meeting, Jiraki wrote, asking how many blows had been struck, and he told her fourteen. When cross-examined at trial, Jiraki would testify that the number of wounds he could attribute to a flashlight was seven, just one more than the number I have always estimated were delivered by me, and me alone. I regard that testimony to be vital, because even though Jiraki was not a neuropathologist – as were two experts who testified for the defense – he was not only the person who performed the official autopsy...he was the *prosecution's* witness. Crazy rumors might fly on the street about Green being pummeled for "an hour." Prosecutors might tell jurors that I hit Green more times than I did – and still find room to tell jurors that Walter Budzyn also inflicted a "beating" on Malice Green. But *their* expert, when put to the wall on how many of the supposed fourteen wounds and lacerations on Green's head could be attributed to a flashlight – supported *my* testimony. That's why another passage in Jiraki's manuscript is astounding. Count the supposed flashlight blows in your mind as you read the following paragraph.

Jiraki wrote, without citing a source and as matter-of-factly as if he had witnessed it himself, that the confrontation began with Walter beating Green unconscious. Walter then climbed into Green's car, Jiraki wrote, and "continued to beat him on the head and face with his flashlight." Then, Jiraki wrote, I climbed into the backseat and – *holding my flashlight with both hands* – started beating Green on the body and face. And there's more. Then, Jiraki's manuscript says, I went around to the driver door and began to beat Green some more on his head.

The fact that none of this is true is *not* what's astounding. What's astounding is that it is so *far* from the truth it's hard to imagine where it comes from, and that it was written by the prosecution's lead expert witness – the same guy whose cross-examination testimony about number of blows lines up with my own testimony. It's also astounding that the Free Press did not quote Jiraki citing the most hysterical street rumors as fact. How many flashlight blows do you suppose the above paragraph adds up to? Fifty? A hundred? It's a ridiculous picture. If Jiraki believes it, contrary to his own allegedly expert courtroom testimony, that tells you something. If somebody else, with his own agenda in this case, wrote the passage for Jiraki, then that also tells you something.

Meanwhile, back to the autopsy. On his report, Jiraki – without waiting for toxicology results – listed "blunt force trauma," period, as cause of death. The toxicology report would not be available for ten days, but even after it was in hand Jiraki refused to tweak his findings in the smallest way. His boss, Bader Cassin, who had passed the hot-potato autopsy off to Jiraki, was immediately troubled – even without a toxicology report – that Jiraki had not taken the obvious into account. The obvious being that Green was a drug user with an enlarged heart, that Green had confronted police outside a crack house, and that rocks of cocaine were in his possession. It is like autopsying that guy who steps in front of a train, if not quite so obvious. Jiraki ignored the obvious. Whether he ignored the autopsy-room chatter about "white cops with a history" and a "police flashlight beating" – or whether he plugged that into his theories about cause of death being influenced by "experience relevant to the locality of the office, and the community it serves" – you be the judge.

Cassin was troubled enough that he returned to the autopsy room Saturday morning and did his own examination of the body and the tissues that Jiraki had removed. If Cassin drafted his own autopsy report, it never saw light of day. In fact, the defense didn't even know about the phantom second autopsy until Jiraki – smoldering with some kind of conspiracy theory about his boss and suspicious, as you will see, of the entire white establishment – spilled the beans on the witness stand. Whatever private battle was going on between Jiraki and Cassin, the bottom line was cocaine. Far be it from me to figure out the behind-the-scenes personality clashes and office politics. The only thing that mattered, and still matters, to me is the bottom line. Cassin, the medical examiner, had let a junior staff member do the autopsy on a case that was about to make headlines across the country when Stanley Knox and Coleman Young went on television to tell the world that Detroit had a fatal Rodney King case on its hands, but never fear – we'll get the cops who murdered Malice Green. And Cassin had put himself in a bind because the junior staff member wouldn't even go so far as to say that maybe – just maybe – cocaine had something to do with Green's death. Cassin, who despite being top dog at the morgue was himself a relatively inexperienced forensic pathologist, knew it was wrong to ignore the cocaine. And while our fate was being sealed, Jiraki and Cassin sparred like amateur boxers pushed into the ring at Madison Square Garden.

Jiraki believes Cassin wanted to dump the original autopsy report and replace it with one that not only cited other factors in cause of death, but which eliminated blunt-force trauma as a contributing cause. In Jiraki's mind that didn't happen only because he had kept photographs and a copy of his own autopsy records. We'll never know what Cassin's report would have said if he, rather than Jiraki, had done the first autopsy. Cassin says he wanted to cite cocaine as a possible contributing factor. He admitted that much in a deposition after we were convicted. I don't for a minute think Cassin wanted the truth out any more than Jiraki did. I think Cassin just wanted to recover from his monumental screwup in giving the case to Jiraki, and keep the prosecutors from being embarrassed in court because the cocaine connection was so obvious. As it turned out, prosecutors loved Jiraki's version, and jurors in our first trial would have found us guilty if the official cause of death was listed as heart failure – which, as a matter of fact, one much more experienced pathologist testified was true.

Jiraki wrote that the sparring with Cassin included the matter of which of them would testify at our trial. Cassin, Jiraki says, saw no reason both of them could not testify. In the end Cassin, the medical examiner, did not testify. You will recall the meeting in the prosecutor's office attended by Homicide Sergeants Danny Maynard and Lee Caudill, the one where Caudill was asked to leave the room when Cassin brought up the matter of cocaine. The one where Maynard remembers Cassin saying: "I'm not so sure that had those injuries been on someone else they would have been fatal." And where Maynard remembers assistant prosecutor Kym Worthy saying: "It [the cocaine] doesn't matter. They beat him to death." The prosecutor's office did not want anyone mentioning the word cocaine with even a "maybe" attached to it. So Jiraki would testify solo.

Here's Jiraki talking about his sparring with Cassin on the cocaine issue, as reported in the Free Press:

"He kept on insisting to me: 'Say one word – "may" – meaning cocaine may have caused Green's death or contributed to it?'" Jiraki wrote. "Besides the fact that this was wrong, it would also mean losing the case in court. I had enough experience to know that saying this one word would mean a different cause of death. I would be hammered on what percent cocaine contributed to the death of Malice Green, and this would open the door for all sorts of speculation."

Jiraki, whose distrust and dread of professional humiliation rose to the level of inventing conspiracy theories, put up an absolute wall on the subject of cocaine – going against common sense and, as it turned out, against an army of nationally respected pathologists. In other words, except for his lack of experience and stature, Jiraki's stonewalling and commitment to a senseless beating by two white cops was exactly what the prosecutors wanted. Like the prosecutors, Jiraki wasn't interested in exploring the truth about Green's neuropathology; he was interested in getting a conviction.

When the toxicology report that Jiraki didn't care about

came back, it measured the cocaine in Green's bloodstream at 0.50 micromilliliters per milliliter. There was alcohol in Green's bladder and his bloodstream contained an important interactive byproduct of booze and crack known as ethyl cocaine. Jiraki would testify at our trial that the lowest blood-cocaine level he had reported as a cause of death was 0.90, almost twice the level found in Green's body. In response to the judge's request for clarification, Jiraki testified that cocaine "had no bearing on the cause of [Green's] death, on the mechanism of his death, and it is an incidental finding similar to the color of his eyes." To Kalil Jiraki, cocaine was not part of the science explaining Green's death, but part of some kind of conspiracy to clear two white cops of wrongdoing. But you don't need to look past Jiraki himself for reasons to ridicule his testimony.

Four months before the Malice Green incident, in a smokestack suburb called Ecorse, a man named James Brooks was subdued by Ecorse police officers and was dead on arrival at a hospital. Police reports said Brooks had gone berserk and crashed through two closed windows while screaming that his back was on fire. He was under the influence of cocaine. Brooks's death attracted no interest outside Ecorse until after Walter and I were long gone to prison. The attention came when Brooks's family had the Oakland County medical examiner, Dr. Ljubisa Dragovic, take a look at the case. Two Detroit News reporters, Ann Sweeney and Brenda Ingersoll, reported a story based on Dragovic's findings.

The parallels between the Brooks case and the Malice Green case were considerable. Both men were high on cocaine, both confronted police officers, both sustained contusions, tears and abrasions to the head. An Ecorse deputy police chief told the News: "My recollection is that he was injured through his own actions." Dragovic said Brooks's injuries were sustained by blunt force and could not have been caused by shattering glass – implying that police officers must have escalated force to subdue him. "I'm not surprised he went berserk with that level of cocaine," Dragovic said, adding that resisting arrest can be fatal to drug users. "They're extremely fragile in a cardiovascular sense. Cocaine primes up the brain and heart when an individual is constrained."

Malice Green's bloodstream measured 0.28 content for ethyl cocaine, the dangerous byproduct of mixing cocaine and alcohol. Ethyl cocaine can heighten a coke user's bizarre behavior (as if jumping through closed windows while shouting that your back is on fire is not bizarre enough) and pump adrenaline at life-threatening levels. Brooks's toxicology report, unlike Green's, showed no presence of ethyl cocaine. Brooks, unlike Green, had not mixed cocaine and alcohol.

No charges were filed against the officers who arrested Brooks. They were black, which doesn't prove anything about anything, but which is interesting. More interesting is the cocaine toxicology report in both cases, which leads to the reason I am telling Brooks's story here, out of sequence. Brooks's blood cocaine level was measured at 0.38, just three-quarters of the 0.50 cocaine level measured in Green's blood. Keep in mind that Jiraki testified at our trial that the lowest level he had ever cited for cocaine as cause of death was 0.90. After we were in prison, however, the News story revealed that Jiraki had performed both the Brooks and the Green autopsies. Green's cause of death – despite the 0.50 cocaine level – was listed as blunt-force trauma, and manner of death homicide. Just a few months earlier, Jiraki had ruled that Brooks – after struggling with police, with a 0.38 cocaine level, and no ethyl cocaine on board – died of cocaine abuse, and that manner of death was indeterminable. Ecorse is in Wayne County, adjoining Detroit's Fourth Precinct, and is served by the same prosecutor's office that came after Walter and me, and which fell in love with Kalil Jiraki – who refused to connect Green's death with cocaine even though Jiraki had ruled a lesser amount of cocaine as the cause of another man's death during a struggle with police.

The News reporters tried to interview Jiraki for their story. He faxed a reply: "I am not obligated to answer any questions to anybody except in court. If you agree to pay the fee for consultation, the format of the interview is determined by me: send written questions and you receive written answers."

Dragovic is a former assistant Wayne County medical examiner, an experienced forensic pathologist and also a board-certified neuropathologist – meaning he has special expertise in brain injuries. To the public nationally, Dragovic is probably best known as the M.E. who bravely wrote "homicide" on the autopsy report every time his fellow pathologist, "Doctor Death" Jack Kevorkian, performed an assisted suicide in Oakland County. First as an assistant M.E. in Detroit, and then as the top guy at Oakland County's morgue, Dragovic has been the medical investigator in countless cocaine-related deaths. Even after he left Detroit, the Wayne County prosecutor's office frequently used Dragovic's expertise at trial. And that is why he came to be at the 1992 Wayne County prosecutor's Christmas party, a month and a half after Malice Green's death. Which is where the trail apparently begins in the prosecution's shopping spree for a heavyweight expert who would support the inexperienced Jiraki's stonewalling on the cocaine issue.

Dragovic says assistant prosecutors Doug Baker and Kym Worthy approached him at the Christmas party and put out feelers about Dragovic testifying for the prosecution in the Malice Green case. Dragovic says his response was: "You have a problem with cocaine." In the end, Dragovic testified for the defense.

Meanwhile, the graybeard of Michigan's forensic pathologists – and a familiar face nationally – was Werner Spitz, author of one of the two standard texts that help American lawyers and doctors speak to each other in the same language. Like almost every nationally known forensic pathologist, it seems, Spitz appeared as an expert witness at the O.J. Simpson trial. Spitz had been chief medical examiner in Wayne County for decades until being eased out amid controversy largely centered on his moonlighting. The third leg of the tri-county area, Macomb County, happily signed Spitz on as its new medical examiner.

In an interview for this book, Spitz revealed that, like Dragovic, he was approached by the Wayne County prosecutor's office as a potential prosecution witness. Spitz says he had looked at the Green file and likely would have ruled cause of death as blunt-force trauma, but he also said cocaine could be a contributing factor. That opinion, no doubt, would have soured the prosecution's interest in Werner Spitz, but it never got that far. "I told them," Spitz said, "that where I grew up, when a policeman orders you to open your hand, you open your hand." Werner Spitz has testified more times than most people have been to McDonald's. But he said "no thanks" to the prosecutors' invitation. Spitz said the Green case should have been first and foremost not a matter for pathologists to wrangle about why Green's body shut down, but a matter for city and police to investigate administratively and determine whether Walter and I were just doing our job which, of course, sounds very much like the board of review we did not get.

Spitz said that contrary to common opinion, the O.J. Simpson jury's innocent verdict was not a racial thing. "O.J. was a celebrity, a hero on trial," Spitz said. "That's why he was found innocent. Now, the Malice Green case...*that* was a racial trial."

Spitz also revealed the answer to the question: "How did the 800-pound gorilla wind up testifying in the Malice Green case?" Spitz said that when he declined to appear for the prosecution, he was asked who they might get to do so. "Why don't you call," Spitz suggested, "my old friend Michael Baden?"

Baden is another nationally known forensic pathologist and TV-show talking head, which, of course, means he also testified at the O.J. trial. If O.J. was this generation's most famous celebrity defendant, Michael Baden might be this generation's most famous celebrity pathologist. So much so, that the honorable Judge George Crockett III described him, in the jurors' presence, as "an 800-pound gorilla." And when Baden had finished his testimony in a trial that had featured a Yugoslavian-born pathologist (Dragovic), an Indian-born pathologist (Haresh Mirchandani), and an Iranian-born pathologist (Jiraki), Crockett said to Baden: "More doctors should comport themselves in the courtroom as you do, (and) speak English."

Baden, who was well-paid for his testimony, went even deeper than Jiraki into the forget-about-cocaine theory the prosecution wanted to hear. We'll get to that shortly.

Despite recommending the court-anointed 800-pound gorilla, Spitz was helpful to our case. Defense lawyers interviewed him early on (he described one of Green's scalp wounds as being no more meaningful than "a bad shave job"). More important, my union-appointed attorney John Goldpaugh recalls how, when he first entered the case, the most perplexing thing in his eyes was Green's behavior when Walter and I tried to arrest him. "The meeting with Spitz," Goldpaugh says, "is where I first began to understand the meaning of cocaine to this case." One might say that anybody able to sit up and take nourishment would see the presence of cocaine and alcohol in Green's body as having something to do with Green's behavior; but Michael Baden would answer the prosecution's fondest dreams and testify otherwise.

Even defense lawyers are not as interested as I am in cocaine's role in Malice Green's death. That's because lawyers know the legal doctrine of "taking the victim as you find him" is going to be a problem in court. The doctrine, simply put, says that if you do something that would be harmless to most people, but might kill a person with a special condition – such as inflicting a minor cut on a hemophiliac, or over-exerting or even simply frightening someone with serious heart problems – then you are at fault. I think that doctrine is crazy when applied to police officers trying to arrest a stubbornly belligerent citizen, but there you are. To use an actual example, the doctrine has been applied to police officers who used pepper spray to subdue a suspect who, unknown to the police, had asthma. So it's a legal problem for police defense lawyers, even if it is no problem for common sense. As is well understood by Richard Thompson, the Oakland County prosecutor who said he would not have charged us with any crime; or Werner Spitz, who said my case was about police procedures, not cause of death; or even the Wayne County prosecutor himself when he took a pass on the James Brooks case, with all its parallels to the Malice Green case – everything changes when you take reality into a courtroom. Lee Caudill, the Homicide sergeant, summed it up when he said: "The courtroom is a different world. It's very difficult to move the street into the courtroom." The doctrine of "taking the victim as you find him" does not mean a whole lot in a fast-moving situation out on the street, when you know the other guy is not thinking good thoughts about you, and you know you are likely to be the victim if you lose control of the situation, or he pulls a gun out from under his car seat – or gets hold of your gun.

Besides which, look at the "victim I found." I'm supposed to do what – add "do toxicology test" to the Manual as a step to take before escalating force? Whether Green was struck six times or six hundred times with a flashlight, the fact is that a normal person would have (a) submitted to arrest before I hit him one time, or at the very least (b) submitted to arrest before I struck him a second time. Which puts cocaine at the center of what caused Green's body to shut down, no matter how you analyze it, and no matter what the medical experts say. If the doctrine of "taking the victim as you find him" somehow means two good cops become murderers because the guy they tried to arrest was stoned, then why did the prosecution try so hard to bury the cocaine?

I believe we should have had a mistrial the moment Kalil Jiraki blurted out in court that his boss had performed a second autopsy – of which there is miraculously no written record, no notes of any kind. The prosecution should have told us about the phantom autopsy, instead of telling Jiraki's boss Bader Cassin to go sit in a corner and be quiet. You don't need a law degree to understand that; all you need is a little sense of fairness and concern for the truth. We should have known about Cassin's second autopsy even before the preliminary exam, which bound us over for a murder trial. And we never would never have known about it if Jiraki didn't have the most incredible delusions. I didn't know about the phantom autopsy until right in the middle of our trial. It would be several years before I learned about the delusions.

Michael Batchelor, Walter's trial lawyer, was cross-examining Jiraki, who had been wandering so far into non-responsive "soliloquies" that even Judge Crockett warned him to stay on track. I want you to imagine sitting there as I was, with my freedom on the line, and hearing Jiraki spill the beans. In the Q and A that follows, Batchelor is "Q" and Jiraki is "A." All Batchelor intended to explore was why the autopsy wound up in the hands of such a junior forensic pathologist. Then Batchelor stumbled on this:

Q: "You asked for help, didn't you?"

A: "It is not help. That was my choice telling him [Cassin], please come and do this case because you are the one who usually talks to the media. Not me."

Q: "You wanted somebody else to take this case from you. You asked your boss to come and take it from you, didn't you?"

A: "Yes, and he did take it."

Q: "He did?"

A: "Yes."

Q: "Did he perform the autopsy?"

A: "He reexamined the body the following day."

Q: "After you did?"

A: "After I did."

Q: "Did he prepare a report?"

A: "He said he is going to prepare a report."

Q: "Has he prepared a report?"

A: "He never told me."

Q: "Doctor, when your boss does an autopsy would

your boss formulate their own opinion as to cause
of death?"

A: "Yes."

Q: "Have you had the opportunity to review your boss's
opinion as to cause of death?"

A: "Yes."

Q: "You have?"

A: "Yes."

Q: "You just told this court that he didn't tell you if he
made a report, didn't you?"

A: "On the day that I did the autopsy, Friday, he refused
to do it. The following day, on Saturday, when I was
leaving to L.A., in my absence he came down and
reexamined the body. And he told me when I came
back…"

Q: "I don't want you to tell me what he told you. I'm
asking you…"

A: "So we are talking about…"

Q: "Let me ask you a question."

A: "There are no lies."

Q: "Let's cut this one off."

A: "Okay."

Q: "Do you have with you your boss's opinion as to the
cause of death?"

A: "No."

Q: "Did you at any time consult that report in giving
testimony at either the preliminary examination or
at this trial as to your boss's [opinion of] cause of
death?"

Assistant Prosecutor Doug Baker: "I object. That assumes a
fact not in evidence. There is no evidence that there is such
a report."

Q: "Well, doctor, have you seen a report?"

A: "I have never seen a report."

Q: "You have never seen it, but you asked him for it?"

A: "I never asked him."

Q: "You never asked him?"

A: "Because I had mine."

(Jiraki testifies that after his trip to L.A., Bader Cassin told him of the phantom autopsy.)

Q: "Now doctor, did he tell you whether or not he had produced a written report to his re-examination?"

A: "He said he is going to produce a written report for this examination."

And with that little bombshell dropped, testimony was interrupted by a three-day weekend. After jurors left the room, Judge Crockett said: "Counsel, I think the prosecution ought to be prepared to explore the possibility of the existence of such a report, and if there is one..."

Baker interrupted to say: "There is not."

Worthy, who had told Cassin in Danny Maynard's presence that cocaine didn't matter, also jumped in and said: "There is not."

Crockett: "Well, double-check it so that they may have the benefit of whatever you found out. All right?"

Worthy: "That's fine, judge. We'll check it again but we know that there is not."

Speculation and 75 cents will get you a cup of coffee. But no matter how Bader Cassin spins it to his dying day, I will never believe he examined Green's body without making notes. Jiraki says Cassin was going to write his own autopsy report. Nothing ever turned up on paper. How convenient for the prosecution. Why did this bombshell end there as far as our trial goes? Why didn't the defense call Cassin to the stand? Partly because we only had three days to ponder a surprise we should have known about for months, and because we didn't yet know some of the things we now know about cocaine. Partly because defense lawyers assumed Cassin would get with the prosecution's program and back up Jiraki's testimony – no doubt a good assumption. Besides, we had agreed to let Cassin sit in the gallery while Jiraki testified, meaning Cassin no longer qualified as a sequestered witness. Also convenient for the prosecution. And, most important, we had far more experienced pathologists testifying for the defense. Their opinion versus Jiraki's opinion looked to us like a slam dunk. As for the phantom autopsy being worthy of a mistrial, that's just my opinion. I'm not a lawyer or a judge, just somebody relying on common sense. When prosecutors do everything in their power to ignore and even suppress scientific explanations for what happened out there, I think it's a miscarriage of justice.

After Walter and I went to prison, my appellate lawyers deposed Cassin. He, of course, stood by his signature on Jiraki's paperwork. But Cassin also signed an affidavit, including: "It was and is my belief that cocaine may have contributed in some way to Mr. Green's death. Although it was and is my belief that injuries to Malice Green's brain caused his death, I also believe that the injuries to Mr. Green's brain may not have been fatal to everyone." That is (a) the most grudging expert opinion of the obvious, (b) something the prosecution nonetheless denied in its case theory and hid from the defense, and (c) a very long way from cocaine being no more important than the color of Green's eyes. It's also a very long way from the testimony of, among others, a neuropathologist, a medical examiner with special interest in cocaine, and another medical examiner who is also certified as a neuropathologist. What the world got to hear as the official explanation of Malice Green's death was Kalil Jiraki – who, of all people, testified that a medical examiner must be "one hundred percent certain" about cause of death in a homicide case. Jiraki also testified that the morgue was his sole employer. Meanwhile, he moonlighted at a birthing clinic, where he signed insurance papers under his middle name and became the subject of an attorney general's investigation – which evaporated just like those warrants against the prosecution's junkie witnesses.

In the final chapter of his manuscript, Jiraki sums up his opinion of what the Green case was about. He says Walter and I knew Green before the incident, and were "tracking" him that night for some reason. Jiraki offers one ridiculous "theory" to explain that falsehood – Walter was involved in an affair with Theresa Pace, and "had noticed her going out with Malice Green." Then Jiraki offers a "scenario based on information gathered from witnesses" – that Walter and I were "high and probably drunk." As you know, I have never been drunk or high in my life, but I digress. He describes the color red as "the only similarity" between Green's Topaz and the stolen Tempo, which is like saying skin color is the only similarity between twins. "Basically, they were drunk and confused," Jiraki wrote, "but their blood test results were never brought up in court. This would have been an indictment of the two officers." Jiraki, incredibly, believes the system that lynched us in broad daylight was actually suppressing information favorable to the prosecution and doing everything it could to acquit us.

Jiraki wrote that the prosecutor's office itself was not impartial – something I would of course agree with, except Jiraki believes the investigation was slanted in favor of Walter and me, because "many prosecutors were ex-police officers." Hello? "The next step in covering up," Jiraki wrote, would have been to bring the charges down to manslaughter, and possibly to an 'innocent' verdict." This did not happen, in Jiraki's mind – and who knows, he could be right – only because he refused to admit that the cocaine and ethyl cocaine in Green's blood meant anything whatsoever. All the cocaine science in the world was, to Kalil Jiraki, part of a grand conspiracy to get some murderous cops off the hook.

"The judge was able to get one officer off," Jiraki wrote concerning dismissal of charges against Freddie Douglas, the black sergeant who arrived when it was all over. "After the pre-trial, it was necessary to strike another deal," Jiraki wrote – referencing the fact that Bobby Lessnau would get a bench trial instead of a jury. "The other two had to face a jury, because no judge could dare to give them an innocent verdict." The idea that George Crockett III, lifetime NAACP member and anointer of 800-pound gorillas, was looking for a way to acquit Walter and me would be the most absurd thing you ever heard, except that Jiraki's conspiracy theory goes even further into left field.

The soon-to-be second black mayor of Detroit, Dennis Archer, had many political allies in the suburbs, Jiraki wrote, but these suburban businessmen would not fare well if Detroit made a comeback under the new administration. "The Green case provided a good opportunity to discredit Detroit. If the officers were found innocent, there would be widespread riots. Those who were trying to affect the outcome of the case in that direction were aiming precisely at this."

The white power structure, in the minds of star prosecution witness Kalil Jiraki, wanted Detroit to burst into flame. Furthermore, they wanted to do this by telling the world about the cocaine in Green's bloodstream. But Jiraki would not cooperate with the evil scheme. "When I did not, they tried to make me pay the price. 'They' does not refer to Dr. Cassin, but to those who stood to lose from a guilty verdict. They lost their chance to burn the city."

A comic-book writer could not make this stuff up. The only reason it matters that Kalil Jiraki made it up is that this is the guy who gave prosecutors a freeway on which they could drive their simplistic theory full-speed. Jiraki's stonewalling on cocaine was so complete, and his martyr complex so obvious, that at one point he answered a defense lawyer's question with his own question: "Is this a trial about me?" In some very important ways, it was indeed a trial about Kahil Jiraki. But nobody, especially the jurors, seemed to notice.

Maybe Jiraki has a way with juries. After he was fired for failure to show up at work, among other things, he sued the county. His suit cited some of the same conspiracy theories I just told you. It named the then deputy county executive, Michael Duggan, as a ringleader in pressuring Jiraki to blame Green's death on cocaine (you know, the conspiracy to protect white investments in the suburbs by inciting riots and burning down the city). The judge quickly threw out Jiraki's allegations against Duggan for lack of evidence. Jurors awarded Jiraki

$2.5 million anyway. Duggan, by the way, had won election as county prosecutor by the time I was released from prison for the third time – on parole and on an electronic tether. The news media were really tired of the Malice Green story by then, and took almost no notice of my release. The Free Press ran a small story inside. Michael Duggan, point man in Jiraki's supposed conspiracy to have me acquitted, told the Free Press that the parole board made a big mistake by releasing me and should have kept me rotting in prison. I'll say it again. Detroit is like no other place on the planet.

Telling you this backroom stuff took me a bit off track from the meaning of cocaine to Malice Green's death. But it goes a long way toward explaining how it is that the prosecution could, with a straight face, fuel the myth of Malice Green's martyrdom as an innocent motorist attacked for no reason by two vicious white cops.

In the ten years after Green's death, I learned so much about crack cocaine's effects on arrest subjects that I can't remember where or when or in what order I learned it. It might seem strange now to think that with all my street experience I didn't know more back then. But keep in mind that Malice Green died in 1992 and crack cocaine didn't overrun Detroit streets until the mid-to-late '80s. I was old enough to have been working in the happy days when heroin addicts would get their fix and – instead of holding up a liquor store or fighting with a cop – pretty much go to sleep. It takes a while to learn new patterns of behavior on the street. It took me twenty-four years to run into someone who behaved exactly like Malice Green. And it took me a while longer to begin to understand why a guy I knew was not going to die did die.

As we were preparing for trial, someone in downtown's First Precinct, stationed on the ground floor of police headquarters, called me and said he had heard that the Philadelphia medical examiner disagreed with Jiraki's version of what caused Green's death. It might, the caller said, be worthwhile to contact Haresh Mirchandani. Much to my amazement, Dr. Mirchandani took my call immediately and agreed to meet with my lawyer. John Goldpaugh was about to get his eyes opened not just on why Green behaved the way he did, but on the whole picture of cocaine and deaths in custody. Goldpaugh flew to Philadelphia to meet with Dr. Mirchandani, a former assistant in the Detroit M.E.'s office and a specialist in the then-emerging study of what happens when police officers try to arrest cocaine users.

As a former Detroit resident, Mirchandani paid attention when he saw the Malice Green story on TV news in Philadelphia. Mirchandani called Bader Cassin and asked him if the toxicology report had showed cocaine in Green's bloodstream. The tox report wasn't back yet. Mirchandani, who halfway across the country had immediately seen cocaine involvement without looking at a tox report, asked to be informed of those results. Mirchandani's conversations with Cassin are just one reason I will always believe Cassin's misgivings about Jiraki's autopsy ran deeper than he ever would admit. Don't forget that Cassin felt compelled to do his own examination of Green's body even before getting the inquiry from Mirchandani.

Not just in Philadelphia, but in big cities around the country, the rise of the crack-cocaine culture was introducing medical examiners – just like street cops – to some new realities. People who didn't used to die when they came into contact with police were acting strangely, getting into physical struggles…and dying. The phrase "agitated cocaine delirium," even though I had never heard of it, was commonplace among the small fraternity of skilled and experienced big-city pathologists. The science about what causes junkies to behave the way they do, and what makes their bodies shut down in police confrontations, is complicated. What's not complicated, and easy to understand, is that medical examiners were discovering that when they got a case of death in police custody, they were also finding cocaine. No two cases are identical. But the common ingredients are a heightened will to resist arrest, a sense of great strength, huge adrenaline surges, and great peril to the heart – typically already enlarged and damaged by drug use. In 1993, Dr. Mirchandani knew as much about this new street reality as any forensic pathologist in the country. His knowledge on the subject compared with Kalil Jiraki's knowledge was like the difference between a trip to the corner store and a trip to the moon.

Mirchandani went to work at the Wayne County morgue in 1976 as a trainee, became an assistant medical examiner in 1978, and in 1982 was named deputy chief M.E. He left Detroit in 1988 when Philadelphia recruited him to run that city's morgue. He had testified as a prosecution witness in countless criminal cases in both cities. As a doctor, he was appalled at what he saw crack cocaine doing to inner cities. As a forensic pathologist with special interest in cocaine's effects, he felt compelled to testify on my behalf "because cocaine has a lot to do with the demise of this young man." Mirchandani asked that his witness fee be paid in two separate checks – made out to agencies responsible for looking after crack-addicted babies in Detroit and Philadelphia.

When John Goldpaugh first went to Philadelphia to talk with Mirchandani, the M.E. asked Goldpaugh to meet his colleague Dr. Lucy Rorke – a neuropathologist Mirchandani often consulted in cases involving questions of brain injury. She, too, agreed to testify for the defense.

Goldpaugh had taken Jiraki's autopsy report to Philadelphia, along with tissue slides, photographs and other materials. When Mirchandani took the witness stand, the two of them got straight to the point.

> *Q:* "And after you looked at that, did you make any
> determinations?"
>
> *A:* "Yes, I did."
>
> *Q:* "What were they?"
>
> *A:* "Based on my study of this particular case, based on my
> previous experience, based on the literature that exists,
> based on my microscopic study of the slides, based on
> the photographs, I arrived at a conclusion that – you
> want my conclusion as to cause of death?"

Q: "Yes."

A: "Yes. That Mr. Green died of cardiac arrhythmias caused by a combination of cocaine, superimposed by physical exertion, stress, and blunt-force injuries to the head."

And there is the first puzzle piece to be had from the expert opinion of key forensic pathologists all around the country. They don't all agree on the details. There are, in fact, some major differences in the details. Some say, flat-out, that cocaine was the cause of Malice Green's death. Some say it was a contributing factor. But all except Jiraki and Michael Baden say that if Malice Green had not been high on cocaine, his injuries would not have killed him. And all except Jiraki and Baden take note of cocaine's effect on behavior, the willingness to resist arrest and do battle with police, and apply it to the Green case. The three who came to court and testified on my behalf took the unusual step of criticizing Jiraki's autopsy, sometimes gently and sometimes not so gently. Mirchandani leaned to the gentle side.

"I'm not here to criticize Dr. Jiraki, but I am puzzled," Mirchandani testified. "I am puzzled and surprised that Dr. Jiraki is a board-certified forensic pathologist and he did not see any role that cocaine may have played in his death."

Mirchandani's associate, Lucy Rorke, had been a medical doctor for thirty-five years, a board-certified pathologist for thirty-one years, and a board-certified neuropathologist for thirty years. Like Mirchandani, she was a university instructor in her specialty. She was chairman of the pathology department at Philadelphia General Hospital, and had been named medical staff president at both Philadelphia General and Philadelphia Children's Hospital. Like Mirchandani, she brought a boatload of association memberships, honors and experience to the witness stand. In other words, the Philadelphia pair were not defense attorney's hacks. They were experienced heavyweights who most often testified as prosecution witnesses, but testified for our defense on behalf of truth and science.

Rorke testified that Goldpaugh and Mirchandani had walked the two blocks from Mirchandani's office to hers, bringing the slides, photos and autopsy report. Goldpaugh asked Rorke whether she had reached any "preliminary determinations" at that time. "Well," she testified, "the determination was that the extent of brain injury that was depicted in the photographs and that was described in the autopsy report were not of sufficient severity to have caused the death of Mr. Green."

By the time she took the witness stand, Rorke also had read a transcript of Jiraki's testimony.

Q: "And, doctor, based on all the information that you had, did you form any type of opinion as to the cause of death?"

A: "My opinion remained the same."

Q: "And, in other words, did you form an opinion?"

A: "Yes."

Q: "And what was that opinion?"

A: "Well, again, that the decedent, Malice Green, had not died of head injuries as had been indicated in the autopsy report and in the testimony."

Rorke and Mirchandani both saw fundamental flaws in Jiraki's work. The first red flag for Mirchandani was that there were no fractures, and the dura – the thick membrane surrounding the brain – was intact. In other words, whatever injury Green's brain had suffered, it was a closed-head injury. Jiraki took a tunnel-vision approach to what, as he testified at our preliminary examination, he regarded as a "run of the mill case." To Mirchandani, there are no "run of the mill" cases, particularly a case like this one.

"This man died when he was under police custody or was being questioned by police officers," Mirchandani testified. "In a free democratic society, questions will be raised as to a citizen, however his background may be, what was done to him, why did he die, if he dies while being questioned or approached or apprehended by police."

Doesn't sound like a man biased in favor of cops, does it?

He went on: "And I think extra care, if anything, should be taken in a case like this."

Extra care would be the opposite of the hot-potato toss between Cassin and his junior assistant Jiraki, certain basic failures in Jiraki's methods, and neglecting to consult a neuropathologist with special knowledge of brain injuries, as Mirchandani routinely did in Philadelphia.

Mirchandani described the reason Jiraki's report immediately put up a red flag: "If somebody is going to die from closed-head injuries…it is going to take some time for that person to die." In his own observation and research as the Philadelphia M.E., Mirchandani testified, "I could not find anywhere sudden death in patients with closed-head injuries."

Coming from a whole different perspective, it seems Dr. Mirchandani was just as shocked as I was that Malice Green died a few minutes after our encounter. Or rather, he wasn't shocked that Green died – he was shocked that any knowledgeable person would not instantly say: "cocaine."

In the previous two years in Philadelphia, for example, the M.E.'s office had examined ninety cases of death from blunt-force trauma to the head. Only six cases were dead at the scene or on arrival at a hospital. "If Mr. Green had died of blunt injuries, if indeed the blunt injuries were sufficient to cause death by themselves, in my opinion, I have no doubt he would have survived for awhile."

So that was the first thing that caught Mirchandani's eye. "Of the six cases that were dead at the scene or DOA at the hospital," he testified in a pregnant by-the-way, "all six of them had cocaine in their system."

Mirchandani also went straight to the phantom swelling of Green's brain. I use the word "phantom" again because Green's brain was not swollen, and brain swelling is central to death by blunt force trauma alone. "People don't die from bruising of the brain," Mirchandani testified. "They die from the swelling caused by bruising and trauma. If the trauma or blows or beating is severe enough, it is going to cause swelling.

The swelling is the one that kills people."

Mirchandani marched Goldpaugh through cocaine's effects on the body – notably a surge of adrenaline that increases heart rate, at the same time that the cocaine is constricting blood vessels. He explained how the risk of sudden death spikes as much as twenty-five times higher when a drug user also drinks alcohol, creating the substance ethyl cocaine in the bloodstream.

Goldpaugh asked Mirchandani to sum up what amounted to his concerns about Jiraki ignoring the most basic checklist of observations to be made before writing down "blunt force trauma," not waiting for a toxicology report, and not even being open to revisiting his opinion when the tox report appeared.

> *Q:* "And you started to talk about the certain things you did not find which created some concern."
>
> *A:* "Yes."
>
> *Q:* "Would you tell us again what those were?"
>
> *A:* "As I said, I did not find brain swelling, did not find herniations, did not find any significant contusions, did not find skull fractures, and I did not find that the patient survived for any length of time. That is very significant."

Mirchandani testified that he had shared his Green autopsy materials with Dr. Rorke, and her conclusion "essentially agreed with me."

Then came this exchange:

> *Q:* "Doctor, subsequent to your involvement and to your indication that you would come and help in this particular case, did you talk to anyone from the Wayne County Medical Examiner's Office regarding this matter?"
>
> *A:* "Yes."
>
> *Q:* "Why did you do that, first of all, doctor?"
>
> *A:* "Because I did not see the brain myself. I just have seen pictures and the autopsy report. I wanted to know firsthand as to why cocaine in the opinion of

the Wayne County Medical Examiner's Office did not play into their opinion, [which] still is cocaine had nothing to do with his death. And I was concerned about that. And I discussed this matter with one of the other members of the Medical Examiner's Office with whom I worked for twelve years."

Q: "Who is that, sir?"

A: "Dr. Kanluen."

Q: "Did you and Dr. Kanluen discuss your opinions and his findings, if any?"

A: "I discussed my opinion with him, yes."

Q: "And you indicated, I believe, doctor, that one of the reasons you wanted to talk with somebody from the Wayne County Medical Examiner's Office was because of your concern that they refused to acknowledge the involvement of cocaine in this particular matter?"

A: "Well, as I said, I am not – I don't know what was refused or what the word you want to use, but I, obviously…they didn't think, or Dr. Jiraki still thinks from his testimony that you gave me transcripts, he still thinks that cocaine had nothing to do with his death. That kind of puzzles me and I am surprised by that. Again, there is so much literature available… there's hundreds of people doing research in cocaine, brilliant scientists. It exists. Only one has to look it up. It is not my finding alone. I was concerned from that point."

Q: "After your discussions or talking with Dr. Kanluen, did you change your opinion?"

A: "In fact, my opinion was strengthened."

Q: "Why was it strengthened, sir?"

A: "Dr. Kanluen essentially agreed with me."

Q: "Dr. Kanluen is the deputy medical examiner for the Wayne County Medical Examiner's Office, is that correct?"

A: "Yes."

Q: "Second in charge?"

A: "Correct."

Second in charge and, I might add, with more experience as a forensic pathologist than Jiraki and Cassin combined. You can see why the prosecution fell in love with Kalil "Stonewall" Jiraki.

In layman's terms, Haresh Mirchandani testified that Malice Green's death was caused by heart attack. He believes that happened because of what cocaine's adrenaline rush, further spiked by the ethyl cocaine produced by alcohol, does during the stress and exertion of struggling with police and after receiving non-lethal injuries in that struggle. Lucy Rorke, the neuropathologist, had a lot to say about those injuries.

If any one witness is living proof that our jurors were going to convict Walter and me no matter who said what in the witness box, that might well be Lucy Rorke. Even ten years later, I run into people who talk about how captivating she was on Court TV, using a model brain to describe for jurors exactly what neuropathologists look for in assessing injuries, moving step by step to ridicule the idea that brain trauma killed Malice Green. She pointed at the brain model and took it apart as she demonstrated, sometimes speaking for several minutes without interruption. Her importance to the common sense of the case was not to testify as an expert that cocaine killed Green but to testify that the flashlight blows did *not* kill Green. If that opinion from Professor Rorke didn't lead you to cocaine being more important than the color of Malice Green's eyes, what would?

She began testifying as if she were doing one of her medical school lectures, applying it to the Green case. First, we look at the two hemispheres of the brain to see if they are about equal size (they were). Then, we check to see if the weight is abnormal (it wasn't). Then, we look for obvious evidence of swelling (none). Then, we look to see if there is any blood between the thin membranes closest to the brain (subarachnoid hemorrhage – a "small amount"). Then, we gently separate the two hemispheres, looking for damage to the bundle of fibers connecting the two hemispheres (in significant head trauma they are often torn – they weren't).

Meanwhile, she is testifying based on Jiraki's autopsy report and photographs. She is describing not just the routine approach to examining a brain, but things you'd expect to find in an autopsy that ruled blunt-force trauma as cause of death. Neither the photos nor Jiraki's report indicated any such findings thus far.

Next Dr. Rorke described the search for the smoking gun, brain swelling – which, as Mirchandani had testified, is required for blunt force trauma alone to account for someone's sudden death. Holding and dissecting the model, she told jurors the names and locations of different brain parts, showed the areas of the skull that hold them, and pointed to the places where a swollen brain tries to find room to expand.

"Now when the brain tissue swells," the almost grandmotherly Dr. Rorke explained, "this part of the brain right here which is next to the tentorium is pushed down into this hole. And that wouldn't be so bad except that there are some blood vessels that are also here that are also squeezed and the blood flow through them is compromised."

"So what we are looking for when we are examining the base of the brain is something we call an uncal groove because this part, which is the uncus, is pushed down from the middle fossa into the posterior fossa, a place where it doesn't belong. So our examination then has to determine whether there is any evidence because of brain swelling or some abnormality of one side or the other, hemorrhage or whatever, which may have pushed this brain tissue which did not have room to remain where it should be normally, into this compartment where it does not belong. So we look here to see if there is any evidence of uncal grooving."

That's the almost cheery style in which Rorke went about her lecture. The photographs of the bottom of Malice Green's brain, she told jurors, showed no uncal grooves. I understood. If the jurors understood, I don't think they cared. It's as if "It doesn't matter; they beat him to death" went straight from prosecutor to juror in a transfusion.

She went on:

"Now, more important than the uncal grooving is…evidence of herniations in this area here…And if you look inside the skull – I don't have enough hands – there is a hole in here. And this hole is called the foramen magnum. Right here. Here's the hole. And this is the hole through which the brain stem is connected to the spinal cord. You can see it is a very small hole and there is not very much space for the structures that normally belong there…Now when the brain swells and there is no room inside the skull, this part of the brain is pushed down through this hole."

I thought she was incredibly clear in her descriptions. Brain swells, gets pushed down into hole, leaves herniations on brain – proof of swelling. No herniations on Malice Green's brain. The process described was the same that a neuropathologist follows in every brain examination. Asked how many brains she had examined that way, she said: "Probably twenty-five thousand or close to thirty thousand at this point."

Whatever much smaller number of brains Jiraki had analyzed in his much shorter career, he didn't follow standard procedure in the next step. He didn't make what Rorke described as half-inch slices of the brain for visual observation – or if he did, he didn't say so in his report…and he obviously didn't find anything in this procedure he apparently skipped. In Philadelphia, Rorke testified, the brain-cutting would be done in front of a forensic pathologist in Mirchandani's office. She would then have a discussion with the forensic pathologist as to how her findings and conclusions about the brain related to cause of death. In Detroit, only two neuropathologists (Rorke and Dragovic) reached any conclusions about Green's brain – and both were defense witnesses. And whereas Mirchandani testified that the sensitivity of the Green case would have meant he, as chief medical examiner, would have done the autopsy himself, in Detroit that job was tossed to Jiraki.

Based on Jiraki's report and the photos, Rorke testified, if she had examined Green's brain she would have told the M.E. to "look elsewhere" for a cause of death. "There was no evidence in the brain of any disturbance of those areas of the brain that control heart function and respiratory function.... And in the absence of abnormality in those vital areas, I cannot make a diagnosis of death due to brain injury."

Goldpaugh then asked questions that brought her first observations up to date – that she had reviewed Jiraki's testimony and that she had the previous morning gone to the Wayne County morgue and examined the brain tissue samples that Jiraki had preserved. Goldpaugh asked if any of that had changed her mind.

"No. In fact it confirmed the impression I had before looking at the brain tissue. I found no evidence of injury in any of the vital areas of the brain which could reasonably have been considered to have caused this man's death."

Rorke testified at length about what she regarded as gross errors in Jiraki's testimony – starting with his reference to swelling in Green's brain, which Jiraki later backed away from. And when the neuropathologist who had examined twenty-five or thirty thousand brains was asked if she had an opinion on cause of death, she said: "My opinion is that the cause of death is not primary brain injury. I would ask my forensic pathologist who did the autopsy to make the decision about cause of death because obviously the cause of death is outside of the nervous system."

Lucy Rorke was a good witness. All those Court TV viewers can't be wrong. Her credentials were outstanding. Her presentation was easily understood. Her theory, as far as it went, was in fact the simplest of any expert medical witness – including even Jiraki, who wound up addressing the swollen-brain issue by saying that, well, Green's brain would have swollen if he had lived longer...which is like saying "the bullet would have killed him if he had been shot."

Ljubisa Dragovic's testimony was less simple. It was, in fact, complicated enough that he would have disagreed with Rorke's testimony that "obviously the cause of death is outside of the nervous system," and yet Rorke testified that she agreed with Dragovic "that the cause of death in this particular matter was not blunt-force trauma to the head" – which led Kym Worthy to shout from the prosecutor's table: "Objection. That was not the testimony of Dr. Dragovic." To which Judge Crockett replied: "That is a factual matter for the juries, not me." Maybe even unbiased jurors would have somehow paid no attention to the medical testimony. It was too complicated. But except for Kalil Jiraki and the 800-pound gorilla the prosecution purchased on its shopping tour, all the testimony led straight to common sense and cocaine.

Dragovic took the witness stand before the Philadelphia pair did. I'm telling you about his testimony out of sequence because it's compelling in a different way. It shows how much trouble the criminal justice system has in seeking the truth rather than a verdict.

Dr. Dragovic is a brilliant guy, born in Yugoslavia, university-educated in Canada, and the first forensic pathologist to win the Russell Fisher Fellowship to pursue advanced studies in Baltimore – the "Mecca of forensic pathology," as Dragovic calls it. He is board-certified as both a forensic pathologist and as a neuropathologist, licensed to practice in Michigan and New York. As the medical examiner for Oakland County – a job he still holds at this writing – he runs the morgue for one of the most affluent populous counties in America. A small part of Oakland County is still rural, but most of it is that stack of suburbs running north from the Detroit city limits at Eight Mile Road. The Woodward Avenue corridor reaches up to Pontiac. Most of metropolitan Detroit's night life is in Oakland County. The Pistons play basketball there. Along with pockets of great wealth, there are pockets of urban poverty and crime. In other words, his office sees every kind of case, including many of the region's highest-profile cases. Dragovic never shies away from controversy if that is where his professional judgment leads him. He once told an interviewer: "If there are one hundred conflicting opinions, that leaves just two possibilities – one is correct...or none is correct." He presents his own opinions with passion, flavored by an accent. His opinion of the Malice Green case is nothing the prosecutors wanted to hear. Parts of it aren't helpful to me, not if you follow the "take the victim as you find him" doctrine out the window. But if you accept that a police officer has a right to defend himself and an obligation to make a resisting felon submit to arrest, then Dr. Dragovic's opinion is as compelling as it gets.

Keep in mind that Dragovic is a person the Wayne County prosecutors thought enough of to consult regularly on homicide cases. Wayne County once dismissed charges in a high-profile murder case – after the defendant already had a preliminary examination and was bound over for trial based on forensic evidence from the Wayne County medical examiner – a dismissal based on Dragovic finding errors in the Wayne County morgue's forensic work. In the Malice Green case, prosecutors weren't interested in Dragovic's opinion. The freight train was rolling.

The defense paid for Dr. Dragovic's time studying the case and testifying, but the money went not into his pocket but to Oakland County to make up for time away from his desk there. Why did he appear on behalf of the defense? He testified: "I found enough merit in the case to come out here and state in public certain things that have to be stated, I believe, because of my personal convictions of working in this line of work in forensic pathology. I think there are certain facts that have to be offered to the jurors in this court and to this court to understand, and to do whatever they want with that."

He explained that he first looked at the case when a newspaper reporter faxed him Jiraki's autopsy report and asked for comment. He recounted the Christmas party at which Baker and Worthy put out feelers for his "cooperation" on the case. Goldpaugh asked Dragovic if Baker was his friend. "I believe he is," Dragovic responded. "At least I am his friend. I don't know how he feels right now." And so began Dragovic's quest on the witness stand to tell the world that this case was not what Jiraki and the prosecutors – and the politicians and the riot talk on the street – insisted it was.

Fred Walker – the union-appointed lawyer who showed up at Homicide the night of the incident and told me to rip up the statement I was writing – wound up as Bobby Lessnau's attorney at our trial. He had been the first defense lawyer to approach Dragovic, giving him Jiraki's report and asking questions about how toxicology fit into the picture. Dragovic asked back then to see photographs and slides, and said he would also want to see the preserved brain tissue itself. Even before visiting the morgue to look at tissue samples, as Dr. Rorke did, Dragovic saw big-time problems with Jiraki's autopsy report. There was "a gap between what was described in the autopsy report and the conclusions that were made," Dragovic testified. "And then a gap between the toxicology report which was clear and standing out, and no integration of the toxicology issue…no factoring into all of these issues and putting it together."

He told jurors the tox report alone gave "clear indication" that Green was high on cocaine at the time of his death, and that Green had recently consumed alcohol. Like many other experts, Dragovic emphasized the ethyl cocaine combination of booze and crack, how it heightens all the effects of cocaine, "particularly the effects upon the brain." That was enough to get him involved in the case – involvement that could just as easily have been for the benefit of prosecutors' understanding. Jiraki's paperwork and the tox report were enough for Dragovic to reject Jiraki's claim that blunt-force trauma alone had killed Green. When Dragovic examined tissues and slides at the morgue, he found still more reason to deny Jiraki's convenient killer-cops theory: "The absolute absence of swelling of the brain and herniations."

He walked jurors through some of the same territory
Mirchandani and Rorke would later explain again – how a brain
has only one way to respond to injury, by swelling and seeking
to expand through the hole in the bottom of the skull…and
how this fatally affects vital heartbeat and respiration control
centers. But there were no signs of swelling, and no herniations
on Green's brain. And of special importance to Dragovic, there
was also no "massive accumulation of water, fluid in the lungs,
is called neurogenic pulmonary edema….The lungs become
flooded, essentially, and heavy, and that is the end point in this
situation, the death." By "this situation," Dragovic was testifying
about death caused by blunt-force trauma. Green's lungs were
within normal weight range, not flooded.

Goldpaugh asked: "Doctor, there was some testimony by
Dr. Jiraki…of some slight or little bit of swelling to the brain,
is that correct?"

"This 'little bit' issue is like being a little bit pregnant,"
Dragovic testified. "For the brain to cease functioning and
render someone dead, the brain has to be swollen and show
herniations."

Dragovic presented jurors color photos clearly showing
that the bottom of sides of Green's brain did not "flatten out,"
losing its wrinkles as happens in the first stage of expanding
against the base of the skull, and that the brain had none of
the herniations that occur as an injured brain tries to escape.
This was science but, for whatever reason, it never seemed to
mean much to jurors. The color photographs that did catch
their attention were the images of Green's shaved scalp and
the ugly but superficial wounds on it. Those pictures worked
well for the prosecution, even if they said nothing about cause
of death.

After ruling out blunt-force trauma as a sole cause of
death, and an injured brain as mechanism of death, Dragovic
got down to what to him as a neuropathologist and forensic
pathologist was the heart of the matter. "In the absence of brain
swelling an alternative mechanism, a different mechanism has

to be offered as an explanation, as a scientific explanation I am talking about, to the public. Because the explanation with the brain swelling is no explanation because there is no brain swelling."

    Q: "Doctor, if the brain didn't swell up, what was the mechanism of death in this case?"

    A: "The mechanism of death in this case was seizure activity that went beyond control. The seizure activity is a massive electrical discharge within the tissue of the brain, and this decedent died in that seizure activity. This did not come about as a simple process. This was the result of the brain being wired up. Wired up meaning the brain being primed up by the influence of cocaine."

And Dr. Dragovic went on to explain neurons and synapses – "the relays that allow us to think, to function as human beings....In between the synapses are certain chemicals called transmitters. The transmitters are influenced and disturbed by cocaine." Adrenaline and related chemicals are the transmitters, Dragovic testified. A cocaine high produces a sort of non-stop adrenaline rush. The presence of ethyl cocaine from alcohol magnifies the effect.

    "When cocaine is in the brain, that is in the circulation, it allows the brain to stay wired up. And then if something happens to cause focal seizure, like a trauma to the surface of the brain, like in this case, then massive seizures result. As a result of that, the heart stops and that is the end of life. That is the mechanism of death in this case."

    In other words, head trauma sets off an electrical storm that in a normal person would subside, but in a brain "wired up" by cocaine the storm keeps gathering to hurricane force. In Dragovic's opinion, if Malice Green had not been doing cocaine, he would have been transported to the hospital, given an appropriate medication, and soon be walking the street. But, Dragovic is quick to add in interviews to this day, that's speculation. What matters forensically speaking is what did happen, which is that Green died minutes after receiving what would almost certainly be non-fatal injuries except for the cocaine. That is the biggest of the many holes in Jiraki's testimony – the hole that led him to say Green's brain would have swollen if he had lived longer. Which led both Mirchandani and Dragovic to be instantly astonished, for different reasons, that blunt-force trauma was listed as sole cause of death.

The red flag for Mirchandani – even before he saw Jiraki's report – was the quickness of Green's death, which doesn't happen with closed-head injuries. For Dragovic the red flag was the toxicology report and inconsistencies in Jiraki's analysis – coupled with the lack of brain swelling. I guess that's three red flags. Mirchandani and Dragovic, each of them the top man in a major medical examiner's office, saw more red flags when they studied the case further. Each wound up believing cocaine played a big role in Green's death. Each was astounded at lack of competence in Jiraki's autopsy and said so, in his own way, from the witness stand.

If the testimony explained my shock when I learned that Green had died, Dragovic also explained the questions that kept flashing through my mind as I tried to arrest him: "What's with this guy? Why is he struggling this way over such a minor arrest? How can he possibly still be resisting?" More cocaine and common sense, and in Dragovic's case, expert testimony. "Cocaine is a very potent stimulant and it will affect the whole body through its effect on the brain," he testified. "It will enhance the feeling of physical capability. It has the tendency to make people feel invincible, to make them behave in a belligerent fashion.... As a result, excessive bravery, being unscared of certain things, of any threat, physical threat." In interviews, Dragovic has expressed his observation about coke-high arrest subjects more directly: "They will fight to the death." In other words a thump on the head that would stop anyone else from resisting means nothing to a "wired-up" arrest subject. Except that the blows wouldn't kill anyone else, but could kill him.

Dr. Dragovic agreed to discuss the case with me for this

book, and explain again what he had testified to almost ten years earlier. Nothing about his professional opinion had changed after another decade of experience. If his opinion had changed he would have said so, because to the philosophical Dr. Dragovic, "a petrified concept is the most dangerous thing." More practically speaking, that view applies to autopsy reports, on which, as Dragovic noted, "amendments can be made into eternity." The contrast is with Jiraki, who had no interest in looking at a toxicology report and who, by the evidence as examined by all three defense pathologists, did not properly preserve brain tissue for future study.

Forensic pathologists obviously have room to disagree on details. Mirchandani testified that Malice Green's heart failed after cocaine and ethyl cocaine made a fatal cocktail when added to stress and struggle and non-lethal blows to the head. Lucy Rorke, neuropathologist but not a forensic pathologist, testified that whatever killed Green it was not brain injury, and that she agreed with Mirchandani's heart-failure scenario. Dragovic, both a neuropathologist and forensic pathologist, comes to a different conclusion. He says blunt-force trauma and a wired-up brain led Green into seizure – but that in someone who wasn't high on crack the brain's electrical storm would have subsided. Instead, the cocaine and ethyl cocaine relentlessly magnified Green's seizure to a fatal result. I look at what all three pathologists agree on: that Jiraki screwed up, and that without cocaine on board Green would not have died.

Dragovic says it can be concluded that Green suffered a grand mal seizure based on "distribution of injuries and the accounts of eyewitnesses." The first part means the non-fatal and minor brain bruises were in the area associated with seizures. He's the scientist and I'm just a cop. I didn't see a seizure when Green was on the pavement while other officers got him handcuffed, or after he was attended to by EMS. I just saw a guy struggling against arrest. Other cops who were there say the same thing. At least one civilian witness claims she saw a seizure, but her account doesn't amount to much under circumstances of the struggle and her distance from it. EMS techs – who ought to know what they are seeing, but who have been inconsistent to say the least and one of whom is a court-certified liar – say Green entered grand mal seizure. But I can see it is possible that Green did suffer a seizure. What matters when you stack the experts up against the prosecution's tunnel vision is that prosecutors say Green had a seizure. Dr. Dragovic – whose counsel prior to the Green case was important enough to the same prosecutor's office that they dropped a murder case only because Dragovic's opinion ran counter to the Wayne County Medical Examiner's Office – also says a seizure happened…but that the seizure is explained by cocaine. So you can take your pick of a couple different expert cocaine-based explanations the prosecution chose to ignore.

On the witness stand, Dragovic was direct about that. "Certain things have been taken out of context and placed as a single cause of death," he testified, "which is not acceptable by the standards of modern science and modern forensic pathology." Translated: the cocaine got hidden, and so did the truth.

I told you that numerous respected medical examiners around the country have virtually laughed at the idea that cocaine played no role in Malice Green's death. If you were watching *Sixty Minutes* one Sunday night while Walter and I sat in prison, you caught some of that. Veteran correspondent Ed Bradley sent autopsy records to Dr. Vincent DiMaio, chief medical examiner in San Antonio and at the time editor of the American Journal of Forensic Medicine. Bradley set up the interview with DiMaio by interviewing Jiraki, who said: "Cocaine had no significance whatsoever." Then DiMaio, who said: "He [Jiraki] should have done the toxicology."

Bradley asked DiMaio: "Is he totally wrong?"

"He's wrong," DiMaio said. "I'm sorry, but he's wrong."

Bradley asked: "So he didn't die of blunt-force trauma to the head?"

"No. It's my opinion that he died as a result of cardiac arrhythmia produced by acute cocaine intoxication in conjunction with a violent encounter....He took an awful beating to the head, but not enough to kill him."

Assistant Prosecutor Kym Worthy, who went into our trial with high aspirations and emerged with a judgeship, told Ed Bradley: "If Larry Nevers had beaten his dog Rover to death the way he did Malice Green, every pet agency in the United States would be up in arms. But a human being and we question it? What does that say about the life of a black man?" Bradley, a black man, did a fair and objective piece of reporting. Watching the tape, it looks to me like he has grave doubts about whether justice was served in our case. If you ever get a chance to see it, judge for yourself.

Bradley noted that five witnesses at our trial were among the crack-house customers you have met, and he asked Worthy about that. "There was no evidence," she said with a straight face, "that they were crack-smoking drug addicts."

The street people, Bradley noted, testified they had seen Walter beating Green with his flashlight. Didn't she think, Bradley asked Worthy, that if Walter had done so, blood would have been found on his flashlight? "Not necessarily," she said.

Bradley asked her about the showing of "Malcolm X" to jurors.

"It was dealt with, I thought, very fairly," Worthy said.

"How's that?" Bradley asked.

"I don't remember now," Worthy replied.

Bradley also interviewed Don Johnson, a black cop who at the time of the interview was head of the Detroit Police Officers Association. Don said that for starters, a complete Internal Affairs investigation should have been conducted. Bradley asked if that happened. "No," Don replied. "It wasn't allowed. I believe certain individuals wanted this case to go to trial as soon as possible because it was election time." The police chief? "Yes." The mayor? "Yes."

Johnson, who did his career no favors by stepping to the plate for two white cops who went to prison before he became union president, has since retired. I visited him at his home while preparing this book. He described an encounter he had with a doped-up citizen who had resisted arrest to a surprising and lengthy degree. "I have absolutely no doubt, and never did after looking into your case," Don said, "whether that is what happened to you and Walter. It was exactly the same thing."

Worthy and Doug Baker obviously weren't real confident that even the Recorder's Court jurors would buy Kalil Jiraki's testimony on the cocaine issue. They brought Michael Baden into their case as early as February '93. When we went to trial in July, Baden wasn't on the witness list. It turns out that's not required of rebuttal witnesses, and that's where Baden popped up. He was, in fact, the last witness of any kind heard by the jury. I suppose that's viewed as a master stroke in the games lawyers play.

Baden is the ultimate coast-to-coast celebrity forensic pathologist, based in New York but commuting to California and all points between for the big cases and the cameras. When O.J. Simpson's white Bronco led cops on the most bizarre police "chase" in history, Baden was in L.A. to interview Simpson before appearing as a hired defense witness. In 2003, during the run-up to the Laci Peterson murder trial, you could find Baden strolling the beach with Greta Van Susteren and giving Fox viewers his take on evidence in that case. Ten years earlier, Baden was already famous enough to knock Judge Crockett's socks off just by appearing at our trial, again as a hired hand.

Baden's writings reveal that his mindset in homicide cases translates as "always suspect the cops." In one of his books he wrote: "In a murder, medical examiners who can't figure out the cause of death tend to go along with the police theory." The irony in our case, of course, is that Baden was one hundred percent willing to accept Kalil Jiraki's opinion over Dragovic's or Rorke's or Mirchandani's or DiMaio's, among others. Baden suddenly wasn't interested in protecting justice from sloppy forensic work, not when the targets were cops. Baden flew to Detroit, collected his fee, got time on national television, got fawned over by the judge, and may even have swung jurors on cause of death – though I don't really think jurors cared.

Mirchandani and Rorke had gone home to Philadelphia. Dragovic was sitting in the courtroom. Crockett interrupted proceedings to ask whether the defense wanted Dragovic to leave so he could return to the stand and rebut Baden's rebuttal. Goldpaugh said no, the rationale being Baden would do nothing more than repeat Jiraki's testimony and, besides, Goldpaugh wanted to consult Dragovic while cross-examining Baden. So the very last words heard by jurors were celebrity pathologist Michael Baden telling them to forget about the cocaine.

Baden repeatedly dismissed brain expert Lucy Rorke's testimony on grounds she was a neuropathologist, a hospital pathologist, rather than a forensic pathologist – strange considering that Rorke worked regularly as a member of Mirchandani's forensics team in criminal cases where brain injuries required special expertise. Also strange in light of Baden's pride in being part of a forensics team for the New York State Police, drawing on the expertise of specialists in bite marks and insects, among other things. Baden's message was that forensic pathologists are more in tune with crime-scene circumstances and investigatory procedures, rather than just being lab rats. In Malice Green's death, he saw a case that involved police officers and flashlights, and in his version of common sense and forensic expertise that was enough to sign on with Jiraki, Worthy and Baker.

Almost four years later, Baden participated in a workshop held in New York by the American Academy of Forensic Sciences. Dr. DiMaio began his part of a panel discussion on the Malice Green case by amplifying the same things he said on *Sixty Minutes.* Baden followed by saying: "The reason that sometimes we have differing opinions is because we take different factors into consideration. And I'd like to start this particular story two hours before Dr. DiMaio mentions the altercation…Now this is the car that Malice Green was driving in when it was spotted by two undercover detectives. They followed the car because he was a known drug dealer, the deceased…and the testimony was that these, the detectives, followed this car for about two hours. During which time he [Green] committed absolutely no infractions. You know, he wasn't weaving…he wasn't doing anything that would have permitted them arresting him."

That little flash-forward has everything to do with Baden's testimony at our trial. I can say a lot of things about his remarks at that New York meeting, while I was in prison, but first I'd quote Michael Baden himself: "Medical examiners who can't figure out the cause of death tend to go along with the police theory." Here's a guy who in justifying his testimony is still hung up four years later on stuff that Baker and Worthy undoubtedly fed him in February when they first hired him to testify. Walter Budzyn and I did not stalk Malice Green for two hours. It was more like two seconds, whatever amount of time it took us to pull out from Twenty-Third Street onto Warren Avenue and instantly stop when Green parked in front of the dope pad. That whole stalking thing is a fabrication, only one tick removed from the street hysteria that tried to explain it – that Walter and I were drunk, or high…or that one of us had been "dating" Theresa Pace…or that I had been stalking Malice Green not for two hours, but ever since he was a teenager and I beat up his friend Victor who was still limping years later at his funeral. This whole scenario is insane, not just the street hysteria but the stuff Baden told his fellow pathologists to be facts.

Who cares if Michael Baden doesn't know the difference between a plainclothes patrolman and an "undercover detective," or that a lot of Starsky-and-Hutch haters would gasp to hear Malice Green described as "a known drug dealer"? What does it matter that Baden once again went into his Quincy-vs-the-lab-rats routine, lecturing his fellow pathologists on the importance of circumstances and street realities as opposed to what their lab tests and studies of similar cases tell them? Simple. He doesn't know what the hell he's talking about, not in terms of how the Malice Green arrest came down. And these things he had all wrong obviously had great impact on his opinion – something I know because he says so. So much for the 800-pound gorilla taking "different factors into consideration."

Kalil Jiraki, by the way, was invited to participate on the New York panel but, as the moderator said, "we couldn't locate him."

At trial, Baden testified that Green died of a concussion. When Lucy Rorke could find no meaningful brain damage that would have killed Green, to Baden that just meant that she was looking in the lab instead of on the street, looking at Green's brain instead of at the circumstances, which Baden had all wrong. "This is important in Dr. Mirchandani's testimony and in my evaluations as to why Malice Green died," Baden testified, "to distinguish what the cocaine did to him...versus what the police did to him." Which, of course, is precisely what Rorke, Mirchandani, Dragovic and DiMaio did in their analysis.

"In my evaluations, in my opinion, to a reasonable medical certainty," Baden testified, "Mr. Green did not exhibit any of the signs and symptoms and behavior of somebody who is in a delirium from cocaine...Mr. Green, from my interpretations of the medical findings and the testimonies, was acting in his normal fashion prior to coming into contact with the police." Baden flat-out stated that Green's cocaine use the day he died had been too long before our altercation to affect either his behavior or the way his body responded to the altercation. Dr. Charles Wetli, chief medical examiner for Suffolk County, New York, is a foremost expert – some would say *the* foremost expert – regarding cocaine's effects on behavior. Wetli was in the hallway waiting to testify as a defense witness at my second trial. My lawyer never called him, partly on grounds of how the "take the victim as you find him" doctrine played out in the trial, and partly because of a sense that the medical testimony was confusing jurors. You can see why.

While Goldpaugh was cross-examining Baden, Judge Crockett interrupted and led a bizarre exchange that you might see in a TV movie. Or maybe not. Who knows what the jurors made of it? Crockett read from the Michigan Rules of Evidence, which say that expert opinion "embraces an ultimate issue to be decided by the trier of the fact." And then Crockett said: "This is the hard part. What is treated as criminal under our law, generally speaking, is not what a person does but why they do it. Do you follow me?"

Baden: "Yes, sir."

Crockett: "Do your years of experience as an M.E. and otherwise lead you to that same conclusion, generally speaking – the law does not punish the doing of an act, it punishes the thought process behind it?

Baden: "Yes, sir."

Crockett: "An evil, abandoned, malignant heart is treated as an evil, abandoned malignant heart. And an accident, an unintended wrong or hurt or harm is not treated criminally?"

Baden: "Yes, sir."

Crockett: "Fair?"

Baden: "Yes."

Crockett continued his little speech through a long series of questions, citing graphic autopsy photos, and apparently suggesting, I guess, that whatever expert witnesses say, Green's injuries were a matter of "malignant hearts" versus "unintended wrongs."

Crockett then had Baden read from the Michigan court rules a passage stating that judges will exercise reasonable control to "protect witnesses from harassment or – "

Goldpaugh interrupted sarcastically: "This witness really needs protection."

Crockett: "No, he's about an 800-pound gorilla, Mr. Goldpaugh."

Goldpaugh: "I'm listening. Believe me."

Crockett: "And sometimes an 800-pound gorilla doesn't need as much protection as a 600-pound gorilla."

Before reading the following exchange, keep in mind that

this is the final witness in a long trial. Jurors, the "triers of fact," to the extent they care or are paying attention, are trying to figure out what it means that Kalil Jiraki, and now this "800-pound gorilla," are telling them that cocaine was no more important than the color of Green's eyes. And Baden is telling them Green died of a brain concussion.

Crockett:"Triers of fact...will have to have predicated whatever decision they arrive at in this case on their evaluation of the witnesses who were presented to them, including you. That make sense to you?"

Baden: "Yes, sir."

Crockett: "Common sense?"

Baden: "Yes, sir."

Crockett: "All right, and whichever theories they choose to accept or reject?"

Baden: "Yes, sir."

Crockett: "Largely on faith?"

Baden: "Faith and the experience of all the triers of fact and the common sense of the triers of fact."

Crockett: "Faith is defined somewhere that I have reason to believe you are familiar with."

Baden: "Yes, sir."

Crockett: "Hebrews, 11:1."

And Crockett had Baden read from the Bible.

Baden: "Yes, sir. How faith is the substance of things hoped for, the evidence of things not seen."

Crockett: "Like concussions, for example, is that right?"

Baden:"Yes, sir."

Like I said, maybe not even in a TV movie. And like I also said, Detroit is like no other place on the planet. At least not that I know of.

So jurors had their night-and-day experts, Jiraki and Baden vs. Mirchandani and Rorke, conveniently summed up by the judge having Baden read from the Bible and making strange reference to "malignant hearts" and "evidence unseen...like concussions." Jurors also had Dragovic, who had to be the most confusing of all. But if you listen to Dragovic, even while he was under fire, you have to wonder how jurors could buy the prosecution's tunnel vision.

It was Baker who drew the task of trying to impugn Dragovic and belittle his analysis of the case. In cross-examining Dragovic, Baker asked a lengthy series of questions ridiculing Dragovic's "agonizing" over whether he could rule the manner of Green's death as homicide – which is not a legal charge, but an M.E. term differentiating a death from suicide or natural causes or accident. Dragovic even testified there was a "remote" possibility that he might have arrived at "accident" as the manner of death, under the circumstances – "a death resulting from confrontation with law-enforcement agents, who are given the ways and means to subdue." Baker, of course, was incensed.

Then:

Dragovic: "We are talking the manner. Now you are bringing in causes. The manner is one thing. The causes are blunt-force trauma and cocaine abuse."

Baker: "Okay."

Dragovic: "Those are the causes. Whichever you want to take, if you insist here that this is the primary physical factor first observed, then you can put it on the first line. As contributory, you can put cocaine abuse. Or if you want to put cocaine abuse as first and beating is contributory, that's fine too. Because if you look into the back of this case you will notice that cocaine started prior to sustaining, or cocaine effect started prior to the time of sustaining the blunt-force injury."

Baker: "Doctor, you are not saying that your opinion was Malice Green would have died without the beating, are you?"

Dragovic: "No, sir."

Baker: "The beating was necessary, wasn't it?"

Dragovic: "The beating and cocaine was necessary to render him dead."

Some of Baker's questions, in retrospect, were obvious set-ups for Baden, who wasn't on the witness list and would only materialize later in rebuttal. The timing of Green's cocaine ingestion was meaningless, Dragovic testified. Its presence is all that mattered. The biggest holes in Jiraki's testimony about death from blunt-force trauma – the suddenness of Green's death, the lack of brain swelling – would be conveniently addressed by Baden's theory of a fatal concussion…something no one else, not even Jiraki, proposed. Baker was, unknown to us, previewing the concussion theory when he asked Dragovic.

Baker: "Can't somebody just be hit in the head hard enough that it interrupts the electrical activity and they die right away?"

Dragovic: "No, sir. No."

Baker: "That can't happen?"

Dragovic: "Only your advisers can concoct that. That cannot happen in nature. I'm sorry." Same words Dr. DiMaio told Ed Bradley when asked whether it was possible that Jiraki was totally wrong: "I'm sorry. He's wrong."

No brain swelling, no neurogenic pulmonary edema, no meaningful injuries to brain tissue itself, death came too quickly. It "cannot happen in nature" that blunt-force trauma alone killed Malice Green.

There is art as well as science to all medicine, including forensic pathology. There are opinions involved. You weigh the opinions and their source and the dominant pieces of opinions when opinions differ in the details. And if the 800-pound gorilla wants to talk about the difference between a forensic pathologist and a neuropathologist, maybe you pay extra attention to the guy who is both. And if Walter and I were luckier, maybe you even get the judge to lecture from the bench not about faith and concussions, but about the concept called "reasonable doubt."

Look at the two basic facts of this case that are absolutely knowable by someone who was not out there on Warren Avenue. A struggle occurred. Malice Green died. Then ask: Where did the struggle start? At a crack house. Cocaine. Why did it start? Because Green refused to hand over evidence of a felony. Cocaine. Why did Green resist arrest? Because he had a habit of doing so, and because the junk in his bloodstream makes users feel, in Dragovic's words, "invincible." Cocaine. Why did Green die? His heart stopped through one mechanism or another because his body was poisoned by dope. Cocaine. What did the prosecution do everything in its power to avoid and suppress? COCAINE! It's the ugly open secret about the confrontation that began between two police officers and "motorist Malice Green," and ended with his death.

16

$5 MILLION SAYS THEY'RE GUILTY

I wanted you to know about the Homicide investigation and about the cocaine before turning to what the winter of 1992 and the spring of 1993 looked like from my vantage point. As we moved toward trial, I did not know about things like what went on in Homicide and what went on in the medical examiner's office. By letting you know those things in advance, you will understand just how blindly I sailed through the storm – which might help explain what happened. Take my legal representation, for example.

If I had fully understood how stacked the deck was going to be, I probably would have cleaned out every piggybank, sold every possession, and borrowed every dollar I could to hire the highest-profile, most-experienced criminal lawyer in town. I can say that because I know Nancy would have approved. Instead, with no job and without an income and not wanting to jeopardize what was left of my family's security, I went with the flow. The flow came in a meeting with Tom Schneider, then president of my union, the Detroit Police Officers Association. I asked for the meeting because even early on I was getting signals that my legal defense was not going to be as vigorous and aggressive as it needed to be.

John Goldpaugh's law firm worked on retainer to the DPOA. Goldpaugh took my case, and his associate Fred Walker wound up assigned to defend Bobby Lessnau. Michael Batchelor, later disbarred for misconduct at the expense of his clients, was Walter's lawyer. I don't know exactly what kind of living a lawyer makes on a police union retainer, or how that impacts schedule and performance. All three lawyers, including Batchelor, did have their good moments defending us at trial. Walker, as you'll see, obviously did a good job for Lessnau. But I realized back then that this was not a Dream Team defense, and I realize now that I needed one. I look at all the high-profile criminal cases that have paraded across TV screens in recent years and I see defense lawyers on the attack, up front and in the media, right from the day their clients are named as criminal suspects. I look back at our case, where we were tried and convicted in the media all day every day for months, and I see mostly silence from the defense – especially in those crucial early days. Right from the moment Fred Walker told me to tear up my statement in Homicide, keeping quiet was either part of the strategy or simply the path of least resistance, probably both. All the lawyering, good or bad or indifferent, was saved for the trial. Maybe it's supposed to be that way, but not when you wind up with a GUILTY sign hanging around your neck before you get to court. It's pure speculation, but I often wonder if the freight train could have been stopped if we had a Famous Lawyer taking our story to the cameras every day from the get-go, countering Coleman Young and all the knee-jerk hysteria about a White Occupation Army gone berserk. That's strictly fantasy considering the economics of it. But I've often wondered.

I had other concerns. I suppose my lawyers at both my trials would tell you I tried to micro-manage my own case. Guess what? When you watch a steady parade of liars telling lies that lead in just one direction – prison – then you do tend to jump up and say something. In the spring of 1993, for example, I sat in my backyard on Bretton Drive with the transcript from our preliminary hearing penciling notes for John Goldpaugh, amazed at some of the things prosecution witnesses testified. The number of times I jumped up and said something in notes to my lawyer was equaled only by the number of lies

I was reading. I don't think that is micro-managing. And I got dismayed by how long it took defense counsel to return my phone calls. A fellow police officer, who smelled cocaine through the nose of common sense just like Dr. Mirchandani did, called me one or two days after Malice Green died. It might be a good idea, he said, to have a private autopsy done on Malice Green's body. You know, in hindsight that was excellent advice. Whether a private autopsy could have been done or not, I don't know. When I passed the idea along to Goldpaugh through the fog I was living in, John said something about it being an interesting idea. But nothing ever happened and the next thing I knew Malice Green's funeral was over.

I had my meeting with Schneider, the DPOA president, and told him I was interested in finding another lawyer for what had become the biggest criminal case ever to involve an on-duty Detroit police officer as defendant. Schneider assured me John was the go-to guy, that I would gain nothing by looking for a lawyer outside the union defense pool. On the other hand, Schneider said, I was free to do so if I wished. And, by the way, if I did that, the union would contribute two hundred dollars to my defense. Not per hour. Not per day. But in total. As much as I thought it a good idea to go shopping for the best, most aggressive, highest-profile criminal lawyer available, I was still in the mindset that somehow this was going to turn out all right. So I wasn't prepared to wipe out the family's financial future just to have an F. Lee Bailey sitting at my table. End of lawyer-shopping.

One night I was watching TV news – either against Goldpaugh's good advice to the contrary, or so early on that I hadn't yet gotten that advice – and Detroit's million-dollar anchorman at the time, Bill Bonds, was blathering about the case. If Detroit is unlike any other place on the planet, which it is, then Bill Bonds was unlike any other anchorman on the planet. He was known to show up on the news set with several cocktails under his belt, and he sometimes stepped so far beyond news reporting that it wasn't editorializing so much as it was

circus. He once – during a news report – challenged Coleman
Young to an unfriendly boxing match (I would have paid to see
it). He once was doing a live interview with Utah Senator Orrin
Hatch, who never met a camera he didn't like, and so infuriated
the senator that Hatch ripped off his microphone and walked
away. It's no wonder that Bill Bonds was the runaway ratings
leader in Detroit TV news and the highest-paid "journalist"
in town. On this night as I watched, Bonds sat in his anchor
chair and began slamming a Mag flashlight against the desk,
demonstrating what his peerless reportorial skills told him
had happened on Warren Avenue. I can't remember whether
that was the same night Bonds responded to news of Green's
toxicology report by idly wondering whether Walter and I had
also been tested for drugs. Maybe Jiraki, like much of Detroit,
was watching Bonds that night and that's where Jiraki came up
with his goofy scenario I told you about earlier. I truly hope
you no longer doubt for an instant that our trial was over long,
long before it began.

The Wayne County prosecutor at the time, John O'Hair, is
obviously one of my least favorite people. He never spent a day
prosecuting us in court, but he was the guy in charge, the guy
who signed off on everything that happened. Of all the many
places I would like to have been a mouse in a corner, one of the
top places would be the meetings where O'Hair's subordinates
presented him with the police evidence package and pitched
him on what to do with us. Remember, the Oakland County
prosecutor said outright he never would have charged us with
any crime, and the Macomb County prosecutor said this was
"an arrest gone bad, not a bad arrest." In Wayne County, O'Hair
was spineless enough to instead listen to the street rumble, the
press, the mayor, a Homicide section that played games with
witnesses, and to a staff of assistants who clearly had big-time
ambitions and a racial/political agenda. Sharon McPhail, an
NAACP officer, wanted to be mayor. Kym Worthy – the woman
who told Ed Bradley we had been treated fairly in the matter
of the "Malcolm X" video, but then couldn't remember *how*

280

we had been treated fairly – was one of the most aggressively ambitious young assistants in the prosecutor's office. She saw a brass ring to be grabbed from the Malice Green hysteria, and she grabbed it with a vengeance. Mouse in a corner or not, there can be no question that those two were loud voices in O'Hair's ear. Loud enough that what I am telling you was two police officers running into trouble while doing their job was officially certified, by O'Hair, as two police officers committing murder.

The Homicide investigation package went to the prosecutor's office exactly one week after the incident. O'Hair announced the charges exactly one week after that. Walter and I faced second-degree murder charges. Bob Lessnau was charged with assault to do great bodily harm. Freddie Douglas, our sergeant that night, was charged with involuntary manslaughter and willful neglect of duty. Freddie's charges made no sense even to somebody who thought *any* of it made any sense, except that charging a black cop made it look less like a witch hunt against white cops. With the NAACP and black preachers shouting "no justice, no peace," O'Hair did their bidding even though, when asked whether Green's death was racially motivated, he said: "We found no evidence of that...no racial epithets." Despite O'Hair acknowledging that it was not a racial incident, race took over and drove everything. There was no doubt that even if we were found innocent, the federal government would discover a way to skirt double-jeopardy by charging us with civil-rights violations. Color me skeptical.

O'Hair went so far as to announce he would fight against any change of venue, thereby assuring that although the arrest was not racially motivated, the verdict *would* be racially motivated. O'Hair needn't have worried about that because, as I've told you, the chief judge announced there would be no change of venue even before we asked for one. "If the trial is held in Detroit and we get guilty verdicts," the Detroit News quoted the Rev. Charles Adams – the preacher who in Malice Green's funeral sermon compared him to Medgar Evars and

Dr. Martin Luther King Jr. – "I think the community will be calmed down." It was an endless procession that added up to: "Convict them of murder, or the city will burn." What Detroit juror could vote to acquit with that result on his hands? The charges were filed, and the riot threats trumpeted over and over and over, with no public dialogue whatsoever from the defense. We should have had lawyers all over television telling our story and trying to unpollute the air.

The Detroit News, under the DEADLY ENCOUNTER logo it would use for all its Malice Green stories for the next seven months, ran a reaction story to O'Hair's murder charges that began this way (italics are mine):

"Detroiter Anton Cross was bitter Monday as he stared quietly at the site on Warren Avenue where his childhood friend was beaten to death by Detroit police.

" 'I'm glad they were charged, *but I don't think they were harsh enough on them*, the way they beat him,' said Cross, one of about a dozen people who flocked to the site Monday after learning four officers had been charged in the death of Malice Green."

Harsher charge? There's only one harsher charge: first-degree murder, which in Michigan is punished by life without parole upon conviction. I have absolutely no doubt – not now, looking back at it – that a Detroit jury would have given the prosecution a first-degree murder conviction if O'Hair had asked for it. He probably could have gotten the death penalty, if Michigan had it. I'm told that Sharon McPhail, O'Hair's top deputy, did in fact want to go for Murder One. I suppose the majority of O'Hair's advisers didn't believe justice could be miscarried that far, even in Detroit – even though a headline like 'NOT HARD ENOUGH,' SAYS GREEN'S FRIEND could be printed with a straight face. You could tear the local papers apart and not find a headline reading: 'TOO HARSH,' SAY PEOPLE WHO KNEW THESE STREETS AND THESE COPS Like countless other news stories, the 'NOT HARSH ENOUGH' story had no balance whatsoever. No interviews with anyone who could talk about the realities of such arrests. Not even a paragraph about our records as police officers. I found myself thinking about a jury, in Detroit, that would read headlines like 'NOT HARSH ENOUGH' for weeks and months before sitting down to judge us.

The Free Press almost apologetically reported, under the headline 2ND-DEGREE MURDER CONVICTIONS UNLIKELY, that no Michigan legal official "could remember a case where an on-duty officer was convicted of any offense higher than manslaughter in the death of a civilian." Keep in mind that includes cops involved in the deaths of civilians who were *not* committing a crime or resisting arrest. A national ACLU lawyer said the same thing about criminal cases against police all across the country. Clearly, even the legal establishment had no real clue as to what kind of a freight train had been sent rolling down the tracks by Stanley Knox, Coleman Young, the NAACP, the preachers and the press.

That train moved fast. Exactly a week for Homicide to report to the prosecutor. Exactly a week for the prosecutor to decide to seek murder convictions for Walter and me. Almost exactly a month for us to be in court for our first hearing.

In the Michigan criminal justice system there are no grand juries. Prosecutors review cases brought to them by police and decide whether or not to file charges (something they were reluctant to do when it was just me, a cop, being assaulted and held up at knifepoint in the Teamsters parking lot). The case then goes to a preliminary examination before a judge who hears witnesses and evidence and determines whether there is probable cause for sending it along to a trial judge. The preliminary exam – known to cops, lawyers and newspaper reporters simply as "the prelim" – is largely the prosecution's show. Sometimes, but rarely, the defense lawyers put up a real effort to prevent the case from being bound over for trial. In our case, I can't disagree with our lawyers' – and everybody else's – opinion that we would have been sent to trial if Bozo the Clown had been the chief prosecution witness. Still I wish I had a Dream Team standing on the courthouse steps every day and making a forceful case for the cameras, where the real verdict was being hardened into stone.

Beginning December 14, the prosecution took seven court days to outline its case, which was top-heavy with eyewitness accounts by the junkies whose outstanding warrants had miraculously disappeared from the LEIN machine. Walter, Lessnau, Freddie Douglas and I could only watch and wonder where we were headed.

Typical of the way the press spun the story, in the prelim coverage and forever, this story from the Free Press: "In the second day of testimony Tuesday, Robert Hollins and Theresa Pace – two friends of Green's and admitted cocaine users – told how a typical evening at the home of Green's friend, Ralph Fletcher, escalated into a bloody street attack after undercover officers pulled up behind Green and Fletcher."

A typical evening at *home* with friends? A "street attack"? Undercover officers? I mean, this might seem trivial stuff at a glance, but months and months of Ralph Fletcher's filthy dope pad – with no water and with electricity stolen by jumper cable – being portrayed as if it were every man's castle being stormed by the Gestapo had its effect on readers, I'm sure. Undercover cops? You know the story on that, and you know that most of these street witnesses were in closer acquaintance with the Third's booster cops than they were with their own cousins. Street attack? Does a street attack by rogue police officers begin with a dope user dragging Walter Budzyn into his car? Or does somebody really believe Walter jumped into the Topaz without reason?

Like the Homicide sergeant said, it's difficult to move the street into the courtroom. But one of the Third's hookers tried. She came barging into the courtroom one day, muttering something about my innocence, or Freddie's innocence... *something* positive about one or all of the four cops who were charged with crimes. I think she was muttering about me, because on any occasion I caught her in the act, in a car parked along a street where I'm sure residents would just as soon she wasn't working, I'd send her home and then have a few choice words for her customer. At any rate, it wasn't a long reach from this bizarre courtroom intruder to the people on the stand testifying against me. Theresa Pace was, after all, a hooker herself. One big difference is that the intruder wasn't coached by Homicide or the prosecution. I really doubt she had anything important to say, and she wasn't exactly the kind of character witness who translates well to the witness stand. But, who knows, maybe she was lurking in the neighborhood that night and saw something. At any rate, she was ordered out of the courtroom. Her escort, Monica Childs, was told to get a statement from her. I'm told Childs reported the intruder was too drunk or too high to bother with. I didn't trust Childs, even then. Goldpaugh – one in a long procession of people who would not fully understand that I had countless good reasons to be cynical about such things – was OK with Childs's judgment. Assistant Prosecutor Kym Worthy was more than OK with the street people's testimony, saying: "Just because these people use drugs doesn't mean they can't be truthful." To Ed Bradley, she added that there was no credible evidence that they were junkies. Sure.

Around the time of the prelim, there was another piece of street business that did not make its way into the courtroom. A week before the Green incident, Walter and I stopped a suburbanite just down the street from Fletch Man's dope pad. There can be little doubt about why this guy was in the neighborhood. After he flunked my standard street encounter test (meaning the things he said regarding age, address, his evening's agenda, etc., did not add up), I patted him down and checked his wallet. We ran him on the MDT, which came back with an outstanding felony warrant – probably receiving stolen property, a common enough warrant in and around the drug trade. He begged us not to take him in, and we told him that with a warrant on the MDT we had no choice. Apparently, other than taking him to the station for booking we were courteous enough, because around the time of our prelim a most curious thing occurred. This same guy went back down to the Third station and voluntarily made a report that the neighborhood drug supplier – who no doubt contributed to the "quiet evenings at home" in Fletch Man's "residence" – had put out word that he'd pay $10,000 for a hit on Walter and me. I know the suburbanite came down and volunteered the story because I saw the preliminary complaint report. That PCR is unavailable to me now.

I have no idea if the guy's allegation was true. I certainly have no idea why he would report it if there wasn't something to it. The only time I ever saw him in my life was the night I arrested him. I do know that at the time of the Green incident I was actively looking for the same dealer who supposedly had a bounty out on Walter and me. He had lived in a fortified apartment and was the subject of an outstanding warrant from the Narcotics Section. You never know about the things street people and druggies will say, but it's safe to assume this dealer did not like booster cops who tried to clean up the neighborhood when his livelihood depended on keeping it dirty. At any rate, this story, needless to say, is not one of the stories about Walter and me that made its way into the press.

Regarding the things street people will say, in the case of Theresa Pace, I don't see why anyone would discount her original, unvarnished version of events, the one that said incriminating things about her friend Malice Green. Pace's testimony at the preliminary exam was a careful march-through of her second statement to Homicide, the one extracted by Homicide brass. Except that now Green was not clutching cocaine rocks – and not even the baggie of her second statement – but *a piece of paper.*

The Detroit News was often less stereotyped than the Free Press in the way it approached daily coverage of the case. That is to say, a lot depended on which News story you read. It was the News, after all, that in the first days after the incident quoted anonymous witnesses as saying I had sent an EMS rig away from a dying man. That's the kind of story that comes from a police-beat reporter who plays cards with Homicide brass whose first goal is to string up two white cops. On the other hand, the News story from this same day of the prelim as the Free Press story above, took a straightforward approach to what was said on the witness stand. One of the story's reporters, Ann Sweeney, would, several years down the road, write an impassioned and fact-laden letter to Michigan's governor asking him to commute the sentences Walter and I were serving. Anyway, the News story on the same day that the Free Press talked about a "street attack" outside Fletch Man's "home," reported Pace's testimony that Green "hit the [crack] pipe one time. Malice came to smoke. That's the only time he ever came over there." Pace and Green shared the pipe before he drove down the street to the beer store. What Green was coming back for when Walter and I pulled up behind him was no doubt, as Pace testified, "to smoke." It is really hard to imagine anyone visiting Fletch Man's alleged domicile for any other reason.

That day's News story from the prelim is an example of how some of the truth was put out there for the taking, by anyone who cared about it and was willing to listen beyond all the drumbeats.

Reviewing the street people's prelim testimony after all these years, one thing is amazing. Keep in mind that in the end I was judged to be the most brutal of the brutes, the person whose actions "killed Malice Green." But if you read what these street people testified at the prelim, telling the world what they supposedly saw, it was Walter who savagely went after Green, doing massive damage to him even before I got involved. That is nonsense. If there is anyone in the world who would benefit from saying otherwise, it's me. But that is nonsense and I won't say it.

Robert Knox – the drug user who had given me the nickname "Starsky" – testified at the prelim on the same day Stanley Knox held his chief's hearing and fired the four of us cop defendants, with my own piece of paper saying I was fired "for committing second degree murder." A DPOA spokesman told reporters Stanley Knox had already convicted us on day one, "so this was not totally unexpected." Expected, yes. But also unprecedented, and a gross violation of due process. We had not yet been ordered to trial. It was a week before Christmas. Fred Walker was asked for comment and said: "I expected them to do this. I expected them to treat them unfairly, and they came through." Coleman Young's spokesman justified the firing by saying we had asked for a quick determination of our status, and said that was the main reason for denying our request to delay the chief's hearing at least until after the preliminary exam. Go figure that one.

The three officers who were suspended but not charged with a crime – Gotelaere, Gunther and Kijek – weren't fired that day. They remained on suspension awaiting departmental discipline. Without a foreordained criminal conviction, they would later be able to extract a certain amount of justice from the department. More on that later.

Goldpaugh brought me my dismissal notice before Robert Knox took the stand late in the afternoon to testify that I "came up with" a rock of cocaine while Walter was "beating" Green. Under prosecution guidance, Knox testified he didn't know where the rock came from. Of course he knew. It came from Green's hand, the one I readily admit to whacking, hard, with my flashlight – while Knox and the rest of the street people watched. Theresa Pace saw crack rocks, then amazingly decided she didn't see any, just a baggie, then finally decided she had seen not crack or a baggie but a piece of paper. Robert Knox saw a rock of cocaine, but didn't know where it came from. The prosecution would do anything to paint this scene as something other than what it was. Knox, for example, testified essentially the truth about me tossing around the toy gun. There was absolutely nothing in the testimony, or the news stories, however, to show what this banter obviously meant – that I, with twenty-four years of street experience, had no idea anything had happened that might mean Malice Green was dying. Instead, it was reported I committed a crass act while "Malice Green lay dying in a pool of blood."

Sometimes the prosecution was so enthusiastic about what these street people testified that they called witnesses who said things so ridiculous you'd think they were *our* witnesses. Emanuel Brown, for example, testified he saw me hit Green on the head twelve times – *with a leather blackjack.* Invited by defense attorneys to clarify, Brown was suddenly not certain he had seen a blackjack. Of course he hadn't. I didn't have a blackjack. But if someone's imagination presumes in great, inaccurate detail what a white police officer is going to do to a black citizen, then that is what they see.

Ralph Fletcher, who had been unable to identify Walter in a lineup, testified that he saw me swing my flashlight in two "upper cuts, like a golf swing," as Green lay in the Topaz. Couldn't have happened that way – not the way Green was hanging out of the car during the second half of the confrontation, which you well know by now…besides which, Fletcher was not present at that time. And it couldn't have happened that way in the first half of the confrontation, when Fletcher was present – not unless all the other street people, who did not report seeing me strike Green on the head, were blind. Fletch Man testified that I was using a weapon the length and size of a nightstick – something which, in these folks' imaginations, I might carry along with a blackjack.

Jiraki told the judge at the prelim that Green had been struck fourteen times by flashlights – a number which you know shrunk by half during Jiraki's testimony at trial. Freddie Douglas's lawyer, David Griem, went straight after Jiraki – pointing out that there was a struggle, that Green had been in contact with pavement, saying that microscopic analysis of Green's heart should have been done at autopsy. Jiraki's stonewalling was already apparent – with one newspaper reporting he "held up better than Fletcher under non-stop, painstaking questions." Jiraki testified at the prelim: "There were bleeding and bruises all over the brain." Not true, as you have seen.

Goldpaugh told a reporter after the court day ended: "We have a doctor who didn't do a thorough exam, and we have one of the local gentry who's going to say whatever he wants. He finally admits he never saw Larry – Officer Nevers – hit the man." The paper reported that "the cops' attorneys appeared pleased with the day's events."

Maybe all of us on the defense thought it was a good day at the time. The same story's next paragraph gets closer, in retrospect, to the prevailing belief on the streets: "They're full of it," said Rogell Hawkins, Green's brother-in-law. "They did what they did, and it's murder, and everybody knows that. If I did what they did, I wouldn't be walking around on bond, I'd be in jail." Rogell Hawkins, like most in the community, had his mind already made up.

The most important witnesses of all – more important than the expert witnesses, infinitely more important than the street people – made their first public statements at our preliminary hearing. The four Emergency Medical Service technicians who arrived on the Warren Avenue scene are the *one* set of witnesses without whom I cannot imagine the prosecution selling its version of this case to anyone. For the average citizen, or juror, I am convinced that the medical experts were too complicated. Take away the EMS techs' testimony, and the entire prosecution version crumbles into a heap of assumptions built on testimony from the street people, Kalil Jiraki, and Jiraki's backup gorilla, Michael Baden. That's why these four EMS techs comprise a big, big chunk of the trial story. You already know most of the other important trial testimony. And if you've been following closely, you've already heard me say that one of the four EMS techs was a court-certified non-credible witness. Another one, I am utterly convinced, was covering his ass and/or protecting himself from the court-certified liar. For sure I can show you that both of these two testified to seeing things that they could not have seen, partly because they weren't there and partly because even if a magician had put them there, things couldn't have happened as testified. The other two techs – the two who were in a position to actually see something – came closer to the truth. But even they were not consistent in telling their versions across a preliminary exam, two criminal trials, one civil suit and a departmental hearing. The EMS crews had their own agenda, their own set of events to be accountable for. Passing all accountability off to the street cops was ever so convenient for them. That's all a very complicated piece of business. And it's the next chapter.

The preliminary exam is where the public – at least those in the courtroom – got its first look at the autopsy photos of Malice Green. The photos are indeed a gruesome sight, especially to a layman. You've already seen how respected pathologists found them far less meaningful. But we'll revisit that issue, too, when I tell you about the trial. Just as it was a foregone conclusion that there would be a trial, and that it *would* be on a murder charge, I won't bother walking through the whole week of preliminary exam testimony.

As far as our future jury was concerned, the most important thing that happened during our prelim did not happen in the courtroom. It happened in a backroom. We were midway through the EMS testimony at the exam when a minor little story erupted on every TV screen and in every newspaper. The City of Detroit had settled the Green family's lawsuit. While a district judge heard arguments as to whether we should be tried on a criminal charge, just a couple days after I was fired "for committing second-degree murder," city hall negotiated the family's $61-million lawsuit into a check for the modest amount of $5.1 million.

How astounding is this, in how many ways?

One way is that it was like all the sell-out penny-ante settlements I had watched the city make rather than chance the anti-cop sentiment of a Wayne County jury, except this one was on steroids. That's probably the smallest, least important way of looking at it. But for twenty-four years I had watched it happen. The only bad marks the press could dredge up about my career, in fact, involved sell-out settlements that any fair reading of the record would show were unwarranted: (1) The kid I pulled out of the pickup truck while working the Tiger Stadium detail. (2) The Kentucky Fried Chicken shootout settlement, which so enraged officers of both STRESS crews who had looked down the barrel of the "victim's" gun. I was used to this sort of thing happening. But this was a whole different thing.

Another way it's astounding doesn't even require you to know anything about the law except what you read in the papers and see on TV. Four cops had been charged with a crime in this case. One likes to think that if we were innocent, we *would be found innocent.* What does it say about that modest proposition when the city pulls out its checkbook even before a trial was ordered for us? Maybe I'm wrong about the four EMS techs being the most important witnesses at our trial. Maybe the most important witness was a check that testified: "GUILTY IN THE SUM OF $5.1 MILLION."

Can I possibly over-emphasize this? The police chief had declared us guilty of murder. The mayor had declared us guilty of murder. The press for the most part had declared us guilty of murder. The biggest non-sports celebrity in town, a TV news anchor, had slammed a Mag light on the anchor desk and declared us guilty. Every black preacher in town had declared us guilty. The NAACP had declared us guilty. What in the world could possibly trump all that? How about the City of Detroit making an unprecedented announcement that it would pay the biggest police-brutality settlement in anyone's memory? How could any Detroit juror not file that away as, "Guilty. Signed, sealed and delivered? The city government said so. Money talks; no cop walks."

As news reporters ran around gathering comment, pretty much everybody was astounded.

One of the most interesting comments came from William Goodman, a Detroit lawyer who specialized in going after police officers, handling – according to the Free Press – more than one hundred brutality lawsuits. The settlement, Goodman said, gave the defense "a stronger argument to change the venue" of the trial. Hey, no kidding. "I don't know if anyone involved thought about that before agreeing to settle the case," Goodman said. "It should have been a factor."

Chief Judge Dalton Roberson of Recorder's Court and Reader's Digest "five worst" fame had other ideas. The Free Press reported with a straight face: "Roberson said he doesn't think the settlement will make it easier to get a change of venue. Once the case comes to trial, publicity about the settlement will have died down and it won't be hard to seat a (fair) jury, he said." Sure.

City Council would have to approve the settlement, of course. Jack Kelly, an Irish councilman and holdover from Detroit's old days, told the Free Press that $5.1 million sounded better than $61 million. And everyone, of course, put everything in terms of heading off a riot. Listen, there were no incidents on the streets of Detroit in the wake of the Malice Green incident, other than "vigils" at the "shrine" outside the dope pad. No one was throwing bricks. The only thing being thrown was a ton of talk – mostly from city officials and so-called civic leaders – about Rodney King and the need to prevent another Los Angeles. In truth, I believe I give the citizens of Detroit more credit in this regard than did the Honorable Coleman Young and his police chief. They seemed to live in mortal fear of a riot that they talked about every time they opened their mouths. I don't know. Judge for yourself.

Keep in mind that information needed to file a $61-million lawsuit was compiled and the lawsuit miraculously filed within four days of Green's death. One of the plaintiff's lawyers was Ernest Jarrett, son of Mary Jarrett-Jackson, a police department deputy chief. Whether Deputy Chief Jarrett-Jackson (and, for that matter, Chief Knox) passed her son everything necessary to type up the lawsuit in world-record time, I have no idea. Judge that one for yourself as well. Ernest Jarrett and another lawyer would split $1.46 million under terms of the settlement.

There is simply no way any fair judge could have denied us a change of venue even before this incredible piece of legal business occurred. After the settlement, it would seem like one of the all-time no-brainers in the history of the criminal justice system, in Michigan or anywhere else. But you know that did not happen.

The preliminary exam came to an end the next day. One thing that is clear in memory is how happy I was for Freddie Douglas. The district judge refused to send our sergeant that night to trial on charges of involuntary manslaughter.

Griem, his lawyer, told reporters: "I did not believe there was a public official out there, a judge out there, who had the courage to stand up to a lynch mob. The incident itself I do not believe was racist, but the charging of Douglas I do believe was racist. I believe the mayor and the prosecuting attorney for Wayne County decided to defuse a situation that could have been volatile and charge a black." Well, yes, of course, a salt-and-pepper case would have looked more credible. There was no other reason to charge Freddie, who came on the scene when it was all over but the shouting and, more important, the handcuffing.

So now we were down to three white cops in the dock: Walter, Lessnau and myself. In the space of a couple of days, we had been fired and bound over for trial, and the city had made a $5.1-million announcement that the trial would be a mere formality. It was two days to Christmas, 1992, less than two months after Walter and I made our fateful, split-second decision to pull up behind Malice Green's car and find out what was going on with this stranger, Fletch Man and Robert Knox.

One odd thing about the preliminary exam is that, in retrospect, I really did not see how much of the upcoming trial's unfairness was previewed in that one week of legal formalities. The EMS techs for the most part I just took as one liar and three guys confused by arriving late at a violent scene. Even the two assistant prosecutors, whom I would come to regard as the number one villains of this case, for the most part just seemed like prosecutors doing what prosecutors do. I only saw them as bringing a B.S. case, not as two people who would be willing to do absolutely anything to make sure it reached the "right" conclusion. I'd get to see that up close and personal soon enough.

Robert Knox's testimony at the preliminary exam would have to be read into the record at our trial. He was shot dead during some kind of drug transaction and therefore unavailable as a witness. On the street, of course, the hysterical rumor was that Walter and I had somehow arranged Knox's demise. On the street you expect to hear absolutely anything. Cows can fly in street rumors. In Detroit, as we prepared for our trial, Bill Bonds took scuttlebutt to another dimension when he went on the city's top-rated TV news show and mused about whether Starsky and Hutch had arranged for the death of Robert Knox.

17

SO WHY STOP
THE AMBULANCE?

You'll recall my invitation to name a criminal trial – any criminal trial – that you think deserved…no, demanded…a change of venue more than ours did. Nancy had that in mind when, sometime before our trial began, she looked to the American Civil Liberties Union for some high-powered legal help. Police officers charged with crimes might not exactly sound like a good match with the ACLU. Nancy's thinking was that the ACLU is all about fairness in the criminal justice system, and about the sanctity of due process. So she contacted the ACLU and asked them to step in and help. Turns out the ACLU was not interested in defending a couple of honest cops who were being portrayed across the country and around the world as racist thugs, no matter what the truth was about that, no matter what was happening to due process and fairness. An ACLU spokesman told Nancy our case was "not statistically significant." It seemed to me that our case ranked right up there in the statistics of unfair trials, but what do I know? The ACLU, as it turns out, did get involved from a whole different direction – to complain about witness Theresa Pace being held in the police department lockup. The ACLU rushed in to defend *her* rights. That piece of business disappeared real quick when Pace told the court she was quite content to hang out at PD headquarters, smoke cigarettes, use the telephone, draw her so-called witness fees, and be the Homicide Section's mascot.

You'll also recall how Homicide Lieutenant Bill Presley became incensed that his bosses, Gerald Stewart and Tommy Alston, took an entirely different approach to Theresa Pace than they did to EMS technician Lee Hardy. After returning from his hunting trip the Monday after the Green incident, Presley was troubled by what he found while reviewing what Hardy told investigators. Presley was an experienced homicide cop. Common sense, experience and intuition told him that what this guy had said – which led perfectly along the path the brass wanted to follow – just didn't add up. But the brass refused to re-interview Hardy. Pace, on the other hand, wasn't just re-interviewed – Stewart and Alston got Pace to reverse key parts of what she saw. The proof that Presley was just another good cop doing his job is that his intuition about Hardy turned out to be on the money. This didn't stop prosecutors from calling Hardy as a witness not just at one trial, but three criminal trials – our first trial, Walter's retrial, and my retrial – a civil trial, and various departmental hearings. To my mind, that is the moral equivalent of the judicial system itself suborning perjury.

Details of what the scene on Warren Avenue looked like are not easy to put into words on paper let alone into spoken testimony. There were two EMS rigs, booster car 3-31, Green's Topaz, the two scout cars directly involved in Green's arrest, Freddie Douglas's car, and the scout car with the two phantom patrolmen from Four – plus various cars that arrived still later. There was the dope pad and the vacant lot between it and the corner at Twenty-Third Street, where the nearest streetlight was. The exact relationship of all these vehicles to the dope pad and the street and to each other was obviously important. That's hard enough to describe – and that's without explaining the much more difficult position and movements of all the people involved at any given moment. This was critical because witness after witness claimed to have seen things they could not have seen even if those things had happened. Coleman Young's failure to provide dashboard video cameras changed everything. It came down to parading street people and the four EMS techs through days of conflicting and often imaginative testimony. Just a couple minutes of dashboard videotape would have provided a window on everything except Walter chasing Robert Knox into the darkness at the beginning of it all. Even Green's handcuffing probably would have been captured on tape.

Instead, jurors had to get their entire mental picture of the scene from witness after witness walking to an easel and moving stuck-on figures that represented each vehicle, then going back to the witness box and describing what they claimed to have seen – and often as not telling either a prosecutor or a defense attorney to move a "vehicle" on the board a little to the right or to the left. Trying to keep track of all this testimony left my own mind reeling, and I knew what happened. I can't imagine how jurors kept track and made sense of it. I doubt any could.

EMS techs Albino Martinez, Mithyim Lewis, Scott Walsh and Lee Hardy were key pieces of this jigsaw puzzle. Martinez and Lewis arrived on the scene when I flagged down their EMS rig for help. Walsh and Hardy then either saw lights and vehicle activity from blocks away, or heard radio chatter, or for whatever reason drove their EMS rig up Warren Avenue and joined the scene out of curiosity. By the time all four had testified, I became convinced there was so much ass-covering and intimidation going on that Walsh and Hardy committed perjury even as to which of them was driving their rig. That's a judgment call you can make for yourself. A lot of holes in the EMS puzzle-solving require easier judgment calls than that one. Especially anything having to do with the testimony of Lee Hardy, who had a history of serious problems with white authority figures, a black belt in martial arts, and a long-time passion for finding a disability ticket off his job – which he finally managed to get as a result of his testimony in the Green case. Besides whatever effect Hardy's testimony had on jurors, his version of events was like throwing meat to lions when it came to the news media.

In court, lawyers on both sides question and cross-question witnesses along what seem like the most nitpicking and detailed lines, though the rules prevent lawyers from touching certain larger issues – such as a complete picture of Malice Green's previous encounters with police officers. The lawyers go repeatedly at details they want to be sticking in jurors' minds when it comes time to reach a verdict. Juries come away thinking they have all the details, and have them straight. With the four EMS techs you could hear testimony for years, and it still wouldn't add up. These guys made formal statements to the Fire Department, of which the Emergency Medical Service was a part. They made statements to Homicide. They testified at our prelim, at our trial, at Walter's retrial, at my retrial, at Bob Lessnau's departmental trial board and his civil trial in his lawsuit, and at a civil trial in the suspended officers' lawsuit. There is no way a judge or jury could listen to these four and have the details straight. The four techs themselves didn't have them straight. Their stories conflict at times within a single proceeding, and flip-flop from one proceeding to another. At other times their accounts are so uniform – despite the quick-moving chaos of the street scene and their separate vantage points – that it smells of careful rehearsal. Some of this can be chalked up to honest confusion. A lot of it cannot. Regardless of my take on this testimony, anyone who sat down and studied the record would see glaring inconsistencies. What I tell you here includes things they said in various statements and various court appearances. Any investigative reporter who wants to revisit the Malice Green incident could do worse than to round up everything these guys ever said about what happened, and try to make sense of it.

There is, in fact, a dark side to this crucial EMS testimony that the media storytellers, in the most-covered trial in Detroit history, never understood or even tried to tell. Pretend for a moment that "motorist" Malice Green's cocaine-enhanced injuries resulted from a traffic accident at Warren and Twenty-Third, and that his family was not handed a $5-million check for allegedly being "murdered by police." In that case it would have been interesting to see what kind of civil suit and judgment or settlement might have come down regarding EMS's performance that night.

Albino Martinez and Mithyim Lewis, despite their own confusion and inconsistencies, gave the most credible testimony of the four. That stands to reason, because they were the first to arrive. Lewis was driving the unit known as Impact 5 west on Warren (headed away from downtown) when I flagged them down with my flashlight. This means that in the prosecution's view I used the "murder weapon" to summon witnesses to a murder. Martinez said they were headed back to quarters. Lewis said they were headed to get something to eat. They parked Impact 5 ahead of Green's Topaz. Martinez got out of the rig. So did Lewis after reporting the rig's location to dispatch.

Martinez and Lewis both described Green hanging head-first out of his car, as I've told you, with me crouched between him and the open door. Martinez had Green facing somewhat to the front of the Topaz, Lewis somewhat to the rear. No big deal. Just an illustration of how two different witnesses see different things, even when they are standing five or six feet away from the things they are testifying about.

If you read Martinez's statements and testimony up through our trial, it's clear that he arrived and saw a struggle in progress. In his preliminary statement to the Fire Department, Martinez said: "Police instructed male to stop moving around and kicking. Prisoner would not stop…Police still order prisoner to stop struggling but wouldn't stop." He told Homicide that I instructed Green to "stop moving around." At our prelim Martinez testified that I told Green to "stop kicking." At our trial he was asked whether Green was making "a conscious effort to do something." Answer: "Yes." And asked whether he "was being told not to do it and he did not listen to the directions." Answer: "Yes."

At the prelim, Martinez said repeatedly that he could not see Green's hands until after Lessnau pulled Green from the car. By the time of Walter's retrial, Martinez was seeing Green raise his hands – but only to fend off blows from my flashlight. This would have been soon after Green grabbed at my gun, and mixed somewhere in the sequence of events in which Green was swinging a fist clenching a metallic object. Or maybe also during the time I believed Green to be clenching drugs in his hand, because Martinez in various statements and testimony recounts how I repeatedly demanded that he open his fist – whether for the drugs or the metallic object, I don't know. I was exhausted and struggling with Green, not standing on a curb conversing with two EMS techs.

Martinez, in fact, says he never speaks to me at the scene. It is Lewis who walks up beside Martinez, and asks what happened. Martinez hears me tell Lewis: "I hit him, and if he doesn't stop I'll do it again." At various times, Martinez said it as "if he doesn't stop," "if he doesn't hold still," or "if he doesn't open his hand." Whatever I said, my intent was to let these guys know that this was a police prisoner, and that I was having trouble arresting him. By the time of my retrial, Martinez tells the prosecutor he heard me say simply: "I hit him." The prosecutor repeatedly asks Martinez what else I said. His testimony remains simply: "I hit him."

Martinez says I ordered Green to "stop it, stop struggling." And that he saw me "flick" Green on the head twice with my flashlight. During examination at trial, prosecutors kept using the word "beating," a term Martinez never used. Then Martinez said he saw me – still holding the flashlight by the large end – deliver two more side-to-side flicks to Green's head: "two quick ones." At our trial, Martinez testified that Green never uttered a word. At Walter's retrial, Martinez said Green: "Just, like moans, and 'wait a minute, hold on.' "

At various times, Martinez said he saw me strike Green three, four or five blows. In the end Martinez settled on four. Repeatedly, he described them as "flicks of the wrist," "just a quick flick," "a snapping motion of the wrist." Remember, he was the first EMS tech on the scene, and he walked right up to it. He is, in fact, the first person on the scene other than the dope house visitors and Fletch Man. Whatever any other EMS tech or cop might have seen, it could not be more than Albino Martinez saw – which in terms of me hitting Green with my flashlight is very much in line with what actually happened, with my account at the time, with my memory now. If the EMS testimony consisted entirely of what the first tech on the scene saw, the tech with the best view, then it would probably amount to a few paragraphs here instead of a chapter. Or maybe there would be no murder trial and no book.

Common sense tells you that this bloody scene – and Green was bleeding profusely from his scalp wounds – would be Martinez's absolute focus as he stood there. So it would be no surprise if his attention, let alone memory, got things screwed up in terms of what was going on elsewhere. At various times he has all four blows being struck while the second EMS unit was on hand, or none of them being struck while the second EMS unit was on hand, or two of the four being struck while the other EMS unit was on hand. He says all other vehicles – the second EMS rig and the scout cars – arrived at about the same time. He has Sergeant Freddie Douglas present during all four flashlight blows, but that simply isn't true. I don't remember it that way. Freddie doesn't remember it that way. These people could not and did not all materialize on the scene at the same instant. At any rate, by the time of Walter's retrial when Martinez was asked whether Freddie was present during two blows or four blows, Martinez replied: "I don't know if he had arrived already."

Like other witnesses, Martinez admitted he had talked to prosecutors about inconsistencies in his statements – including the extent of Green's kicking and struggling…shades of Theresa Pace's revised version of events that happened before EMS arrived. Listen to the prosecution and you'd think Green was passive throughout his arrest. Listen to all the witnesses, even pieces of testimony from unfriendly witnesses, and you will realize that Green was resisting from beginning to end.

Mithyim Lewis, Martinez's partner on Impact 5, was twenty-four years old at the time of the incident and had about one year's experience with Detroit EMS. Martinez was also twenty-four, and had been with Detroit EMS about fifteen months. Both reported some kind of prior med tech work, but they were young and inexperienced.

Lewis's various statements and testimony show the same inconsistency of detail. As with Martinez, many of these can easily be written off to confusion. In fact, where Martinez varied only somewhat from the truth of what happened (whereas the two techs from the second EMS unit testified from some address in fantasyland), Lewis got several key facts exactly right. Lewis saw continuous struggle by Green. At one point, Lewis said, he walked away – "bothered" by what he was seeing – and told Dispatch he needed a run number, then returned to stand near the Topaz. This, he said, is the time frame when the second EMS rig, Freddie Douglas's car and the scout cars arrived. Dispatch logs suggest Lewis is correct. Lewis said none of the blows (or just two, depending on which of his testimonies you read), occurred after Douglas or the second EMS rig arrived. Once Green was pulled from the Topaz and lay on Warren Avenue, Lewis described "up to six" uniformed officers struggling to handcuff him. Lewis sees the keys in Green's hand, sees Green trying to reach into a pants pocket, and he sees the large folding knife that was removed from that pocket. At the preliminary exam, Lewis testified that Green was still trying to get a hand in his pocket after he was handcuffed.

I could go into great detail about the Lewis and Martinez testimony, flyspecking it endlessly. Martinez, for example, has me putting my foot on Green's neck for an instant during the handcuffing process. I didn't. I wasn't involved in that process. Another officer did place his foot somewhere on Green's anatomy for an instant – and so testified at trial. It was, after all, a struggle. But in the end, I don't have a major beef with Martinez and Lewis, not as far as what happened as I struggled with Green while he was inside the car. They saw him resist. They saw Green swing at me with the keys clenched in his fists. (At trial, Goldpaugh made a fist with two keys protruding and demonstrated, asking Martinez whether that was the way Green swung at me. His answer: "Yes.") They saw me using the small end of my flashlight in flicking motions, not haymakers. They heard me telling Green to open his hand, to stop resisting. They heard me shout no racial epithets, no shouts of generalized anger, but instead specific commands to an arrest subject. They, in fact, heard no shouting at all, but the muted urgings of an emphysema victim (me) who was flat-out fatigued from a prolonged struggle...and who was worried about Green following through on his attempt to get my revolver. I've got other beefs with Martinez and Lewis, but their testimony about what they saw as I knelt next to the Topaz was close enough to the truth.

Lee Hardy is another matter.

Long before the Green incident, an EMS lieutenant was visiting a crew quarters on a matter unrelated to Lee Hardy when he met Hardy for the first time. The lieutenant says he was introduced, said hello, and Hardy asked him: "Is it necessary that I speak to you? I have no reason to talk to you." It's as good an illustration as any of Hardy's problems with authority, particularly white authority.

Hardy was thirty years old at the time of the Green incident, with five years' experience in Detroit EMS. That was more than enough time to run up a long trail of similar confrontations and worse. It would appear Hardy had an angel somewhere high up in EMS or the fire department or city hall, because his behavior should have gotten him fired. Here are a couple examples. Try to find anything remotely like them in my own twenty-four years as a public servant.

In August 1990, Hardy was the passenger on a Medic #1 run – meaning he was riding with the patient, a seizure victim who had been drinking alcohol for hours before becoming sick. Hardy had the run called in to the hospital as a "Code One," meaning the most seriously life-threatening illness or injury. A nurse at the hospital made a call to an EMS lieutenant, stating that the hospital's emergency room was not at that time open to neurological cases. When Medic #1 arrived, the nurse asked Hardy why he had not taken vital signs en route. Hardy replied that seizure activity had made that impossible. But upon arrival, the nurse said, the patient had been "talking and lying quietly." The lieutenant, Larry Cry, went to the hospital in response to the nurse's call, and she made a complaint. Lieutenant Cry stepped outside the E.R. and told Hardy and his partner to write letters answering the complaint.

The nurse reported that Hardy then "came into our conference room and in front of another R.N. and a tech demanded to know what I had told his supervisor. I told him that I quoted his words regarding code status and (vital signs). He then screamed calling me a 'mother f------ bitch.' I told him he couldn't talk to me that way and got up to call security. I went out and then spoke to (Hardy's) supervisor who was still outside our E.R. Mr. Hardy continued to yell obscenities to me as he was advised to get in the truck and leave." Lieutenant Cry agreed with that account. After a hearing, Hardy was penalized with a *one-day* suspension.

Still another EMS lieutenant, William Brem, sent Hardy home halfway through his shift one night in 1991 because, Brem's report stated, "in his present state and due to his action, Tech Hardy was not capable of working the remainder of his shift. I felt that to allow him to do so would have been detrimental to himself and the EMS Division." At the point Hardy was sent home, according to Lieutenant Brem's report, Hardy had "violated the following rules and regulations: 1. Insubordination and disrespect to an immediate superior, 2. Refused to obey a proper order from an immediate superior, 3. Was driving in a reckless manner, 4. Accepted a run...acknowledged same...was cancelled by dispatch after five minutes and never responded. Was given (another run) and refused run, putting unit out of service, 5. Acted in a way, in a public place (the dock of Detroit Receiving Hospital) that was a disgrace to the whole (department)."

Lieutenant Brem went on: "My attempts at resolving this matter with Tech Hardy were met by alternating loud threatening vulgar arguments, and dull blank stares, and an appearance of total loss of reality." All the above, the report said, were witnessed by another lieutenant, two EMS techs and numerous other hospital staff and private citizens. "Tech Hardy was not suspended on the spot by myself at this time due to the public place, and the potential of escalated actions on his part."

The next day, Lieutenant Clarence Williams, wrote up a more detailed and colorful report of the same incident. Here are excerpts:

"On June 22, 1991, at approximately 0145 hours, I heard Medic #6 requesting a supervisor to their location. Dispatch asked what the problem was and if they could take a run. Medic #6 replied, 'Personnel problems and no.' They were placed out of service by dispatch. Lt. Brem acknowledged response to Medic #6's location. I queried (Brem) via MDT if he needed assistance. He replied yes, and directed me to Detroit Receiving Hospital. I arrived at approximately 0210 hours and saw (Brem) talking to Tech Hardy outside hospital E.R. entrance near Medic #6's vehicle.

"Tech Hardy appeared extremely upset, exhibiting loud, boisterous, coarse and profane language, yelling: 'I'm tired of all of you fucking with me, you got an attitude.' He seemed to flow in stages of ranting and raving, then periods of just glaring at Lieutenant Brem. His anger seemed to have reached a point that I thought he would physically strike Lieutenant Brem. (Brem) was talking calmly to Tech Hardy about putting the unit back in service, and his ability to work the remainder of the shift. He attempted to calm Tech Hardy, but to no avail.

"I approached Tech Hardy and asked him to calm down, take it easy and what's the problem. (Hardy) said, 'My partner refused to drive for the second half of the night. We always change up. It's a common practice in EMS.' He further went on to say, 'When (Brem) got here, he talked to my partner first and then came to me and asked why I put the unit out of service. I'm tired of them fucking with me. (Brem) came on me with an attitude. They been fucking with me all day – Lieutenant Jones, Lieutenant Jayne, now Lieutenant Brem.'

"Tech Hardy seemed to calm somewhat, but suddenly went into another tirade at (Brem). He would then alternate periods of loud, disrespectful language to exhibiting a menacing expression, arms at sides, fingers twitching, staring at (Brem).

"The unit then received a run and returned to the hospital with a victim. (Hardy's partner) immediately voiced concerns about safety, stating, 'Tech Hardy drove 70 miles an hour all the way to the scene and was reckless.'

"(Brem) spoke to Tech Hardy about his driving, and directed the crew to return to quarters. (Hardy's partner) went to the rig, but Tech Hardy went inside the hospital foyer and continued to stare into space."

Lieutenant Williams went on to report that a union steward showed up and had no more success in talking sense to Hardy. Brem's "attempt of logic and calmness," Williams wrote, "was met with a bizarre and inappropriate behavior, bordering on the unnatural." Williams named six med techs at the busy emergency room's receiving dock as among the countless witnesses to all this. The lieutenant named five supervisors and techs with whom Hardy had recent run-ins and concluded: "I have no documentation substantiating other incidents, therefore none is enclosed."

Lieutenant Robin Jaynes, writing yet another report regarding that same evening on Detroit's streets, from a different vantage point earlier in the shift, stated that Hardy requested to speak with him in person. "I have gotten only one or two word replies from Mr. Hardy or just a stare when I have talked to him in the past about hospital times or whatever, so it surprised me when he began speaking with full sentences. He wanted to know why I was picking on him and harassing him. I stated that I was merely doing my job in both instances. I also told him that it finally seemed like I had grabbed his attention since this was the most he had ever talked to me. He became more agitated, a little louder, used 'motherfucker' a couple of times and told me to stop harassing him. I restated that I would do my job as I saw fit and that he could gain my favor by doing his job better. I told him that I was perfectly justified in both actions that I had taken with respect to Medic #6 that night. In the one instance, I was enforcing an EMS rule by ordering them to return to quarters. In the other instance, I was getting a unit back in service when their services were no longer needed on a scene…I told him that if he had a problem with either action he could file a grievance but that I didn't think he had a leg to stand on. He also stated that I was not his supervisor and that I should quit talking to him. I told him that when I was around, I was his supervisor."

This loose cannon Lee Hardy, sullen and intimidating martial-arts expert who accused *others* of having an attitude, would become a star witness for the prosecution against Walter and me. This is the same guy Homicide Lieutenant Presley sought, to no avail, to have re-interviewed because his statement didn't add up. This is a guy who had, by the reckoning of countless fellow EMS employees, some very serious racial issues, particularly when it came to white police officers. And this is the same guy whose MDT message to the supervisors he detested so much – "What do I do if I witness police brutality/murder?" – would cause a sensation in the newspapers and on TV newscasts even before our trial began. Everybody in Detroit had heard the mayor call it murder. Now they heard that a civil servant named Lee Hardy had witnessed a murder. See jury pool. See poison.

The night of the Malice Green incident, a twenty-two-year-old EMS tech named Scott Walsh was assigned away from his normal east-side shift to ride instead with Lee Hardy. Despite his age, Walsh had more than three years of experience and was the only one of the four techs at Warren and Twenty-Third who had completed advanced EMS training. Hardy, when not creating headaches for supervisors, had begun his hobby of looking for a disability exit from the department. He and Walsh made an odd couple. Like Martinez and Lewis they were traveling west on Warren Avenue, but in a more sophisticated rig designated Medic #7. Unlucky for Walsh that he had to ride with Hardy. It would have been lucky for Malice Green if Walsh had been there with a different partner.

Lee Hardy didn't just "see" things he couldn't have seen, he magnified them beyond all credibility. Some of Hardy's miraculous vision, seeing things no one else saw, begins in my opinion with lying about who was driving Medic #7. In one of his early statements, Hardy reported asking Walsh to pull over – obviously something that passengers, not drivers, ask. At another point, he testified that he walked behind our booster car to reach his vantage point – a movement that only would have been made by someone exiting the EMS rig's passenger seat. Meanwhile, only the rig's driver could have seen what Hardy claimed to see. Even if Hardy had been driving, he would have to be at Warren and Twenty-Third simultaneous to Martinez and Lewis arriving in Impact 5. That didn't happen. I say so. Martinez says so. Lewis says so. And Martinez and Lewis did not see what Hardy claims to have seen. And still Hardy was trotted out as a witness – and would be again if this case somehow wound up, for a fourth time, in the criminal justice system.

Could anybody possibly want to be riding an EMS rig with Lee Hardy? I can't imagine it. Could the younger Scott Walsh have been intimidated by this guy? I have my opinion on that. I guarantee you that the short list of people within EMS who had been intimidated by Lee Hardy – or who he had tried to intimidate – was not a very short list. I just don't believe Hardy was driving as Medic #7 approached Warren and Twenty-Third.

As you try to picture all these vehicles and all these people converging on the scene, it's probably a good time to remind you why all of them except the EMS vehicles were there – Walter had radioed for help. And I'll ask you to remember that a help call from Booster Car 3-31 was something that almost never happened. That is why Lessnau, Gunther, Kijek and Goetelaere hauled ass to get there, even after Walter almost immediately got back on the radio to indicate that a difficult arrest was in progress, but it wasn't an officer-down kind of thing. That's not one but two instances of 3-31 asking for help and summoning "witnesses" – Walter on the radio and me signaling Martinez and Lewis to pull over. It is absolutely crazy no matter how you spin it to imagine either of us summoning help if Malice Green was, in fact, not offering resistance, or to imagine us summoning witnesses if either Walter or I was trying to cover something up. Crazy.

Lee Hardy, of course, claimed to see wall-to-wall police brutality and not an ounce of resistance by Green. To Lee Hardy, through all his statements and testimony, I was the image that America saw on Court TV, "that white cop with salt and pepper hair," the one who simply looks mean. Amazingly, beginning from the time Hardy supposedly drove up behind our booster car and stepped from the driver's side of his rig, he claims to have seen me beat Green ten or more times – more than twice the number of times Martinez says I struck him. And Hardy specifically contradicts the "flicks" that Martinez and Lewis say I made with my flashlight. Hardy calls them "short powerful strokes." Hardy says Freddie Douglas was already there. Who knows, maybe Freddie was – because the evidence suggests Lee Hardy arrived a whole lot later than he says he did. Up to seven minutes later, if you go by the dispatch tapes – which would make his arrival not until it was all over. If you listen to Martinez, Hardy maybe arrived when it was half over. If you listen to Hardy, he made all his observations and *then* notified dispatch that he was at the scene. It is *very* hard to pay any attention to Lee Hardy. Remember the medical examiner testimony regarding how many blows could actually be determined to come from a flashlight? According to Lee Hardy's count, he saw every one of them – despite his late arrival on the scene, and despite the fact that careful measurement of vehicle locations and lighting show Hardy's miraculous vision was impossible even if he had been there, and probably even if he were driving the rig.

Keep in mind that despite Lee Hardy supposedly seeing all this happen, the prosecution – depending on who was being prosecuted in which trial – had the dope-house people testifying that Green was savagely beaten by Walter Budzyn even before I left Car 3-31 and went over to help my partner, and long before either EMS unit arrived. Yet Lee Hardy saw every blow. Whatever works. Pile it on. That was the prosecution motto.

Hardy seems unable to tell any story, true or false, without multiplying it by two. The EMS crews say Green had a seizure before he was placed in the rig. I didn't see it, no other cop saw it or even heard the techs say anything about it, but they say it happened, and it fits with Dr. Dragovic's cause of death. But Hardy, and only Hardy, claims to have seen not one but two seizures. Hardy even embellishes the "piece of paper" that supposedly fell from Green's hand as he and I struggled. All I can tell you is that I never saw a piece of paper. At least two of the EMS techs claim they saw one. The alleged piece of paper is not relevant to anything that happened. Even the prosecution did not make anything of it. I don't know how to explain its supposed existence, unless one of the techs thought he saw a piece of paper and it became part of a rehearsed EMS version of the story. No piece of paper was ever recovered from the scene. In Lee Hardy's account, there was not only a piece of paper, but I bent over, picked it up, read it, and then started "beating" Malice Green again. I'm not sure Lee Hardy ever saw a white cop make any arrest he couldn't embellish into a saga of brutality. When this arrest went bad, it was of course instantly "murder" in Hardy's eyes. Very handy for the prosecution.

Scott Walsh, Hardy's unlucky partner the night of November 5, 1992, is a difficult read for me. I told you I thought he was intimidated. In Walsh's version of events, he was last to leave his rig and arrived near the Topaz just in time to see me strike Green once on the head. Walsh claims Green is out of the car face down, not face up, which of course would mean that any blow I struck would have landed on the back of Green's head. There were no wounds on the back of Green's head. That's fairly basic. Interestingly, the face-down position is also the way Walsh's partner Lee Hardy told the story – some of the time. Walsh of course also testified that he was the passenger as Medic #7 approached Warren and Twenty-Third. I simply don't believe that. Whatever Walsh saw he could not be a very good witness – he said I was not wearing a coat (I was), he said I had a gun on my hip (I always wore it in front of me in a cross-draw), he variously said Green had a dazed look or that he could not see

Green's face, heard me say "drop what's in your hand" (one trial) or "drop the keys" (another trial). In his first statement, he said I had mustache (I don't; that would be Walter, and there is no way Walsh could have confused my whereabouts with Walter's). At trial Wash testified, I'm sure with pre-encouragement by the prosecution, that "since I've been working I've never seen that much blood before." In response to cross-examination, he agreed that head wounds bleed a lot, and the amount of blood did not necessarily mean a serious injury.

In his statement to Homicide, Walsh said I also used my flashlight to hit Green in "the chest and back." At the prelim he said this was "in the side and on the back and on the arm." At our trial it was "in the side of the chest and the side of the abdomen." Take your pick. None of these alleged blows, which the prosecution got Walsh to agree were "more forceful" than the "flick" he said I used in the one head blow, resulted in injuries that showed up at autopsy. Walsh – jumping to the end game once again, when Lessnau, Kijek and others struggled to handcuff Green – reluctantly admitted in several different ways, in answer to several different questions, that Green was still resisting at that late point.

That's the gist of what the four techs claimed to see as I attempted to subdue Green. What to make of their all-over-the-map statements and testimony? One of a thousand ways to look at it would be through the eyes of Sergeant Freddie Douglas, who according to the four EMS techs was either there for all of it (Lee Hardy) or for an unknown part of it (the other three techs). The judge at our prelim, of course, tossed out the prosecution's case against Freddie. Freddie, located at his new home outside Michigan to comment for this book, said he arrived at the same time as Lessnau, seeing Bobby approach from the opposite direction. Since everybody agrees that the first thing Lessnau did was dart from his scout car to drag Green out of the Topaz, that would mean Freddie, as he says, saw "nothing except good police work." He doesn't recall making the now-famous "Take it easy, Larry" remark. "I can tell you this much," he said. "If I made it, it had nothing to do with beating Malice Green. From a common-sense aspect, if I did not see him hit the guy, then why am I going to tell him to stop hitting him? All of my people understood that if you screw up, you gotta be willing to pay and there will be consequences. I am not going to sit there and put my livelihood in jeopardy trying to cover up your wrongdoing. Had I seen some wrongdoing by Larry or Walter or anybody else, it would have been very simple for me to handle it. I've got the pen" – meaning a writing utensil and the rank to use it – "and I could let the department deal with it, not try to figure out how the hell I can justify it." That is the view of the only black police officer at the scene regarding the testimony from EMS, and particularly Lee Hardy.

I told you my own view is that some serious ass-covering was afoot by the EMS crews, and an ingrained effort by Lee Hardy to avoid the truth, nail some white cops, and eventually get his own meal ticket out of EMS. How far you want to walk down that road with me is up to you. But whether you go an inch or the whole nine yards, you will see a lot wrong with what EMS did that night.

Walter's struggle, my struggle, the struggle by Bob Lessnau and the other uniformed cops to get cuffs on Green, is the story of an arrest. After that it is a story of EMS treatment and transport. Regulations require police officers to conclude a felony arrest by handcuffing the subject behind his back. EMS regulations require that techs not get involved with an injured felony subject until the arrest is complete. That's exactly what happened after Green's long, dope-driven, mindless struggle with Walter, me, and the uniformed officers. The cuffs came off Green and the techs began to treat him. It might seem like a crazy sequence. But that's regulations, and crazy is what resistance to arrest is all about. That can have no good end, just degrees of bad. Green was subdued, the keys were removed from his hand, the knife was removed from his pocket, he stopped protecting precious rocks of cocaine that already had fallen free – and he was in very bad shape. Far worse than I had any idea he was.

Even Lee Hardy – who had testified that Green was dazed and lethargic as I struggled with him – said that after Green was handcuffed and the uniformed officers walked over to search his Topaz, Green on his own rose up and sat straight despite the cuffs and his ordeal. So much for Green being "for practical purposes dead," as the prosecution described Green's condition even before Lessnau dragged him out of the car.

I observed almost nothing directly about EMS's preparation and transport of Green. I was first catching my breath, then telling Freddie what happened, then being involved in the search of Green's car and its movement a few feet, by hand, to look beneath it.

One obvious thing is that in a city where EMS at 10:30 p.m. has plenty to do, four techs and two rigs remained at a scene where only one person needed to be transported. Another obvious thing is that Medic #7, at least in name and, in fact, by virtue of Walsh's advanced training, was a more sophisticated unit than Impact 5. Which immediately raises a couple questions. Why was Green transported by Martinez and Lewis in Impact 5, rather than by Walsh and Hardy in Medic #7? Just because it was first to arrive and be assigned a run number? Then why didn't one of the two rigs go straight back into service rather than hanging around the dope-house scene? Remaining out of service was, you'll recall, part of Lee Hardy's problem in incidents mentioned earlier. Whether any injured or wounded citizen elsewhere on the west side was left waiting for a rig, I don't know. I'd guess yes, because at that time of night in Detroit it would be common for EMS runs to be stacked up. As for why Medic #7 didn't make the transport, I doubt Scott Walsh was very interested in making the hospital trip with this particular patient and the volatile Lee Hardy. I wouldn't want to myself. Walsh testified that even though he was trained to start IVs and intubate patients it didn't matter, because Medic #7 for whatever reason was not equipped with anything but the basics that night – in other words, it might almost as well have been the 1960s and a ride in the back of a police station wagon. But it's not even clear whether Impact 5 had a backboard on which to place Green. The techs' statements disagree on whether Impact 5 borrowed one from Medic #7, or not.

Paul Goetelaere, Jim Kijek's partner assigned by Freddie Douglas to keep traffic moving past the scene, recalls it seemed like a long time before Green was bandaged, C-collared, loaded and taken to the hospital on Impact 5. It was 10:20 p.m. when Martinez and Lewis notified Dispatch that I was summoning them to stop. It was 10:40 when Impact 5 radioed Receiving Hospital that they were about to leave with a Code One. That's twenty minutes from the time the first vehicle other than Booster 3-31 arrived on the scene until Impact 5 departed for the emergency room. I don't know how you split those twenty minutes between the arrest process and the treatment and loading-for-transport process. I really don't. Half and half? There has been a world of investigation, speculation, and accusation as to whether seven police officers did anything wrong in their half of that time. I don't know how much, if any, investigation went into whether EMS did anything wrong in their half. Let me be clear. I'm not saying they did do anything wrong. Not at the scene. But it's the kind of thing you wonder about when your world gets turned upside down by a Lee Hardy. It's not even speculation. It's just one thing I've got to wonder about. Particularly after what happened next.

Walsh helped Martinez put on the C-collar. He says that's when a seizure occurred, lasting about 30 seconds. It's possible, because at that point police officers had turned their attention elsewhere. Green's head was then bandaged, he was placed on a backboard, wherever it came from, and then placed onto a stretcher, then loaded onto Impact 5. Walsh says both he and Hardy helped inside Martinez and Lewis's rig, four guys working on one patient whose biggest need is to get to a hospital in a timely way. The bandage slips off, and they apply a thicker bandage. Walsh said that by the time they got Green on the backboard his respiration has slowed down. Walsh thinks he told Martinez and Lewis they had "better get going."

Gotelaere rode in the back of the rig with Green and Albino Martinez. Kijek followed in their scout car. Walsh and Hardy hung around the dope-house scene for a few minutes, and Walsh supplied the peroxide Walter requested – probably on my account – to clean blood off myself and my flashlight. Remember, our regular sergeant was not working that night because he was at an AIDS seminar, where he was being reminded, among other things, that cleaning up blood was a vital piece of routine. (Hardy first testified that he had dispensed the peroxide; then testified that it was Walsh.) I was in fact a mess. Not just from Malice Green's blood. I was exhausted physically by the struggle, and mentally because it was unexpected and seemed never to end and had come just a tick too close to that scene in front of the Book-Cadillac Hotel. If I had thought Malice Green was, at that instant, dying…I would have been much more of a mess. But you know that and you know the rest of my actions as the night ended and Friday began.

The run from Warren and Twenty-Third to Receiving Hospital on the other side of Woodward Avenue should take six-and-a-half to seven minutes via the route Impact 5 took. It's freeway driving virtually the entire way – a couple blocks east on Warren, then down the ramp onto I-96, then over onto I-75 and then up a ramp onto the Mack Avenue service drive just half a mile from the emergency room. At that time of night I think – *I know* – they could have gotten there quicker taking a direct route on surface streets, but I was a cop with twenty-four years on those streets, not a rookie EMS driver. Anyway, even on the route they took you could practically fly. Jim Kijek expected to do just that. Driving his scout car behind Impact 5, he was up the ramp onto the service drive for the last quick leg to Receiving Hospital when to his astonishment Impact 5 pulled over and stopped.

Gotelaere, riding with Green and Martinez, says Martinez yelled to the driver "something like, 'Pull over and get back here! I need help.' "

The dispatch log says Impact 5 radioed at 10:46: "We'll be at

Receiving in another two minutes. Please let them know that the patient has no vitals now."

Kijek stepped out of his scout car, watched Lewis move to the back of the rig, asked Gotelaere what was going on, then stood "scratching my head" and staring at Receiving Hospital, wondering why they hadn't continued straight on to the emergency room.

Gotelaere says: "For the life of me, I don't know why he stopped. I thought it very odd that these guys who were not doctors would pull over a thousand yards from the hospital and work on this guy. Even if they lost a heartbeat. If we had something like that, we'd have gotten on the radio and asked the docs to stand by, not stop and work." Kijek, who was fully trained in CPR, wondered the same thing, with the added question of if it was CPR they were doing in there, why two guys to do it? Gotelaere, his attention diverted by Kijek, never did figure out what they were doing. "They were talking so low I couldn't hear them."

Both officers, years after going their separate ways, agree that Impact 5 sat there, within sight of the hospital, for about five minutes. It had taken approximately six minutes to get from Warren Avenue to this fateful stop within sight of the hospital. Even allowing one minute to travel the rest of the way to E.R., the total run would have been about seven minutes – almost exactly the six minutes and forty-five seconds a police officer timed for me in a dummy run a few years later. Instead, Impact 5 took twelve minutes or more to get Green from Warren Avenue to waiting doctors, and at least five of those minutes passed after Green had lost vital signs. The dispatch log puts Impact 5 at Receiving at 10:57, a full seventeen minutes after leaving the scene. The crew claims they didn't call in their arrival until after they wheeled Green into the trauma room. Radio and MDT messages from both rigs had a way of not being made when they should have been, for whatever reason. Who knows? What's known for sure is that two guys with no relevant skills spent five minutes within a softball throw of one of America's finest emergency medicine centers rather than bringing in their patient, and a six-and-a-half-minute run (which could have been shorter if they had gone another route) took at least twelve minutes. Might Malice Green otherwise be alive today? That's not the kind of question, and the kind of liability, that anybody got around to investigating.

So why did they stop on the service drive? Follow this bouncing ball. Martinez testified at the preliminary hearing that Green actually lost his vitals about one minute into the run. "I said, 'First stop you come up to I'm going to need you to give me a hand to stabilize him.' " At our trial, it was needing help "to strap him down a little bit better." What are you supposed to make of that? That five minutes after Martinez says they have to pull over, they finally stop when they're practically at the hospital doorstep? That "stabilizing" a patient without vitals means tying him down tighter?

Impact 5 driver Mithyim Lewis, who said nothing about Green having a seizure when he notified dispatch that he was inbound with a Code One, testified that vitals were lost two or three minutes into the run and that Martinez "needed my help in the back." First he says they were stopped only about a minute, long enough to do two reps of CPR. At Walter's retrial, he mentions Martinez wanting help inserting an airway. One assumes that whatever they were doing back there, Scott Walsh would not have needed any help.

As Kijek wonders, why would somebody require help to deliver CPR? Especially under the circumstances. Kijek and Gotelaere were patrolmen whose nightly duties required a good sense of elapsed time. They are haunted to this day by what both of them describe as five unexplainable minutes while Impact 5 sat parked beside the road. Martinez testified at our first trial that "I think (Lewis) came out to the back to see if I had needed help, but I told him that the straps weren't tight enough on the stretcher, just tighten those and I'll be all set to go." You could flyspeck the testimony from various proceedings and just keep coming up with stuff that makes no sense at all.

Just like stopping the rig made no sense. Unless there was something wrong with the way they had prepared Malice Green for delivery to the hospital. There is just so much about the EMS crews that night that smacks of cover your ass. And, of course, Lee Hardy's off-the-wall agendas.

Back up to EMS's very first contact with the incident, when I flagged down Impact 5. One partner says they were on the way to quarters, the other on the way to lunch. Could it be it was neither, that like a lot of inexperienced EMS crews they were still "trauma junkies," milking clock time on false alarms before putting themselves back into service...so they could meanwhile look for something more exciting to do than take a sick old person to a hospital? Some crews carried police scanners (not standard equipment) and even listened in on booster-car channels. It's possible Impact 5 was scoping out Warren and Twenty-Third because of Walter's call for help. For sure they were not on their way both to quarters and to lunch.

Then Medic #7 gets involved, and two units are out of service. Miraculously, their paths keep crossing all night long.

Hardy and Walsh say they drove Medic #7 to Receiving Hospital after hearing Lewis radio that Green had lost vital signs. All four techs moved around the loading dock and the E.R. with ample time to compare notes after Green was delivered, and before EMS Captain Rick Hughes arrived and ordered them to write incident reports. The world knows that Lee Hardy "saw" things he didn't see. If he wanted to coach the others in any way about any detail or generality about what *they* saw, this was the time and the place.

Hardy was either parked or not driving when he sent out his famous MDT message about witnessing "police brutality/ homicide." The message went both to Lieutenant Bill Brem, who was Impact 5's supervisor that night, and to Captain Hughes, Medic #7's supervisor. Whenever the message was sent, Hughes told Homicide that he opened it at 11:07. "I sat for a few minutes thinking," Hughes's Homicide statement said. "Then I heard Medic #7 calling that they were at (Receiving Hospital). I went directly to the hospital." Brem paid not much attention to the message because Hardy – who another lieutenant once thought was going to attack Brem on this same loading dock – was Hughes's responsibility.

The first tech Hughes saw at the hospital was Scott Walsh standing on the dock. "He said that he saw a police officer clubbing a guy with a flashlight," Hughes said in his Homicide statement, "and he (cardiac) arrested in the truck on the way to the hospital." Keep in mind Scott Walsh's testimony, and whether it amounts to me "clubbing a guy."

Hughes told Homicide: "I then called Lee Hardy out of the hospital, who was standing at the hospital front desk, and I asked him if he could confirm what Scott Walsh had told me. And Lee said, yes, that's what happened." Hughes then ordered all four to write reports. In one of his statements to investigators, Lee Hardy said Captain Hughes told the techs: "Cover yourselves, cover the city and cover EMS." Like anything Lee Hardy had to say, who knows whether it was true?

Hughes says he ordered the four of them separated as they wrote their reports. Hughes, however, was busy making notifications. He talked with several police officers at the hospital, he called police headquarters, and he talked on the phone with Homicide in the direct person of Lieutenant Alston. Hughes, after talking to Walsh and Hardy and viewing Green's body, was gung-ho to get Homicide on the case. (Jim Kijek had already, following regulations, called Homicide...which would soon be interviewing Kijek as a felony suspect.) Hughes is convinced I "lost it" and unintentionally used enough force to kill Malice Green. That obviously puts him on the other side of this case. But he is not a medical examiner. And Hughes once told an interviewer: "I never thought (Nevers) was guilty of murder." Which is a logical conclusion even for someone on the other side. Tell that to the prosecutor's office.

Lieutenant Brem, meanwhile, recalls that the four techs – who already had opportunity to talk with each other – were not separated in any meaningful way as they wrote their reports.

"One was sitting in a car. They were in a circumference of twenty feet of each other."

Brem had come to the hospital not because of Hardy's MDT message, or about the Green arrest, but on a piece of business related to a fatal shooting run Impact 5 had made.

What to make of this hospital scene? Or the fact that Medic #7 kept cruising around the dope house into the night, or that *both* units were logged together back at the scene? How much ass-covering was going on, or how much seed-planting by Lee Hardy, or how much script rehearsing? Or whatever? I have my suspicions. A quest for truth rather than a quest for murder convictions would have pressed those suspicions real hard, don't you think? Consider this: In a murder trial where the prosecution called all kinds of peripheral witnesses who had no knowledge of what happened out there...in which the only direct witnesses were the junkies and the four EMS techs ...neither Brem nor Hughes took the stand. I would imagine that the prospect of airing Brem's other contacts with Lee Hardy must not have had great appeal to prosecutors. Despite Hughes's stated opinion of the case, I have no doubt he would also have testified honestly about the loose cannon who claimed to have seen more than anyone else on Warren Avenue, and who was trolling on his MDT to whip up a "murder" investigation against supposed rogue white cops.

You didn't have to be me or Walter to know something smelled bad about the EMS techs' escalating and inconsistent stories and how these four guys, including Lee Hardy, became top prosecution witnesses in the only murder convictions you ever have heard of against two cops making a lawful arrest. I'm sure that's why the techs met with some harassment out on the street, by officers who did not know me personally – even cops in the suburbs. There were cold shoulders at trauma scenes, there were some incidents of overzealous traffic enforcement, there was at least one "keying" of a private car. Lee Hardy even claimed his car was set on fire by police officers trying to intimidate him – something you'd expect an official report would have been filed on, but none was filed. This is not good stuff. It shouldn't have happened, and it certainly did us no good. Walter and I had nothing to do with it and we didn't condone it. You can go round up one hundred cases of criminal charges brought against police officers without finding this sort of thing happening. But in our case there was anger in blue about this runaway freight train bearing down on us because of a good arrest that went bad, and anger at the bad odor rising from the EMS testimony. Everybody knew it could only come down this way in Coleman Young's Detroit, and everybody knew our fate was sealed from the get-go. Police officers who serve justice like to see justice for their own. Any harassment that occurred was a bad thing. But you have to put it in context.

Hardy was successful in his trolling. All the white cops wound up being fed to the hysteria machine. And Hardy's various attempts for a disability settlement finally found one that stuck. He left EMS on a "stress-related" leave of absence. Then on September 20, 1993, the city worker's-comp lawyer, Terri Renshaw, wrote to Hardy's worker's-comp lawyer and offered $20,000 to settle Hardy's claims. Less than three weeks later Renshaw sent another, most interesting letter to Hardy's lawyer. "While we are still willing to redeem this case," the letter said, "another wrench has been thrown into it. You may have read in the paper that Robert Lessnau has filed a lawsuit against the city of Detroit and, among others, Mr. Hardy. Once Mr. Hardy is served, I assume he will be requesting representation and indemnification…Should City Council vote to represent Mr. Hardy, and I am not making any statement regarding this office's or his department's position regarding representation, I would like some assurances that Mr. Hardy will cooperate with his defense regardless of his status vis a vis the City of Detroit. In other words, if Mr. Hardy's case is redeemed at some point, will he be cooperative with counsel in defending this litigation?"

Then the payoff paragraph: "That having been said, I am authorized to increase the City's offer to redeem this matter from the $20,000 originally offered to $35,000. Please let me know your thoughts."

The "I am authorized" had to come from the top. Probably not just the top of the law department, but from the mayor's office. The city not only was fond of repeatedly using the least credible person on Warren Avenue as a witness – it would pay him to testify. You don't often see a bribe paid with a worker's-comp check. As it turned out, of course, they could have paid Lee Hardy $35,000 a word for his testimony and Bobby Lessnau still would have won his lawsuit, and Walter and I would still be sitting in prison. We were there in no small part because of testimony from Hardy and his three colleagues. With Lessnau's case being heard as a bench trial, even Judge Crockett found Hardy to be a non-credible witness. But for Walter and me, enduring our jury trials in the same courtroom at the same time, it wasn't up to a judge. It was up to jurors who had been listening to the hysteria – including Hardy's "police brutality/murder" MDT message – for months.

Like I said, Detroit is like no other city on the planet.

18

"BEYOND
REASONABLE DOUBT"

What's it like to sit at a table, looking guilty, for two months on national television? At the time I didn't realize how typecast I was for the prosecution's script. Unlike the "real" Starsky, I wasn't an actor and wasn't thinking about my appearance, other than being – as always – uncomfortable in a sport coat and necktie. I was a police officer of Armenian heritage, naturally dour-looking and tending to look even more dour with the rest of my life in this court's hands. By now I've watched the trial videotapes. The fact is, central casting couldn't have found anybody in Hollywood who would have done better at sitting in that chair looking like what was advertised – the most brutal police officer in the United States. I couldn't have put a different face on the TV screen if I had thought about it and tried. That's the mug I was born with. I didn't play a cop on TV; I was a real cop on the street. My weeping when the trial ended was real, too.

Speaking of real-life roles, the trial was such an unbelievable role reversal it seemed unreal. I felt like I was on display in a cage every long minute the criminal justice system and Court TV's cameras took aim at me. Before opening arguments of "The Malice Green Trial" on June 18, 1993, I had been completely at ease in a courtroom. Being in court was the second half of my job, the overtime part of it, where I helped put behind bars the felons I brought in off the street. I'm pretty much a shy person in formal settings, and there aren't many settings more formal than a courtroom. But I made so many court appearances as a police officer that testifying actually became a part of my comfort zone. Sitting at the defense table in *this* trial, instead of comfort I felt a cross-fire of emotions that came and went in machine-gun bursts. Disbelief. Dismay. Anxiety. Anger. Occasional hopefulness. Even flat-out fear, that worst of emotions, which on the street I had learned to keep in my pocket. I felt all the feelings you would imagine, almost none of them good. Except that right up to the end some part of me kept feeling that common sense somehow would prevail and nobody could possibly think of me as a murderer. When it finally ended on August 23, common sense never did step forward, and I put my head down and cried. Nancy has said many times that she expected I would buy the farm chasing a bad guy into a building some night because in her mind I was fearless out there, and that she never would have believed our life as we knew it would end at a defense table. She was wrong about me being fearless on the street. Everybody who does real police work has fear, and controls it. At my trial I controlled my fear, too. But, in truth, I had more fear in this court than I did rushing out of a booster car. This wasn't one or two guys in a dark alley. It felt more like the entire world against Larry Nevers. If that sounds – if this *whole book* sounds – like "me, me, me," try being a murder defendant in this particular trial in the unique place called Detroit.

The racial hysteria was about role reversal, too. It wasn't even Walter and me, particularly, who were on trial. We were stand-ins for every white police officer who ever – in reality or in imagination – mistreated a black citizen. As in, "Finally, we've got a couple white cops charged with murder." It was in the air. I think that's where a lot of the crazy rumors about my record as a police officer came from. If you're going to be cast in the role of every brutal white cop who might or might not have walked the streets, then you've got to have a record of racist brutality. I didn't have that kind of record. Neither did Walter. That part of the typecasting didn't fit, so out on the street they just made it up. The NAACP could go peddle the Free Press the story of a teenaged Malice Green watching me beat up one of his friends, and how that friend was still limping many years later as he attended Malice Green's funeral. The story would be printed and broadcast. Everyone would assume it to be true. No reporter would ever follow it up. Ever. But every juror would take those kinds of stories into the jury box. Testimony on the street was more important than testimony in the courtroom. I don't know how anybody could say otherwise. And on the street, reasonable doubt is not exactly a high priority.

The street and the courtroom were two different things, of course. On the street outside Fletch Man's dope-house-turned "shrine," there were no rules of evidence for the TV reporters who flagged down cars every night and built up the myth of Starsky and Hutch. But no matter what decorum and what rules of evidence applied in court, no matter what rulings the court might make, nothing on the street could be kept from the jurors, and the court didn't really try. So the air in court might have seemed cleaner, but it was polluted. For one major example, no one said in court that Malice Green's death had anything to do with racism. That's what the trial record shows. But who are we kidding here? You've read what was said at Green's funeral, which had intense media coverage. *They* killed Malice Green and Rev. Martin Luther King Jr. and if you're not careful *they* will come in the night and get you. Endless, wall-to-wall coverage of Malice Green's death as a racial incident... even though the only "evidence" of such was that Green was black and Walter and I were white. White cops were *they* and Walter and I were every white cop ever presumed guilty for policing while white. Detroit reached that verdict in the first days after Green's arrest in November 1992 and talked about it non-stop until the day our trial began. Then it heated up.

The jurors weren't found in some vacuum-sealed pouch; they came off the streets of Detroit. Not from all across metro Detroit, as in "I live in southeast Michigan, so when people ask me where I'm from I say, 'Detroit.'" Every juror lived within the city limits of Coleman Young's City of Detroit, which was then nearing its current racial composition of more than eighty percent black. The entire municipality was the inner city of America's most racially separated metropolitan area. (I should remind you that I, too, lived in the city I grew up in, refusing to break the rules by having a phony Detroit address while living in the burbs.) And every night our jurors went back onto the streets of Detroit, to their neighborhoods, and listened to what their families and friends and TV news and the newspapers had to say about the trial. If they wished, they could spend each night watching the whole trial, including the parts they weren't supposed to see and hear, replayed on Detroit cable TV. All this was against the court's instructions, of course. No matter. Jurors even talked about the case amongst themselves. The court's instructions not to discuss the case or follow it in the news were a bad joke. The refusal to grant a change of venue was such a racial power play that you can't even think of it as a bad joke. It was more like a crime. Conspiracy to deny justice.

In many ways, I don't have to tell you about the trial. You already know what kind of police officer I was, my perspective on what happened out on Warren Avenue, the avalanche of hysteria that destroyed due process, the racial politics that drove the case against us, the big problems with key prosecution witnesses. You know in detail what the medical examiners said about Malice Green's death, and how desperately the prosecution tried to suppress and spin that testimony – to say nothing of what common sense tells you about cocaine's role in Green's arrest, behavior and death. That's enough, if you followed this story in the papers or on TV, to show you that the story is not what you thought it was. I think you also now know enough to have big questions leading straight to those key words in the criminal justice system – "reasonable doubt." That's without taking my word for anything. It started as a justifiable and routine interview of a citizen outside a dope house. No doubt is possible about that. We were not "stalking"

Malice Green, and Malice Green was not someone I decided
– just for the hell of it and for the first time in twenty-four
and a half years on the street – to hassle and beat senseless,
meanwhile summoning EMS techs to witness it. He was not
"motorist Malice Green…pulled over for a traffic stop." He was
a felony drug suspect making a repeat trip on the same day to
the same dope house – according to his dope-house patron
friends who testified against us. He resisted arrest repeatedly
and persistently (something investigators and the prosecution
did everything in their power to hide). It all went bad. Green
died. The investigation and medical evidence are as you now
know them. No other police officers, to my knowledge, have
ever been charged with murder in the course of making such
an arrest. That means that, thanks to Detroit being unlike
any other place on the planet, the entire history of the entire
country's criminal justice system stands at two-for-two in
convicting police officers of murder in such cases.

But despite having already covered the most crucial parts
of the case presented against us, I need to tell you a few things
about what happened in court.

First, I need to tell you the only good thing that happened to
me at trial. A plainclothes police officer I barely knew phoned
me a month or two before the trial began. Paul Fitzgerald
worked in the Fourteenth Precinct on the northwest side of
town for almost his entire career. He spent many years doing
surveillance work, which he was doing out of the Fourteenth
during my brief stint at the Headquarters Surveillance Unit
in my post-STRESS days. We crossed paths once or twice
in person, and like many detectives or plainclothes officers
around the city he was likely to call the Third and ask about
some perp I had in my mug file. But I really didn't know this
guy at all. That was about to change. Paul knew Detroit's
streets and what can happen out there. He was a wise man, a
funny man, a compassionate man, a deeply religious Catholic,
an eternally optimistic man – but also realistic and strong. As
the trial approached, Paul recognized that I was a fellow police

officer in a different kind of distress and he came running to help.

As little as I knew Paul, he seemed to know me from day one. He had that way with people. Paul called and announced that he was going to pick me up and drive me downtown not only the first day of the trial, but every day. He followed through on that. We became close friends. He was a very special guy. Multiple sclerosis had already begun taking its toll on Paul, forcing him to move to a desk job, to walk with a cane, and finally to retire in the spring of 1993. That summer, during our trial, is when we became close. A few years after the trial Paul would be in a wheelchair. Ten years after the trial, Paul would be dead. My trial was the wrong way to start a friendship, and that long and painful decline was the wrong way for Paul to go. I will forever be grateful for knowing him, and everything he did for me…which was a lot more than playing chauffeur.

I've had more than a decade to look at criminal trials from a whole new perspective. I notice things I never paid much attention to before 1993. The lawyers who yak all day on the cable news channels, for example, always say nobody ever has any good words for the people who prosecute them. Now there's an understatement. I'm sure hardly anybody I arrested felt good about the assistant prosecutor who put them away. I've thought about this a lot. After all, I keep telling you I was just a police officer doing his job. And many people say Doug Baker and Kym Worthy were just doing their jobs when they prosecuted me for murder. Sorry, I don't buy it. Especially Worthy's performance. Then, down the line, Baker got a chance to do it all over again. Given the passage of time before Trial Two, the partial cooling of the hysteria – and the things Baker told the jury knowing them to be wrong – he winds up in my mind as doubly guilty of misfeasance, malfeasance and all-around sleazy prosecution. Just to be clear about my thoughts. Doug Baker got his convictions, but I thought his job was supposed to be a fair quest for the truth.

John O'Hair, the elected chief prosecutor at the time of

Trial One, never set foot in our courtroom. But he was the front-man in the investigation and the charge decisions, along with his top assistant, mayoral candidate Sharon McPhail. You know I believe I was guilty of no crime. Maybe you don't accept that. But choose one hundred rational people at random and ask how many would say Walter and I should be charged with murder. Then ask, if the prosecutors were so eager to turn the arrest of Malice Green into a murder case...what does that say about their willingness to overstep every inch of the way, to pile it on, to obscure, to spin or even avoid the truth? Keep in mind that the chief prosecutors in metro Detroit's other two counties famously went on record as saying this prosecution was a mistake. That's still another first about our case. And it gives you an inkling why Recorder's Court, the City of Detroit's now-defunct criminal court, defied common sense and refused to allow this trial to take place anywhere else.

I can't believe Doug Baker thought I was guilty of murder, despite his best efforts to "prove" it. Maybe I'm wrong, but I'm serious about that. Baker did a lot of good work over the years as top courtroom dog for his office. A lot of police officers liked his work. I didn't have any reason not to feel otherwise until I wound up in his sights. I want to think that what he did to put me in prison, not once but twice, wasn't typical of his work. Maybe I'm wrong about that, too. Who knows – I've had lots of reasons to readjust my thoughts about the criminal justice system. Ms. Worthy? Ambition run amok. Baker came into our case as the lead prosecutor. Before you knew it, Worthy – wearing green nail polish and visiting with the Green family in the gallery each day – had the spotlight. I now know the trial was over before it started. Some say it didn't end until the day Kym Worthy, cross-examining Walter, shouted: "Couldn't you smell the blood?" She parlayed the Malice Green case into a judgeship. By the time this book went to print, she had left the bench to take her old boss's job as chief Wayne County prosecutor.

You've seen Baker and Worthy at work in my detailed

account of the pathologists' testimony – and before that in shopping for a pathologist who would back up Kalil Jiraki... the guy who aside from ruling out cocaine as a factor in Green's death has written that powerful forces were working to get Walter and me acquitted so as to cause a riot in Detroit, thus driving up the value of these powerful forces' suburban business ventures. You've seen how the nationally respected graybeard of Midwest pathologists, Werner Spitz, declined to testify for prosecutors. You've seen how Dr. Dragovic, the pathologist and neurosurgeon, told Baker, Worthy and their colleagues, "You've got a problem with the cocaine"...and wound up testifying for us. The prosecution's whole case followed that pattern of seeking not truth but a conviction, and on the highest possible charge. I honestly believe they would have gone for first-degree murder if that would have passed Detroit's low standards for a smell test when it comes to race-based accusations. And when you stop to think about it, if the screwy story they tried to peddle – that Walter and I were stalking Green that night – had been true, then I guess you'd have to think they were negligent *not* to pursue a first-degree murder charge. I even believe they could have won a first-degree-murder conviction, but the stench level would have reached far enough outside Detroit to finally attract some serious attention for our side.

The courtroom was a crowded place. Not just a full gallery every day, but two aggressive prosecutors, three defendants – Walter, Bob Lessnau and me – our three lawyers, and two juries (Walter's and mine). Overseeing the circus was Judge George W. Crockett III, whose father had also been a judge and social activist...one of the black heroes listed in the Reverend Adams's fiery eulogy for Malice Green. Crockett – hand-picked by chief judge Dalton Roberson rather than by blind draw as was customary – was, of course, a member of the NAACP, which had been doing its best to convict us in the newspapers. When we actually got to court, it was almost like being at an NAACP meeting – though I can't remember whether Sharon McPhail, an NAACP officer as well as an eager candidate to replace the soon-to-retire Mayor Young, showed up as an observer to make a quorum.

One of the first acts of Judge Crockett and Prosecutor Worthy was to seat a juror who was second vice-president of the local NAACP chapter. This gross violation of fairness floated right through voir dire, the jury selection process, without anyone saying a word. Everyone pretended they didn't know each other. Cozy. Merlyn Washington sailed onto Walter's jury despite denying she knew any of the lawyers or was affiliated with Coleman Young's administration. In fact, she worked in the city DPW under Young's nephew...besides which there was no such thing as an NAACP officer who was not affiliated with the administration. After the trial as we prepared appeals, our investigators came back from juror interviews reporting that Washington had gone so far as to solicit NAACP membership in the jury room, campaign for McPhail, and let jurors know she had an inside pipeline to the current mayor's office. Nice touch. Crockett made Washington the spokesman for Walter's jury. Every time there was a housekeeping issue – Does anybody need a bathroom break? Will this arrangement be satisfactory? – he turned the query to "Juror Number Nine," his fellow NAACP member. There was also a famous case of intimidation involving the only white on Walter's jury, but that gets ahead of the story. Here you just need a taste of who sat in the jury box – the "judges," as Crockett constantly addressed jurors.

The magic poison word "STRESS" was not allowed in open court, but just as race was not to be mentioned as a motive in open court, this was a sham. The news media had been full of my brief tour as a STRESS officer. Just to be sure, jurors talked about it outside the courtroom. And someone made sure Walter's jury knew that *he* also had served in STRESS, which shouldn't have mattered if he had, which he had not. The very mention of STRESS would have been enough to poison a Detroit jury pool even if Walter and I had been STRESS clerks who never set foot on the street.

My jury – after alternates were discarded at the end and the field reduced to twelve in a most interesting way I'll tell you about shortly – wound up with ten blacks and two whites. As Detroit residents, every juror had to live and work among the kangaroo court that the entire city had been ever since Green's death. I imagine all the jurors who voted in the previous election had contributed to the usual landslide victory by the mayor who had proclaimed us to be "murderers." All had heard their police chief assure the world that "we will convict." All had been warned endlessly that without a conviction there would be a riot. I never thought Walter was smarter than me, but I have to admit that he took one look at the situation from day one and never at any moment held out even a small sliver of hope. No question that on this point he was smarter than me. Bob Lessnau, being tried on charges of assault with intent to commit great bodily harm, was smarter than either of us, getting a bench trial and leaving his fate in Judge Crockett's hands. But if either Walter or I or our lawyers had thought that was the way to go, we wouldn't have gotten it. No change of venue, and just one cop avoiding a gauntlet of Detroit jurors, was all Recorder's Court had to offer.

Right at the outset the prosecution pursued a bizarre path. Wade Rayford, the black patrolman who had wrestled down Benny McCoy in a righteous drug arrest only to see it portrayed on TV as a "Starsky and Hutch" operation, was called to the stand. His sole purpose in being there was to testify that a little more than an hour after Green died Rayford had recovered the red Tempo that Walter and I were looking for when we saw Green's red Topaz. The "carjacking" victim himself was called to the stand, and we got our first look at how willing the prosecution was to withhold evidence and testimony they were supposed to share with us. This was the moment Walter and I discovered for the first time that this guy had filed a false armed robbery report, and that his car had not been stolen. We were dumbfounded. The guy – whom we had driven around the neighborhood looking for his alleged assaulter – had committed a crime (filing the false report) after using his vehicle to pay off a debt. Worthy did handstands to make sure it wasn't made clear what kind of a debt was being paid – just as she would do handstands to accomplish the impossible and try to make the dope-house crowd look like upstanding citizens congregating at Ralph Fletcher's "home."

If you put the above together with the prosecution spending hours spinning the fact that we had run Malice Green's license plate on our MDT earlier that evening, you can see what they were throwing against the wall – planting the idea that Walter and I were stalking this man we had never heard of. As you've seen, we ran license plates almost endlessly while patrolling the streets, and we paid no attention to a result unless the car was hot. And you know that when the red Topaz flashed in front of us again shortly after 10 p.m. it was just another candidate to be the missing red Tempo – though this time the car had observable bullet holes in a fender and door on our side...and was pulling up in front of a drug house with Fletch Man himself as a passenger. The stalking theory is a joke. You can take my word for that, because you will be hard-pressed to find anyone who believes it, even after it was laid out, more or less, in a court where people were willing to believe anything the prosecution said.

It's worth recalling that one of the few people on the planet who bought the stalking theory was celebrity pathologist Michael Baden, the same guy who lectured his fellow pathologists about accepting the word of street cops. By the time Nancy attended that pathologists' convention to confront Baden, while we were in prison, Baden was *still* telling the world that Walter and I had been stalking Green – something Worthy and Baker must have told him back when they convinced him to come to Detroit and back up Jiraki's pipe dream that cocaine meant nothing to the Malice Green case.

You know what the street people and Fletch Man testified. Worthy insisted that the dopehouse be cleaned up before photos were shot, continued her routine of insisting that these were upstanding citizens whose word was to be taken at face value, and generally portraying them as poor black people living under the thumb of harassing white police, and an asset to the prosecution's credibility. Baker and Worthy even presented the tale of Theresa Pace as a heroine who endured weeks of hardship down at police headquarters while waiting to testify – totally avoiding whether her drug and hooker habits made her a credible witness, and that Pace spent her unusual weeks at police headquarters at *the prosecution's* insistence because she was a flight risk. All in all, you'd think this group of witnesses was a Rotary Club coming in to testify as a civic project. Robert Knox, shot dead in a drug deal gone bad, testified posthumously via transcript from the preliminary exam. As you know, street talk had Walter and I involved with Knox's demise.

A police department self-defense training specialist was called as a prosecution witness. She talked about the extensive training all Detroit officers get, and about use of techniques such as "pressure points." I have no blessed idea why this witness was called. Though the witness was at the front end of middle-age, she still would have been in public school when I passed through the Police Academy, which at the time taught none of the things she talked about.

There was expert testimony and counter-testimony on blood-spatter evidence. To my mind it proved not much of anything except that there was, in fact, blood-spattering. This kind of evidence involved so much tea-leaf-reading that it would later become part of the prosecution's effort, at Walter's second trial, to treat him as if I wasn't even at the scene.

There was the EMS testimony, which I've already covered in depth. Of the three police officers at the defense table, this testimony became most vital to Bob Lessnau. Judge Crockett found Lee Hardy to be such a problematic witness that Crockett declared Lessnau not guilty. It would have been interesting – though probably not very good for Bobby – to see the result if *his* case had gone to a Detroit jury.

And, of course, there was "testimony" that never was heard. Many people probably were left with the impression – on the basis of the magic "STRESS" word alone – that I desperately wanted my record as a police officer off-limits to jurors. That's horsecrap. Baker and Worthy no doubt would have spun the KFC holdup and such for hours, but I wouldn't care. My record was clean, meritorious even. I would *love* to have had my entire career on the table. But that isn't the way the legal team saw it ("STRESS" *is*, I cannot emphasize enough for non-Detroiters, a powerful word even now). John Goldpaugh had my regular sergeant, Randy Martin, on the stand and was moving toward asking him whether I was an assaultive police officer. We weren't allowed to bring in Malice Green's history of resisting arrest and scuffling with police in Illinois because that's something I didn't know about the night of the incident. But we could bring in my record as a non-assaultive cop. Right at that point, though, all the lawyers wound up in a sidebar with Crockett. Baker and Worthy told the judge that if Goldpaugh went in that direction, they were going to go after citizen complaints against me – even though none had been upheld after investigation...all of which I have told you about.

Goldpaugh told Crockett, "You can't do that" (allow the prosecution to put unfounded complaints in front of the jury). Crockett said: "I'm going to do it." Goldpaugh decided he didn't want to conduct a mini-trial on every phony allegation against me. That could include, ironically, Billy Polk, who brought the phony complaint against my black partner and me and filed the unsuccessful civil suit (which he attended with a phony limp)...the same guy who wound up with a shotgun in his hand as I entered that living room two nights before the Green incident and right down the street from Fletch Man's pad. So Randy Martin basically testified nothing except that I was a good cop who showed up for work on time. I would rather have had all of my history and Green's out on the table. Everything in my history said, "No indication that the story portrayed by the prosecution would ever happen – let alone that it was a case of "Starsky and Hutch finally getting caught." The history of Malice Green's relationship with law-enforcement pointed in a quite different direction. But there was no way to get it into evidence without making a one-for-one trade with the prosecution. No way were Baker and Worthy going to allow testimony that suggested anything other than "motorist Malice Green pulled over for a traffic stop outside Ralph Fletcher's home." In some ways, the unexamined pages of my history and of Malice Green's history were the most distorted part of the whole distorted trial.

My severely bad attitude toward Crockett starts with the obvious behind-the-scenes stuff like the unspoken racial-political connections that ran all the way into the jury room. But what about actual judicial conduct? What of the phantom autopsy that medical examiner Bader Cassin made the day after Jiraki performed the official exam? Sounds like a mistrial to me. Not just because the prosecution failed to tell the defense about Cassin's involvement, but because the prosecution had no intent of *ever* letting us know about it. Only when Jiraki's personal issues caused him to blow up on the witness stand did he blurt out the fact that his boss Cassin had doubts about Jiraki's "cocaine-doesn't-matter" verdict and felt a need to reexamine Green's body himself. Can you imagine how stunned we were at the defense table? Or how about that incredible exchange between Crockett and celebrity pathologist Michael Baden – where Crockett suddenly stepped in and started questioning the witness, overseeing a recital of Bible scripture, demeaning defense pathologists in comparison to this "800-pound gorilla"...all but telling jurors: "Look, when you get to deciding reasonable doubt regarding the medical evidence, *this* hired gun is *the man!*" Not just bizarre and unconscionable, but obvious – anywhere but Detroit.

Baden was coincidentally at the heart of one of the court's biggest screw-ups. If you recall, he was sprung as a surprise witness – legally, because he was a rebuttal witness – and would be the very last person to take the stand. The trial was winding down at midweek, a day or two quicker than expected, and Baden couldn't show up until Monday. So the jurors would get some unexpected time off. Meanwhile, the good judge decided jurors should come down to the courthouse every day anyway. This baffled Goldpaugh, considering it hadn't been a sequestered jury. But it happened. And the bored jurors asked for some movies to watch. Crockett ordered it, and a bailiff rounded up some videos. On Saturday, with Crockett out of town, Goldpaugh got a phone call from a reporter wondering what he thought about jurors whiling away some time on Friday by watching *Malcolm X*.

Maybe you just take that as probably the most stupid movie choice anybody could possibly make. Or maybe you are on my page and strongly suspect it was an intentional attempt to sway jurors, as if they needed swaying. Either way, it happened. Just two days before seeing and hearing Crockett play the celebrity pathologist, and the Bible, like a violin…jurors were handed a video of white cops subduing Rodney King – choreographed into a rant about white police brutality. Of all the times in your life you have said, "Beyond belief!" – how many times could you mean what you said as much as this time?

Defense lawyers, of course, saw it as instant grounds for a mistrial. Who wouldn't? Well, our old friend Recorder's Court Chief Judge Dalton Roberson, for one. He told reporters, for their stories in Sunday's papers, that showing jurors the Rodney King videotape at the ultimate moment of a trial of three white police officers accused of beating a black man to death was no reason whatsoever to squelch the trial. Crockett reportedly was livid when he returned to Detroit on Sunday night. You'd hope so, no? Livid or not, it was *his* court, he ordered up movies, and his bailiff made the selection.

Roberson assigned Judge Vera Massey-Jones to rule on our request for a mistrial. During that brief encounter, she allowed as to what a fine actor Denzel Washington is, how she herself had seen the movie more than once, and how she was considering purchasing it for her children. Goldpaugh

– who not just as my attorney but as your ordinary rational person – saw the incident as an obvious cause for mistrial. In frustration, he told Massey-Jones that jurors might as well have been given a screening of "12 Angry Men." This was Detroit Recorder's Court. The idea of a mistrial got shot down very quickly. Crockett may have been livid to learn about the movie screw-up, but when we got back to his courtroom and Walter's attorney made one last complaint about the incident, Crockett got seriously testy. One reason the judge gave for his testiness? Unlike the Malcolm X movie, the Malice Green trial *had nothing to do with race*. Yeah, right. Pretend there's no elephant in the living room, and you don't have to clean up its mess. When the trial was over, Worthy would tell an interviewer that she couldn't imagine anyone hadn't already seen the movie. As if the idea of watching it while judging two white cops wasn't a somewhat different proposition. You'll remember that when Ed Bradley asked Worthy about the incident on *Sixty Minutes*, she said she thought it had been taken care of fairly. And when Bradley asked her how so, she said she couldn't remember.

After the debacle with the 800-pound gorilla Baden, it was time to shed alternate jurors and decide which twelve souls would be chosen as finalists on each of the two juries. My sixteenth juror had been hospitalized the night before, so when Crockett's clerk went to draw names from the plastic fishbowl, on a counter above the clerk's table and just a few feet away from me, it contained paper slips bearing fifteen names. He would draw three names to be discarded as alternates. I've seen this routine done countless times. Just like at a raffle, it's traditional to stick your hand down into the paper slips and fish randomly for each name you draw. The clerk drew one, two, three names – all off the top of the pile. They were precisely the three jurors whose courtroom demeanor and attentiveness had led me to believe they might be leaning to my side: one black male, one white female, and one Hispanic male. That left two whites and ten blacks, none of whom had given me any signs of being open to a not-guilty verdict, to decide my fate. The draw occurred exactly as I have described. It's your choice as to whether you wish to join my suspicions about what was going on. Even before deliberations began, all the jurors were communicating. I can't help thinking someone on the jury knew who was leaning which way, and let someone on the outside know. The "coincidence" of these three being selected as alternates is just way too much for me to believe.

John Goldpaugh came to me to find out how I'd feel about asking Crockett to include involuntary manslaughter as an option for the jury. I gave a resounding "No!" We had been charged with second-degree murder and were at the end of a long and difficult trial defending ourselves against a murder charge. We had prepared and presented a defense against the murder charge, not a manslaughter charge. The proofs required of the prosecution are quite different. Besides, and just as important, offering a jury the option of a "lesser included charge" is a prosecutor's dream. If a jury can't agree on guilt, the pro-"guilty" jurors can always convince the pro-"not guilty" jurors that conviction on the lesser charge amounts to a break for the defendant. Lesser-included charges allow prosecutors to throw accusations against the wall to see what will stick; and even if nothing is going to stick, jurors might compromise a defendant straight into prison. I mean, think about it. I forcefully told Goldpaugh thanks, but no thanks.

Walter's attorney and Goldpaugh started double-teaming me on this, claiming it would be in my best interest to ask for the manslaughter option to be included. They told me the prosecution would "go along" with it. How could that be in my best interest? A police officer defending himself during a lawful arrest cannot be guilty of murder. Of course, I don't believe I was guilty of manslaughter, but even in a fair trial there would be reason to fear jury compromise on the lesser charge. So if Baker and Worthy and Coleman Young wanted to call me a murderer, and try me in court and in public as a murderer, then murder damned well ought to be the charge. The prosecution in my eyes didn't prove any phase of their case, didn't disprove that I had acted in self-defense, and they looked like fools where cocaine was concerned. I wouldn't budge.

When instructions were given to the juries, I was dismayed – and livid – to hear jurors being told that manslaughter was an option. Baker for obvious reasons had wanted *me* to ask for a manslaughter inclusion. When I didn't, *he* asked for it. Crockett of course agreed, over my objections. I asked Goldpaugh if Baker and the court could do this. The answer was "yes." Two different charges for the same actions. One charge defended, the other not at all the focus of the defense. A chance for compromising jurors to pretend the lesser offense is somehow a "break" for the defendant. Big problem with the criminal justice system. As things turned out it didn't matter. Down the road the same unfair process would turn out to be a *big* problem.

Walter's jurors got the same instructions as mine. The two juries were sequestered at last and disappeared for nine days, leaving Court TV with air time to fill and leaving three police officers to ponder their fates. Walter's jury reached a verdict on a Saturday. They were brought into the courtroom and delivered their written verdict. Crockett polled them without revealing their decision. One juror, a young man and the panel's only white, lowered his head and was barely audible when he said "yes," indicating he agreed with the verdict. If you didn't know right then that the verdict was "guilty" you weren't paying attention. But there was still hope – always, I thought – and the matter of "guilty of what?" Crockett had Walter's verdict sealed until my jury finished deliberations. Crockett also sat on his own decision regarding Lessnau. All three verdicts would be read at the same time.

For anyone who somehow thought a manslaughter conviction would be a good result, I suppose nine days of deliberation was a good sign. What I know for sure is that second only to a video camera on the dashboard of our booster car, the thing I would most like to have is a videotape of what went on in the jury rooms. A copy of sentencing guidelines got left in jury rooms, against all rules. I suppose that could be construed as an honest mistake; but the guidelines "book" magically got up and walked with jurors from room to room. Our investigators' interviews with jurors produced stories of pre-judgment, of blatant disregard for Crockett's orders not to follow news reports on the case or discuss it…every sloppy and unfair piece of jury conduct you could imagine. One juror convinced other jurors he was a medical expert, and on that panel it was him – not Jiraki, Baden, Rorke, Mirchandani or Dragovic – who carried the most weight on the medical evidence. Saturday morning, before Walter's jurors returned a verdict, news reporters heard jurors shouting from behind closed doors.

On Monday, my jury signaled that it was through talking. We all gathered for the reckoning. Nancy, my rock through the entire trial, had a seat in a very crowded gallery. I was the only defendant with family in the room. Besides Nancy, my brother and his wife were there. My cousin, Richard Howe, who had provided the wheels for our first date, was there with his wife. I had forbidden my daughter Kelly to attend a single day of the spectacle. This was the same little girl I sometimes took with me on days I had to sign a warrant against a perp I had arrested the night before. Those outings would have been to the prosecutor's office on the eleventh floor, where it had been decided to charge us with murder. One prominent spectator from the other side was Dennis Archer, the former Supreme Court justice who back in November had told TV cameras he understood there were bone fragments on Warren Avenue. Why not – he was a leading candidate to replace Coleman Young in the next election. The other candidates criticized Archer for being "opportunistic." It didn't hurt him. Archer won two terms as mayor, and became the first black president of the American Bar Association. Good things happened to a lot of people who somehow saw justice in the verdict that was about to be read.

Walter turned his head toward the jury box and blinked once, barely, as he was told that twelve citizens unanimously agreed he was guilty of second-degree murder. Walter then turned his gaze forward again, as if he were sitting through a boring committee meeting of some kind. I knew Walter very well, in the sense that street cops know each other's strengths and weaknesses. In many ways I didn't know Walter at all. To this day, I don't understand how anyone could respond that way, even if he "knew" from day one what the outcome would be. But who knows? They tell me Nancy, with whom I had shared so many emotional hours and days since the night Malice Green died, was almost as stoic as "stoic Walter Budzyn" while the verdicts were read.

Not me. Walter's verdict told me all I needed to know. I was next.

Waiting for my jury foreman to read the verdict I began taking involuntary quick, deep breaths. Maybe the same reason Court TV captured me, as one local news anchor described it, "almost hyperventilating" had something to do with everything ending this way. I don't know. Possibly. A lot of things could have, just like getting stopped by a traffic light might make you miss a collision at the next intersection. But for sure my lung capacity hadn't helped me out on Warren.

I had first become aware of it in July of 1991, ten months before the Malice Green arrest. My partner and I were sitting in the booster car in an alley near Tiger Stadium, working days because of a ballgame. The night before I had found an unoccupied car that had been used in an armed robbery. We set up surveillance on it that night, but then had to abandon the scene because the city wasn't about to pay overtime. We could have recovered the car, of course, but I was more interested in recovering the armed holdup man. Next day, sure enough, the car was still there. I decided to sit on it once again. I began to feel bad during the couple hours we sat there hoping the felon would materialize before the ballgame started. The appeal of the arrest overpowered my feeling of illness. The perp came out of a house, I drove out of the alley, and we arrested him without incident. After doing the paperwork I told my partner and a supervisor I was sick and going home. That was a rare event.

When I got home I felt as sick as I ever had in my life. I was having trouble breathing and it got worse by the hour. I tried to lie down but couldn't get any air at all, so I spent the night sitting in a chair. Next day, I went to a walk-in clinic where the doctor prescribed an antibiotic and some kind of steroid. It was a couple of days before I was able to lie down. Several times I thought I was about to buy the farm. Tests revealed double pneumonia. The medications got rid of it. Back at work I noticed I got out of breath easily, especially when under stress. I had quit smoking five years earlier, a few days before my dad died of complications from emphysema. So I told myself that in a few weeks or months I'd be back to normal. Meantime, the only "normal" that mattered to me was driving a booster car, the one job where I ever excelled and made a difference. Eventually I went in for a follow-up exam and on November 12, 1992 – seven days after the confrontation with Malice Green – the diagnosis came back: emphysema. On the calendar, this was only months before I should have been getting the gold watch and the retirement party. In the real world, it was only months before my murder trial. I never told the department about the emphysema, and wouldn't have if there had been no Green arrest and no trial. Damned if I would spend my last days as a cop shuffling papers.

Sergeant Freddie Douglas was talking to the emphysema when he came on the Malice Green arrest scene and was heard to say, "Take it easy, Larry." I was sagging against the booster car gasping for breath after struggling with Green. Did the lung trouble impair me in the struggle? Well, I was fifty-two years old and a few pounds overweight, too. Did emphysema have anything to do with my sense, after Green put his hand on my gun – several minutes into the struggle – that there was a limit as to how long I could keep this guy under control? Probably.

Did my experience outside the Book-Cadillac Hotel make me wary of situations where somebody might get my gun while I am running out of gas? Probably. Would I not have hit Malice Green if I had been twenty-nine years old and in top shape? Who knows, and what's the difference – the fact is I *wasn't* twenty-nine and playing flag football anymore.

So waiting my turn to be found guilty of murder, I started, as the TV guy said, "hyperventilating." I needed the oxygen. The circumstances and the emphysema had sucked it all out of me. When the foreman read the words, I put my face in my hands and sobbed. That's one part of the Malice Green story that does exist on videotape. It got played a thousand times on television around the world.

No way could I reconstruct the thoughts I had at that moment. I was ashamed. I was afraid for Nancy and Kelly's future. I was confused. My first thoughts of "we must have done something wrong, a guy died" had long since been overtaken by clear thought about Malice Green's actions that night. I felt remorse about his death in the way I have described, but I had begun the long trip down the road toward anger at how the system refused to see any of the incident from two booster cops' point of view. At all. I believed I was guilty of nothing. I used my flashlight under high-stress circumstances. I was under control and conscious of how hard I was striking Malice Green. Was it my fault no one was there to see him put his hand on my gun? I hit his hand with much more force than I hit his head, and did not so much as cause a fracture in a pinky finger. Why was this happening? Why did any of this happen? How many thousands of arrests had I made without anything like this happening? Twenty-four and a half years come to an end this way? I'm sure I thought all those things and a thousand more. I'm sure I thought about a whole string of things from being advised not to make a statement at Homicide that night in November to watching those three jurors' names magically rise to the top of the fish bowl the following August. I probably had more thoughts in those few minutes than in any few minutes of my life. The same thoughts still come and go, all day every day. Just not so many at one time.

Crockett pronounced that Bobby Lessnau – whose chief accuser, Lee Hardy, no doubt impressed Walter's jury and mine – was not guilty. "I am not satisfied, in my head or in my heart," Crockett intoned, "that Mr. Lessnau has been demonstrated to be guilty" of any crime with which he was charged, or any lesser included offense, or any cognate offense. I suppose I heard Crockett say some of that. Bobby was free to go. I felt all kinds of happiness for this dedicated young officer who had gotten caught up in the racial frenzy just because he answered a call for help.

Walter and I were neither a threat to the community nor a flight risk, Crockett said, so we were to be free on personal bond until sentencing on October 12. Theresa Pace had been locked up to make sure she would not flee instead of testifying against the two "murderers" who now were being sent home, however briefly. I can't say I didn't want the month and a half of freedom; but it was obviously going to be the worst month and a half of my life. So far.

Starsky and Hutch had been the biggest news story in Detroit almost every day for ten months. So it was no surprise that all the TV channels expanded their news shows that day – by several hours in some cases – and pretty much made our verdicts the *only* story of the day, interrupted occasionally by sports and weather. Live news crews were, of course, dispatched to Fletch Man's dope house, where demonstrations and rallies occurred throughout the day.

Bennie White, the guy who painted the Malice Green mural on the front of the dope house, was interviewed. Speaking of Bobby Lessnau, the artist said: "As far as I'm concerned he was obviously guilty and something is wrong with Judge Crockett."

A socialist political party and some out-of-towners who called themselves the Justice for Malice Green Coalition – both groups almost all white – got into a scuffle partly with each other and partly with the black demonstrators. A bottle or two got tossed at a passing scout car. The crowd got big enough at one time that the street was shut down, mostly for reasons of traffic control. A few people sold T-shirts and reproductions of the "shrine" mural. My least favorite executive deputy chief, James Bannon, circled overhead in a police helicopter.

On the courthouse steps, one young black man was interviewed and said: "We have police out here killing people for no reason – some we don't even know about. No real justice has been done."

At a rec center on the site where the 1967 riot began, a man told the camera: "They should have got life because they've been beating a lot of blacks." Actually, Crockett would be able to give us anywhere from one year to life at our next scheduled trip to Recorder's Court on October 12. I think what this man was complaining about, as were many on camera, was the fact that two police officers would have this little window of freedom before sentencing. Many of those interviewed were, in fact, clamoring for life without parole and complaining the charge should have been first-degree murder.

Even thugh we had been convicted of murder, much air time that afternoon and evening was spent worrying about a "civil disturbance" and congratulating the level-headed citizens of the city for not rioting. I shudder to think what it would have been like if we had been acquitted. But then, riot prevention was one of the main points of our trial.

In one telephone interview from his retreat at the Manoogian Mansion, Coleman Young himself said: "I think justice was done. I think the city is cool, as we fully expected it to be." And then the man who called us "murderers" on national TV amazingly said: "I think there have been attempts on the part of the media to aggravate, agitate, and stir up trouble…the constant reporting and talking about it."

Huel Perkins, an anchor at Channel Two, congratulated Detroiters for being prepared for any trial result. Then Perkins said this was because of the great wisdom of trying us before "predominantly black juries and a black judge."

Dalton Roberson – the chief judge who denied us a change of venue – went on camera and said: "I had thought as a lawyer the verdict would probably be manslaughter. You can't predict what a jury is going to do." Well, judge, sometimes you can't and sometimes you can.

Kym Worthy said she was "a little surprised – very pleasantly surprised" with the verdicts. Baker said he was not surprised. I don't believe him. After all, he asked that jurors get the option of a manslaughter verdict.

The police officers' union issued a statement declaring that the verdicts were "a victory for the drug dealers, addicts, pimps and prostitutes in the city." It was one positive message in the mix, but I had never exactly been thrilled with the DPOA's lukewarm support for us. And as you know, my career wasn't about arresting prostitutes.

Mike Lewis, a street reporter for Channel Four, was asked in late afternoon by the anchor desk whether Chief Stanley Knox had made a statement. Lewis said: "No. It's hard to explain why we haven't heard from Knox. He was very quick to speak out after the incident occurred but very slow after the verdicts came in." Stanley Knox always had one thing right. Detroit wasn't Simi Valley.

A legal analyst for one channel, when asked about possible appeals, said dryly: "This case will perhaps make some important law on the issue of change of venue." I wish.

The various mayoral candidates were given air time to snipe at Dennis Archer for showing up and working the courtroom for votes. As for the trial itself, every candidate was unanimous: The verdicts were righteous and Detroiters deserved a gold star for not going out and burning down their city. For any politician in Detroit, the "truth" about the Malice Green case was as obvious and one-sided as the need to kiss a baby at a Fourth of July picnic.

A few jurors spoke to the news media.

One Rosey Brooks, who served on my jury, said that the

most difficult part of the jurors' ordeal was "being locked up and away from our families" for nine days at a hotel. I would have had the priorities a little different, but what do I know.

Then there was "Karl," the white kid on Walter's jury. He cheerfully told the cameras that he disagreed with the verdict and didn't think the charge "was proven." Asked why he voted "guilty," he shrugged and said "duress." All the shouting on Saturday morning, it turned out, was directed at "Karl." Roberson and the prosecutors all pointed out that Walter's jury was polled twice, once when they reached a verdict and again on the day all three verdicts were read. If "Karl" had a problem with the verdict, they said, he had his chance to speak up about it.

And then there was Sadie Roberts, the woman on my jury who was sent to the sidelines when her name was pulled out of the fish bowl. She welcomed the cameras and said, forcefully: "I feel cheated. The way I feel is not the verdict that came out. I thought the evidence speaks for itself."

Would Sadie Roberts have succumbed to "duress"? Would she have played the Henry Fonda role from *12 Angry Men*? Would she have prevailed on a "compromise" verdict? What would she have done if the only choices were murder and "not guilty"? For that matter, what would she have done if the only choices were manslaughter and "not guilty"? We never got a chance to find out. No way would she have swung a Detroit jury. But maybe she would have held out.

There was nothing left to do but wait for sentencing day. I certainly can't say I expected Crockett to sentence lightly. I can't even say I had real hopes for a fair shake. But, ever the optimist, I kept Bobby Lessnau's fate in mind and focused on our October 12 date with what we'll just call wishful thinking.

19

SOME GOOD NEWS,
A LOT OF BAD NEWS

A few weeks after Malice Green's arrest somebody called and said there was a guy on the radio I ought to hear. I had never listened to Mark Scott, a conservative talk-show host who at the time had a very popular show on WXYT. I hadn't yet gotten "politicized." My whole adult life before the Malice Green incident I would rather listen to somebody – anybody – talk about sports than politics. But I followed the caller's advice, turned on WXYT, and thus began my relationship with an honest voice who made sure at least one media outlet was telling our story front and center. To this day, it's unusual for me to circulate in a public place without running into someone who has heard Mark Scott talking about Walter and me.

I was dumbfounded on that first listen to hear this radio host telling everybody to take a wait-and-see attitude about our case, talking realistically about a police officer's life on the streets of Detroit, denouncing all the hysteria, urging against any rush to judgment. He talked about us often, and needless to say I became an instant regular listener. I sent Mark a letter thanking him for his level-headedness and sense of justice. I didn't include our home phone number, which I had learned to guard zealously, but I did include Nancy's work number. One day Nancy called from work and said: "Guess who I have on the phone – Mark Scott!" Nancy connected us, and I told him how refreshing it was to hear a public voice who was not screaming for a conviction without knowing any facts, or without thinking about them very much. Mark invited Nancy, Kelly and me to join him and his wife for dinner. We did. I told him everything about the night of November 5, but asked him not to mention the gun-grab. It was just about our only ace in the hole against the prosecutors' creative version of events. Besides, I didn't want a bunch of talk-show callers stretching the facts into a suburban version of street buzz with Malice Green aiming a .357 magnum at me. That would have been just like the wild stories going around Detroit from the other side. Mark honored my request, though he told listeners he had information he couldn't share. Meanwhile, anyone in southeast Michigan who had sympathy for our situation – a much larger number than reflected in the prevailing media – made *The Mark Scott Show* their main source of information and commentary. Repeat callers to the show included the quiet but strong plainclothes cop Paul Fitzgerald who was soon to become such a great friend.

I've made it pretty clear how the *overwhelming* majority of media coverage and commentary wasn't just tilted toward the prosecution but was badly distorted, especially television news. More important, anyone who wanted to lynch us was given direct access not just to talk shows but to the news, on the air or in print, no matter how many credibility problems they had. To be fair about that, the occasional column dared to suggest that due process was being trampled, or cautioned against pre-judging us. And one newspaper reporter in particular covered our trial straight down the middle and believed we were two cops just doing their job. In the end this Detroit News reporter did an amazing rare thing on our behalf that I will never forget and will tell you about in Chapter 21. But it was Mark Scott who had a microphone he used as an advocate for justice from the get-go, and stayed with the story all the way. Almost every show, before signing off with his famous cry of "Excelsior!" he spent at least some time discussing our case. Often enough, he gave our story a *lot* of time.

So that's two good people – Mark Scott and officer Paul Fitzgerald – who came on the scene as we prepared for our trial, and who played important roles in helping preserve my spirits as best as possible. A third appeared on the scene immediately after the verdicts were read. Darin Chase jumped into our cause with so much energy, and did so much work for us in so many places, that naturally he also became a close acquaintance of Mark Scott. Darin was a twenty-seven-year-old mortgage banker at the time. His age no doubt helped account for the energy. But he also brought a sharp mind to our side. He was a member of a conservative Republican group in suburban Macomb County and was following the case closely. Shortly after watching the verdict on live TV, he got a call from a coalition board member. Why don't we, the question was put to him, get involved to help these two railroaded cops? The coalition was a political group, and governors are politicians, and governors can grant pardons or commute sentences. So they saw a direction in which they could help. It was Darin's turn to lead the group's next project. He never takes on a project he doesn't believe in. And he took on our cause like a bulldozer looking for some earth to move. What Darin, his group, and everyone who rallied behind them did in the short time before sentencing was incredible.

    That first day, the Macomb coalition faxed out a press release declaring the "Budzyn-Nevers" murder convictions to be a railroading, calling for public support, and launching a petition drive calling on Governor John Engler to pardon us. That was such an audacious pronouncement compared to the story line the public had heard for nine months, and amid the cheerleading for our convictions, the news media couldn't avoid reporting it. Darin left his house for a bit and when he came back he found messages from a dozen reporters seeking interviews. The Macomb coalition held a press conference at its modest headquarters, and that was all it took to get the ball rolling. The coalition office had three telephones and a fax line. From that moment until after our sentencing, the phones almost literally never stopped ringing. The response was enormous, and even came from our own families who were delighted to see this happening. One of the very first to call and offer help was Diane Budzyn. Nancy was close behind. It was the support group, really, that led Diane and Nancy – two great advocates walking the same ground along separate paths – to become close partners in the effort.

Darin Chase energized the drive to connect supportive police officers from across Michigan with this rush of ordinary citizens who responded to word that someone out there was organized on our side. With barely a month to our sentencing date, the coalition gathered 40,000 signatures before we faced Judge Crockett. Most signatures were turned in on sheets with just four or five or a half-dozen names – meaning someone had rushed to get a petition, signed it along with his or her spouse and a neighbor or two, and then sent it right back in.

Darin's group and the loose-knit coalition of police officers got together on fund-raisers that were phenomenal, which is exactly the right word. The police officers were willing, but it was Darin who brought political expertise and PR savvy to the equation. For one thing, he stepped up and told it like it was – blaming the NAACP and Coleman Young for the hysterical atmosphere that knocked justice off the tracks. "We were doing the unthinkable in calling out the NAACP for being corrupt," Darin said years later. "That struck a chord with the suburban public. It had been underneath the surface for a long time." In short order, the support group organized three major fund-raisers, drawing 3,000 people twice and then 4,000 to one incredible event at the Father Solanus Casey Knights of Columbus hall in Roseville. One reason I'll never forget the location of that event is that Father Solanus was a priest I had never heard of until Paul Fitzgerald came on my scene and in his optimistic way, fighting his own tough battle, quoted the good father at least once every time we had coffee together.

The rallies did a whole lot for my spirits as we moved toward what I knew was not going to be a good day on October 12, sentencing day. They also raised money – some toward legal appeals expenses but mostly, and this was where Darin came in, for serious public-relations efforts, getting the word out and keeping it out in an effort to keep Walter and me from rotting in prison while no one noticed. Even after Walter and I went to prison Darin would find a way every month or two to get the case back into the news in ways big or small. There were even some radio commercials. By 1996 when John O'Hair ran for re-election as prosecutor, Darin put together commercials opposing him and noting the NAACP role in what happened to Walter and me (some of which you won't know until later in this chapter). Darin even sued the biggest TV station in town seeking to get an O'Hair commercial knocked off the air for claiming a misleading conviction rate. That included, at my suggestion, going after O'Hair's promise to "continue" diligent enforcement of illegal handgun-possession prosecutions in the city. Hell, I knew up close and personal that the prosecutor's office had been relentlessly dropping gun charges from a four- to five-year felony down to a misdemeanor. "Guns and drugs off the streets" had been the plainclothes cop's marching orders almost my entire career, and was the stated goal of no less than Coleman Young himself. We brought in so many perps that we couldn't get the prosecutor to take that mission seriously. And of course, Darin could count on Mark Scott to re-light the fires whenever Darin had news about what was happening in the courts or with the support group. Darin Chase is a fine young man.

I'll jump way ahead to tell you here about Darin's worst day on our behalf. Bobby Lessnau had never in his life wanted to be anything but a good cop. He loved the job as I did, and he was already a good one, which made it especially painful for me to see him caught up in all this. And after being fired and wrongly prosecuted, all the way through a sensational criminal trial sitting next to Walter and me, the department, though obligated to take Bobby back after his not-guilty verdict, didn't really want him. He sued, as much to guarantee he could continue his career as for damages. The city Law Department was so fond of settling nickel-and-dime phony lawsuits against police officers rather than defend them, thus leaving the cops' names sullied for no good reason. Now, with Bobby's suit, the Law Department found itself looking at a legitimate case that went in a police officer's favor. The lawyers recommended the city settle with Bobby for $400,000. The City Council, of course, wanted none of that, and all the old hysteria about racist white cops started flowing all over again. The city council scheduled time to debate the settlement recommendation. Walter and I were in prison at the time, but Darin was no wallflower in his endless efforts to keep our story alive.

What he did was dial up a city council member and ask to be put on the agenda as a citizen coming down from his auditorium seat to give public comment. Apparently, the councilwoman who put him on the docket assumed anyone asking to speak would be speaking against that brutal cop Bobby Lessnau. At any rate, Darin found himself near the top of the list, sitting at a table just a few feet from Joann Watson, the NAACP chapter's executive director who had done everything in her power to get us convicted of murder, right down to convincing news media to run the story of Victor. After Watson finished her diatribe insisting that Bob Lessnau – found not guilty by no less than Judge Crockett – was guilty, it was Darin's turn to speak. And all he said was: "What part of 'innocent' don't Joann Watson and the NAACP understand?" Diane Budzyn had suggested the question. When Darin walked back up to his seat he was kicked and called various names. He heard someone spit but "didn't feel any wetness." The name-calling went on from the surrounding audience for as much as a half-hour as Darin looked around for security to escort him out. TV cameras and print reporters were there, but if the incident got even a brief mention in the news media I never saw it, and haven't been able to find it. Surprise. Darin's another of those I'll never forget. How could I? He's still in touch and still offering whatever help he can in trying to clear the record.

"Karl," the guy on Walter's jury who briefly told the TV

cameras that he had voted guilty only under duress, did a more lengthy interview when he called in to Mark Scott's radio show the next day. I don't have a transcript of that interview, but I do have a transcript of Mark talking about it the following day on his show – two days after the verdicts were read. The reason I have *that* transcript is that *The Mark Scott Show* had just one guest two days after our trial ended – me. When it came time to read the news, Mark skipped the headlines and told listeners that on this day, his show was the news. Turns out he was right.

I wound up paying for it – which is one reason you need to read some of the supposedly unfair, improper, inflammatory, outrageous stuff I said. From my view I was just a guy telling it like it is after being railroaded on a murder charge in full public view – national and international view, even. Maybe it's not wise for a defendant awaiting sentencing to speak out in public, but I pretty much figured it was my right to step up and tell the truth, just like I did on the witness stand. I think I was rational, composed, and more dismayed than angry. Mark was pretty worked up. But that's his style. It was interesting stuff, and I'm going to give you a chunk of it. The transcript runs to sixty-eight pages. The highlights that follow include, I guarantee you, the most controversial – if you can call it that – things I said. I've inserted a couple comments in parentheses. Otherwise, it's the same words that went out over the air in 1993, edited only for length.

MARK SCOTT: Well, yesterday in talking about the jury trial of the three police officers here in Detroit we had a caller who identified himself as "Karl" and he was Juror Twelve and apparently captivated the news in this marketplace for all of yesterday.

In the studio with me this morning is Officer Larry Nevers, and he is going to tell you exactly what went on that night and what happened.

Yesterday, in talking with Karl on this broadcast, one, he came on the broadcast to apologize to Michael

Batchelor, Walter Budzyn's attorney, in saying that during voir dire he was asked, when it came down to the eleventh hour in deliberations, would he hold on? Would he not fold? Well, he didn't hold on, he said, and he was apologizing for that. He believed that Officer Budzyn didn't get a fair trial and his – his thoughts on that probably had to do with, no doubt, the fact that he – he did not stand tough in all of this. And there may have been some other things, because Juror Twelve told us that at least two jurors violated Judge Crockett's orders not to watch TV news. According to Juror Twelve one juror went so far as to try to catch up by watching Court TV.

And Karl said that he got frustrated over deliberations; that he had been without income for a couple of months. In a way, he said here on my broadcast, he copped out and he rushed to judgment. Karl also said that he changed his mind on the stand Saturday (when the jury was polled the first time, after reaching a verdict but before the other jury came in), almost changed his mind, that he wished he had. He didn't feel comfortable with the verdict as it was.

He said he was intimidated by the other jury members; that he was – they said he was playing games. In essence calling him a racist as well. And that definitely, he was pressured and intimidated. He said he would have come in with a lesser verdict...perhaps manslaughter at most.

Karl said he believed some of the jurors had a preconceived notion of guilt on the part of the officers. Now, see, this is important, because you're not hearing this out of the news media again. They did not report this. You only heard this on this broadcast...Karl pointed out that certain jurors offered affirmation like the A-men choir. The utterances of "uh-huh," or "oh-

358

yeah," to confirm what they already thought, body language, turning away, the wave of a hand like I need to hear no more.

He asked them to bring to up the issue of the medical testimony. In other words, Dr. Lucy Rorke. Karl was told he was out of order because he wasn't a forensic pathologist, and yet that goes at the heart of what happened. Cocaine issues go at the heart of this trial...The central issue in the Malice Green trial was the role that cocaine played in his death...They decided to just brush it away and evade it. It still sits there... And Karl believed racism was introduced when other members of the jury said they believed the officers' intent was "to teach this," and I will not use the big N word, "a lesson."

Juror Twelve said he would go to Judge Crockett and relay under oath what he told us here on this broadcast.

(NOTE: So far as I know, nothing like that ever happened.)

You saw immediately the closing of ranks in the black community yesterday. And they first tried to taint Karl as some kind of psycho. That was the first thing coming out of Judge Roberson. And of course you heard the parading of the people on television yesterday who tried to say this (what Karl said), this simply wasn't so. And they even talked about how they prayed about this. Who did they pray to? What was the prayer? What was the content? They prayed about it. They prayed and thought that they were going to get an answer to the fate of Larry Nevers and Walter Budzyn out of the cosmic conscience up in the sky. That somehow that cosmic conscience was going to tap into their minds and they were going to come up with the right answer. And they didn't, and they came up with the wrong one.

WXYT News Talk time 9:24. Officer Larry Nevers. The first thing I want to do is thank you for the number of years of service that you have given the Detroit community, some twenty-four years.

LARRY NEVERS: Thank you.

SCOTT: In this corner you know that we salute you and make no bones about it. I've put my money where my mouth is on that score and I did that a long time ago and watched this trial with a great deal of interest to see how justice is served in the United States of America today and what is going on.

The night of the deadly encounter, Officer Nevers, was a horrendous night for everybody concerned. Not only for Malice Green, who lost his life. Could you tell us, first of all, why you're not guilty of murder?

NEVERS: Well, before I get into that, Mark, I would like to publicly thank you for all these months of your support. It's meant an awful lot to my family and I and the people that have showed their support with cards and letters and phone calls. I'll never know how I can repay you and the people out there that supported my family and I in that regard. And as far as the religious aspect – the Man Upstairs and I kind of…I kind of shied away from a long time now, but there are so many people that intervened in my regard and I appreciate all the prayers and the support.

SCOTT: Well, you don't owe me anything. I think anybody who would do less would be dishonest, most certainly. Look, look, the issue here was the fact that you said you did not kill Malice Green.

NEVERS: That's right, Mark. I believe that with all my heart. And I'm a police officer. I don't kill people. And I did not kill Malice Green.

SCOTT: We'll find out what was going through your mind at some steps of the way during that evening. But what brought you to that point?

(Mark Scott walked me through the night of November 4 and the carjacking report that set us looking for the red Tempo. He asked about the nature of booster-car work, my years in the Third Precinct, the beginning of our work night on November 5 [starting with punching the red Tempo's license plate into the MDT to make sure the "stolen" car was still hot], the radio run where we confiscated the toy gun. He jumped back to the Billy Polk incident on election night, two nights before the Green incident. Then we went back, in detail, to the surveillance the uniformed cars had put on the missing Tempo and how we took over the surveillance but then had to make our radio run, and how on the way back to that area we saw Malice Green's red Topaz cross in front of us just a matter of feet away from the dope house. I answered Mark's questions like a cop who has been writing personal complaint reports and testifying in court for twenty-four years. In other words, it was real dry and matter-of-fact. Absolutely nothing that would offend anyone. In fact, it sounded like the PCR I would have written in Homicide if legal counsel hadn't ordered me to tear it up. Much of the radio show transcript would make pretty dull reading for you in the parts where I was talking, because, first, it's almost all matter-of-fact reporting of what happened, and you know all of that; and second, because I was reciting it all in such a dull fashion. Microphone fright, maybe. Mark at times, however, was very much the opposite.)

> *SCOTT:* So you saw a man run from (Green's) car. Now, you see, I know that Chief Knox would say, well, he didn't violate any law so why would you pursue a guy who is running from a car? Why would that cause any curiosity in your mind? In a police officer's mind who is working the Third Precinct in Detroit who has been on the force for twenty-some years plus, a guy who has received all kinds of commendations, who has been in it when the capital S with a hit has hit the fan, why would that cause curiosity in your mind, officer Nevers?

NEVERS: Well, Mark, for a number of reasons. I guess the basic reason was, obviously, the man in the back seat that ran away did not want to come in contact with us. And I'm not putting aside that the vehicle did have bullet holes in it and –
SCOTT: That's not against the law either.
NEVERS: That's true. That is very true. Nothing – nothing that was done at that time was a violation of any law that I know of.
SCOTT: Of course, in this day and age, why would you guys be concerned if you saw a car with bullet holes in it and a guy running away from it and you're sitting outside of a crack house? I mean, why would you even give it another thought? Oh, I forgot. You're there because you're looking for guys who are committing a felony. Gee, I forgot that. I suspect that so did your chief of police and some of the other people forget it, sitting up there, top-heavy brass shuffling papers and collecting some pretty hefty paychecks.

We'll continue this because I find this very interesting. Officer Larry Nevers, one hell of a man here on Mark Scott, News Talk 1270.

(Scott continued taking me through the arrest. And as I review this transcript after all these years I am surprised at how very un-dramatic and un-angry I was in telling the basic facts. But to Detroit listeners in that time and place – with me getting a chance to tell the whole story across an entire radio show, it probably did sound pretty dramatic. Neither Walter nor I had ever done an interview like this, never had a chance to put it all out there uninterrupted. So, coming just two days after the verdicts, it probably struck a lot of listeners as dynamite stuff. When Mark and I started talking about the struggle with Malice Green, Mark took the conversation back to the Book-Cadillac incident where I was almost shot with my own gun. Then as we returned to the details of the Green arrest, I kept sounding like a straightforward police report and Mark kept getting more sarcastic and fired-up in his commentary. After establishing that Walter and Green were struggling in the confines of a small car with bucket seats and a center console, and reaching the point where Green tried to get out the driver's door and I went around to that side of the car, Mark's commentary became even more pointed.)

SCOTT: And you started struggling with him and is that when Walter Budzyn got into the back seat at that point? Or what?

NEVERS: You know, I said this on the stand, Mark, I absolutely don't know exactly what Walt did, or when he did it –

SCOTT: Well, why don't you guys police each other, Larry? When you're going through this and you're wrestling with somebody, why aren't – why don't you guys have your eyes on the other partner? Why aren't you examining what he's doing? You mean to tell me that things are that tough out there when you're wrestling around with someone else that it captures all your attention? Why could that be? Why would it capture all of your attention – you and Walter couldn't look at one another and see what each other was doing here? Because in the minds of a lot of people here in this metro Detroit area, they seem not to be able to understand that you had your hands full. Why, Malice Green was only 145 pounds.

NEVERS: Well, Mark, you said that very eloquently. I couldn't – that's exactly it. I was paying attention to Malice Green trying to get my gun and –

SCOTT: Not to worry. He's only 145 pounds. I mean, forget about your past experiences in your life as a police officer. You know what, Malice is just – he probably was going to ask you to enter into a game of Russian roulette with him. And maybe even offer you a little crack, a little speed, the two of you could freak out. You know how you police officers are. You all go into those crack houses and freak out with those speed freaks, don't you? Isn't that what you guys do? I mean, doesn't the police officer – the police department never tests you guys to see whether you're on drugs. I mean, you guys just run around like a bunch of wild yahoos, man, hey, this is my street, out of the way. Isn't that it? Isn't that true? Isn't that what you police officers are about? Especially in Detroit?

NEVERS: No, Mark, they're not like that. As far as drug testing, we – I've been randomly drug tested and I'm sure that I know other officers have been randomly drug tested. All officers –

SCOTT: Yeah, but you guys know this ahead of time so you can clean yourselves up . . .Well all right, so we've been misinformed, misled. There's been a lot of half-truths and myths in this trial, most definitely. And the media have just had a field day over it. They really have. It's been a feeding frenzy and this is discussed as the top story and it's probably the biggest story this city has seen in years.

But nevertheless, back to Malice Green and he is wrestling around with you and you are now having some thoughts and serious reservations as to what is going on. You've struck him several times. The medical examiner said fourteen times. We don't know whether he was struck fourteen times or not, really, according to what you were saying, there's ample evidence here that he might have hit his head a couple of times – at least a couple of times while he was wrestling with both you and Officer Budzyn.

So now we have a man who has gone for your gun, what did you think as soon as he went for your gun? And why didn't you tell Officer Budzyn that he went for your gun? I mean, I probably wouldn't have said anything either, I would have been reacting just as you did, but you're the police officer. This is – this is your story, this is what happened. Why didn't you tell Officer Budzyn and why didn't you tell everybody else? Why didn't you tell the news media, why didn't you tell all the hierarchy in the police department? Let's hear that. Why didn't you tell them about Malice Green going for your gun?

NEVERS: Well, part of this I told on the witness stand. My main concern was my livelihood at the time that he grabbed my gun. I didn't have time to tell Officer Budzyn, by the way, "Walt, he's grabbing my gun, do you want to shoot him in the head? Do you want to shoot him in the stomach?" I didn't at that point feel that it was necessary and I didn't even have time to think about telling Walt. Had Mr. Green removed my gun from its holster and had it in his hand, I certainly would have told Officer Budzyn.

SCOTT: Why didn't you draw your gun and shoot him?

NEVERS: I did not draw my gun, number one, because he had a hold of it. And once he released my gun, I certainly had no reason.

SCOTT: What do you think he would have done if he had got your gun? Do you believe he would have shot and killed you?

NEVERS: Mark, I've asked myself that question so many times. The man was desperate. I couldn't understand, what are we missing here? Why is he putting up this fight? Why is he struggling so hard against a cocaine arrest? Is this man a murderer? Is there a dead body in the trunk? Why is he resisting in this fashion? That played on my mind. Why is he trying to get my gun out? What makes this man so desperate? Plus, all the things that happened to me in my police career. Things were popping in and out of my mind. I just could not understand the motivation of this man. Why was he resisting in this fashion? I still don't know the answer to that. I have to say it's – it had to be the cocaine. It had to be.

SCOTT: I remember talking with the police chief, and he had what I think is a legitimate concern of what's going on on the street and that is, that any police officer does not see himself as king of the block, that he is controlling that street and everybody's got to live and walk in fear of him. What do you think of that?

NEVERS: Well, I certainly don't put myself in that position.

SCOTT: Why not? Wouldn't it serve you for people to be in fear of you?

NEVERS: No, definitely not, Mark. We are unlike, say, the Narcotics Section or the Commercial Auto Theft Unit or a lot of specialized units in the Detroit Police Department or other police department that are given funds to pay informants. We have to rely on street people that we come into contact with, maybe someone we've given a break to, not to run roughshod over people.

SCOTT: So it's a quid pro quo. Something for something. In other words, there's a mutual agreement here and if they burn you on the street, then what?

NEVERS: Well, if they were to burn me on the information, the next time I would not give them a break probably. I might take them to jail for that misdemeanor they committed. But by and large, I don't ask for much – I didn't ask for much. A lot of the things I was given, like the Billy incident with the shotgun, that person just came up to me and said don't use my name but –

SCOTT: But given the way the prosecution in Detroit painted you and Officer Budzyn…And yet there was reason to believe when he went for your gun that he would use it, wasn't there? I mean, why would he go for your gun? Maybe there was something sticking out of the floorboard. He didn't want to hit his head on it and he thought he could use the gun butt to pound it down. Foolish of you not to have realized that, Officer Nevers. And Officer Budzyn as well. You guys were not sharp enough to really read Malice Green's mind.

Of course, you could have interviewed him along the way. You guys carry a notebook, don't you? Couldn't you have asked Malice Green, "What's on your mind?" You know, I am being a horse's ass here. That's all right. It's my show. I can do that.

But that being said, why didn't you tell anybody – or did you tell anybody that he went for your gun? Because everybody has the impression that you never told anybody until you hit the witness stand. Of course, you and I talked about it and you told me that long before you said it on the witness stand. Of course, I couldn't say that because you asked me not to say it on the air. Did you tell anyone else?

NEVERS: Yes, Mark. I told several people. I told my family. I told my lawyer. I may even have told a lot of people I work with.

SCOTT: Some police officers?

NEVERS: Yes.

SCOTT: You told some police officers?

NEVERS: Yes I did.

SCOTT: Why didn't you want to say it? Why didn't you say anything? Why is it that the police department did not hear from you and to my knowledge Officer Budzyn as well and Officer Lessnau? Was there a board of review that heard from you guys? Did you tell them anything?

NEVERS: No, there was nothing convened on our behalf.

SCOTT: But there were some people who knew about it. There were some people you talked to. I was one of them and I did know about this. And I have to say

that, because there are so many people – some of
my colleagues even have been condemnatory of you
because it came out on the witness stand.

And so it went. I answered questions about pepper spray,
and training, and the academy. Mark said: "Unbelievable,
unbelievable." And he went to listeners' calls. And at no time
did I say anything more "inflammatory" than what you see
above. In fact, as above, the callers and the host did almost all
the talking. I can't say it occurred to me at the time that I would
not be doing another interview with Mark Scott until after I had
been to prison on three separate occasions. After the interview
several reporters were waiting, and I talked to them. When
they asked questions, I answered. The result was a headline in
the Free Press that read: NEVERS VENTS RAGE, FRUSTRATION ON
AIR. If you read the story, it shows no on-air rage. The quotes
are all from the "press conference," not – as the headline says
– the on-air interview. I had just spent three hours on the radio.
I was tired. I was not media-savvy. I wanted to go home. The
show was over, and I guess I had a sense that my real "press
conference" was over. At any rate, when the reporters started
asking questions I was honest and direct. From the Free Press
account:

> In a cracked and weary voice, Nevers, convicted
> Monday of second-degree murder in the beating death of
> Malice Green, was himself, in a sense, a beaten man.
> "I feel as if I've been in a nightmare and I haven't
> awakened yet," Nevers said quietly. "I don't know... I could
> never imagine in my mind anything as bad as this."
> Nevers was outraged that while there is a memorial to
> Green at the site of his death, less than a mile away there's
> just a wreath to note where State Police Trooper Kermit
> Fitzpatrick was killed in 1991 by a motorist on the side of
> the Jeffries Freeway.
> "Kermit was gunned down by scumbags and what do
> they have? A Malice Green memorial. And this is a state

police officer. But people over there are afraid to walk out their doors at night, they're afraid to sit out on their porches. But nobody cares about us, nobody cares about the police."

"I certainly did not intend to kill this man; I'm a police officer. I don't intend to kill anybody unless they are trying to take my life," he said, his voice rising.

"I'm old, I'm not in the best of shape, I'll admit that. But I certainly could have generated enough force to crack somebody's skull and his skull wasn't cracked. Why doesn't that go to my intent?"

He said Detroit police officers are not well-trained, and are hampered in their ability to fight crime without Mace (or) pepper spray…Beyond more tools, Nevers said Detroit police need yearly physicals and ongoing self-defense training.

"There has to be something in between deadly force and whatever else, but it's not. It's just you and your wit and your flashlight and your gun," he said.

He said prosecutors Kym Worthy and Doug Baker "had their jobs to do…and they did it in a classless way, underhandedly. I guess I'm naïve; all I wanted them to do is be fair. Everything in that trial hurt me."

I am not a student of legal history. I don't know exactly how often a defendant speaks his mind after being found guilty. It might not be smart, but I know it does happen quite often. I know it ranges from some nutcake being dragged kicking and screaming from the courtroom while making death threats, to jailhouse interviews as a newspaper reporter seeks to prove a wrongly convicted man's innocence. How about cases in which someone does hard time for years, sometimes on death row, only to be totally cleared by DNA evidence? Are those defendants supposed to keep their mouths shut until the system stumbles onto its errors? I believe I had a right to talk. I was, am and always will be someone who obeys the law. If the law, even this court and this jury, said I had to go to prison, then I would report to prison. But no way could the law – and most particularly this sham investigation, trial and conviction – tell me what to think. I was dismayed, frustrated, disbelieving of the verdicts. I couldn't comprehend how jurors could do what they did. And keep in mind that at this point I didn't know some of the things I've been telling you about here.

When Kym Worthy said she was "pleasantly surprised" at the murder verdicts, I'm sure she meant *both* of those words. I believe Dalton Roberson, the chief judge, meant it when he said that "as a lawyer" he was not expecting a murder verdict. It's no accident that the TV legal analyst, minutes after the verdicts, speculated that our case might "make some new law" regarding change of venue. I *know* I have seen countless news stories about black defendants claiming they were railroaded by a "white judicial system," and I know I have seen the NAACP go loudly to bat for them. But in my case, the NAACP went totally ballistic about my appearance on *The Mark Scott Show*. Rest assured that nowhere on that three-hour show, including the parts you haven't read, was the word "NAACP" mentioned. The word "black" was barely mentioned, and never in a remotely racist way. I said nothing disrespectful about Judge Crockett. I was disrespectful of the juries – but, you tell me, who wouldn't be? I expressed my dismay. I answered questions honestly. And that's all.

Still, the NAACP – which first sought to hang us in the media and then was represented at the prosecutor's table, on the judge's bench, and even in the jury box…which pretty much covers every facet of a trial – could not believe the audacity of a convicted white police officer protesting his innocence!

Two days after I went on air, the Rev. Wendell Anthony, president of the Detroit NAACP chapter, sent a letter to Prosecutor O'Hair. Rev. Anthony complained that two such dangerous criminals as Walter and I were free on bond pending sentencing, and more or less accused me of trying to provoke a riot. It's a tad ironic that by addressing O'Hair "on behalf of the officers and members of the Detroit Branch NAACP," Rev.

Anthony was writing on behalf of those who prosecuted us, found us guilty, and were soon to pass sentence.

"The NAACP has grave concerns," Anthony wrote, "about the decision to allow these individuals, convicted of second-degree murder, to remain free on bond, ostensibly 'for their safety.' The decision to allow convicted murderers to remain free has provoked and incited an already tense community."

"Ostensibly" for our safety? Perhaps the good reverend would like to make 5,000 felony arrests and then spend a month and a half in the Wayne County Jail awaiting sentencing.

Anthony went on: "Also, since the verdict, radio, television and print interviews by the media have provided extensive coverage featuring reaction and condemnation of the jury and the City by those convicted. This publicity has included one three-hour talk radio interview during which Larry Nevers announced he would be 'leaving the area until October 12, 1993, the day of the sentencing.'"

"These and other post-verdict developments have generated hundreds of calls and protests to the NAACP from Detroit residents who are unwilling to be taunted and disrespected by convicted murderers and shameless, exploitative media practices.

"Furthermore, the special efforts put forth by many of us to maintain calm and peace in the community is jeopardized by the inflammatory developments that have occurred during the past week.

"We request, therefore, that you, as the Prosecutor of Wayne County, execute a directive which will remand the individuals who have been convicted into custody. Notwithstanding Judge Crockett's assertions regarding their safety – we are also justifiably concerned about the safety and climate of the total community. In addition, we believe that the correctional system can provide the safeguards necessary to facilitate the immediate imprisonment of these individuals. We believe the severity of the crime, the verdict, and the need to be sensitive to the total community fully substantiate this urgent request.

"We urge careful consideration, and anxiously await your affirmative response to this request."

Whatever Reverend Anthony was talking about, note that he made the same accusations against both Walter and me. If Walter gave any interviews, I don't know about it. I don't recall doing any interviews other than to Mark Scott and the reporters who were waiting afterward. I did appear at a couple fund-raisers and answered requests to stand up and speak briefly. But that wasn't until after Reverend Anthony wrote his letter. I also don't know what Anthony was talking about in asking the prosecutor to lock us up. So far as I know in this country, only a judge can do that. And as for "leaving the area," the only travel I thought about was camping out at my in-laws' home in Dearborn Heights so as to get away from the TV cameras and curiosity-seekers. In the end, we stayed put on Bretton Drive. I don't know what conversations O'Hair and Anthony might have had as a result of Anthony's formal request; but when O'Hair got around to asking Judge Crockett to take action on behalf of the NAACP, it was only me, and not Walter, he was after. O'Hair sent Judge Crockett the following letter, which I believe played a big role in my fate. Or rather, I should say that the NAACP's anger at my exercise of free speech played a big role in my fate. O'Hair wrote to Crockett:

> Permit me to express my appreciation for your fine handling of the trial on the death of Malice Green. The case was a tragic, difficult and stressful one for all involved, and you deserve credit for your efforts.
>
> I am writing to bring to your attention community concerns about the post-trial behavior of defendant Larry Nevers after the court's decision not to remand him following his conviction. Rev. Wendell Anthony, president of the Detroit branch of the NAACP, has shared with me that he has received hundreds of letters from individuals who are intensely upset with Mr. Nevers' conduct since his trial.
>
> As you are probably aware, since his trial Mr. Nevers has made a number of public statements and appearances in

which he has sharply criticized the criminal justice system's handling of his case. Rev. Anthony relays complaints that Mr. Nevers has used derogatory terms to describe members of the Detroit community, has evoked a generalized disrespect for the court and the criminal justice system, and otherwise has created a great deal of anger, bitterness and tension in the community at large. Indeed, Mr. Nevers' activities seem unusual for a convicted defendant awaiting sentencing, and stand in stark contrast to the post-trial behavior of defendant Walter Budzyn.

I am sharing these concerns with you so that you are fully aware of various sentiments in our community as you make decisions regarding conditions of bond and sentencing in this case.

In a case as tragic and significant as this one, it is terribly important that impact on the community be considered in making those decisions, which will reflect the integrity and effectiveness of our criminal justice system.

I don't know what business a prosecutor has sending a judge a request, on behalf of the NAACP, to revoke my bond and to pile on at my sentencing, but there you are. Down the road when I sought a criminal investigation of this, I was told it didn't amount to *ex parte* communication because O'Hair sent my lawyer a copy of the letter. Big deal. The prosecutor, at the stated behest of the NAACP, requested a life member of the NAACP to throw the book at me. My belief is that the judge listened, even though we remained free on bond until sentencing. In the Free Press, James Neuhard, director of the state Appellate Defenders Office, said that O'Hair injecting himself into Crockett's decision was "as rare as hen's teeth." Judges routinely receive letters about people coming before them for questioning, the Free Press wrote, but "the question is whether O'Hair's will carry any added weight." Neuhard told the paper: "I don't question for a second that if you get a letter from – essentially – the top cop…is somebody going to pay attention to that? Of course they would."

Reverend Anthony wrote about concerns in "the total community." O'Hair wrote about "the community at large." What both really meant, of course, was the black community. Maybe my going public isn't what bothered these guys so much as the fact that many members of the actual *total* community had sat back for nine months like good citizens and waited quietly for the criminal justice system to give us a fair shake, like it was supposed to. Then, astounded at the verdicts and tired of the hysteria, this part of the total community found *its* voice. Just a thought. Maybe Darin's PR efforts, and the response to it – which were just beginning – made these guys nervous about a city rioting over two cops who were convicted of murder for running into trouble while making a difficult arrest. Or maybe the riot talk was mainly coming from the same people who were patting themselves on the back for stopping a riot. I honestly don't know. I don't know how you determine something like that, or if anybody ever tried. But nine months earlier it all began with public officials in the highest places shouting that Walter and I had to be convicted or there would be a riot. And now that I was convicted, the shouting was that I had to keep quiet or there would be a riot. How about those TV cameras that went out to Fletch Man's dope house every night for weeks on end, asking bystanders if anyone had seen any signs of a riot? How much did *that* contribute to a stirring up "an already tense community"?

Maybe somewhere in the days before sentencing, not in an interview but in a meeting with supporters, I said that if Walter and I had been black there probably would have been no criminal charges and few people ever would have heard of Malice Green. I don't remember saying that so soon after the verdicts. I didn't yet understand just how true that was. I know I said it many times after I went to prison. That's where I was when I said it to Ed Bradley on *Sixty Minutes*. But many other people, including the Detroit News's only black columnist at the time, have said pretty much the same thing. I can point you to black police officers who will tell you the same thing. I know I've showed you examples of that, like the two gang squad cops who shot to death the same unarmed Cuban who Walter and I took a real gun away from and arrested without incident. It's as if Reverend Anthony and Prosecutor O'Hair and the shouters didn't even understand that these juries had found us guilty of *murder*, something that surprised even Dalton Roberson. I can't help it if I'm repeating myself. All the hysteria and the piling on had been repeating itself from the day of Green's arrest, and it was still repeating itself as we prepared to go to prison.

It's amazing how little I remember about our brief window of freedom. I guess I just savored the moments while dreading their end. I imagine I read a news clip I stumbled across while writing these pages. Coleman Young, with four months to go in his twenty-year reign, on September 2, 1993, announced the promotion of seventeen police officers to sergeant or lieutenant. None were among the top ten scores on either promotion list, and most had close ties to the mayor or his hand-picked police hierarchy. One officer promoted to sergeant ranked 325th on the merit-based list. A lame-duck mayor and a lame-duck sergeant were rewarding their friends. At the bottom of the story, it was revealed that Gerald Stewart, who had moved on to head the major-crimes unit, was denied promotion and sent back to the Homicide Section where he had skillfully helped get a revised second statement from Theresa Pace while refusing to re-interview Lee Hardy. I have no idea what that was about, but I'm sure it made me smile.

Meanwhile, the support-group rallies, fund-raisers and petition-gathering were taking place, whether the NAACP liked it or not. About a week before sentencing, two busloads of supporters took the fifteen boxes of signatures up to Lansing, delivered them to the governor's top aide, John Truscott, and returned to Roseville for that rally of 4,000 Budzyn-Nevers supporters. Then, on the night before sentencing, somebody decided Balduck Park on Detroit's east side would make a good place for a candlelight vigil. The gathering was heavily patrolled and there was no trouble. A box of church candles got distributed; a pickup truck and a bullhorn became a speaker's platform. Anyone looking out at the crowd saw nothing but a sea of tiny lights. Walter and I didn't attend. People who did attend say it was a moving experience. If no one really understood what happened on Warren Avenue the night of November 5, 1992 – and you know there are some things that even I do not fully understand – there were nonetheless lots of people who somehow understood that justice had not been served at this trial.

The next morning Nancy, Kelly and I made our tearful goodbyes inside our Bretton Drive home. I still held out a sliver of hope that Crockett would come around. You've heard me say that sort of thing both ways – that I knew nothing good was coming, and that I hoped for the best. Contradictory but true. Both were there in my muddled thinking, my apprehension, my hopes. I made sure my pockets were empty before I left the house. No wallet, no comb, no wrist watch, no handkerchief. I even took off my wedding band and gave it to Nancy. Kelly went to her grandmother's home for the day. Nancy and I drove ourselves down to court, knowing she would have to drive home alone. On this day, Paul Fitzgerald – who stayed with me almost to the end, but by now walking with a cane – could not chance trying to navigate the circus of protesters and media. He stayed home, and I'm sure said a prayer or two, and probably made some mention of Father Solanus.

Our fate was in the hands of a man I kept thinking of as the guy who coached Michael Baden through a witness-stand Bible class that almost anyone would interpret as the judge's roadmap to "the truth," and as the guy who ordered up movies for the jurors. George Crockett III's personal style throughout the trial had been strange, but then lots of judges have strange styles. However, Crockett far more often than most I've seen would interrupt witness-lawyer exchanges to ask his own questions. He generally spoke in a slow, dull voice that

would sound like he was out of touch if not for the fact that he
obviously was on top of every word spoken in court and was
in fact quick to suggest words he thought should have been
spoken but weren't. He played the jurors like a choir, always
calling them "judges." If he had something to say to the juries,
that would be his first word: "Judges?"

Crockett's father, George W. Crockett Jr., had been Coleman
Young's lawyer back in the '50s. When Crockett III first ran
for the Recorder's Court bench, the Detroit Bar Association
rated him unqualified and his father privately said the son had
personal problems and wasn't ready to be a judge. Publicly, the
elder Crockett said judges don't endorse judges. Still, when
Crockett III presided over our trial he had just one picture
besides Martin Luther King Jr.'s hanging on the courtroom
wall...a picture of his father. In April 1993, looking forward
to the Green trial, Detroit's largest newspaper, the Free Press,
ran a profile of Crockett III. I don't know if the personal
problems in that profile are the personal problems his father
was referring to, but they are interesting. From the Free Press
story (I'm going to put one sentence in bold):

*In 1976 he announced his candidacy for judge and
opened the door to his troubled private life. Crockett revealed
he had undergone treatment for severe mental illness for
about a dozen years, including several commitments for acute
psychotic paranoid depression, a condition marked by extreme
swings from periods of hyperactivity and elation to bouts of
overwhelming gloom.*

*In 1980, his illness resurfaced and he took medical
leave to enter Henry Ford Hospital for several weeks,
followed by three months of recuperation at home.*

*Since the early 1980s, his condition has been under
control through continued psychiatric therapy and
medication, including Lithium. Lithium is a medication that
helps moderate the mood swings. "I feel it's under control as
long as I am faithful to my medical regimen – and I am."*

Crockett said his disorder, when untreated, was

*characterized by periods when he felt unmatched exhilaration and brilliance. During those episodes, he said, came an absolute belief that his mind was a powerful engine of logic, learning and sheer laser-like clarity and insight. The accompanying thrill was so powerful that there was resistance to treatment, he said. **He likened the experience to the grip of cocaine on an addict who knows the drug is ruining his life, but can't fight the lure of the euphoric state.***

The manic peaks are followed by bitter lows, during which life seems worthless and futile. Lithium helps maintain an acceptable emotional balance by limiting the intensity and number of swings, said Dr. Kenneth Edelman, medical director of the Michigan Health Center. Crockett said he is able to carry out his duties by faithfully taking his medication and attending regular weekly sessions with a psychiatrist.

I don't know what kind of mood swing Crockett might have been having when he dressed down Walter's lawyer for refusing to let go of the Malcolm X fiasco, but the judge looked to me at the time like he was on the edge. Almost seven years after our trial, the medication issues didn't look like they had gone away. From another Free Press story, on August 18, 2000:

Detroit police interviewed Wayne County Circuit Judge George Crockett III on Thursday in their investigation of the alleged attack and sexual assault of a Detroit woman.

The 51-year-old woman, who has known Crockett for more than 20 years, told police she was beaten in the head and face, forced to perform sexual acts and held against her will in Crockett's east side home Tuesday night.

Two investigators went to Crockett's house Thursday afternoon and took a statement from him. Investigators said Crockett's story differs from the woman's, but would not elaborate.

"We have talked to him and we are conducting a very

unbiased, fair investigation," said Cmdr. Dennis Richardson, head of the Detroit Police major crimes section. "At the conclusion of that investigation, if we think it is appropriate, we will submit a warrant to the prosecutor's office."

Police said the visibly bruised woman, who filed a police report late Wednesday afternoon at the 1st (Central) Precinct, told investigators she is Crockett's ex-girlfriend.

She said she went to his house to console him over his recent breakup with his fiancee. The woman told police she and Crockett drank a few glasses of wine, and an argument ensued.

The woman said Crockett beat her, forced her to perform sexual acts and would not let her leave. She said she was able to escape only after Crockett calmed down and fell asleep.

"It is an allegation of a sexual assault in addition to a physical assault, but beyond that, we are not going to comment," Richardson said. "It's important that we be fair to both sides."

The woman could not be reached for comment Thursday. Her name is being withheld in accord with Free Press guidelines about sexual assault coverage.

Crockett's attorney, Gerald Evelyn, said the woman had ulterior motives for filing the police report, though he would not be specific.

"The judge is very concerned about the allegations and has cooperated fully with the police department," Evelyn said. "He is awaiting the results of the investigation. We fully expect him to be vindicated of any allegations that were made."

The charges went away, for whatever reason. At least all I know about them is what I read in the newspapers, and that's all I can find. I was dealing with the shuttle bus to prison at the time.

On October 12, 1993, I was focused on Judge Crockett but not on his personal quirks. I was deep into the wishful thinking I mentioned earlier. After all, Crockett had seen the truth of the testimony against Bob Lessnau and had set Bobby free. That was a good sign, no? He had appointed a three-judge panel for guidance in determining a sentence for Walter and me. That suggested even-handedness and a quest for fairness, no? The standard pre-sentence investigation by the probation department had produced nothing against me, as it should not have since I was an upstanding citizen with no prior record. I was given no negative points for priors, drug or alcohol abuse, or for an item often used to single out a defendant for especially harsh treatment – being the alleged "ringleader" of a criminal act. I was probably thinking, hard, about these good signs while Walter and I sat silently in the witness room waiting to be led in to hear our fates.

The highly unusual three-judge sentencing advisory panel had sounded particularly promising when Crockett announced it on September 20. The Detroit News noted that "whatever sentence Crockett hands down is expected to be controversial. Some segments of the community are calling for the maximum penalty – life in prison – while others advocate minimum time or say the verdicts should be set aside." The News said Crockett had used an advisory panel at least one other time, in 1982, after he found a News reporter guilty, in a bench trial, of the shooting death of his girlfriend, a police officer. The reporter was charged with second-degree murder. Crockett found him guilty of manslaughter and sentenced him to five years' probation. The reporter had to serve a mandatory two-year sentence on a felony firearms conviction. Even without knowing the details, it was the kind of case that caught my eye. Whatever had happened, for sure the reporter wasn't trying to arrest the dead woman for committing a felony and resisting arrest. Fact is, however, the announcement in the newspaper was the last I would ever hear about the three-judge panel. If their findings were ever released, my lawyer and I never heard about it.

It was a Tuesday morning as Walter and I waited to be summoned. In Saturday's paper, the Free Press ran a story speculating about what was going to happen to us. The top of the story noted that Judge Crockett had received "pounds and pounds" of letters on the subject, but the story didn't note the crucial one from O'Hair. The story went on:

Pre-sentence reports prepared by probation officers call for eight to twenty-five years – within state guidelines. Crockett is not bound to stay within those guidelines, but the law requires him to sentence Nevers and Budzyn to "some term of years."

Whatever he does, his decision is sure to leave many people unhappy.

Malice Green's family wants Nevers and Budzyn to get life in prison.

"They deserve it. They took life," said Monica Green, sister of the 35-year-old man who was beaten to death last November 5.

But Nevers's attorney will ask for a year of prison at most. The only reason he won't ask for probation is that the law won't let him.

"Larry has no prior record...He is one of the most commended officers in Detroit," said John Goldpaugh. Budzyn's attorney declined comment.

The story reported that Crockett, wading through public comment about what to do with us, had not yet made a decision as of Friday. The paper said the judge "is reading every letter, every report." And then it said that he "was halfway through the transcript of Nevers's post-conviction appearance on a WXYT radio talk show."

The story noted that I intended to speak at sentencing and Walter did not; and that the minute any prison time was ordered, notice of intent to appeal would be filed. The final words of the story were: "Even if Nevers does end up serving a long prison sentence, his attorney is confident he will come out alive, healthy and ready to live out the rest of his life normally. 'Larry's not a quitter,' Goldpaugh said. 'As long as there's a light at the end of the tunnel, he's going to be fine.'"

If I had read the papers before reporting to court that morning, I would have been told that "there are 135 ex-cops in federal prisons, and none is serving time for murder in the line of duty.... Murder is not a federal crime, but police officers convicted of major crimes are almost always sent to federal prisons for their own protection." The story rounded up various commentators who suggested that the reason police officers aren't convicted of murder in the line of duty is that prosecutors and juries are reluctant to convict cops. And the story included this interesting line: "Los Angeles police officers who shot a man in the back ninety-six times in 1990 – a year before the videotaped Rodney King beating – were never charged." Another story noted that the Michigan Department of Corrections was already geared up to put us in the federal prison system. A Corrections spokesman was quoted as saying: "The only way we can keep them safe in a state facility is to hold them captive in their cells for twenty-four hours a day. And we're not proponents of keeping people locked up in a box." There would come a time when I would like to have had that quote in neon above my cell door.

But reading the papers was not high on my priority list that day. If I glanced at them while trying to forget, for a moment, what was about to happen I certainly wouldn't remember a word I read. I barely remember speaking in court that day, and don't remember anything I said. In fact, except for the numbers of years that Judge Crockett pronounced, I don't remember any words that were spoken by anyone after we were led into his courtroom. I had to look them all up to write this chapter.

Green's sister Sherry addressed the court. She said: "Since the verdicts, we have been hurt and insulted by many who support these ex-officers and act as if my brother, who they never knew, did not have a right to live. We speak on behalf of all human beings, employed or unemployed, black, white, brown, yellow or red, who have a right not to be beaten to death simply because they suffer from an illness known as drug dependency."

I look at those words today and can only ponder how many thousands of times I came into contact with drug-dependent people on the street. Fifty thousand – ten times for every felony arrest I made – might be as good a guess as any. Think about it.

When it was my turn and then Walter's to speak, according to the Free Press report, it went like this:

>Nevers, wearing a necktie bearing stars and stripes, shuffled to the bench in front of Crockett and spoke in a voice thick with tears.

>"I never had the opportunity to express to the Green family my sincere apologies for the loss of their son, husband and father," he said. "Your honor, I did not kill Malice Green. I never intended to hurt him, to do anything to him other than to arrest him for a felony."

>Under questioning from Crockett about an arrest Nevers had made two days before Green's death, of a man who had shot his father, Nevers replied:

>"Every single arrest I've made in my twenty-four years – every single one – was non-confrontational if I could possibly make it so. If I were some kind of a brutal, killer cop running wild in the streets of Detroit casting my will upon everyone that I came in contact with, and if I was out there just to kill a black person, I certainly could have shot that man that had just killed his father. I'm not that type of an individual, your honor. I've never been that way."

>When Budzyn's time came, he brushed away uncharacteristic tears and spoke quickly in a nearly inaudible voice.

>"I'm sorry for what has happened. There's nothing I could ever do to change it – nothing. I was just doing my job and I was arresting him for narcotics. I never struck Mr. Green. Never."

And here is some of what Crockett told each of us.

To Walter: "I believe from the evidence I heard that you

did in fact strike Mr. Green. I believe from the evidence that I heard, the jury could have, as it did, find you guilty of creating a situation that exposed a person, Mr. Green, to serious physical injury or death and which did result in his death. The fact the jury found you guilty of murder in the second degree I cannot and do not quarrel with. However, sentencing is an individual thing and many, many factors can, should, frequently must be taken into consideration. The individual who gets killed, the result of that killing on his family, the community, you, what your life has been, the motivations that give rise to your actions and the result thereof. I don't think that you should be treated as a person who intended to kill someone. I don't think that was ever your intent."

Bottom line: Eight to eighteen years in prison.

I'd only be guessing if I tried to tell you what I thought as I heard Walter's sentence. For sure I was thinking about myself, as would anybody, because I was next. So I imagine I was reacting to being told that I was heading off to prison at age fifty-three (I'd had a birthday since the incident), short of breath, leaving a wife and daughter to make do while I could contribute nothing but a partial pension, and moving in with a population of felons – no matter how much care my jailers took in putting me in a "safe place." I think it's safe to say it was a more stunning moment than the verdicts. Crockett was not going to leave us free on bond pending appeal. This was it.

The judge turned his attention to me: "Mr. Nevers, you were the senior officer that evening, the most experienced, the elder. Yours were the blows that resulted in the death of Malice Green in all probability from the evidence that I have heard. I do not believe from the evidence that I heard, that you offered as well as was offered by the other witnesses, that you intended to kill Malice Green. I don't think you are an ordinary murderer, but what you did was excessive in the extreme. To strike a person, obviously seriously injured, and to tell persons that you would continue to do it further if the individual continued to struggle, which persons were uniquely qualified to provide medical assistance immediately, is a circumstance that cannot be overlooked."

Bottom line: twelve to twenty-five years in prison. I would be eligible for parole in nine years. The fact that I got a stiffer sentence than Walter stunned me. Every officer on the scene that night except Sergeant Freddie Douglas was a lowly patrolman in rank. Walter and I were doing the same job – trying to arrest Malice Green, a process which Walter began, which I tried to finish, and which was finally completed by Bobby Lessnau – though he needed help in putting the handcuffs on. The pre-sentencing report had rightly cleared me of any "ringleader" role in the events of November 5, 1992. I had struck Green on the head in self-defense and the struggle to subdue him – including the couple of times I used my flashlight after I summoned EMS to pull over. The whole thing stunk, but why was I being singled out as "the man who killed Malice Green"? I probably didn't think too deeply on this subject at the moment. The fact was, I was going to prison, and for longer than I had hoped, and for longer than Walter, and it all just ran together in a despairing moment. It wasn't until after I was in prison that I got the full meaning of O'Hair's and the NAACP's urging that Crockett throw the book at me. Of course, the black community thought I was getting off easy. And the editorial writers would say that Crockett had showed great wisdom in a sentence that was going to make neither side happy. And my side – including all 40,000 signers of that petition for a pardon – thought both sentences were a travesty. Again, I really have no idea what I was thinking at the moment, except making peace with the hard truth that I was gone.

Crockett's last words before rising and leaving the courtroom were: "The circumstances that gave rise to the loss of life of Mr. Green touched all of us. I have abiding faith in the cool heads that live in this community, in its sense of fair justice and fair play. This trial has demonstrated this city is without peer in this nation. This *is* Detroit, Michigan."

Well, yeah. Even after being one of the first two cops in

the nation that anyone could remember being found guilty of committing murder in the line of duty, even after being sentenced to hard time, everybody was worried about all those "cool heads" out on the street.

And just like that, I *was* gone. I turned and tried to catch Nancy's eye in the crowded, buzzing, media-filled courtroom. She was lost in a sea of faces and we never did make eye contact. Nancy on the other hand was forced to listen to some of those faces as they shouted niceties like: "Boy, they're waiting for those two cops! Wait till they get in there, then they'll get what's coming to them!" I think I actually went into some kind of trance. With the reality of it staring me in the face, suddenly nothing seemed real. Being scared of the unknown no doubt had something to do with it. Walter and I were taken into a hallway. A deputy handcuffed us. Then it was onto an elevator and down to the sub-basement in the Frank Murphy Hall of Justice. As many times as I had been in the building, I had only heard about the tunnel that led to the Wayne County Jail. Now I was seeing it for the first time, being led through as a prisoner. It was a long walk. I was getting tired. We emerged near the jail garage. The handcuffs were taken off and we were given some clothing to put on, including shoes. My suit, shirt and shoes were put into a bag and retained by a deputy.

Two identical mini-vans were waiting in the garage. A deputy put a bullet-proof vest on each of us. We were Public Enemy #1 and Public Enemy #2. I got the longer sentence, so I must have been #1. They put us in one of the identical vans. When the garage doors were opened, one van went in one direction and we went in another. Nobody spoke. Not the deputies, not us. I suppose Walter and I had reached a point where we couldn't do much except sit and wonder how we wound up where we were. We would have a lot of time for that.

Nobody handed us a travel agenda, and we really didn't know what was about to happen to us. I had some thoughts, none of them good, about a place seventy miles west of Detroit. Jackson Prison is Michigan's old main prison, and the gateway to the correctional system for common criminals. It used to hold the distinction of being America's "largest walled prison." Not a good place for a police officer convicted of murdering a drug user. We were apprehensive as the van rolled west. At least I know I was apprehensive, and it's a safe bet that Walter was, too. When our van pulled into the front gate of Jacktown, as the prison was known in street parlance, a wave of fear washed over me, but I held it in. My thoughts were that I would never survive this place. I had played softball in the prison once when my General Motors team visited to play the inmate team. Since becoming a police officer, my only connection with the place had been to send the warden many of his residents.

We were unloaded and led into an intake building of some kind. We were told to strip, given a small piece of soap and a small towel and ordered to take a shower. One of the guards – corrections officers, they prefer to be called – "closely" examined me head to toe, outside and inside. We were again given a completely new set of clothes – right down to shoes, socks and underwear. Maybe even a coat. I can't remember. But it was October in Michigan, so it would be a necessary part of any wardrobe. I was trying to make light of the situation, which is always a good way to go when you are scared. We were sat down in a cubicle near the shower room. A nurse gave TB tests, and asked about any health problems I might have. I knew about the emphysema, but that was it.

When the health interview was completed, we were taken back to the area where we entered the prison. Two uniformed guards stood holding long chains and a special restraining device. Each of us got the complete hog-tied-with-chains treatment – legs shackled together, then hands. Then they used what they call "the black box," a rectangular-shaped piece of metal maybe five inches long and three inches high. The belly chain traveled through the black box, which attached in front of your stomach. A set of handcuffs was concealed inside the black box with one cuff coming out of each side of the box. Once the belly chain, which wrapped around your entire body, was in place, one hand was placed in one of the cuffs and the other hand in the other cuff. There were only a few links protruding from either side of the black box. Therefore, when cuffed in this manner, you could not raise either arm more than six or eight inches. To scratch your nose, you had to lower your head to meet your fingers. With most prisoners, this kind of detailed description would sound like checking out the equipment to assess escape possibilities. With me, it was just a matter of familiarizing myself with tools related to my former profession, but not exactly something I'd ever see or use on the street. There was good news in all this. It meant we were being transferred somewhere else. Anywhere would be better than Jackson.

They loaded us in a different van and drove for at least two hours. If Walter and I spoke this time, I don't remember it. The feeling must have been a weird sense of relief at leaving Jackson, then recalibrating our apprehension about still another place. We had no idea where that might be. The first glance was oddly like pulling into the circular drive of a Marriott. It wasn't a Marriott. And to this day I have no idea why the guards couldn't have told us where we were headed. I didn't exactly have a cell phone to call a jailbreak mob to get us, and was no risk to do so anyway. It turned out to be Oaks Correctional Facility in Manistee, a Level 5 prison – Michigan's highest security rating. Maybe I was sleeping when we passed through the outer fences. I did a lot of sleeping those first few days of incarceration. It was, after all, a nightmare. Maybe I was hoping it would be over when I woke up. Maybe I was exhausted. Who knows? But I did sleep a lot.

They took us inside and into what looked like a board room, took off the cuffs and chains and seated us at a long table. A couple prison officials talked to us, but all I remember is asking if I could call Nancy and tell her where I was, since she had no idea. They allowed a quick call – but first I had to ask where I was, because I didn't know either. Quick as the call was, I'm sure Nancy wouldn't have told me, even if we had time to talk, that Kelly had launched into inconsolable scream-crying at her grandmother's house when she heard the sentences.

They gave us a couple of sheets and a small plastic pillow and case and led us into a courtyard where I could see five or six buildings. We were led to the second floor of one building and we were put in different cells, separated by a cinderblock wall. I put a sheet on the gym mat that served as a mattress atop a six-foot concrete slab. The only other features of my new surroundings were a stainless steel sink with attached toilet, a stainless steel mirror bolted to the wall, and a barred Plexiglas window about seven feet off the floor.

I was inside the correctional system, feeling like the things that needed correcting were on the outside. No matter how often I fell asleep, I was still inside when I woke up.

20
LIFE AS #124259

O ur temporary stay at Oaks, shorthand for the Manistee prison, lasted exactly a month. It was a foggy month spent getting used to loss of freedom, something you of course never get used to. But you adjust to reality, make adjustments and keep the faith, or you die.

As painful as the shock of incarceration is, the pain isn't half as deep – not a tenth as deep – as what sets in after your time served gets longer and longer. Besides, once Nancy and everybody else found out where we were, somebody on the Oaks staff claimed we set a record for visitors and mail. Probably not true, but a lot of people did make the long drive up from Detroit. Nancy, Kelly, Paul Fitzgerald, my old partner Woody Horne, Mark Scott, my brother and his wife, my cousin and his wife. I talked to Walter's ex-wife and daughter when they visited. Doing time is about hope of getting through to the end, and often – as in our case – hope of winning your appeal, which had been put in motion. More on that later. So my introduction to life as an imprisoned felon was numbing and disheartening, but I'd have to say that – with Nancy's help – I found a way to make hope a part of every day. Well, most days.

Walter and I met our fate together at the corner of Warren Avenue and Twenty-Third Street. Somehow the criminal justice system seemed determined to keep us partners. We stood trial together, and we would be shipped around the prison system together. We didn't know this when we got to Oaks. In fact, we didn't know much of anything except that at some unknown time we would be transferred to some unknown place or places. Ultimately, we would spend four years together in the same seven-foot by ten-foot cell many miles from Michigan. But this first month we had separate accommodations as we awaited transfer. We were totally segregated from the rest of the population and never saw another inmate except through cracks in our cell doors. We got an hour a day of yard time, during which we could walk or use the outdoor phone. Yard time for us two special guests was 10:30 p.m. The long walk to the visitors room was a welcome diversion, at least at first.

After a couple of weeks, they revealed that Walter and I both would be going to the Fort Worth Medical Center in the federal prison system, but didn't say when. Neither of us needed special medical attention that we knew of, but the last thing the criminal justice establishment wanted was to have its two infamous killer cops murdered on their watch. Texas was their choice of a safe place to warehouse Walter and me.

A few days before the transfer – though we still did not know when that was going to be – some federal honcho, a former warden at the Texas prison, showed up at Oaks. We were taken from our cells to an office, and introduced. He told us about our destination and answered questions (we didn't have many). Scuttlebutt was that we would be flown to our destination, so I requested some Dramamine for the trip. The Oaks doctor gave me a couple of tablets and told me to hold onto them for the flight. Early the morning of November 11, 1993, Walter and I were gathered up for the trip. The first thing they did was retrieve my two Dramamine pills. We would not be boarding a plane.

We packed our meager belongings and were walked to the administration building. The warden and a couple of other Oaks staff met us, along with two guys who were not wearing any kind of uniform. They turned out to be our rent-an-escorts. I named them Mutt and Jeff. They were our chauffeurs for twenty-three scenic hours headed south in another paneled van from which we could see nothing except hazy glimpses through the heavy police screen separating us from Mutt and Jeff, peering between their heads and out the windshield. Even that much required movement that wasn't easy while in chains. I think Mutt and Jeff were armed. Trying to get some conversation going, I asked. They refused to answer. No doubt they were afraid the ever-dangerous Starsky and Hutch would, despite their shackles and black boxes, make a run for it at the next pee break, or at the two McDonald's stops we made along the way.

Unlucky for me, I was the only non-smoker in the van. Mutt and Jeff kept lighting up. Walter even managed to smoke while in shackles, bending his head forward to take a puff. One way I passed time was to calculate, using the dashboard clock, that there were only seven minutes in every hour when new smoke wasn't circulating through the vehicle. Mutt, who was driving at the time, managed to make one of our gasoline stops hilarious. We were in Missouri, the Show Me State. Mutt went in, pre-paid, came out, and started pumping gas. He climbed back in and was ready to drive off when the loudspeaker at the pumps blared that he should come back inside. He was in there a long time when a highway patrol car pulled up, which is how I figured out we were in Missouri. Even knowing what state you're in is not the kind of thing you learn from a couple of lip-locked rent-an-escorts. The trooper went inside, and it was a few minutes before Mutt came back out. Seems he had passed a phony twenty-dollar bill. Mutt told the clerk and the trooper that he must have picked up the bogus bill at our previous stop in another state. Apparently, one and all believed Mutt's story, because Mutt and his human cargo were quickly back on the road to Texas.

When we pulled into the prison parking lot, rent-a-Jeff stepped out and took our paperwork into a building. When he emerged, he told us it was shift change and we would have to sit tight for a few minutes. We were now almost twenty-four hours in chains and black boxes, and more than a little stiff when it came time to get out of the van. As we did, a prison vehicle came flying up a gravel drive, scattering stones as it ground to a stop. The driver jumped out and stood in front of his car with a 12-gauge shotgun held in military position. Thousands of times I had jumped out of a government-owned vehicle and into genuinely bad situations. Now here's this guy staring back and forth at Walter and me to detect the slightest move of two police officers – chained and road-weary, inside a prison, taking hunched baby steps to move a couple of inches at a time – as if we are about to make a break for it and blow away a few guards in the process. I thought: "What a puss." What little humor I could find in this new life, I found in the damnedest things.

The complex included, up front, a pair of two-story housing units including the one Walter and I would be in. Three housing units that were really sections of one big building sat in the back. There was a chow hall and an attached commissary, an administration building that included the visitors' room, a central building where crafts were taught and where inmates could, on free time, play pool or table tennis or cards, and the "jail" or "hole" where rule-breakers were sent. A free-standing hospital was built while we were there; when we arrived it was a section of one of the housing units. There was a running track, a soccer field and an outdoor weight "room." I'm not sure how much detail I could see at first glance standing in chains with an armed guard, but it was clearly a "campus" and not just one big pile of walls and bars. I would sink into real despair in this place, but it was a country club compared to Oaks. Of course, like every step in my life as a prisoner and as a Ping-Pong ball in the criminal justice system, I had no idea what lay ahead. All I knew for sure is that I wasn't free. I was no longer Badge #2034. I was federal inmate #124259.

I'm being honest when I say this was a "country club" by comparison. But let me say no one would pay ten cents a year to be a member of this Club Fed, even if they were free to come and go as they pleased. The buildings were surrounded by two razor-wire fences, and armed guards circled the compound endlessly in prison vehicles. Daily life inside was a mind-numbing regimen of menial labor and boredom. We called our cramped quarters our "room," not our "cell." The room had no door, and there were bars on the windows. If we stood and looked out, we saw a fenced-in visiting yard where visitors and inmates were usually allowed to meet if the weather was good. Any inmate who broke the rules wound up in the hole – not in a metal box like in the movies, but locked down twenty-three hours a day in a one-man room with no access to the TV room or a few minutes' conversation with a Mafioso or a drug kingpin or even a couple infamous killer cops. Texas was a place where I dug in to survive, to try to make at least some kind of phony life within the smothering routine, and to as often as possible stay on top of appealing my case. That was enough to keep me going. It would be a very long time before I wound up believing the criminal justice system would never recognize that Walter and I had been railroaded. Meantime, I used my wits and played the game, much as I had on the street all those years.

After two weeks locked down in the prison hospital – I guess to "ease us into the system" – they moved Walter and me to one of the housing units, in the same room. We were put on the second floor of the "Fort Worth" unit (every unit was named after a Texas city). Years and years of driving separate and competing booster cars in the Third Precinct. Then just a few days working as permanent partners in the same car. Then one arrest gone bad. And now we were about to spend an unknown number of years in the same seven-by-ten, Walter looking for rescue by his appeals lawyers and me looking for rescue by mine. It wasn't a renewed competition, just separate paths. All those endless days trapped together in close Texas quarters, and the only time Walter and I ever talked about the Malice Green incident would be whenever a snippet of news made its way to Forth Worth about his appeal or mine. That's it. Period. Kym Worthy and Doug Baker, who sneered at the idea that Walter and I didn't know exactly what the other was doing within the close quarters of Malice Green's Topaz, would sneer again if they had learned this fact. Let them sneer. That was Walter, and that was me. I can hear Worthy barking: "Do you think this jury was born yesterday?" But the truth is, Walter and I didn't talk much about anything – he didn't get a reputation as "stoic Walter" for nothing. And we simply did *not* talk at all about that night on Warren Avenue. There was one notable exception. I'll tell you about it now, even though we must have been inside a while before it happened. I don't know exactly how long. At least six months, I'd guess.

Walter blurted out: "You know, if it weren't for you I wouldn't be in this (various expletives deleted) place!"

I cannot remember well enough to quote verbatim the heated but brief conversation that ensued. I know the gist of it. I responded along the lines of: "What the hell are you talking about? You're the one who lost control of the situation. You're the one who needed help. What was I supposed to do? Stand there and watch this guy take your gun and shoot you? I didn't put you in here – Crockett and that #&^@*# jury put you in here!"

There wasn't much more to it. Walter calmed down. I calmed down. We never talked that way again. Walter was a good cop. I was a good cop. Neither one of us has ever figured it out completely, even today. It would have been nice if more people had understood how some things that go bad cannot be figured out, and you have to look at a bigger picture. Not a picture of white racist cops running wild, but a picture of a struggle with a coke-using felon outside a dope house. Sorry, Ms. Worthy. That's all there was to it.

I worked my way through a succession of prison jobs before I finally found the closest thing they had to a booster-car shift. Night shift, independent, not getting up early with the herd. It was a laundry detail, but not a half-dozen guys standing around a big room full of washing machines like in the movies. Every orderly was issued one towel a day, along with various cleaning products, to clean up our housing unit.

These towels got as dirty as a towel could get, and at the end of the day the orderlies would toss them in a bin. My job was to pull these rancid towels out of the bin, clean them up spic and span, and fold them nicely for the next shift. It only added up to maybe thirty towels a day, but there was no hot water in the place; so getting them clean wasn't easy. Now this is not exactly the Tiger Stadium detail, but I worked alone and I was able to avoid as much contact as possible with the guards, whose main job seemed to be to make our lives more miserable. There wasn't even much contact with other inmates, as we all had to wash our own clothes, and I was using the laundry room when no one else was. In fact, the guards listed my job as starting after midnight. This meant I could start my work any time after 10:30 a.m. (by which time the orderlies were done with their cleaning) until 7:30 the next morning, when they started their work again. Besides that, my "work week" began on Sunday and ended on Friday morning, so I pretty much had weekends to myself. Finally came a time when because of postage stamps and a deck of cards, I rarely did my laundry job at all. I'll tell you about that in a minute.

Besides regular assignments, prisoners had tasks such as stripping floors whenever an inspection team or some prison system honcho was scheduled to visit. Floors would have to be waxed, and first we'd have to get rid of the previous application of wax. We'd get down on our hands and knees and scrape away with a single-edged razor blade, often as not without a blade-holder. Of course, all the blades were carefully collected and counted when we were finished.

Walter had been a workaholic as a cop, and he wasn't about to change in prison. It was his way of helping time go faster. While I was trying to avoid the system and the drudgery, he seemed to make contact with it wherever possible. He was always helping somebody with something, just like he was always in to work early at the Third, fiddling with our radios. In prison he pretty soon worked his way into being clerk of our housing unit, which was damned near like reporting to work on the outside. He had hours of maybe 7:30 a.m. to 4 p.m., and was subject to being awakened by a guard in the middle of the night to register a new arrival. It got to the point where guards would wake up Walter (and me) just because they needed help doing some piece of paperwork. Naturally, some inmates began to wonder if Walt was a snitch, like the guy in "Stalag 17." I set them straight. As unit clerk, Walter was entitled to have a twelve-inch color TV set in his room, which was also my room. Never once did he ask me what I wanted to watch. I guess it was his way of defining the place as "his room" even though it contained two people.

Only a handful of the Forth Worth unit's seventy or so rooms had television sets. Anyone who worked on computers in the administration building had one. Anyone who worked a specialized job in "prison industries" had one. The unit clerk, Walter, had one. Everybody else watched TV on 25-inch sets in one of the three TV rooms (bring your own chair), exception being that anyone working as an orderly got to have a TV for a week at a time on a rotating basis. Pro and college sports broadcasts were when the TV rooms filled up. There was a lot of betting on the games (against the rules, of course), as well as on the "football cards" that somehow made their way into the prison. The only other time I can recall the TV rooms filled to capacity were the nights A&E did a Malice Green special on *American Justice* and the night *Sixty Minutes* ran its piece. Walt and I watched in our room with a friend or two. The only reaction I remember from the inmates was a few of them coming up to me and saying that Walt and I "really got screwed."

There were vending machines in each unit. Soda pop, candy bars and chips. Each room was assigned one commissary night per week, and on that night you could go to the PX and spend up to $40 out of your prison account – if you had the account funded – to buy things like socks, underwear, toiletries, stationery, reading material, postage stamps, whatever. When we first got to Texas, you were also allowed to buy one roll of quarters a week for use in the vending machines. A few months after we got there, they upgraded the machines to include doughnuts, popcorn and peanuts. And they eliminated coinage, issuing vendor cards – which, again, required you to have a funded prison account. They also installed microwaves, one on each floor. We were cashless, we had no refrigerator and no stove. But we did have ice machines and now the microwaves, which quickly became an important part of the culture.

Breakfast was 6 a.m. By the time I had the laundry job, I rarely bothered to roll out of the sack for breakfast. Except when hard-boiled eggs were on the menu. I like hard-boiled eggs. Word got around, and even if I stayed in the sack somebody occasionally would come by with a few hard-boiled eggs and we'd settle up with postage stamps (lots more to come about postage stamps). Lunch was around noon and I usually went. Dinner was at 5 p.m. Housing units went to the chow hall one unit at a time, with the unit rated cleanest on inspection going first. Our unit went first for a long time, then we got a new unit manager and the inspectors apparently didn't like him. Suddenly, we were last to the chow hall. A vegetarian in the unit consumed far too much garlic, but was good for trading a couple pieces of fruit for a second piece of chicken.

Having food in your room, other than stuff from the vending machines or commissary, was forbidden. So you'd find ways of hiding a small stockpile. On some occasions, I'd have a dozen hard-boiled eggs stashed away. One day an inmate stopped outside the room and asked: "Wanna buy two dozen raw eggs?" I have no idea how he managed to get two dozen eggs out of the chow hall kitchen, or how he had hidden them for the seventy-five-yard journey without breaking any. I got another guy to buy a dozen and I bought the other. Both with stamps, of course. I had become friends with a Hispanic guy in the unit, a couple of years older than me. He had shown me how to make perfect hard-boiled eggs in the microwave, a process that required making a tiny puncture in each egg. So now I had a dozen raw eggs I wasn't supposed to have, no refrigerator, and therefore no way to keep them very long. I decided to make four trips to the microwave over the next day or so, taking three at a time. Each time I made the trip the microwave was in use. I even went down to the first-floor microwave – same problem. Finally, I found the coast clear, put the three eggs in a plastic bowl with a little water, made the tiny puncture in each, and hit the start button. Shortly before the eggs were supposed to be ready there was an explosion of water and eggs that blew the door open, spreading egg-and-water goo everywhere. I hustled to clean the place up before a guard came on the scene and I had to explain what I was doing with raw eggs. I wasn't sure if that was an offense worthy of being sent to the hole. I didn't get caught, but the first floor was without a microwave for a couple weeks.

Speaking of the hole, most of the unit would have been up and to breakfast and back by the time the workday began at 7:30. There were a few, like myself, whose work schedule meant they were still in the sack, and a few more any given day who skipped breakfast. An old guy on our floor became somewhat overzealous with his responsibilities in mopping the floor each morning, which were supposed to include *occasionally* buffing the floor with a waxing machine. This guy loved his waxing machine. He used it every day and instead of starting at 7:30 like everyone else, he'd start about twenty minutes early. And every morning anyone still in the sack would yell at him to "turn off your #%@^$! machine!" This didn't deter him. In fact, he'd yell back. The corridor was L-shaped, and when he went around the corner, someone would run out and unplug the damned thing. Undaunted, he'd walk back, plug it in, and challenge whoever unplugged it to come out and "face him like a man." Somebody got at the waxer one night and messed with the wiring trying to make it short out. Didn't work. The morning noise continued. We started calling this guy "the Uni-Buffer." Finally somebody – while the Uni-Buffer was buffing – went into his room and set his mattress afire. The rules are that if your mattress burns, you go to the hole – no matter the story behind the burning. As they led the Uni-Buffer off in cuffs, he was shouting threats at anyone within earshot. But that was the last morning the waxing machine ever got put into operation before 7:30.

Our unit and the "Dallas" unit directly across from us looked to be inhabited mostly by middle-aged inmates. Units at the back of the facility – Austin, San Antonio and Houston – seemed to be filled by younger, maybe more violent types. No one ever said so, and I never asked, but that's the way it looked. The Dallas unit is where Detroit Police Chief William Hart was incarcerated for his indiscretion in the disappearance of a million dollars from a secret department fund. Walter, that notorious racist rogue cop, often would pass time by wheeling Detroit's first black chief around in his wheelchair. I occasionally passed time chatting with them, usually on my commissary night when I could buy the chief ice cream. Fate can be a strange thing.

When I got to Texas, my intention had been to go into the prison industries operation and try to send a few bucks back to Detroit to help out Nancy. I think you could make a couple hundred dollars a month over there, but the warden wouldn't allow either Walter or me to work outside our unit. Apparently, there too many of the younger, more violent prisoners from other units would have enjoyed the opportunity to introduce a police officer to a piece of industrial equipment. Meanwhile, orderlies made seven dollars a month for jobs like cleaning towels. I did find a way I could send a piddling few bucks back home occasionally; but that involves postage stamps – which, as I keep saying, I will be telling you about shortly.

The house on Bretton Drive was no mansion, but it was as solidly middle-class as it gets in Detroit. I didn't make a fortune as a street cop, but because of the kind of cop I was the time I spent in court by day went a long way toward helping make the house payments (we had remortgaged to pay for Kelly's tuition at Sacred Heart Academy). Now I was contributing nothing but a partial pension check, and an entire Detroit pension check would only have been half a suburban police officer's pension check. So Nancy and Kelly were basically hanging on with what Nancy made on her own job. For a while we were given a $500 monthly check from a fund raised by other police officers and distributed among all seven cops suspended in the Green case. By the time I was in Texas, it was obviously time to give up the Bretton Drive house. It had been Nancy's dream place, but it had to go. Then Nancy's mother died and I talked Nancy into selling the house. She and Kelly moved in with her father in Dearborn Heights, where she could live for free but had a much longer commute.

Nancy and I talked almost every day. It was a weird thing about the regimented life in the Fort Worth unit that I had to hide hard-boiled eggs in my locker, and couldn't have twenty-five cents cash, but I could make phone calls every day from, as I recall, 8 a.m. to 10 p.m. There was a short approved list of people I could call, but as long as the call was paid for I could place it. The time limit was fifteen-minutes, but if no one was waiting to use the phone you could call again. Calls were subject to monitoring by "them," so, of course, I could not plan any jailbreaks. But we soon found a way of talking to Darin, who wasn't on the approved list. Nancy – even if she was at work – would say something like, "Darin's here and wants to talk to you." And she would call out to Darin on a three-way hookup, and he would fill me in on all the efforts on our behalf back in Detroit. Nancy was incredible. She had a daily goal of coming up with one positive thing each day to plant in my head, almost like me making my daily quota of taking guns and drugs off the street. I'm a pretty resourceful and determined guy, and Fort Worth wasn't Devil's Island, but I really don't think I would have made it the way I did without her incredible support.

Nancy and Kelly came down twice to visit. The first time they brought my brother and his wife, and Paul Fitzgerald. The second time they came alone. Saying goodbye was always difficult, to say the least. The second time they visited I watched

Kelly as she walked away, and caught her bursting into tears. That was it. I ordered no more visits from either Nancy or Kelly as long as I was in prison. As much for me as for them.

Before the no-visitors order went out, Rita Petranovic drove all the way to Texas with her kids and her friend Vicki Duff. Both were hard-working members of the support group. Rita's ex-husband had been my partner briefly, so she knew about my pride-and-joy wheels, the Lincoln Mark VII. I had Nancy sell the Mark to Rita before she sold the house. By driving the Mark to Texas, Rita put more miles on it in a couple of days than I would have in six months.

In the end, I was only allowing one person to visit, the Rev. Harold Elliott, chaplain of the Arlington, Texas, police department. I met him when he read about our case and paid an unsolicited visit. As you know, I am not religious. But the good reverend is a very special guy. He visited once or twice a month, we talked a lot, and his visits served me well. What I liked about Harold was that he never talked religion (unless I did). We talked about the case, we talked about his family, we talked about his involvement with the Arlington P.D. He *always* (at my urging) came to our visits with a pocketful of quarters that got spent in the visiting room's vending machines. These machines were nothing like the ones in our housing unit. They contained hot dogs, hamburgers, cheeseburgers, pizza, ham-and-cheese sandwiches, etc. This stuff was a genuine gourmet quality treat.

A father-and-daughter lawyer team from Detroit, sympathetic to our case, came down, and offered to give Nancy any advice that might be useful. Donna Barbera, a reporter from Detroit's biggest radio station, WJR, came to do an interview. Rich Fisher, the anchor from Channel 2 and son of a police officer, did an interview. There was the *American Justice* interview for A&E. And, of course, there was the Ed Bradley interview for *Sixty Minutes*. Court TV asked for an interview. I told them sure, if they would provide Walter and me with videotapes of the entire trial. They pleaded poverty, so I said no thanks to the interview. Clearly, there was interest in our case. Particularly, the cocaine part of it. But those interviews were spread across several years, not several months. Everything about our case came to be measured in years, not months.

There were piles of letters and cards. A few crank letters, but mostly encouraging. One letter was the beginning of a golden friendship. It came from a housewife named Lynne Krueger who, like a lot of people, had become incensed about our situation just from reading the facts of the case. Lynne was and is a remarkable woman, a very religious and bright mother of ten kids, all of them home-schooled. She began clipping and gathering every story she could find about the Green case. And then she wrote to Nancy, who forwarded me the letter, as she did with many others. I answered Lynne's first letter, and in answering her questions I wrote down what became the beginning of this book, something she encouraged. Lynne became a champion of both Walter and me and put together a web site accessed by police officers and others from all around the country. Her incredible attention to detail made her the unofficial archivist for the Budzyn-Nevers support effort. By the time of my second trial, she was an official member of the defense team, sitting at the table and helping my attorney with her carefully compiled and indexed collection of articles, documents and transcripts – all the while pregnant with her tenth child. I hope she's glad there's finally a book. Her work is no small part of that.

So there were a lot of things going on the outside, and a lot of people keeping me informed about it and helping me keep faith of getting another chance in the court system. I'm going to tell you how that went in the next chapter; but first, as promised, let me tell you about postage stamps.

The thing about money is that in places where there literally is no money, people invent money – and ways to accumulate it. You've figured out that postage stamps became the inmates' money. This "currency" was deflated the instant you spent it – a Postal Service booklet of stamps cost $5.80 at face value when

I arrived in Texas, but if you used it as money in prison it was traded as a $5 bill. The most the money supply could increase per week would be two times the number of prisoners, who each were allowed to buy two books of stamps per week at the commissary. So 80 cents per booklet ($1.10 after a rate hike that took effect while I was inside) just kind of disappeared into thin air when you used stamps as cash. That's because among inmates who accumulated this "money" in various ways, very few stamps got put on letters or got passed to the outside and sold for face value. At least not as long as you were a prisoner. Theoretically, if you had a warehouse full of stamps you could not get out the door with them, because it was against the rules to possess more than three booklets of stamps. This made gathering wealth a little dicey. Forbidden food, like my hard-boiled eggs, I usually would just put in my locker without trying real hard to hide it. I assumed that if a guard found my eggs I'd just lose them and not be slapped with punishment – though you never knew. Stamps were a different matter. For one thing, if stamps were confiscated you lost your money – which is one place the phantom 80 cents per booklet disappeared to. For another thing, you were liable to be punished. Eventually, I accumulated more stamps than almost anybody in my housing unit. Stories going around said that a guy in the Dallas unit had been busted with three hundred books of stamps. I never had anything like that in my treasury, but I did OK. To explain my success in accumulating this phony money, I have to explain the gambling that went on inside.

Let me start with Walter, who had a close personal relationship with gambling before he went to prison – but who amazingly didn't gamble at all, so far as I know, while he was inside. I shouldn't say Walt was a gambler on the outside. He was a lottery player. He loved to play the state's numbers. He was one of those guys who you might say blew a big chunk of his paychecks on the lottery – except that, of course, he got some of it back. A few times, in fact, he scored some very nice payoffs. For all I know, Walter was ahead of the game, though considering the nature of the game and the gusto with which Walt pursued it that seems unlikely. Anyway, Walter being Walter, he wasn't slow to share his good fortune when lady luck smiled down on him. Several times after a nice lottery payoff Walter took almost everybody from our shift (plus a few supervisors he liked on the afternoon shift) out to dinner at Carl's Chop House, a very nice place to chow down. This was Walt's nature – a workaholic who liked to help people, whether it was Rosa Parks and her stolen car or Bill Hart in his wheelchair…and who liked to hammer the lottery, and be generous when he won. But during his years in prison, Walt somehow just walked away from any opportunity to take a chance, unless he hid that from me, which is not probable. With Walter, postage stamps in Texas mostly meant a way to send a letter.

I, on the other hand, fell full-bore into a sort of permanent floating prison gambling circuit. I even helped create it. There are two reasons for this. First, I love to play cards. Especially blackjack. I've never been a vacation-taker, but give me a chance to fly out to Vegas for a couple of days spent mostly playing blackjack, and I'm in heaven. Second, the way you survive prison is to take every opportunity to make prison life as "normal" as you can. Playing cards is something I loved to do on the outside. Finding a way of doing something in prison that I loved to do on the outside was a way of fighting the boredom, doing the time, and pretending I had a life in there. It didn't hurt that I was good at it, even though blackjack wasn't one of the games we played. Gambling was, of course, strictly forbidden.

When I arrived in Texas, it took me a while to fall into the laundry job, to find my bearings with the routine and the inmates, to feel out how and how far one could press the rules. All those things eventually led to my extensive card-playing life, but that took a while. It all kind of overlaps, and I can't remember the time line very well. For instance, once I got the laundry job I had huge flexibility in my hours. And sometime after I got that job, I began hiring other people to do it for me. This gave me still more time to play cards – when I wasn't walking five miles every day on the prison track, or working out in the outdoor weight "room" – something I did three or four times a week until I injured my shoulder. How did I pay somebody to do the laundry job for me? Stamps. Where did I get the stamps? Playing cards. That's three offenses right there – gambling, possessing too many stamps, and paying somebody else to do my work. I was lucky about not getting caught. Except once.

Everything we owned or purchased at the commissary had to be kept in our lockers. This didn't leave much storage space. There was a hook on the side of the locker where I hung my coat and a white mesh nylon laundry bag. Instead of dirty clothes, I used the laundry bag to store large bags of potato chips or pretzels. One day, we got word that guards were going to empty the unit and shake down the rooms. We'd be searched on the way out, so I couldn't take any stamps with me. Among other hiding places I put one stash of twenty stamp books – $100 "street" value – in my bag of pretzels. A guard found them. I was penalized three weeks of commissary privileges. And, of course, I lost $100. I had a few other, better hiding places, including in the ceiling above a light fixture. Anybody hiding things had to do a good job of it, not only because the guards were constantly looking for stamps and other contraband, but because the place was, of course, filled with criminals – who knew all the usual hiding places and a few more. One day I found a TV set at the bottom of my laundry bin. Who'd ever look under a pile of filthy towels? The guard who found stamps in my pretzels, by the way, was a decent guy and he apologized a few days later. If I had been the guard, and knew they belonged to an ex-police officer railroaded for murder, I would have ignored the hidden stamps.

When I first started playing cards for "money," it was mostly gin rummy. We played one-on-one, or partners, and we also had little tournaments. Most of the time I won, and most of the time I got stiffed on what was owed me. The games were usually the same bunch of players but were open to anyone, and word got around to other units that gin was being played. During this gin rummy phase, one guy who loved to play was a Mafia type who was dying of lead poisoning. The real kind of lead poisoning, not the kind Mafia types are usually associated with. He was a mean guy, and he was convinced I was cheating. Maybe that's because I usually won. You have to know that I have never cheated at cards in my life. I don't even know how. I'm just a steady player who pays attention to what you are supposed to do when you have any given hand. I don't play impulses. I play what you are supposed to play. Always. At any rate, I cleaned this Mafia guy's clock at partner gin one night and it resulted in the closest I came to being a victim of physical violence while in Texas. No way could I have handled this guy – he was 5-foot-9 at most but about two hundred and twenty-five pounds and built like concrete. More important, a fight was like a mattress-burning – it didn't matter what the story was, you get in a fight and you go to the hole. So when I wanted to quit playing around midnight, and he pinned me in a corner in his idiotic rage over imaginary cheating, I stayed cool and talked my way out of a real confrontation. Just as I always had on the street whenever possible.

I think the card games started gravitating toward seven-card stud after I had been in for about two years, around the same time a youngish Texas drug-dealer – an unusual profile for our unit – got housed there. He liked to play. When you're playing poker, it's a little harder to keep up the façade that you're not gambling. So pressure from the guards would run hot and cold, and we'd back off when necessary and return to playing gin. But for much of my last two years in Texas, I played a *lot* of seven-card stud. If I had been able to collect more of my winnings, I could have sent a few meaningful grocery checks back to Nancy. I did manage to get a couple of bucks sent into the Detroit treasury in circuitous ways.

One player had somebody in prison industries make us some chips out of cardboard. This lasted maybe two nights before the guards confiscated them. Then we tried to keep track of all the bets on paper – a total disaster. Then for a long time we used old playing cards as chips, each one worth a quarter or a dollar depending on the stakes. Winners were paid in stamps or "goods" – or a promise to pay. Sometimes these IOUs would hit $100 or more. There is at least some honor among thieves, because I did collect on some of these debts. The debtor would contact someone in his family and have the money sent to Nancy, or in a money order to my prison account (the prison wouldn't accept checks; probably a smart idea). Because the phones were monitored, this all had to be done by mail, which might take a month. If payment was to be in "goods," and a loser owed me four books of stamps, I'd give him a $20 shopping list of items for his next trip to the commissary. And, of course, most of the time I never got paid. A couple "goods" IOUs did get paid off with a new pair of gym shoes and a radio. Over time, we got wise to the deadbeats and started requiring a stamps-for-poker-chips buy-in right up front.

Sometimes we held tournament play, where an inmate might buy, say, 100 chips for a book of stamps. It was winner-take-all, and when your chips were gone, you were out of the tournament. The winner might collect six or seven books of stamps for his efforts. When the heat got on and we reverted to gin rummy, the tournaments were actually bigger – often twenty or more entries, each playing a two-out-of-three or five-out-of-seven game. These tournaments were big enough that we could give the second-place finisher a book or two as a consolation prize. I did quite well at both gin and poker. It was good to be recognized as good at something again. And good, at least for any minutes when the cards were running my way, to get my mind off the reality of where I was.

Because I was walking and working out, and because prison food wasn't the sort of thing to make you want to overeat even if you were allowed to, I lost weight and probably got in better shape than I had been in years. The emphysema didn't go away, of course, so shortness of breath and a little coughing were no surprise, even though I was in better trim. But after a routine X-ray, the prison doc said I had spots on my right lung that might be cancerous. He ordered a CAT-scan. This would not be good news anywhere, anytime; but one of my real fears about prison – and I imagine one of any prisoner's real fears – was dying inside the fence. Waiting for the CAT-scan results was not a good period. After spending a couple of weeks getting a consensus on what the scan meant, word came back that there was no cancer. Sometime after that I was blessed with shingles and wound up in the prison hospital for eleven days. I came very close to losing an eye as the infection spread down from my scalp onto my face. And that, in a paragraph, was my health history in Texas. It would come back to haunt me soon enough.

So those are my war stories from my first trip to prison. I wasn't chained to a wall in a dungeon. I didn't get killed, or even beat up. I'm sure I'm supposed to be grateful for that. I finally did come out – for a while. I'll tell you about that in the next chapter. For this part of the story, just please know that living by your wits, keeping your sanity, being able to get out of your cell for many hours a day, being able to play some poker...nothing changes the fact that you're in prison. You already know that; but not really. You have to experience it to understand what it means to suffer the greatest loss a person can suffer without dying: *time*. It's not waking up one morning and discovering you are years older than you were the day before. It's watching those wasted days take a month apiece to slip by. When you believe in your heart you don't belong in that cell...the loss is impossible to describe.

21
ONE JUDGE
GETS IT RIGHT

The appeals process began immediately after the verdicts, even before Walter and I were led away on October 12. The notice of intent to appeal was filed. A request for bond pending appeal was made and, of course, denied. In my few weeks of freedom before sentencing, Nancy and I set to work trying to figure out what legal path we could follow once Recorder's Court got through with us.

The first and obvious thing we did was interview appellate lawyers. We had no idea what we were doing. We didn't know anything about appeals lawyers, and didn't know how we'd finance an appeal. The police union, once again, had a very small budget. Our own budget was smaller and shrinking. We interviewed several lawyers. One, Mark Kriger, told us we should have Neil Fink handle the appeal. Neil was one of the highest-profile – maybe the highest-profile – criminal attorneys in Detroit. By now we had figured out that appeals work was a specialty, and we didn't even know Neil did appeals work. The morning of October 12 we still hadn't figured out what we were going to do, mostly because of the money situation. And we certainly hadn't talked to Neil.

Nancy was still in the courtroom on sentencing day when word got to her that Mark Kriger had some people who wanted to talk about taking our case to the next step. After Walter and I were driven off to Jackson Prison, Nancy went to a lunch meeting in Greektown just a few blocks from Recorder's Court.

She found Mark Kriger there with Neil Fink and another lawyer named Carol Stanyar. My brother, his wife, and Darin Chase also attended the meeting. It was decided that Carol would write the appeals brief with input from Neil. Nobody talked about money. We figured the reason Carol and Neil agreed to do the work for DPOA "union scale" was the publicity. That was fine with us, both from the financial side and because that sounded to us like someone who was confident of victory.

I'm not even an *amateur* lawyer, not even after spending more than a decade bouncing around the courts and the prison system, with lots of time to ponder all the stuff that came down around me. I was even less of a lawyer the day I went to prison. When the appeals process began, I was about as naïve as it gets. For one thing, the process is slow. Very slow. And, I of course, thought that the minute some court outside Detroit got a look at our trial, things would change very quickly. Instead, the politics of the Malice Green case got fed all the way up the courts' food chain. You can believe that or not as I tell the story. But one thing I've learned is absolutely undeniable. The way justice works, if you've been stamped "guilty" in big, bold letters from day one – by your boss, by your mayor, by the commentators, by the NAACP, by a $5-million settlement paid out to the Green family even before anyone had any idea what happened out there, by endless propaganda that Detroit will go up in flames if any juror finds reasonable doubt, and finally by a couple juries in one of the all-time biased trials…then it's going to be real difficult to get a fair hearing. And if you wind up in a new trial, then all that baggage of being a famously convicted felon – plus giving a jury the option of a "compromise" verdict – is going to make it *impossible* to get the verdict you're looking for. Fact is, when Walter and I went to prison the first time, we became – in every sense of the word – history.

We had lots of grounds for appeal, obviously. The first step would be the Michigan Court of Appeals and then, if we failed there, the Michigan Supreme Court. Our hopes were high for succeeding on the very first round, and getting a new trial

quicker than you can say "Stanley Knox and Coleman Young."
It didn't go that way. The Court of Appeals ruled on March 22,
1995, sixteen months after our arrival in Texas. I got the news
on the phone when I called Nancy. I don't remember much
about that moment except being devastated. I'm sure Nancy
told me we'd win on the next round and did her usual best
efforts at cheerleading.

The Court of Appeals is a big court that appoints smaller
panels to hear cases. A three-judge panel heard our case, two
appellate judges and one lower-court judge. Walter and I,
having faced separate juries, had some shared appeals issues
and some separate appeals issues. The appeals judges shot
both of us down on every one, beginning with several points
we raised about Judge Crockett's jury instructions.

First, when a defendant says he acted in self-defense, as I did,
the burden of disproving self-defense falls on the prosecution.
We cited Crockett's failure to remind my jury of this when
he gave them instructions. The appeals court said that didn't
matter because "not only was there no timely objection to
the omission when the jury was instructed, defense counsel
expressed approval of the instructions."

Second, on the matter of judging our use of force, we cited
reversible error when Crockett asked jurors to think in terms
of "a reasonable, prudent person" and failed to cite the full
standard that includes, "with the knowledge and in the situation
of the arresting officer." It's the old matter of a guy in a bar
fight not having the same obligations as a police officer trying
to make an arrest. The appeals judges said: "We disagree."

Third, regarding the second-degree murder instruction, we
said that intent to do great bodily harm is an empty phrase
when, as police officers, we were lawfully entitled – in fact
required – to use whatever force necessary to subdue Malice
Green. "Again," the judges said, "this issue is not preserved
because defendants failed to object to the instruction."

Fourth, we argued that Crockett screwed up when he
refused to give an instruction we requested that would have

pointed out there can be more than one cause of death and that "it is not enough that the defendant's act made it possible for the death to occur. In order to find that the death of Malice Green was caused by the defendant, you must find beyond a reasonable doubt that the death was the natural or necessary result of the defendant's act." The three judges said Crockett was right. Our complaint didn't matter, they said, because of the take-the-victim-as-you-find-him doctrine. In other words, it wouldn't matter if cocaine contributed to Green's death, or if a pre-existing heart problem contributed to his death. Besides, the judges noted, "it was alleged that the defendants were acting in concert."

So much for Crockett's errors in instructions to the jury.

And so it went with all of our complaints. You could sum it up with one sentence from the court's decision: "We also reject defendants' claims of juror bias, juror taint/misconduct, and prejudicial media publicity or community sentiment." Things like the mayor calling us "murderers" didn't matter because voir dire had produced two fine juries who would proceed fairly without respect to the hysteria and the media overload. Yeah, right. We had, by the way, asked Crockett for individual, sequestered voir dire. The appeals judges said this was "not necessarily required as long as the method of questioning is adequate to expose bias and to avoid taint." Right, like seating an NAACP officer on a jury.

We also, of course, appealed Judge Crockett's unusual questioning of the 800-pound gorilla, Michael Baden. The judges in their wisdom said this circus "did not unfairly bolster his credibility or denigrate the defense experts or defense...In a similar vein, the trial court's occasional use of phrases '800-pound gorilla' in reference to experts and 'spirited discussion' with counsel in chambers, brief expression of gratitude to Dr. Baden for using easily understood language, and encouragement of Dr. Baden's use of the well-known definition of 'faith' from Hebrews 11:1 were relatively innocuous matters." Uh-huh. Telling the jurors that an 800-pound prosecution gorilla will now lead us in Bible study, which will lead you to truth and righteousness in your verdicts, is…innocuous.

The appeals judges found our charges of prosecutorial misconduct to be "without merit." That would include the mess with Jiraki and Cassin. We also objected to the prosecution withholding results of other autopsies made by Jiraki in which he miraculously found cocaine to be not only more important than the color of the deceased's eyes, but the cause of death. No matter, the appeals judges said, because "the prosecution was not required to undertake discovery on behalf of the defense." Nor did the prosecution's failure to tell us about Theresa Pace's $600 in walking-around money while held at Homicide mean anything, according to the appeals panel.

Lee Hardy's report to his supervisors of having witnessed "police brutality/murder" had been admitted as evidence. That struck us as grounds for overturning our trial, especially when Bob Lessnau was acquitted by Crockett himself on grounds that Lee Hardy was not a credible witness. The appeals judges, however, denied us that one issue on grounds that "the witness provided sufficient testimony regarding his factual observations…"

That's just part of it. All rejected.

As for the *Malcolm X* videotape, the judges confessed to being "concerned" about the movie's screening. "We disagree with the trial court's determination that the impact of viewing this footage was likely to be negligible at best. Even though it was probable that most, if not all, the jurors had previously seen the footage, the act of providing the videotape for entertainment was highly inappropriate." No kidding.

But, sayeth the appeals panel: "Notwithstanding, we believe that reversal is not warranted on this basis given the overwhelming evidence against defendants in favor of the convictions." Crockett's denial of my request for a change of venue wasn't even something the Court of Appeals cared about. Walter's side hadn't asked for a change of venue, presumably to avoid upsetting Crockett over something they knew they would not get. So much for our case "making some new law" regarding change of venue.

By the time a copy of the Court of Appeals ruling made its way to Texas, I didn't have even a paragraph or two of good reading. I was devastated. Walter probably found some extra work to do that day to take his mind off it. The lawyers regrouped and went at it again, this time to the Michigan Supreme Court. Step two would take more than two years, and this time I again heard the result the hard way. Real hard.

Almost two and a half years after the Court of Appeals ruling, the last day of July 1997 was also the final day of the Michigan Supreme Court's session. Big cases have a history of being announced as courts recess, and it was widely expected that ours would be one of them. That would account for Channel 4's Roger Webber hopping a plane for Texas, and for prison management notifying Walter and me that Webber was there and asking for an interview. Typically, I agreed and Walter did not. Then Walter and I were both summoned to the Fort Worth Unit office and – while being told nothing about what was going on – were asked to fill out forms with instructions for forwarding our mail back to Detroit. Is this exciting, or what? I was so wound up that I wrote down the address for the Bretton Drive home we had sold, then had to cross it out and write in my father-in-law's address in Dearborn Heights. Three years and ten months in Texas was enough for me. Back home. New trial. *All right!*

Cops are skeptics, but that seemed like a reasonable attitude under the circumstances.

In a couple hours, I was summoned to the visitors' room. The first words out of Roger Webber's mouth were: "How does it feel that Walter's getting out, and you're not?" I've got to admit it was the legitimate question of the hour. I didn't feel capable of answering, so I terminated the interview and walked back to my room. I couldn't believe it.

I must have called Nancy at her office after the interview request and then the mail-forwarding thing. But she wouldn't have answered because she heard a flash on the radio that she interpreted as meaning both Walter and I had been granted new trials. She instantly ran out the door, drove to Neil Fink's office, burst in and said how excited she was. Darin was there, and was the one who told her it would just be Walter leaving Texas. Nancy was my news line to Michigan, so I had been left in the dark until Roger Webber gave me the news.

I lay on my bunk as Walter unloaded his locker and packed up. What to say? Nothing. I suppose Kym Worthy would ask if I thought the jury was born yesterday on that one, too. But Walter and I didn't talk as he packed. When he was ready, he walked over, shook my hand, and said: "We'll never stop fighting for you." I stayed on my bunk, feeling an emptiness like I felt the morning after Green died. Things just weren't supposed to turn out this way. Walter was a good and innocent police officer. I was real glad he was going home. I was incredibly sad that I was staying in Texas.

In short, the Michigan Supreme Court ruled that Walter had an unfair trial, and therefore would be released and given a new trial. And, by the way, I *also* had an unfair trial – but the evidence against me was "overwhelming," so I would not get a new trial. There are lots of ways to read this. One way is to remember what I said about what happens if the die is cast on day one, and also what the criminal justice system does whenever it has a way to compromise on a controversial and politically charged decision. No one with an IQ above room temperature could claim that I had a fair trial, and certainly not that a change of venue hadn't been called for. But despite all of its population loss, Detroit was still the biggest city in the state, with the most political chips to be counted. And you don't, on the hottest day of the year, announce that both Starsky and Hutch are going to be leaving prison. So they compromised. One cop goes free; another cop stays in the slam. The one who talks too much.

The Supreme Court was very interested in a number of things the Court of Appeals had found to be meaningless. That includes the *Malcolm X* videotape. The Supreme Court majority opinion said: "The film begins with the voice of Malcolm X's character giving a provocative speech charging 'the white man with being the greatest murderer on Earth' while the viewer is shown footage of Rodney King being beaten by Los Angeles police officers, interspersed with a picture of an American flag. The Rodney King videotape is shown in slow motion, in eight segments, as the American flag begins to burn. The voice-over makes an explicit reference to the City of Detroit, the location of the incident in the instant case, by stating that the black community has been deprived of democracy in the 'streets of Detroit.'" Yeah, that seems important. The court's "by the way" said, as Walter and I had always said, that by putting us on trial in Detroit we were being prosecuted for every misdeed, real and imagined, of every white police officer who ever wore a badge in the city.

The justices also noted that: "A juror in the Nevers trial indicated that he had learned from news reports and other sources about the city's preparation for a possible riot. There is no indication that the Nevers jury ever discussed this point during deliberations. Yet, according to an affidavit, the Nevers jury did discuss, before deliberations, the 'similarities between Rodney King and this case' because 'it was cops beating a black man.' Like the exposure to the film, the fact that the city braced for a riot should be irrelevant to the juries' deliberations because they are bound to issue their decisions in accordance with law. They should not consider whether there would be a riot if they acquitted. The reality is, however, that the jurors' knowledge that the city was preparing for a possible riot may have caused them to fear an acquittal."

The justices also, being well aware of Detroit realities in addition to Detroit politics, were unable to ignore the fact that jurors had been made aware of the magic word STRESS. "This extraneous influence creates more than an emotional reason to convict," the court wrote. "It suggests, if the perceptions were true about the nature of the STRESS police unit and defendants' participation in it, that these officers may have been acting in accordance with their *preexisting racist predisposition* to target young black men for abuse when they encountered Malice Green." Isn't it interesting how that language nails down, more than these justices ever intended, how assumptions about white police officers drove everything in this case?

The Supreme Court also pointed out, in passing, that the case was all about whether you believe the EMS techs and the junkies, or you believe seven police officers. The opinion said of the STRESS scuttlebutt: "This evidence was never introduced at trial. It is the kind of evidence that has a direct and rational connection between it and an adverse verdict…The jury's duty to resolve factual questions is severely impaired when it improperly receives information that besmirches the defendants' character…Similarly, in hearing that defendants were members of an allegedly violent and racist unit, the juries' ability to resolve the factual questions before them may have been severely impaired." Like I've said, I wish my actual record as a police officer had been part of the evidence introduced at trial, that witnesses had been called to testify to my actions and character while wearing a badge. I'd have taken my chances with that, gladly. But the court hung me on the four EMS techs, "who had no apparent motive to lie." We've been through that. We've been through my use of the flashlight. We've been through the medical testimony. But to the Michigan Supreme Court, this was "overwhelming evidence" against me. So I stayed in Texas.

Neil, of course, turned to the federal courts, and that became Nancy's new focus for her pep talks every time I called her. Before I tell you what happened on that path, let me tell you about the efforts to get Governor John Engler to step into the case. Besides the petitions gathered by Darin's group, and personal urging from various supporters, the governor was sent a remarkable letter I want to share. It went to the governor's desk halfway between the day we entered prison and the day Walter was released to stand trial all over again. It was a long letter, and I'm editing it for length. Most of it covers familiar ground. But note the letter's source, and how well it gathers everything together. It wound up doing us no good, but I'll always be grateful to former Detroit News reporter Ann Sweeney for knowing a cesspool when she saw one:

Aug 7, 1995

Gov. John Engler
The Capitol
Lansing, Michigan

Dear Governor:
It has been two years since a trial in the Malice Green case ended with stiff prison sentences for Larry Nevers and Walter Budzyn. Not a day has gone by that I don't think about the injustice that was done to these police officers. And not a week passes without queries from readers, law enforcement officials or journalists around the country.

I am writing to ask that prison sentences for Nevers and Budzyn, who have already served two years in addition to the ordeal of a lengthy trial, be commuted. And I am asking from the vantage point of someone who covered every moment of the trial from start to finish, as a reporter for the Detroit News.

In hindsight, it is my personal opinion that these men were scapegoats for a political machine which used them for its own ends by setting off a racially biased frenzy for conviction. Within 48 working hours of the November, 1992, tragedy that ended Green's life, city officials had supplied Green family lawyers with enough confidential information – much of which was later proved wrong – to file a $5.25-million suit. Within days, then-Mayor Coleman Young went on national television to call the officers murderers. Police Chief Stanley Knox added inflammatory statements in suspending the men, and refused to allow a police review board to investigate, thus denying the officers due process or *a chance to explain the incident to the public.*

According to court testimony, police officials got to assistant medical examiner Dr. Kalil Jiraki before the autopsy, telling him that Green died from a "police beating." Without waiting for the toxicology report, Jiraki made that finding. During trial, he stuck to his story that Green died from "14 blunt force trauma blows to the head," in the face of contradictory medical evidence that showed that Green's seizures were a result of his consumption of alcohol and cocaine....Jiraki (later) reduced the number of blows to seven, which fit with Nevers' testimony of the number of blows struck in self-defense when Green grabbed his gun.

At the time of the trial, Jiraki was under investigation for medical fraud in connection with his moonlighting activities, and was later fired by county officials who called him emotionally troubled. Under oath, he said his boss, Dr. Bader Cassin, agreed that Green's drug consumption was as "insignificant as the color of his eyes." From the depositions of Cassin and others, we know that Cassin, who performed a second autopsy on Green, had argued the cocaine issue vigorously with both Jiraki and with prosecutors. With the machine still in high gear, prosecutors chose to produce the testimony that most closely fit the now widely accepted scenario of events – that Green, who was black, died from a racially motivated beating by aging white police officers who stopped him without cause. Meanwhile prosecutors kept the defense in the dark about the opinion of Cassin, the chief medical examiner. Other nationally known medical experts testified that Green's injuries were superficial and not sufficient to cause death.

The so-called "eyewitnesses" also were not what they seemed. Well-coached, they all adapted prosecutor Kym Worthy's version of a car "flooded with light" by an overhead dome – until an evidence technician testified that the dome light had been removed, presumably to cloak drug deals in darkness.

After giving an incredible version of events, witness Gregory Simms admitted on cross-examination that he had paid a neighborhood prostitute $10 for information, presumably to enhance his standing in the neighborhood.

The witnesses, of course, were not random people at a bus stop but friends of Green who frequented the same drug house at Warren and Twenty-Third. They had congregated there that night when Green drove up with Ralph Fletcher, the drug house proprietor. There was testimony that Ralph Knox was in the back seat. Knox, known to police as a drug dealer, ran from the car when police spotted him and pulled in behind. Some witnesses denied Knox was in the car, apparently in an effort to protect the drug man. Soon after the preliminary examination Knox was killed in a drug deal gone bad but the witnesses were then stuck with their cover story and repeated it at the trial.

Green of course was never "a motorist" as some sensational TV coverage has suggested in an effort to draw a parallel to the Rodney King affair in Los Angeles. He, Fletcher and Knox were dealing when Nevers and Budzyn pulled in behind them, as evidenced by the crack cocaine in Green's hand and car.

NAACP officials, fighting internal political battles of their own, seized on the Green case as a cause celebre and the machine snowballed through both the channeled public perception of the case and private manipulations.

Just how far the tendrils of this all-encompassing political machine reached was shown when the Nevers/Budzyn appeal was denied. Before the decision was filed with the court clerk, and before a date was even set for its release, the prosecutor's office knew the decision. It was leaked to the Free Press, which had toed the party line in coverage. The News also was able to report the story in even earlier editions after the leak to the Free Press was discovered. I later reported my suspicions on the leak to Judge Martin Doctoroff.

Nevers and Budzyn deserve better from the system than the turbocharged railroading they got to federal prison. In assessing the trial and Green's death, I believe that there was no crime and no intent to commit one, just two dedicated officers doing their mandated job. That Green died of seizures was certainly a tragedy, but the result of forces sadly set in motion by his own lifestyle.

Larry Nevers and Walter Budzyn have now served two years in prison. I hope you can see your way clear to commuting their sentences.

Sincerely,
Ann Sweeney

The governor never "saw his way clear." I think at the very end maybe he helped out a little. Every little bit counts.

After Walter left Texas, for a week or two I was assigned a roommate who weighed about three hundred pounds. I refused to give up my bottom bunk despite his protests that his health problems made it difficult to climb into the upper. I told him to put in for a medical slip. I won the battle for the lower bunk, but when he was in bed his weight sagged within about two inches of my face and – part of his medical problems – he snored louder than a chainsaw. It was good when he got transferred to the Dallas unit. For the remainder of my stay I was assigned a good guy, from out west somewhere. Part-time law enforcement of some kind. I don't remember his case, and despite the notoriety of the Green case and my growing stack of documents related to my appeal, we didn't talk about it much. Talking about "your case," in my experience at least, is not a real big item with most inmates. You got your troubles, I got mine. Rightly or wrongly.

With Walter released and my case shot down all the way through the state Supreme Court, I reached bottom. Well, at least I thought I did. Let's say "reached bottom – so far." There would be more bottom to come; but first there would be incredible joy. Neil Fink went to federal court and filed a writ of habeas corpus, which means, essentially, he claimed that my incarceration violated the United States Constitution because I had been unfairly tried, convicted and sentenced. It had taken the state courts four years to rule that this wasn't true. It took less than six months for a federal court to stand those courts on their head.

A courageous U.S. district judge named Lawrence Zatkoff shredded the prosecution, city officials and my trial court into little pieces. It was as if Judge Zatkoff were the person in "The Emperor's New Clothes" fable who finally has the guts to speak up and point out that the entire city power structure from Coleman Young on down was standing naked. Most everything I've said about the railroading of Walter and me can be found in Zatkoff's ruling. Appropriately for me, the hearing that produced it was held on December 19, 1997, as last-minute Christmas shoppers bustled through the suburban malls. Downtown, in a federal courtroom, Zatkoff was preparing to wrap the best present I ever received.

Nancy, of course, attended the hearing and gave me a full report by phone to Texas. The other side must have sensed what was coming when Zatkoff showed up knowing the Green case inside and out and firing pointed questions at the prosecution. He almost snickered at the "overwhelming evidence" and witnesses cited by the state Supreme Court, reminding everyone that police officers' testimony counted for something, too. He took note of the 800-pound gorilla's Bible reading on the witness stand. And he seemed to be downright angry at the state Supreme Court's characterization of all the trial screw-ups as "harmless error." He listened to the oral arguments, asked his questions, and promised a quick ruling. Neil came up to Nancy and told her that the way it had gone he almost expected Zatkoff to order me released on the spot. Nancy had thought the same thing. You can't imagine what it was like for both of us to be verging on confident after so much time struggling just to find hope.

It didn't take long. Zatkoff issued his ruling on December 30. It was even more blistering that we had hoped for. After first noting that his habeas corpus ruling was not about my guilt or innocence but about whether I had received a fair trial, Zatkoff proceeded to trash our sham trial on every imaginable front.

He wrote a long passage about the "firestorm" of media coverage supporting my futile request for a change of venue, noting many of the stories you've read about here – from the mayor calling us murderers (and calling us "Starsky and Hutch"), to Malice Green's mother saying we "should get the electrical chair," to a News and Free Press analysis two days after Green's death headlined ABUSE OF POWER AN OLD PROBLEM, to the NAACP's Joann Watson complaining that the police department still had "holdovers from STRESS," to a headline three days after the incident that read ACCUSED COPS ARE FEARED ON THE STREETS...In fact, Zatkoff cited several pages of passages from newspaper stories that made a fair trial in the city impossible. And he didn't even mention the even more volatile and probably more influential television coverage.

As for Stanley Knox's rush to judgment in his public remarks, Zatkoff was particularly blunt: "Although Chief Knox's intentions may have been virtuous, the result was plain; within hours of the incident, the seven officers were indicted, tried, found guilty and suspended in the name of riot prevention. However, the Constitution of the United States does not bend to placate an enraged citizenry."

As for the Green family lawsuit: "Approximately one month after the incident the city agreed to settle a lawsuit filed by Green's estate for $5.25 million. Both the amount of the settlement and the quickness with which it was reached was shocking...As if the petitioner's immediate suspension did not clearly communicate city officials' belief that Nevers was guilty before he was even charged, the substantial and swift settlement removed any doubt."

As for all the riot talk: "Shortly before the trial, media reports surfaced that described preparations taken by the

Detroit Police Department to defend against potential rioting in the event that the defendants were acquitted. The Green case was repeatedly compared to the King case in Los Angeles.... The message in these comparisons is abundantly clear; jurors could avoid intense public scrutiny from community members and a riot in Detroit by convicting the defendants."

And: "Many of the widely publicized facts were not admissible at petitioner's trial. Immediately after the incident, reports began to circulate that petitioner was a former member of STRESS (Stop the Robberies, Enjoy Safe Streets), the controversial police squad allegedly responsible for the deaths of twenty Detroit residents seventeen of whom were young black men. Petitioner's involvement in STRESS was recounted in the media on numerous occasions. Further, reports also surfaced that Nevers and Budzyn were known in the southwestern Detroit neighborhood where Green died as 'Starsky and Hutch,' a comment on their reputation as 'rough-and-tumble' police officers. In addition, mayor Young validated the reports when he publicly referred to Nevers and Budzyn as Starsky and Hutch."

Did it really take all this time, and a federal judge, to recognize outrageous and pervasive pre-trial publicity? In Michigan, yes. "This Court finds that the refusal to change venue upon petitioner's request was 'contrary to or involved an unreasonable application of clearly established federal law, as determined by the Supreme Court of the United States.' Both the Michigan court of Appeals and Supreme Court...relied upon juror statements that they will be impartial. However, the adverse publicity so prejudiced petitioner that the juror claims should not be believed. Moreover as this Court will discuss in detail in the following section, while the jurors claimed to be impartial in front of the judge, behind closed doors a significant amount of inadmissible extrinsic evidence invaded their deliberations and thoroughly tainted petitioner's trial. Therefore petitioner's request for a writ of habeas corpus is granted."

Zatkoff's ruling is a long document. At every turn, it ruled in our favor – often with some stunning words for the other side. Here are a few samples:

"This Court has grave concerns that petitioner was convicted not because of his involvement in the Green incident, but instead because of his reputation in the community and community discontent with the lack of administrative control in the police department.

"The community was so permeated with hostility toward petitioner that his trial was nothing more than a 'hollow formality.'

"The Michigan Supreme Court found that the constitutional error in petitioner's case was harmless beyond a reasonable doubt because of 'overwhelming evidence' of petitioner's guilt. In reviewing the record in this case, the Court has no doubt that the state court determination that the error was harmless was an unreasonable application of federal law.

"The viewing of the movie (*Malcolm X*) by the jury cannot be dismissed as mere entertainment...The timing of the jury being shown the film and the fact that it was supplied by the Court added to the harmful effect...The fact that the Court failed to give a curative instruction after the movie was viewed left the impression on the jury that the movie was 'sanctioned' by the trial court judge.

"The Court cannot imagine a more prejudicial extraneous influence than that of a juror discovering that the City he or she resides in is bracing for a riot – including activating the National Guard and closing freeways – in the event the defendant on whose jury you sit is acquitted. The magnitude of such extraneous influence cannot be overlooked.

"This was not simply a case of one or two minor instances of extraneous influence finding its way into the jury room, but, rather, serious, repeated encroachments of the petitioner's constitutional right to have a jury decide the case solely on evidence submitted at trial.

"Needless to say, merely stating that the evidence against the petitioner was overwhelming does not necessarily make it so…The Michigan Supreme Court apparently found the testimony of the EMS workers to be 100 percent accurate and completely true and thus overwhelming evidence of petitioner's guilt. However, the only way the Michigan Supreme Court could so find is by ignoring the significant inconsistencies in EMS workers' testimony, and by completely disregarding the testimony of petitioner."

Judge Zatkoff's entire ruling is good reading. You can find it on the Internet.

The result was that I missed, by less than twenty-four hours, being in prison, where I had been since October 12, 1993, for the first day of 1998. The morning of December 31, 1997, I filled two cardboard boxes with almost fifty pounds each of correspondence, news clips, notes, magazines and documents related to my appeal. This amounted to the bulk of my personal possessions after more than four years in Texas, where there is more land to see than anywhere else in the Lower Forty-Eight, but where I had seen nothing but razor wire and convicts and guards and laundry and a deck of cards. This collection of paper was important stuff to me. I also had postage stamps in quantities I was not supposed to have. I gave twenty books of stamps – a hundred bucks in prison money – to an inmate along with instructions to get the cash to Nancy via the usual back channels. We never, no surprise, got the hundred. The rest of my stamps I stuck in envelopes and elsewhere in my stash of correspondence. To my great regret, the inmates I was leaving behind owed me more than two hundred books – one thousand dollars – worth of stamps.

I lugged all my stuff, under escort, to the intake/outtake building, wondering how I was going to haul those two boxes through an airport and onto a plane. This was not the biggest thing on my mind, of course, but it was on my mind. Because I was outbound, the guards didn't bother searching my possessions. The guard processing me out the door remarked that I could always mail my boxes north to Detroit, if I had enough postage. I don't know if it occurred to me that this might have been a good piece of jive talk aimed at making confiscation easy, but I really wasn't interested in trying to carry one hundred pounds of stuff with me. So I rifled through various hiding places and produced enough stamps to get the two boxes sent home via the U.S. Postal Service. The guards surprised me by not saying a word. I *still* had a couple books of stamps stashed away. Eventually Nancy or I used them to send letters or to pay bills just like any other stamps lying around anybody else's house. No souvenirs.

Going all the way back to Jackson Prison, Oaks, the ride with Mutt and Jeff, and all the time in Texas, being told almost nothing about what is happening is one hallmark of being a prisoner. I had maybe two hundred dollars they gave me from my prison account. I wore sweat pants and white T-shirt, and a red jacket the guards had given me – for which I was grateful, even though it was about two sizes too small, because it was a cold day in Texas. I was told a cab had been called for me and that the fare to the airport would be thirty or forty dollars. I was told the time of my flight. And I sat in the waiting room outside the steel doors and razor wire, waiting and feeling – despite my outfit and lack of luggage – as free as a millionaire waiting to catch a flight to Paris. It felt good, antsy as I was to step off a plane in Detroit. After maybe forty-five minutes of waiting in this hyped-up state I asked somebody if they would re-call the cab company because my flight left in less than an hour. Turns out the cab had arrived while I was still inside being processed. Nobody told me. Meanwhile, a couple guards and my unit counselor passed through and congratulated me on my release. About thirty minutes later another cab showed up. I walked out into the sun and felt reborn, a 57-year-old kid in sweat pants.

As the cab drove off the prison property several cameras and people I assumed to be reporters were standing beside the road. The driver asked if the cameras were for me. They all turned and aimed at the cab as it went by, and I said: "I guess so." The driver asked if I was famous. I said: "No, I'm a nobody."

I knew by then that I would miss my flight. I was glad in a way, because I wanted to get a new pair of jeans, and maybe grab some airport food. The driver dropped me at the appropriate entrance, and pointed me to an escalator leading to the proper ticket counter. The line was long and my plane was long gone. As I queued up, several reporters and at least one TV camera came over to interview me. I told them all the expectable things about how glad I was to be free. And I told them I hadn't seen Nancy and Kelly for more than three years. When I finally got to the ticket counter, they asked for I.D. and of course I didn't have any. A reporter from the Free Press said: "He's who he says he is." The reporter asked for another interview. It was about an hour before my new flight and I wanted to get some clothes and a bite to eat. I told him to wait a few minutes, and I went for a walk. No clothing store in sight. So I set out to find a Burger King or McDonald's. Hey, when's the last time you went four and a half years without a fast-food burger? But all I could see was a Pizza Hut, and I was too excited to handle pizza. So I settled for just a Coke.

Sitting there with my soft drink I suddenly realized that a TV camera, aiming through the Pizza Hut window, was recording each swallow. That made me uneasy, so I carried my drink out into the concourse looking for a phone to call Nancy. I found a bank of phones, but it was like Tarzan emerging from the jungle. I didn't know how to use them. I asked a TV reporter, who said only with a credit card. No help there. I tried to make a collect call, but was doing something wrong and that didn't work either. So I walked over to my flight departure area and took a seat. A Dallas print reporter came over and asked for an interview. I told him the same things I had told everyone else. A quick rush of inbound passengers must have been from a Detroit flight. One woman came up to me and said: "Boy are they waiting for you up there." She was smiling, so I knew to take that as a good "they are waiting for you" rather than a bad "they are waiting for you."

The plane was only about one-quarter full. That was great.

I had a window seat by myself and could stretch out. Once airborne, the Free Press reporter wandered over and asked to sit down and do an interview. I was reluctant because of some of the coverage and all of the editorials the paper had written about the Green case. He assured me he would only report on our conversation and said I could look at the story on his laptop. I told him to sit down and we talked. It was a direct flight and the interview lasted almost all the way to Detroit, interrupted a couple times when flight attendants came over to congratulate me.

I really didn't know what to expect when we landed. As I walked past the cockpit door, both pilots said: "Welcome home." I was wound up and anxious, and at the same time I felt good in a way I hadn't felt in many years. And onto the enclosed mobile ramp I went, making my way around and through until it opened into the concourse. Things immediately became almost unreal. There was the usual throng of people. But it was clear that many were there for me. And it was all skewed by lights, which I didn't instantly recognize as TV cameras. Nancy and Kelly came running toward me out of the lights. We embraced, the tears flowed, and we began walking toward the lights. I wondered how we were going to make it through the crowd, which looked like maybe one hundred people. A couple of sheriff's deputies materialized and took all three of us by the arm, back toward the ramp and out a door. We found ourselves in the Metro Airport sheriff's station. The rest of the welcoming committee straggled in, away from the crowd. My cousin and his wife. My brother and his wife. Mark Scott and his wife. And two of us seven police officers who had been together in the wrong place at the wrong time, Karl Gunther and Bobby Lessnau. I couldn't remember being so happy – except a few hours earlier when I caught that cab in Texas.

My brother *always* had a New Year's Eve party for family and friends. The party was still a go and we were all invited. I protested, being in sweat pants and gym shoes. That dispute never got decided, because Mark Scott said: "You are coming with us! You can go to Bill's party later on!" You don't turn down someone who has done as much for you as Mark had done for me, so Nancy, Kelly and I hopped into his car along with his wife, Leslie, making one of the most exuberant parties of five ever to descend on the Ginopolis restaurant on Twelve Mile Road, about twenty minutes from the airport. It was downright festive. Mark knew I loved ribs and ordered them for me, saying they were the best in town (they were). Pete Ginopolis came over with congratulations and bought dessert for the table (none for me; I pigged out on ribs). Afterward, Mark not only drove us to brother Bill's party, but came in and mingled – which surprised me because Mark tended to avoid crowds. My sister-in-law Diane had stopped somewhere on the way home from the airport and bought me a Detroit Lions T-shirt to wear. I was still dressed like a weirdo compared with everybody else. In the end I didn't care. What I was wearing more than anything was my freedom.

I borrowed Bill's car and drove the three of us "home" to Dearborn Heights. Kelly, too, had moved in with Nancy's father after rooming with a friend for a while. It was a small house – three bedrooms and one bath. This night, past 3 a.m. and into a new year, it might as well have been a mansion. We were all exhausted, but if I somehow woke up in the middle of my sleep and wanted to walk out the door...I could. There were many things I still wanted to see in my lifetime, but Texas was not one of them.

22
TRIAL TWO AND DÉJÀ VU

We didn't live in pop-in-law's house very long. When we moved out, he – in failing health – came with us. We had lots of room in our new place. In fact, our housing story and some other news we got around the same time make for quite a good-news, bad-news double-header. First, the good news.

My first few weeks after Texas were mostly spent visiting with old friends and family. One invitation was to dinner at my cousin Richard Howe's home. His wife, Carlene, told me that a very good friend of hers named Dick Lambert was one of my strongest supporters, and how he had said if there was ever *anything* he could do to help, I should let him know. Carlene went on to say that Dick was a very successful real estate developer and owned a number of single-family homes. I said, mostly in jest, "Well, maybe he could lend us one of his houses." Carlene said: "We can talk about that at dinner. I've invited him and he really wants to meet you."

The dinner date came. We had a nice meal. Dick Lambert and I hit it off, and Carlene or someone steered the conversation to the matter of housing. Dick said he had one house sitting vacant that he might let us live in rent-free, and would we be interested in having a look at it? Well, of course. And off we went, Nancy and I following Dick and the Howes on a drive to look at we didn't know what, but knowing that stumbling into a rent-free home would be a blessing for us right now, and anything with more than one bathroom would seem like a mansion. To our utter amazement, we were led into the circular driveway of...a genuine mansion.

We were in Bloomfield Hills, the ritziest, most desirable suburb in metro Detroit. The prestigious Cranbrook Academy was a few blocks up the street. I figured maybe this was a joke, or Dick had made a detour to show us one of his prized properties. No joke. Once inside, it was even more mind-boggling. Almost 6,000 square feet, a beautiful home without a stick of furniture in it, and looking – despite its classic design and interior finish – like no one ever had lived in it, which turned out to be true. Dick built the place intending to live there, but a divorce occurred and he never moved in. As Nancy and I explored for a few minutes, pretty much disbelieving everything we were seeing and hearing, Dick said he would consider letting us live there for eighteen months as long as we kept the place up and paid the utility bills. We drove back to my cousin's for dessert, and I asked – still, I think, mostly in jest: "Well, when can we move in?" Dick said: "Anytime you want." And so began the bizarre but wonderful stay of an ex-convict and his office-worker wife in a Tudor mansion just down the road from Cranbrook Academy.

That was the good news.

The bad news was medical. It started immediately after Texas and played out over a year and a half. I went for a physical exam soon after returning home. My doctor told me I should see a pulmonary specialist. I did. There were X-rays and CAT-scans and biopsies and consultations and, finally, a diagnosis of lung cancer. Whatever those prison docs had spent two weeks discussing wasn't good. If it wasn't cancer back then, it was obviously about to be. I hadn't smoked for years by now, but the old habit crept up and hit me anyway. After the diagnosis was finally made, the surgery came in August 1999. They removed most of my right lung. The pain was intense enough that I thought I was buying the farm, and there were moments I almost wished I did. Between the surgery and the emphysema, I measured out at 31 percent lung capacity, and would be that way the rest of my life. By now I've passed the magical survivor period. I'm ever so grateful for that. With lung cancer you always keep your fingers crossed.

So amid the joy of being free, almost every day of 1998 and 1999 was built around a steadily increasing worry about what was going on inside my chest and whether it was about to kill me. I was on the road to recovery just in time to confront the criminal justice system's dogged pursuit of Starsky and Hutch. There were some miles for Walter and I to travel after Texas, this time on entirely separate paths. And even when they were done with us they would say "not enough."

Some important legal scenery had changed while we were in prison. In 1994, Kym Worthy rode her fame from the Green trial into election as a Wayne County Circuit Court judge. Doug Baker remained, however, as the prosecutor's top trial attorney. In 1997, the state Legislature disbanded Detroit Recorder's Court and merged it into Wayne County Circuit Court. I'm sure our trial played a part in Recorder's Court disappearing into the sunset. In any case, the city of Detroit power structure will forever accuse the Legislature of racism because the end of Recorder's Court meant the end of all-black and nearly all-black juries.

The prosecutor's office, as widely expected, was not going to let Walter's punishment stand at time served – much less accept the rebuke the Michigan Supreme Court dealt the prosecution by ordering Walter released. So when I got home from Texas, Walt was within weeks of facing retrial on a murder charge. Carole Stanyar, Walt's co-counsel this time around, came to the house in Dearborn Heights to discuss his case. I told Carole I was prepared to take the stand and tell the truth, same as before – that I never saw Walter strike Malice Green with his flashlight, and didn't believe he did. She was very happy to hear that, but she wanted me to testify that I struck Green fourteen times – the number Jiraki had first come up with at autopsy. I pointed out to her that we had forced Jiraki to admit he could only ascribe half that number to a cylindrical object such as a flashlight. Meanwhile, for six years I had been explaining to anyone who would listen that I struck Green a half-dozen times. But Carole refused to understand, or accept. I was dumbfounded that she was buying into the prosecutor's script when we had proved it false. She pleaded for agreement that half the money left in the support group treasury be freed for Walter's legal expenses. Up to that point, any funds available had gone toward a monthly newsletter, the PR campaign, advertising, the pardon petition drive and such. There was only about $15,000 in the checkbook, and, of course, we freed half of it up for Walter.

Walter's retrial began in February 1998, this time in Wayne County Circuit Court. The hysteria was at a much lower pitch than five years earlier, but anyone who thinks the jury pool had forgotten the 1993 circus was crazy. Even with the lower decibel level in the media, the prosecution managed to get at least one "extraneous" piece of "evidence" planted without ever having to bring it to court and expose it for what it really was. Just as the trial was about to begin, the media ran with a story saying an ex-Detroit cop named Jefferson Burgess would be testifying that he had gotten a jailhouse "confession" from either Walter or me or both of us. Burgess had served time in Texas for possessing and distributing cocaine. Burgess never took the stand, and the prosecution never said why. The reason, of course, is that there was no jailhouse "confession." Anyone who thinks the jurors didn't hear about it anyway must have been smoking some of Jefferson Burgess's cocaine. Neither one of us knew or even met this guy in Texas or anywhere else. Chalk it up to another drug inmate trying to find a way to shorten his time. Even Doug Baker must have figured out what a crock this story was.

I never heard from Walter's lawyers and realized they were not going to call me as a witness. I probably knew right then what they had in mind. I wasn't real pleased to see it unfolding on Court TV. What Carole and her co-counsel James Howarth did was play good-cop, bad-cop to the jury – with me being the very bad cop. The defense portrayed me as responsible for any injuries inflicted on Green, and hung their case on whether Walter could have stopped it from happening. Doug Baker meanwhile portrayed Walter as a vicious, mad-dog assailant – leaving any rational observer wondering whether there was room for me to have done all the things he claimed, at the first trial, I did. Still another example of how criminal trials are not about seeking the truth, but about seeking a result. Cocaine and cause of death were barely mentioned. It looked to me like neither Walter's lawyers nor the prosecution were much interested in the truth. That's aside from the fact that the defense tried to win acquittal by throwing me under the bus.

They were successful only in that the judge instructed jurors they could not find Walter guilty of second-degree murder on grounds he failed to intercede in his partner's actions. Some victory. It only helped grease the skids for a manslaughter conviction – which is exactly what the jurors did, in March 1998. I don't blame jurors for that. It was a real strange way for the defense to mount a case – trying to deflect any alleged crime onto Walter's partner instead of standing up and saying a difficult but lawful arrest that went bad was no felony. This is all layman's talk, of course, but that's what the trial amounted to.

Stoic and silent Walter, by the way, was a good police officer but a lousy witness. When everything about your manner says "I am going to take whatever life throws my way," that includes whatever crap a lawyer – in this case, a prosecutor – is throwing at you. One of our very worst moments in the first trial came when Worthy started shouting at Walter that he must have known what happened out there was "wrong." Walter replied: "Yes." Hey, even I think what happened was "wrong." Malice Green died. That wasn't supposed to happen. We didn't want it to happen. We didn't want anything to happen except for Green to give up his cocaine and submit to arrest. That's what we tried to make happen, just as we had many thousands of times before. Malice Green himself, and his bad habits, had a lot to do with what went "wrong." That is *not* what Kym Worthy had in mind by "wrong." Anyway, in a case that pretty much consists of nothing except "who are you going to believe?" – which is what the Malice Green case was – Walter was not his own best friend as a witness. The world never did understand that Walter and I *both* felt, and will always feel, remorse that Malice Green died. Which is quite different from feeling legal guilt for what went wrong. Walter would give you the same answer to that question as I do. His demeanor as a witness gave a different answer.

Some say Walter's second trial wound up the way it was supposed to – with Walter guilty of involuntary manslaughter and sentenced to time served. Maybe the lawyers thought of that as a victory. I didn't. And Walter appealed the verdict. You won't believe what happened after that played out. But I am getting ahead of the story.

As for my case, the Wayne County prosecutor first tried to get Judge Zatkoff's writ of habeas corpus overturned, which would have sent me back to Texas without a new trial. But in March 1999, a federal appeals court upheld Zatkoff's writ. Then in June the U.S. Supreme Court also let it stand. So if Doug Baker wanted me back in prison he would have to do a third Malice Green trial. The result of Walter's second trial would have some bearing on my own second trial, no doubt. But I honestly was optimistic. I didn't think much of Walter's defense strategy. I was grateful I wouldn't have to face a Recorder's Court jury – or judge, for that matter. I was confident in my own testimony. I was confident in the cocaine experts who would be called on my behalf. This was all lining up for *after* recovery from lung-cancer surgery. Maybe I thought that if I could conquer lung cancer, I could conquer anything. For whatever reason, I felt good about prospects for my second confrontation with the criminal justice system. Not cocky, not at all. Just believing that the Recorder's Court trial had been such a farce, and a Circuit Court jury would see the common-sense truth of it all. And I had Neil Fink as my trial attorney.

There were countless things I didn't foresee – especially

including what it means to already have been found guilty in Detroit's most famous trial…and all the unfair baggage that went with that. They don't call me Naïve Larry for nothing. I also didn't seem to have good timing when it comes to anti-police sentiment in the media and the public. Our first trial came just six months after the Rodney King riots in Los Angeles. And now, I was about to stand trial again just a few weeks after a New York jury found those four plainclothes officers not guilty of even reckless endangerment after emptying their guns into Amadou Diallo in his Brooklyn apartment building. To say nothing of the infamous LAPD Ramparts corruption scandal that had been playing out for months in the media. Those cases, and Jefferson Burgess's phony jailhouse confession story, were the police stories anyone had read recently in the papers as my Trial Two began. Fortunately, I was old news as far as Court TV goes – or at least not headline news. There would be no full-time TV coverage.

Because of my medical condition, I couldn't have done much real work during 1998 and 1999 even if I had found someone who wanted to hire an aging ex-convict. I gave a few speeches about our case before Rotary Clubs and that sort of thing. There was that appearance before a junior college criminal justice class where one student showed me a textbook that badly twisted the facts of our case. Much of my time was spent maintaining the "mansion," where Dick Lambert let us stay past the allotted eighteen months, and taking care of my infirm father-in-law while Nancy went to work. Every other minute I devoted to getting ready for Trial Two. Lynne Krueger, with whom I had exchanged correspondence from Texas, became invaluable. She has to be the most organized person on Earth. Her archive of Nevers-Budzyn material was complete and cross-indexed so that even someone like me could find it in an instant – and if I couldn't, she would. Lynne and her husband Jerry became close friends. We wanted to have absolutely everything at Neil's fingertips as we took on Doug Baker for a second time.

Baker was ready to go in mid-summer 1999 but would have to wait for my cancer surgery and recovery. Crockett refused to accept the case because he had "heard all the evidence, and it would be humanly impossible" not to have some reactions and impressions. The court's chief judge then assigned the trial to Judge Thomas Jackson, who had presided over Walter's second trial and sentenced him to time served. But by the time I had my surgery and the trial was finally put on the docket, for March 2000, Jackson also disqualified himself. My fate was assigned to the hands of Judge Ulysses Boykin – the third straight time an African-American judge had been assigned, rather than selected in the usual blind draw, to try my case. I didn't know anything about Boykin. Neil had appeared before Boykin at least once and was satisfied. Before Trial Two was over, Neil would be demonstrating – very publicly, in court – that his confidence in Judge Boykin's fairness and racial blindness did not mean much when a white police officer was on trial in the Malice Green case.

Securing Neil's services for Trial Two turned out to be a financial nightmare. When I got home from Texas, we assumed Neil would be my lawyer for Trial Two, just as he had been my lawyer in getting that far. I'm not sure why we assumed that. The police union certainly wasn't going to pick up the tab for going first-class, and we knew we had to go first-class in this case. Maybe we thought Neil would continue to work for "scale," though in retrospect I guess that would have been unthinkable. Mounting a trial defense is different than filing an appeals brief and showing up to argue it. So as the trial drew nearer, I enlisted Lynne Krueger's husband, Jerry – a very successful businessman – to meet Neil and me for lunch and maybe help me bargain. No such luck, so far as I could tell. Let me just say that the fee was, for our budget, astronomical. As high-profile lawyers go, it might have been modest. For us it was impossible. Besides, we'd need additional money for a young assistant counsel. Besides that, Neil's fee did not include other considerable legal expenses – the jury consultant we hired, expert witnesses and their travel expenses, the hefty cost of buying transcripts. Plus, we would have to pay the attorney fee up front – common practice in criminal law, but no less stunning when you are the one who has to come up with the money.

We paid about a tenth of the fee to get preparation for trial started. Days before the trial Neil asked for the rest and we didn't have it. He was about to ask Boykin to take him off the case when we asked for a couple more days. We borrowed the money from Nancy's dad, who had sold the house in Dearborn Heights. I suppose these financial unpleasantries are common in the trade; but just in case you've never had to defend yourself against a murder charge, I thought I'd point it out. In the end, our total legal costs for Trial Two alone were about $200,000. We would have been wiped out – including my father-in-law's nest egg – if the DPOA hadn't contributed $80,000 and we didn't get $100,000 from a godsend known as the Law Enforcement Legal Defense Fund. That group, organized by publisher Al Regnery and including board members such as former Attorney General Edwin Meese, saved us from bankruptcy. Not that we didn't appreciate the DPOA help, or Dick Lambert's free-rent mansion. And everybody else who helped in various ways. The Law Enforcement Legal Defense Fund helped Walter, too – something Nancy suggested when the LELDF came to us.

When we got to trial, I discovered I had some strong differences of opinion with Neil about how best to defend myself. I suppose that's hardly unique, either. You hire a top guy and you find out you've got some serious disagreements. Happens with brain surgeons, too, I suppose. That's why God invented second opinions. But you don't get second opinions while you're under the knife. On the other hand, you don't get anesthesia when you go to trial, so my lawyer and I argued. At least once we argued loudly. If it had turned out different, I probably wouldn't even be telling you about this. And the truth is, I can't blame Neil for what happened. Trial Two was as pre-ordained as Trial One, just more subtle. So my idea of how we should have argued the case probably wouldn't have made any difference. Nancy, Lynne Krueger and the young lawyer who assisted on the case all say Neil had it right. I'll tell you about my differences with counsel anyway.

Trial Two turned out to be the Reader's Digest version of Trial One. Instead of moving like a glacier it moved like a speedboat. Lynne and I – especially Lynne – had spent months and months compiling every contradiction, every lie, every misleading spin brought forth by the prosecution and its witnesses the first time around. We were eager to expose every last one of these things and build up a mountain of credibility problems for the other side. Neil – and I have to admit, he's the lawyer, not me – saw it differently…something I didn't realize until we were in court.

To me, the medical evidence regarding cocaine and Malice Green's lifestyle is the whole key to understanding what happened. That's because it's the only way I can understand what happened. I know how hard I hit Green, and how many times. He should not have died. I know how bizarre Green's actions and resistance were. The drugs explain it. I know how long he refused to submit. The drugs explain it. Any street cop these days – and I would think any layman – understands all that. But neither judge nor jury in Trial One cared at all about the cocaine. The judge and the prosecution went straight to the "take the victim as you find him" doctrine. Baker and Worthy, just to be sure, tried to hide and suppress the truth about how drugs took Green over the edge. Crockett tried to build up the 800-pound gorilla who was hired just to disagree with common sense and cocaine. They were all scared to death that a jury would use their common sense and see that a police officer trying to make an arrest has different obligations than a citizen in a brawl with somebody who is high. The jury in Trial One, of course, would have found me guilty if Malice Green *had* gotten hold of my gun and used it to shoot *himself.* At Trial Two I wanted to go back to the drug testimony in full, and make cause of death a prime part of my defense.

Neil, as it turns out, didn't believe any of that mattered much. Not as a lawyer. He knew "take the victim as you find him" would be enforced by the court, and the judge would make sure jurors were steered away from a complicated cause of death. Neil believed that in the end all any jury would care about, even if cocaine played an important role in Green's death, was the question of whether I used excessive force. To Neil, it was strictly a self-defense case, a matter of a police officer defending himself while trying to bring in a stubborn felony suspect. As far as communicating our case to the jury, he believed "clarity" was the only way to go. "Confusion" is the enemy in presenting a case, Neil believes, unless you don't have a genuine case. So he kept it simple, and he kept it short. I wanted every last piece of chicanery exposed. I wanted every sorry prosecution witness from Trial One on the stand and exposed in every way. If the cocaine evidence was confusing, I didn't care. So almost from the get-go, Neil and I quarreled about what was happening on the witness stand. He may have been right – because he understands, as he told the jury several times, that Malice Green "was up to mischief" that night. One way he re-enforced that was a piece of evidence not introduced at Trial One – the knife that was in Green's pocket, a pocket several witnesses said he tried to get at even as he was being handcuffed.

Despite the move to Wayne County Circuit Court, the trial was still all about race. In fact, race got put front and center more openly than it did in Trial One. It happened even before the trial began, during jury selection. The Honorable Ulysses Boykin made his feelings clear on the subject. Doug Baker was determined to seat as many black jurors as possible, no matter what kind of obvious bias they displayed. If Neil used a peremptory challenge to remove a prospective black juror, Baker was going to portray it as racism. I suppose I should have known right then how the trial was going to wind up. There are other reasons to take you inside jury selection at Trial Two.

This isn't the part of a trial they make movies out of, but it's a part that – in this case, at least – tells you what it's all about and how it ends up the way it does. You know, for instance, that the whole idea here was for me to get "a new trial." If you watched my jury get put together, you'd understand that for "Starsky" there could never be a new trial. So I'm going to tell a good deal of the Trial Two story by telling you about jury selection, and letting you hear the jury pool talk.

Change of venue wasn't something we thought of asking for in Trial Two. For one thing it wouldn't have been granted; and for another the trial would be in Circuit Court instead of the defunct Recorder's Court. We were still in downtown Detroit – in the same building, in fact; but now the jury would include not only Detroiters but also residents of mostly white blue-collar suburbs.

Jury selection meant the court summoned several groups of seventy-five Wayne County citizens down to the Frank Murphy Hall of Justice. All filled out a lengthy written questionnaire. Lawyers (and our jury consultant) got to read the completed questionnaires. Then, in the first phase, known as individual voir dire, these panelists were kept in a different courtroom and called in one at a time – supposedly at random – to be questioned by Boykin, then by Baker and Neil. Attorneys for either side could challenge for cause, and Boykin would rule on the challenges. Sometimes cause was so obvious that no challenge – or even any questions – were necessary. Sometimes it was maddening that the system, as interpreted by Boykin, didn't see any cause to keep a juror out of the box. Individual voir dire would "qualify" fifty prospective jurors from the pool. This took four days and reached deep into the second group of seventy-five. Then all fifty qualified panelists were brought into the courtroom. Sixteen were blind-drawn to sit in the jury box for final voir dire, and Boykin read them a set of questions. The other thirty-four sat in the room listening, because they would be asked the same questions if their name happened to be drawn to replace an excused juror. Baker and

Neil could once again challenge jurors. And if a challenge was denied, either Baker or Neil could exercise one of their twelve peremptory challenges – theoretically, at least, ousting a juror without having to say why.

Getting down to the fifty during individual voir dire was like an archeologist digging through the history of the Malice Green case. Almost every prospective juror not only had heard of the case, but had watched chunks of Trial One on TV, or read about it in the newspapers, or talked about it. No big surprise, even though the incident happened almost seven and a half years earlier. The least credible jurors were those who seemed to have been visiting Mars on November 5, 1992. Many on the panel, when asked what they knew about the incident, recited incredible detail from news stories. The gist of voir dire was to discover what each panelist thought he knew about the case, and ask whether they thought they could nonetheless deliberate fairly and reach an unbiased verdict. For Baker and Neil, of course, priority one was trying to weed out anybody biased against their side, and priority two was trying to retain any juror who revealed signs of being able to reach the right verdict. One might have expected jury selection to go long and deep. But it ended a bit before most anyone, especially Doug Baker, expected.

Here are a few snippets, as revealed during individual voir dire, of what the Malice Green case looked like on the streets of Wayne County as we entered my "new trial." All panelists during this first phase were identified only by number.

Prospective Juror #36 was living in Houston at the time of the Green incident, but still had heard enough about me ("you can hear people talk about it at restaurants, anywhere") to have an opinion that I was probably guilty. Baker waltzed through the usual line of "can-you-reach-a-fair-verdict-anyway?" questions. Then Neil dug a little deeper. Juror #36 said she knew someone with personal knowledge that I was a "bad cop" who had "a tarnished reputation for, you know, robbing people and stealing…and being aggressive with beating them." After a few other questions she declared she had heard that I "raped" people, and that: "It would have to be proved to me that he was not guilty of what he did." Baker pursued with her the novel idea that she could be a good juror anyway. On Neil's request, #36 was dismissed for cause.

Baker asked #50 if despite his opinion, formed by media coverage of the incident and the first trial, he would ignore the evidence at Trial Two and "still convict him." The answer was "Yes sir." Baker: "No matter what you heard in this case?" #50: "Yes."

Prospective Juror #62 was asked, by Boykin, whether he had formed any opinion about me. The answer was straightforward: "That he is guilty." In the lengthy questioning that followed, #62 opined that the Malice Green case was "no different than Rodney King case," that his sister-in-law was an employee (and perhaps the director) of the prosecutor's victim-assistance department, that it would be up to the defense to prove me not guilty, that he did not believe my testimony (which he remembered) from Trial One about Green putting his hand on my gun. Just to be sure about #62's opinion of the gun grab, Neil asked him: "Nothing is going to change there, is it?" The reply: "No." Question: "As you go into this trial you think he is a perjurer, fair enough?" Answer: "That's fair enough, yes." Boykin, however, believed that #62 could, as he claimed, set his feelings aside and render a fair verdict. The judge refused to dismiss #62 for cause.

When #62 left the room, Neil addressed the judge: "Well, I can't do anything more than make a record. I'm a lawyer. You're the judge. But in my opinion you've got now a juror that you qualified whose law firm represented the Green family, (and you've) qualified a juror now whose sister-in-law works for the prosecutor's office and who thinks my client is a perjurer and came here and compared him to Stacy Coon and the Rodney King trial. I started with twelve challenges. I guess I've got ten now. I'm taken aback, Judge, and I'll accept the ruling. I've got no other choice."

Keep in mind as this little jury-selection drama plays out, it is Neil – and me – who will be portrayed as unreasonable. And racist.

Prospective Juror #46 when asked what he knew about the case gave a pretty straightforward recital of all the news stories, even knew how long we had served in Texas, opined that I ought to get the same verdict and sentence Walter had gotten in his second trial – "with the sentence they already received, everything they already went through. My thoughts at this point are that it ought to be over with." Can you by chance see sentiment for a compromise verdict? Neil, who made a careful record on what would be the key part of our appeal, addressed #46: "If I'm correct, neither side would look for a verdict that was rendered in the Budzyn trial. They are asking for second-degree murder. I'm asking for not guilty." And Boykin took the occasion of #46's voir dire to hint at the little surprise he had in store for me: "You mentioned something about the sentence that both Mr. Budzyn and Mr. Nevers had already served. Do you understand that I will instruct you further on the law that possible penalty in this case should not influence your decision because if there is a conviction it is up to me as the judge to set the penalty, and not up to you?"

Prospective Juror #4 offered this not very promising proof that there is no such thing as a "new trial," at least not when everyone knows about the old trial: "He was convicted the first time around and I'm kind of having a hard time getting past that. If the jury convicted him that many years ago, they had facts based upon that."

Looking back through the transcript, I find I had forgotten how many jurors were excused without a single question from either Neil or Baker because they flat-out believed me to be *innocent*, and couldn't even conceive reaching a different verdict. Most sounded like Werner Spitz – that when a police officer orders you to unhand evidence, you unhand it or there are likely to be consequences. That was the view of #24, who added: "I feel that criminals have too many rights and that this man was breaking the law and on drugs." There were lots of those. It seemed those who obviously leaned in the prosecution's direction were about one-tenth as likely to admit their bias.

For example, #49 waltzed through the opening questions saying that she would have no trouble reaching an unbiased verdict. Then Neil started asking her about the written questionnaire on which she said that police officers' testimony couldn't be believed because "they stick up for their friends" and "think they are above the law." Boykin upheld Neil's challenge for cause. Baker objected.

The lady known as #74 was first questioned by Baker's assistant, Robert Donaldson, who asked several pages of those long "wouldn't you say?" leading questions that lawyers ask to get nothing but "yes" or "no" answers. Then Neil questioned her and let her do the talking, and it emerged that often on trips to visit her mother-in-law's grave she and her husband would stop to pray at Malice Green's grave. She and her husband would discuss things, and her husband "didn't believe (Green) had to die that way. I don't believe he had to be beaten or anything like that." Neil, of course, challenged for cause on grounds that it probably was not a good idea to seat a juror who prayed at Malice Green's grave and who agreed with her husband that too much force had been used. Boykin said: "I don't agree with that at all," and qualified her as a juror.

Panelist #40 allowed as how he had not made up his mind on guilt or innocence and could give a fair trial to both sides. Neil reminded him of his questionnaire on which he had written that the legal system was "all corrupt," and the Green case was an example of corrupt law enforcement. Panelist #40 said: "Right." He said he believed the sentences for Walter and me would have been longer if Malice Green were white. And, referring to the *Malcolm X* screening he said: "I mean, you know, people see a movie, all of a sudden now the movie is the very reason that everybody is back here today...It doesn't make sense that there is another trial because of that." In a long series of questions from Neil, it was brought out that on his questionnaire, #40 had indicated he was not willing to treat a police officer's testimony the same as anyone else's testimony. He compared the Green case to the Rodney King case. He was twice a defendant in criminal cases, and twice exonerated. He said that taking so long to seat a jury was an example of how the system didn't work. With #40 out of the room, Neil made a long challenge for cause in which he called #40 a disturbing malcontent who shouldn't be "sitting in the jury room with other jurors and spreading that view around. I don't think he should be here." Boykin noted that various studies had shown that whites do, on average, serve shorter criminal sentences if their victims are black – and denied Neil's challenge.

Prospective Juror #3 made it clear that a judge's instructions to jurors not to discuss a case among themselves can be basically useless. When asked why he thought he could not give a fair verdict, he said: "Well, first of all, I been here two days. I heard a lot of hearsay discussions. I understand that you are not supposed to at this point." The next day #34 said: "Everybody is talking in that jury room." So much for bailiffs.

A woman identified as #57 said she had visited the Green "shrine," and that if I were "a black officer, I would not be getting all these trials." She was excused.

If there ever was a juror attempting to qualify herself for a seat on a big case, it had to be #67 – who answered Boykin's standard questions straight-up "yes" and "no"…no doubts, absolutely able to be fair and impartial in every way. Knew almost nothing about the case because she had been busy getting ready for, and staging, her daughter's wedding at the time. "The two gentlemen were on trial. They were found guilty. That's about all I remember of it." She never discussed the case with friends, family or co-workers. Not even her husband. ("He's very quiet. He very seldom talks to me.") She worked as a board of education safety officer at a middle school. She remembered that Walter and I were accused of murder, but did not read or hear anything about it: "Because like I said, I was dealing with my daughter's wedding and every waking hour besides being at school, being at work, I was at the stores or malls or whatever getting things, preparing for her wedding." The wedding was in June of 1993. Did she recall reading anything about the incident when it occurred in November 1992? "It takes a year to plan a wedding" – and no, she had not heard Stanley Knox or Coleman Young say a word about the death of Malice Green. She said she was a regular newspaper reader, but only glanced at any Malice Green stories because she was "doing other things." She was apparently the only person in Detroit who never read about the case, never watched anything about it on TV, and never talked to anyone about it. Neil made no challenge.

As a final sample, I offer #71, a genuine piece of work. He was absolutely certain he would be a fair juror. Baker had no questions. Here are some snippets from #71's exchange with Neil:

Fink: Have you ever had any problems with the police?
#71: No, sir.
Fink: They never stopped you illegally or harassed you?
#71: Well, I have been harassed lately, you know.
Fink: Can you share that with us?
#71: Okay. Say, for instance, Thursday of last week. Sitting in front of the day care, you know, with my old lady and the kids in the car. An officer approached us and said, you know: "What are you doing here at this time of the morning?" I said: "I am here to drop my kids off at the day care."

He said: "What time do they open?" I said: "4:30." Then, you know, he proceeded to ask me for I.D. I gave him I.D. He said: "Do you have any guns or dope in the car?" I said: "No, sir." I said: "Is there a reason, you know, for you stopping over here?"

He said: "Yeah, because you are a prime candidate to be robbed." So I said: "I'm not worried about that, because, you know, I can take care of myself. I've got something to handle somebody, you know, if they are trying to rob me."

So he said: "So are you trying to tell me you've got a gun in the car?" I said: "No, sir. I'm not trying to tell you I've got a gun in the car. I can defend myself." You know, that was basically it, really.

Fink: That's the only time you have ever had a run-in with the police?

#71: Couple other times, but nothing major, you know.

Fink: Do you feel your friends were treated fairly, the ones who were convicted?

#71: You know, it's still pending really. You going by the jury sheet?

Fink: Yes.

#71: It's still pending, really. I don't know the outcome of that.

Fink: All three of them or is this the same friend?

#71: One of them, he shot his girlfriend's father. That is the felonious assault, I believe. And the other one was for rape. I think the other one is for drugs. All those are still pending.

Fink: Those are three different guys?

#71: Yes.

Fink: Are you still friends with them?

#71: Yes.

Fink: You had "yes" you favor lawsuits for victims of police brutality, and then you put dollar signs next to it. I don't understand.

#71: Okay, well it's like this. Sometimes, you know, police, they do abuse that badge that they have. You know what I'm saying? I'm not saying that all of them are like that. You know what I'm saying? Because there are some out there that, you know, "I own the world and I can do this and I can do that." You know what I'm saying?

It goes on for several pages. Panelist #71 believed police and prosecutors get a conviction "damned near every time...

but that doesn't mean the person is guilty, you know." Neil asked: "White cop, black deceased. You never discussed this case with your friends?" Answer: "Never." Question: "You want to sit on this case, don't you?" Answer: "I would like to."

With #71 out of the room, Neil complained to Boykin that the prospective jurors were not being led in randomly, that too many were being "self-selected." And he asked that #71 be excused for cause. Boykin denied the challenge.

By qualifying #71, the court had, after four days, assembled fifty potential jurors for final voir dire. The next step would be to assemble all fifty in the courtroom, seat sixteen in the jury box and go through the final voir dire process – with more questions and each side's twelve peremptory challenges until the final jury was set to be "the triers of fact" who would determine my fate. Naïve me was still feeling hopeful.

Boykin had his own mostly standard set of questions: Where do you live? What is your occupation? Are any of your relatives police officers? Etc. Both sides get to propose additional questions for the judge's approval. Baker came up with a laundry list that shocked Neil – questions that quizzed potential jurors on their ability to comprehend and judge almost every single point of law in the prosecution's case and previewing the judge's final instructions at the end of testimony. We already had the detailed written juror questionnaire. Neil told Boykin the question list was so exhaustive it amounted to arguing the trial even before jurors were seated. Neil said if the judge was going to allow such an unusual list of questions, he wanted an hour or two to produce his own parallel list. Baker's laundry list even took up the issue of whether someone can resist an illegal arrest – an interesting question for Baker to raise because he had spent his entire Malice Green career telling the world that Malice Green did *not* resist arrest, and because by the end of this trial the prosecution would once again stop pressing their idiotic position that this was not a legal arrest. Boykin, Baker and Neil debated and hammered out a list of questions for final voir dire.

The fifty qualified panelists were led into the room, and names were drawn to take the sixteen seats in the jury box. Suddenly every prospective juror had a new number, from one through sixteen. Boykin started going through his standard list of questions – starting with whether anyone had served on a jury before – plus questions that came mainly from Baker's laundry list. A woman now identified as Mrs. Tyner was one of those who had served on a jury. She "thought" she had heard an assault case, and she "thought" the verdict had been "guilty."

After a recess, and with the potential jurors still out of the room, Neil looked at the glass box from which juror names were being drawn for the sixteen seats and told Boykin: "I'd sure like to have those juror names covered up when they're in shuffle. I mean, they are just displayed and shown."

Boykin took affront on his clerk's behalf. "Just a matter of style," Neil said. "My client did a lot of time based on a trial that went wrong in one hundred different ways. All I am worried about is appearance. I am not worried about anybody personally."

The jurors returned, and a few began to be excused by Boykin as he ran down the question list. Panelist #71, the one with numerous felonious friends and who really wanted to sit on this jury, was one of the sixteen in the box, now with the name of Mr. Cain. He, of course, had his hand up when Boykin asked whether anyone had been a crime victim and whether anyone had close friends who had been convicted of crimes. Mr. Cain had been shot in the hand during a mysterious drive-by while at work. His partner at work, meanwhile, "shot his girlfriend's father three times and I think it was felonious assault." And there was another friend who "shot his girlfriend in the chest with a .25 automatic pistol." And there was a friend on parole, who got caught with an illegal gun, and "got forty-five days of community service." And he recounted his "harassment" outside the day-care facility. And he assured Boykin he would be a fair juror and judge a police officer fairly. And Boykin left him seated in the jury box.

No one in the box raised a hand to indicate difficulty in following any of the legal instructions in Baker's questions. Boykin asked each juror the name of their city of residence and their occupation. Boykin asked if either Baker or Neil had any challenges for cause. Baker had none. Neil renewed the same ones Boykin had denied during individual voir dire. Boykin denied them again. Neil pointed out that several of Mr. Cain's interesting answers about felons in his acquaintance had changed since the day before. Baker said this still didn't merit challenge for cause. Neil exercised his first peremptory challenge and Mr. Cain was gone. A replacement took Mr. Cain's seat in the box, answered the same questions, and the hunt for a jury was under way in earnest.

Neil used another peremptory challenge to dismiss a black woman named Ms. Corr. Another juror was seated and questioned. Neil burned his third peremptory on a white juror named Mr. Zutek. The jury was sent home for the day. Neil made a record on his complaints about Boykin not dismissing Mr. Cain for cause – and being forced to call Cain a liar in front of the other jurors, thus immediately casting the defense as the heavy and denying us a fair trial. Boykin was not impressed. "I don't want the court to take this wrong," Neil said. "But you know, this community is very interested in this case. And – well, I am not going to do anything I said I wouldn't do before by talking to the press. It's very frustrating to put a self-imposed gag on myself, and sit here and watch Larry Nevers go through this." Boykin remained unimpressed.

The next morning, after Boykin asked the jurors an additional question that Neil had proposed regarding reasonable force in making an arrest, the last juror called the previous day was given her round of questions. Baker passed his opportunity for a peremptory. Neil used one, thanking and excusing Mrs. Tyner. And that is when it hit the fan. Baker asked Boykin not to dismiss Mrs. Tyner, and asked for the jurors to be removed while he made a motion.

With the jury gone, Baker went straight to it. "Malice Green is black. The defendant is white. We have a jury pool that we started off with fifty prospective jurors, eleven of whom are black. We think the defense is using its peremptories to excuse those members, you know, of that group to basically end up with an all-white jury."

Baker went on a tirade about my outspokenness, saying "the defendant himself has gone on record in many different forums and in many different ways concerning his view of this case and this prosecution...He feels he is a victim of black racism." Baker was particularly taken by a Detroit News interview I gave after the state Supreme Court freed Walter but left me in prison. I had blamed five white justices for following one black justice (and the whole Detroit power structure) in refusing to grant the very trial at which Baker was now speaking. The fact that a federal judge saw it my way didn't impress Doug Baker very much, nor did the fact that he had unsuccessfully appealed that federal ruling all the way to the U.S. Supreme Court. In that same Q&A article, I was candid about my Trial One jury (asked whether I knew I was in trouble when I saw the number of blacks on the jury I said: "Of course. The jury was made up of Coleman Young peers, not my peers.") When asked what I meant by "radical blacks," I said: "Black people already have a bias against police. (They believe) every white cop beats up black people. That is the false premise put forth by the NAACP and these other race hustlers around the country. Not all white cops beat up black people, but nobody seems to think about it if the black people are out there committing crimes and the police go to arrest them and they say, 'No, I'm not going to be arrested.' What are the police supposed to do?"

Basically Baker, citing my interviews and what he called "my" web site, told Boykin that I was a racist whose whining had no basis in fact. He said the public record of my comments showed my view "as to black people in the community and (my) beliefs about them." Then he appealed to Boykin's regard for his clerk, alleging racism in our request regarding the blind draw of jurors: "We have, for example, through his attorney suspecting this staff of possible wrongdoing. We have the clerk in this court, Freda, who is black, and this suspicion being leveled that she is going to somehow improperly draw from those fifty names to seat jurors in this case and the whole to-do about trying to blind her or hide the names on the slips so that if they're pulled out she is not going to pull them out unfairly."

Baker complained that in individual voir dire Neil had asked only black jurors whether they would be able to take an innocent verdict back to their community. "I think it's clear, Your Honor," Baker said, "abundantly clear, that this defendant and his attorney are paranoid about any blacks seated on this jury and they are now using their peremptories I think to exclude them improperly...(to) get the all-white jury they want."

Baker noted that three of the four peremptories Neil had used so far were black jurors. He said Mrs. Tyner and Ms. Corr "gave no real reasons to kick them off" – though he conceded that "Mr. Cain, I can understand that." Baker asked Boykin to overrule the peremptory Neil had just made on Mrs. Tyner, saying: "There is nothing about her answers which would disqualify her or stand out." Baker argued that Neil had illegally established a pattern of trying to stack the jury with whites.

Neil, not only a gifted lawyer but one with a long record in civil rights activism, was, of course, outraged. He began:

"I suppose the court is going to let me defend myself here personally and legally, because this is a personal attack, also. First of all, I would say that from my personal standpoint I am the one in Coral Gables, Florida, who got beat up protecting an Africa-American's right to go to an all-white bathroom when Mr. Baker was probably in knee pants. And Mr. Baker is the one who has made a career of putting young African-American men in jail. So from a personal standpoint, it is very offensive what he said.

"From the standpoint of this case, the first judge that was chosen was not blind-drawn, George Crockett III. Longtime personal friend of mine...Larry Nevers did not get a blind-draw judge. The second judge that was chosen, again, was not blind-drawn. It was a second African-American, Tom Jackson. Great federal defender, a person I consider a friendly acquaintance …again not a blind-draw. Chosen for public perception, I suppose."

Neil said he had been "overjoyed" to see Boykin on the bench for this trial "because you are not only an academician, but you are low-key. That tends to defuse a volatile situation. But the point is we have had three African-American judges chosen to try Larry Nevers's case, not blind-drawn. So if Larry Nevers is a little paranoid, you know, it's understandable."

Neil was just warming up.

"Attacking me, Mr. Baker, does a great disservice to manipulators. To call him a manipulator would be to insult manipulators. To try to manipulate this situation to my attacking Freda is obscene. What I am trying to do is preserve the integrity of the entire process so that nobody can say later on something went wrong or something could have gone wrong…. If Your Honor was picking out of the box himself, that glass box with names exposed, I would have raised the same issue."

Neil pointed out that "we have spent a great deal of money and done a great deal of begging to get the top jury consultant firm in the country to help us pick a jury. We would not be spending this kind of money if all we were looking to do is to kick African-Americans off the jury."

Neil told Boykin "with all due respect" Mr. Cain should never have been qualified as a juror (who could possibly disagree?). Ms. Corr "wore a T-shirt with Psalm 19 printed all over it. Fire and brimstone and the poor shall succeed and the powerful shall die. I mean, it was fire and brimstone. I don't want a fire and brimstone juror on my jury." As for the third black juror Neil had bounced, Mrs. Tyner – whose dismissal Baker was challenging – Neil noted that she lived two miles from Warren and Twenty-third, and had a son who served a year on arson charges (in voir dire she said "even though the judge felt he did not do it…he was with the young man who did it"), Neil said: "She has a son that went to prison at the hands of the police and (she) made a point to tell us that he has turned his life around. I don't want her on my jury for that reason. It has nothing to do with her being African-American…I've spent seven years of my life on a death-row case for the NAACP, and to have a person like Baker accuse me of something like that I find is beyond belief, the ultimate irony." And he reminded the court that a full complement of reporters were on hand for the day's voir dire: "I think somebody in (Baker's) office dropped a dime and said, 'Be here today for an interesting motion.' This is way premature. There has been no pattern established."

Boykin did everything but grant Baker's motion, no doubt stopping short because he didn't want to set up obvious grounds for appeal even before the first witness was called. He warned Neil that he would be watching closely for a pattern of excluding black jurors – including questions about whether black jurors felt they would be able to return to their community with a "not guilty" verdict. Personally, that seemed as valid a question as asking whether somebody had a relative who was a police officer. As for Neil and his anger at being accused of racist tactics, Boykin said: "I don't think that this is really indicative of your true feelings. But then by the same token, you are also directed and guided by a client who has certain beliefs." In other words, I was about to go to trial before a black judge who was calling me a racist. And we got to that point because my very expensive jury consultant believed Mrs. Tyner, whose son had turned his life around after being arrested and serving time, would be inclined to think of Malice Green as someone who would have done the same thing but wasn't given a chance to do so.

Neil's next move stunned most everybody in the room. He withdrew his peremptory challenge of Mrs. Tyner and said: "We are satisfied" – meaning there would be no more questioning, no more challenges…we had a jury. Racially speaking, it was nine whites and three blacks. Neil turned to the prosecutor and said: "Sometimes be careful what you ask for. You might get it."

So much for removing racial politics from the case by getting out of Recorder's Court. The part of a trial that movies and TV shows are made out of was about to begin. It would, of course, be described as a "new" trial. Maybe if it had been moved to another state, it would have been new.

The major blowup between Neil and me occurred after Bader Cassin testified as one of the first prosecution witnesses. Neil treated him gently, got Cassin to make his lukewarm and ass-covering statement that cocaine *might* have had something to do with Green's death, and dismissed him. I was furious. Lynne and I had compiled chapter and verse on Cassin dodging the official autopsy, doing his own phantom autopsy the next morning, his meeting with prosecutors at which Danny Maynard heard them reject Cassin's concern about cocaine, and Cassin's jousting with Jiraki on the subject. I wanted to know why Cassin was suspicious of a cocaine role even before the toxicology report came back, and Jiraki on the other hand didn't care about cocaine even after seeing the tox result. I wanted to know how Cassin could do his own examination without preserving so much as one page of notes, and whether that had anything to do with the fact his medical license had expired. Jiraki had long since been fired from the M.E.'s office. Cassin soon after had resigned under pressure, but reaching back into history and putting Cassin on the stand was the best Doug Baker could come up with for his theory that Green died from blunt force trauma, period. That whole Wayne County Morgue operation was suspect. We had Lucy Rorke and Charles Wetli, the Long Island medical examiner who handled the TWA Flight 800 case and one of the nation's foremost pathologists in cocaine issues, waiting to testify. I wanted to destroy Cassin on the stand. Neil didn't want to embarrass him in front of the jury. So we had a lively discussion in the hallway during a break. Nancy and Lynne and Marla McCowan, Neil's assistant, all helped convince me – then and over the years – to accept Neil's approach. I still like mine.

In the end, cause of death would be addressed only by

Cassin for the prosecution and Lucy Rorke for the defense. Neil never called Dr. Wetli, who was left sitting out in the hallway at our financial expense. Neil's view was that any expert who said the flashlight blows contributed to Green's death – even if the flashlight blows would not have been fatal without the cocaine – did us no good under the "take the victim as you find him" doctrine. This meant we didn't even call Dr. Dragovic, the only forensic pathologist *and* neuropathologist who ever examined the Green case. Dragovic maybe offered the best and most common-sense theory of Malice Green's death, and the most expertise, of anybody. Plus he could testify about Baker and Worthy ignoring Dragovic when he told them they "had a problem with the cocaine." But Dragovic's explanation was complicated, lacked the "clarity" Neil wanted in the defense narrative, and – despite saying cocaine and alcohol killed Green – said it was the stress, exertion and flashlight blows that triggered his "wired-up brain" into shutting down his body. Neil felt Wetli did us no good for similar reasons.

So Dr. Rorke testified her opinion, as she did at Trial One, that any brain damage was superficial, and that blunt-force trauma was *not* the cause of death. Despite Neil's warnings to Lucy that Baker would be on full attack mode trying to fluster her, and that she should not go too far in trying to simplify her findings for the jury, she fell straight into the trap. Baker rattled her into agitated defensiveness, then asked whether she was saying Green would have died that night if he stayed home and watched television. She said "yes" – her way of saying that in her professional opinion, as a brain expert, whatever killed Green it wasn't my flashlight. Cause of death as a serious piece of my defense probably went in the tank right there. I will go to my grave believing – *knowing* – that this is where the legal system…not just judges and lawyers, but the law itself… sabotaged the quest for truth in Malice Green's death. I'm not a lawyer, and I'm not in court. I'm just trying to write a book that explains what happened out there, and afterward. By the way, Baker told the jury that Lucy's expertise didn't pass the laugh test. So I probably ought to note it was Lucy who pointed out that Cassin testified while using a brain-section photo that was upside down.

Bobby Lessnau was a major defense witness in describing what happened, especially in terms of how much resistance Green still mounted long after I last touched him. Several times as Baker badgered him, Bobby looked Baker – or jurors – in the eye and reminded: "*I was there.*" Neil said after the trial that Bobby was "probably the best witness I've seen in thirty-five years. Ex-Marine. Clean-cut. Brave. The kind of guy you'd want your daughter to date. That knife never came out in the first two trials. Larry was an old man with emphysema, fifty pounds overweight, hanging on for dear life."

During Lessnau's testimony, black jurors often crossed their arms and looked the other way. During my own testimony, while I described Malice Green's arrest as I always have, as you've heard it here, Malice Green's mother sat in the gallery and chanted beneath her breath: "Murderer. Murderer. Murderer.

Doug Baker's approach to my testimony was simple. His cross-examination and his closing statement told the jury I was lying about everything. I do mean *everything*. The prosecution's position was that I lied about being focused on finding the carjacked red Tempo, lied about confiscating the toy gun from the kid in the housing projects, lied about not "stalking" Malice Green, lied about even having reason to ask Green for his driver's license, lied about Green putting his hand on my gun, lied about my concern for the metallic object in Green's hand when he swung at me, lied about how many times I struck him with my flashlight and how hard I hit him, lied about not walking over and punching and kicking Green while other officers handcuffed him – among other things. According to Doug Baker, I was another defense witness who did not pass the laugh test. He made the trial into a credibility contest between his "testimony" and mine. And he was absolutely fixated on the toy gun. He spent an incredible amount of his time chasing the idea that I invented my encounter with young Damon Davis, and that instead of taking a toy gun from him that night I was already carrying it as a plant – a "drop gun." The only thing that got planted in the Malice Green case was the idea that I was a crooked rogue cop who could be expected to phony up a crime scene. That is a powerful idea to plant with a jury. Baker knew better. In twenty-four years as a police officer, no one ever alleged that I was a crooked cop – except as I faced trial in the Malice Green case. So let's talk some more about Damon Davis and the toy gun – starting with me telling you what happened, and then with Doug Baker telling my jury his creative version of what happened.

The plastic 9 millimeter replica came into my possession only because we were assigned by dispatch to answer a B&E alarm in the housing projects. It turned out to be a false alarm. But that is why we wound up in the area. While there, I heard a call for a volunteer car to take a run, practically around the corner, regarding "man with a gun." We didn't get on the radio and accept the run, but we cruised into the area for a minute. After all, if somebody really was engaged in armed larceny, catching him in the act would be booster-car work. That's when Damon Davis emerged from between two buildings, we stopped the kid, and when I saw a bulge under his shirt I took the toy gun from him. We warned him it was bad news to be carrying such a "weapon" and sent him on his way. I did that for several reasons. For one thing, if he was in fact the "man with a gun" we couldn't take him with us while trying to find the complainant – if in fact the complainant had identified himself when he called 911 – because it amounted to setting up an improper identification. For another thing, we had no idea whether this kid had actually done anything illegal with his toy gun. For another thing, confiscating toy guns from kids wasn't booster-car work. At *most*, the kid would have been turned over to a juvenile officer and then sent on his way. For another thing, getting back to looking for the red Tempo was on my mind. I wasn't interested in doing paperwork on a toy gun instead.

I gave Damon Davis a slide after writing his name, his stated date of birth, and his stated address in our run book. He was too young to have a driver's license. Remember, the run book was the car's bible, not official department paperwork. The run book was a place for useful future reference by me and my crew. I can to this day go to the stack of filled run books in my closet and find most of the meaningful citizen encounters I had over the years – shorthand descriptions and license plates of suspicious cars, notes on unusual street activity, a note on an interview that led nowhere but smelled of going somewhere in the future, an address I wanted to remember as an address not as "ya know, that place on Trumbull where two guys ran last week when we approached." I paid no attention to the radio during the brief encounter with Damon Davis, so I assumed someone had taken the volunteer run. I got on the radio and told dispatch words to the effect that "we have information for whichever car in Three took the 'man with a gun' run." Almost immediately a marked car pulled around the corner. I drove toward it. We stopped car-to-car beside each other, driver's windows down, and talked. I told them about the kid and his name. I observed the passenger writing down everything I told them – or, let's be precise, I saw him writing as I talked. They never said they hadn't taken the run, so I assumed they did. Which is one reason we didn't put it on our official activity log as well as in the run book. Turns out, apparently, no one took the run. Walter and I left the area and headed out for where the red Tempo was last sighted. When we came to Warren Avenue is when Malice Green and his red Topaz crossed in front of us.

That's the way it happened, and I am swearing that is what happened. Doug Baker told my jury that *none* of the above happened. You can make up your own mind.

On the stand Baker showed me a list of uniformed patrol officers on duty that night, and by process of elimination I named the two officers in that car. They didn't testify, but Baker informed the court that they had not been in the area. In his closing statement, Baker said: "I'm not going to chase them down. I have their activity log. They were nowhere near that place." Furthermore, there was no record of such a "man with a gun" run going on the air, or of my own call about information for whoever took the run. Conveniently supporting Baker, dispatch records showed a thirty-nine-minute period around 10 p.m. in Detroit's Third and Fourth Precincts with no activity on the street and *nothing* on the air. Well, OK. Meanwhile, Lee Hardy testified that he tried to call dispatch that night but the airwaves were so busy he couldn't get through. EMS has its own radio frequency, but most EMS runs also generate a police run. I later got hold of the two phantom police officers' activity log. It shows that they took a "missing person" run and milked it for several hours, at two different addresses not far from the housing projects. Between time logged at those two addresses are fifteen unlogged minutes roughly coinciding with when our cars sat side by side. The missing-person report shows up on these two guys' activity log as their *only* activity for the evening. They were, in fact, the only car in the precinct that did not respond to Walter's call for help. So I call them lazy. As for the thirty-nine minutes with no activity of any kind in the Third and Fourth, I can only call that miraculous. Or selective tape retrieval by the prosecutor. I have no idea how this can be. I have no idea how Doug Baker thinks that as a twenty-four-year veteran, if I wanted to make up a story, I would be dumb enough to say I was on the radio when I wasn't – and invite investigators to go listen to the tapes. Or say I interacted with a marked car when I didn't. Anybody devious enough to carry a drop gun would be smarter than that, don't you think? But we are just getting started with the toy gun.

Sometime before the trial I made half a dozen copies of my run-book page for November 5, 1992. I kept at least one. I gave at least one to Lynne Krueger, my very religious and straight-arrow then-mother of nine and about-to-be-mother-of-ten archivist. I gave one to a guy who was helping me with this book, and to whom I had showed the run book several months earlier. And I gave at least one copy to Neil, who was expecting a discovery visit from the prosecutor's office. I told Neil to be sure Baker got a copy. I assume Neil passed it along. The truth is, I desperately wanted to *find* Damon Davis to prove where and when I picked up the toy gun. I wanted Damon Davis subpoenaed to be in court on the very day Baker cross-examined me. I asked police officers in two different departments to see what they could find on this kid. They came up with nothing. Then I asked an Oakland County sheriff's deputy, and within a week or two he called me at our "mansion." He had information. I grabbed the run book and turned to Page 371, because I wanted to be certain we were talking about the same guy with the same date of birth. As the deputy read me the information, I wrote in the run book adding Davis's middle name, a more recent address, the number on an outstanding warrant, and the word "drugs." Despite this information, we never found Damon Davis. Those copies I had passed around did not include a middle name, or a new address, or a warrant number, or the word "drugs." I hadn't yet gotten the call with that information when I made the copies.

As Baker cross-examined me, he picked up my run book, turned to Page 371, and we had the following exchange:

Baker: And doesn't that look like it (the information given me by the sheriff's deputy) is written with the same pen as "Damon Davis"?

Nevers: That would be impossible.

Baker: Right. You didn't keep the same pen for eight years to write this in?

Nevers: I couldn't keep that.

Baker: If it looks the same that's a coincidence?

Nevers: Very much so.

Baker: You wouldn't doctor anything?

Nevers: Absolutely not.

Baker: Other people might doctor evidence, but not you?

Nevers: Absolutely not.

Incredible. He didn't subpoena the two lazy cops to testify under oath that I hadn't run into them in the projects that night. He just said it was so, relying on their activity log. Maybe they weren't just lazy. Maybe they wanted Starsky and Hutch to go down. And instead of having a handwriting analysis done on the two Damon Davis entries, Baker just announced in court that it looked like the same pen. I *did* get a handwriting analysis done, but wasn't able to arrange that, of course, until after the trial. If I had a *third* trial, being aware what Baker was going to allege, I'd have the handwriting expert on the stand. But it gets better than that.

Seven years earlier when I testified at Trial One, Baker sneered when I told about confiscating the toy gun, and sarcastically said words to the effect of: "And I'm sure you can tell us the name of the person you took the gun from?" I told him I couldn't at the moment, but would do so the next day. I did in fact that night pick up my run book and copy Damon Davis's name and date of birth onto a piece of paper. Next morning I gave it to Goldpaugh, who gave it to Baker. I watched as Baker said "I don't need this," and ripped it up and tossed it. Ask John Goldpaugh. But it gets better than that.

With the passage of time and personnel changes, Homicide had named a new officer in charge of the Green case for my Trial Two, a policeman who wasn't involved in the original investigation. Sergeant Dale Collins, a black officer, showed guts and honesty. Part of his job was to round up physical evidence, much of which had disappeared. But he found Green's folding knife, and there it sat on the evidence table – four inches folded and eight inches opened, as I recall. Dale Collins also played an absolutely crucial role in demonstrating just how far Baker would bend the facts to call me a liar. Collins came over to the defense table and informed us that Homicide had tracked down Damon Davis, interviewed him, and the young man had said that, yes, I confiscated a toy gun from him. I assume Homicide had tracked down Damon Davis only by phone, what with the matter of an outstanding arrest warrant and all. And though I thank Homicide for finding him – no longer a kid, but now a young adult – and I thank Dale Collins for letting us know,

I wish they would have asked him the obvious question as to when our encounter occurred. I think he would have been able to remember it happening, as it did, on the most infamous law-enforcement night in his young life.

More basically, why on Earth would I lie about *when* I confiscated the toy gun? What's the point? I'm charged with second-degree murder and I'm worried about being charged with having a toy gun in the car? One that has absolutely nothing to do with the Malice Green incident...except that I tossed it to Mickey Williams, in a typical piece of street banter (and attempt to defuse a potentially volatile situation) after Green was taken away (and I had no idea he was dying)? What does this have to do with when I got the gun? Where's the relevance? Neil, of course, objected to going to this subject even before I took the stand – with the jury out of the room. Boykin overruled the objection. So Baker not only got to portray me as callous in tossing the gun to Mickey Williams, but he also got to go fishing and portray me as a callous rogue cop, a liar and a forger. And the toy gun became a big piece of Baker's pitch to the jury that my account of November 5 was not credible.

You have to understand that at both Trial One and Trial Two, the prosecution started its case by trying to convince jurors that this arrest never should have happened, that I didn't even have valid reason to ask Malice Green for his driver's license. I can't imagine prosecutors themselves believing this to be true, any more than I believe they honestly thought I was carrying a drop gun. It's as if the dope house didn't exist, and Green wasn't chauffeuring the proprietor. Let alone Robert Knox running from the car. The prosecutors made much of the fact that no one else would admit to seeing Knox run from the car. That was also, Baker said, a lie. It wasn't a lie. But let's forget whether Robert Knox ran from the car or just materialized out of the shadows, as Fletch Man testified. Car with bullet holes pulls up in front of dope pad. Dope pad proprietor steps out onto sidewalk with an open bottle of beer in his hand. I mean, please...if this was Grosse Pointe instead of Detroit, and it was a Burger King instead of a dope house, even then *no one* would question a simple request to see a driver's license. But Baker told the jury I was lying about our grounds for sticking our noses into this social gathering on a Warren Avenue sidewalk.

Baker remained hung up on the theory that we were "stalking" Green, based on the fact that we had run his license plate number earlier that evening. I've explained that. More nonsense. If we wanted to "pull Malice Green over for no reason," we would have done it the first time he crossed our path. We didn't. Didn't even think about it. We just ran his plate number. It wasn't hot – and it certainly wasn't the "carjacked" red Tempo, so we ignored it and wouldn't even have looked at the owner's name, because he had no outstanding warrants. But that, Baker told the jury, was a lie. According to the prosecution script, *everything* Walter and I said about our shift that night was a lie, and even the dope house itself was a lie – it wasn't a dope house but Ralph Fletcher's "residence." Baker was terrified some juror just might decide that it all began with two police officers trying to make a lawful arrest. Terrified, in other words, of the truth. Neil said after the trial: "Baker's main case was that Larry was a racist rogue cop looking to show his strength to a new guy in town."

Baker said I lied about Green putting his hand on my gun. I told you back at the beginning that this was something no one can possibly know except me, and that after reading my story you will believe me – or not. Baker's "proof" was that I didn't tell anybody about it. It's true I don't recall telling anyone until I told Fred Walker, the DPOA attorney, later that night at Homicide. Walker testified at Trial Two that I did tell him, even as I was tearing up the report he advised me not to write. Why wasn't I talking about it before then? I don't know. I can only guess. Mostly, I suppose it's because Baker is talking about a time period when I didn't know Green was dying. When I learned he had died, there were a whole *lot* of things I wasn't real articulate about. On the other hand, right

in the middle of the struggle – after Lessnau removed Green
from the car – a streetload of witnesses heard me shouting
at the other officers to watch out for something in Green's
hand. Baker couldn't say I didn't tell anyone about *that*, so he
pretended there was no reason for me to be concerned about
a guy swinging his fist with something metallic in his fingers
– deep into a struggle in which I am losing wind badly and
not wanting to lose control...much like in front of the Book-
Cadillac Hotel a decade earlier, a struggle whose relevance to
November 5, 1992, is something Baker also didn't want to hear
about. Boykin, for his part, refused to allow into evidence a
criminology book containing material on the use of keys as
weapons. The whole idea that I was defending myself, Baker
told the jury, was another lie.

Neil's closing argument appealed to the jury to see it my
way. Some sound bites:

"The reasonableness of the force must be judged in the
light of the circumstances as they appear to the officer at
the time...It's not Rodney King because this man was never
helpless, ever. And we don't have a film. So what we rely
upon is your mind's eye as the lens, and looking at this case
frame by frame, and then understanding how fast it was going
at the time...Does a guilty man go and try to round up the
witnesses who he knew would probably be hostile to him? As
Mr. Fletcher said he came into their house, got their names
and addresses, and documented them in this (run) book? Is
that the way that somebody who has a guilty conscience acts?
Going to get witnesses, bringing EMS drivers to the scene?...
Listen to Walter Budzyn on the tape (when Walter called for
help). Listen to his breath. Listen to how much strain – Walter
Budzyn was in better shape than Larry Nevers...This was not
a case of being bludgeoned. These were 'flicks' by everybody's
testimony (except) Lee Hardy. Reasonable force. He was
flicking, he was doing what he had to do to get the man under
control to make the arrest, to defend himself, he was doing his
job – for all the people of the City of Detroit...The prosecutor

calls Dr. Cassin in this trial, and winds up arguing with him about the role cocaine played in the death. Even Dr. Cassin said that cocaine primed the brain to be put in that position to asphyxiate Malice Green...The road less traveled in this case is the road to the truth. It's a hard road to take to think a man has been incarcerated, his family destroyed for nothing but doing his job."

Baker, of course, moved once again for the jury to be given the option of a lesser-included charge, involuntary manslaughter. Neil, of course, objected. Boykin, of course, approved giving the jury an opportunity to "compromise." The idea of all three black jurors finding me not guilty of anything, including murder, was – major understatement – unlikely. The idea of all nine white jurors finding me guilty of murder was equally unlikely. So any court observer would have predicted a hung jury if the trial had been, as advertised and defended, a murder trial. And any observer except me probably would have guaranteed a manslaughter conviction once that option was offered. The city was tired of the case and wanted it over, and every juror in the box knew that Walter had been found guilty of manslaughter at his second trial. Despite Boykin's warning to one of the prospective jurors back in individual voir dire, I think it's safe to say that some jurors thought they were doing me a favor by finding me guilty of manslaughter – that I would get time served and the streets would remain peaceful, something the whole region had been told for seven years would never happen if I ever were found innocent. But objecting to allowing manslaughter as a compromise verdict wasn't just about trying to get a not- guilty verdict. The facts don't fit the lesser charge – either I murdered a man or I did my job and a man happened to die. And the Michigan Supreme Court had been practically begging the lower courts to send them a case where they could eliminate unfair lesser-included offenses, something the federal courts and many states already had done. This would be the backbone of our appeal if I were found guilty of manslaughter.

Which, of course, I was. It was April 18, 2000, the second day of deliberations. Before deciding, jurors had first requested a copy of Stanley Knox's memo on use of force – the one that didn't change any rules or regulations but just said, in effect, "Watch your ass." As the verdict was read I sighed, lowered my head and shook it from side to side. Once again, my world stood still while the jury was polled individually and I pondered this trial I had fought so hard to get, how it was over and I was still a felon, and how my family had given up so much to see me through this far. Bond was continued pending my sentence date of May 16. And I went home.

I can't honestly remember what I expected to happen on the May 16 sentencing date. Probably I had no idea. Walter had been sentenced to time served. I had served more time than Walter. There was a lot of speculation that I, too, would be a convicted felon but a free man, or soon at least. Malice Green's sister, Treise, told the Associated Press she was satisfied with the verdict, that the word "guilty" was important, and that I "should just go back to prison, even if it's fifteen days." Baker told reporters the prosecutor's office had not yet decided what sentence to recommend, adding that: "In this case, we have Mr. Nevers delivering most, if not all the blows." Walter's jurors probably were surprised to read that. Dennis Archer, by now the mayor, was called upon for the obligatory "civil unrest" comment and said: "I think this verdict will be accepted."

The probation officer's interview was my first bad sign. Somehow – despite having done nothing to warrant it – I was given a worse score than when I was awaiting sentence for murder. Suddenly, for instance, I was given points for being the "ringleader" – unlike the first time around. It would be part of my "paranoia," I suppose, to note that the worse score came from a black case officer, the better score from a white case officer. These scores are important to a judge who is looking for a way to stick it to you. But even with the magically worsened score, I was still within range of a "time served" sentence. I was, as always, hopeful.

Sentencing day began with Neil arguing against various scores on my pre-sentencing probation report, noting – to no avail – the discrepancies from Trial One to Trial Two, and discrepancies with Walter's scores in his Trial Two.

Then Sherry Green, another sister of Malice Green, spoke to the court, reading a first-person statement on behalf of their mother, Patricia Green. Sherry Green spoke of the family's grief – and who could not feel some of that grief along with them. Malice Green was not supposed to die, was not intended to die on my shift. Listening to Green family members has always been an emotional roller-coaster for me. One moment I am drawn into the grief caused by November 5, 1992; the next minute I am wanting to shout: "You have it wrong!" The family statement said I beat their son and brother to death because he refused to open his hand. That it would have been impossible for Malice Green to knee me in the chest when I reached into his car and grabbed his wrist. That I was on a "bizarre" quest to clear my name by lying about what happened out there. And: "The defendant has stated he asked my son for his driver's license because my son was parked in front of a dope house. My question is, who in this courtroom has never parked in front of a dope house?" That last sentence led numerous audience members to look around the room, almost as if they were counting heads. The family expressed anger that our side had produced testimony about Malice Green's history of resisting arrest while living in Illinois. "My son was never a problem child or in trouble with the law," the family said.

And then Sherry Green recited a name you will remember from a few chapters back. "What is true about my son as a child," she read in her mother's name, "is when he was a teenager and riding his Moped with Victor Rogers, who was also riding a Moped. They were chased down about half a block from where this defendant finally killed my son. Victor Rogers was beaten savagely and he received a City of Detroit settlement." Sherry Green, standing directly in front of me, turned and looked at me to emphasize that I was the police officer who allegedly beat Victor Rogers so badly that a decade and a half later he was limping at Malice Green's funeral. Every news organization and TV station in Detroit was present in the courtroom. Not one mentioned Victor Rogers in their stories that night or the next morning or ever. No reporter went out and did the legwork to determine whether the Green family was, in fact, baring a terrible chapter in the long history of a brutal racist cop – or putting an exclamation point on my impending sentence by citing another fictional piece of "Starsky" hysteria. How could any reporter, let alone all of them, ignore this? I have no idea.

Baker recommended that sentencing include at least some period of incarceration. "There has to be a message sent," he said, "that no one is above the law."

Neil's pre-sentencing remarks were lengthy and very good. Inspired, even. He revisited testimony from multiple witnesses that Malice Green was still struggling, forcefully, after Bobby Lessnau removed him from the car. "Three people to handcuff him. So this Rodney King imagery is false. The truth has never been told about that. Some people can't stand the truth. It is politically incorrect to tell the truth...One newspaper reporter portrayed it as a 'pen knife.' If that's a pen knife, I would hate to see a street knife...It's difficult to pick a fight with the Free Press or the media. It's hard to fight people who buy ink by the barrel...But coming down to what the sentence should be, even Mr. Nevers's powerful adversary, the Detroit Free Press, recognizes that the community has had enough. (The Free Press has) been his most powerful adversary since November 1992. They have remained so through this verdict. They say time served would be an appropriate sentence."

And Neil went on. "Some people are judged because of their deprived background. Abused as children. For a variety of reasons. Inevitably, you wind up in front of a criminal court judge. It's just the way it is. Other people will wind up here because of a simple twist of fate. Twenty-four years plus, with some seventy citations, two life-saving citations. He had two disciplinary problems. One was the blue flu and the other he went home for lunch. He was not one of those 'killer cops' we've been reading about the last three days in the papers. Something would have manifested itself before the twenty-four years' and three months' time. It was Fate...Fate brought him to that corner. Fate brought him to this courtroom. And now his Fate lies in your hands, Judge."

And: "You know, my father was a college graduate, but he never really made anything of it. He was a clothing salesman. But he was a very wise man. He told me when I feel strongly about an issue I should work all the harder to see the other side of the issue. And I've done that in this case. I have been on the other side of this issue. I have been involved in racism from the other side, white racism. And I don't say this is black racism, but the racial aspects of the case – the way people lined up – should not be ignored. The truth is a great disinfectant. I understand the strong feelings on both sides. It has a 250-year history to it. But he is not the white police officer that comes in and looks to dominate the black community."

And: "Walter dove into the car and, according to citizens, Walter delivered the first blow. They saw his arm going up and down. What is there about this case that endeared Mr. Budzyn to the media, and to Judge Jackson, that makes everybody hate Larry Nevers? He spoke up after the first trial. He was very frustrated. He couldn't believe that the jury had convicted him because he had given so much to the community. Cancer has a way of humbling people. And I go back to where I started; even the Free Press recognizes this should be a time for healing, the time when both sides say they can never agree, but enough is enough. The community suffered enough. The Nevers family suffered enough."

And I spoke, saying among other things: "Even if I had been found innocent I would be intensely remorseful for the rest of my life about Malice Green's death, or any person's death for that matter. But the remorse I feel about the death of Malice Green and about the waste of twenty-four years as one of Detroit's best street cops deals with the true enemy of the community – cocaine. Malice Green was the victim of cocaine abuse. Crack cocaine brought him to that dope house. Crack cocaine, not a willful obstruction of the law but a crack cocaine high, drove him to disobey a police officer's verbal command. A senseless, drug-driven impulse drove Malice Green to resist what began as a non-physical effort to control him and to arrest him. Things happen quickly on the streets, Your Honor. When someone resists arrest you don't stop and take notes. But among the images of those moments I will carry with me forever there is this. I asked myself repeatedly, why is this man resisting like this? It was about nothing except a few rocks of cocaine, Your Honor. That's all. But cocaine possession is a felony and my job was to take guns and drugs off the streets."

"Some people," I said, "have expressed resentment that I would stand up and tell the truth as I see it. And as I lived it. But telling the truth about this is my only compulsion. I am suffering from emphysema and recovering from lung cancer and whatever time I have left I would like to spend with my family."

Boykin said: "All right. Anyone else have anything to say?"

Neil and Baker dueled a bit more, with Neil pointing out Baker's history of making Walter a mad-dog assailant whenever Baker was trying Walter, and making me the cause of all damage whenever he was trying me. Boykin said none of that mattered and none of the media coverage mattered. And then he gave me, essentially, another murder-two sentence on my manslaughter conviction.

"Mr. Nevers," Boykin intoned, "it is the sentence of this court that you be incarcerated for a period of seven to fifteen years with the Michigan Department of Corrections. This is eighty-four months to fifteen years. You have already served 1,543 days. That credit will be applied to the minimum sentence of seven years."

Neil asked, unsuccessfully, for bond pending appeal. He asked, unsuccessfully, for two weeks to appeal Boykin's ruling on the bond and to firm up the prison's knowledge of, and preparation for dealing with, my health condition. Boykin remained unimpressed by anything the defense had to say.

And they handcuffed me and led me away once again.

23

FREE, AND NEVER FREE

The legal pundits estimated Boykin's sentence meant I would serve another eighteen months in prison, counting time served in Texas and time reduced for my highly predictable good behavior. What with the cancer uncertainty, it crossed my mind maybe a thousand times a day that I might never go home alive. Meanwhile, there would be no Mutt-and-Jeff escort to Texas, no poker games, and the only postage stamps I'd see were the ones I used to send grim letters from Oaks Correctional Facility. The state of Michigan had decided that this time they could guarantee my safety right here in the Great Lakes State. Of course they could. They sent me to Oaks, a maximum-security prison, even though I was eligible for a facility with a lot more "freedom." Whether it was going to be eighteen months or three years or more, I would be practically in "the hole" the entire time, locked down in a one-man cell except for one hour of yard time per day. On the other hand, I did get to talk with a couple of other prisoners in the "yard" – such as that black patrolman in for an off-duty shooting death, who told me he had become a cop because that rogue white cop "Starsky." Oaks was definitely going to be the second worst time of my life, after those late hours of November 5, 1992, when I grappled with the news that Malice Green had died.

I hadn't yet gotten my bearings for this second trip to Oaks when the criminal justice system reached into its bag of tricks again. Neil Fink, you'll recall, had argued with Boykin, to no avail, against the prosecution's request that the jury be allowed to consider the "lesser- included cognate offense" of involuntary manslaughter. Then, when the jury found me not guilty of second-degree murder but pounced on the "compromise" and found me guilty of manslaughter, Neil had argued with Boykin – again to no avail – that I should remain free on bond pending appeal. The rationale for an appeal bond was that the Michigan Supreme Court had been all but begging for a case that would allow it to prevent trolling for compromise convictions by giving juries the last-minute option of lesser-included offenses. This was the main basis of our high hopes for overturning Trial Two's result on appeal. On May 26, 2000 – just ten days after they led me away for the second time – the Michigan Court of Appeals agreed with our argument in a roundabout way. The appeals judges read the Supreme Court's smoke signals the same way we did and ordered me freed on an appeal bond. Do I need to bother trying to explain how much joy I felt? After just ten days in virtual solitary, and with at least a year and a half or more of the same ahead of me, I was at bottom and sinking. Then, just like that, I was an optimistic guy headed back home to get ready for the appeal.

This time the good news lasted forty-nine days.

The Michigan Supreme Court's signals were perfectly clear to my lawyers and to the Court of Appeals (no friends of mine, having refused to overturn Trial One while I was in Texas). But the state Supremes declared that an appeal bond could not be granted on an "assaultive crime" unless there is clear and convincing evidence that the appeal raises a substantial question of law or fact. I thought we had a number of clear issues, such as Baker getting a jury to believe I had forged my run book . . . but, hey, I'm not a lawyer. And I suppose you have to be me to believe these guys were influenced by the politics of my case, or the fact that I had very publicly said what I thought of them. At any rate, on July 17, 2000, the Supreme Court revoked my appeal bond and ordered me to surrender by 3 p.m. the next day for return to Oaks Correctional Facility and the remainder of Boykin's sentence. My appeal would go forward, but because the appeals process does not break any speed limits I would no doubt serve out my time even if eventually I were to be found "not guilty." Keep in mind that as an eternal optimist I had high hopes for winning my appeal, and imagine the devastation I felt at going back to prison anyway.

So for the third time in the matter of Malice Green's death, I extended my wrists to be handcuffed, and was transported to prison. I would have plenty of time to think of how if Malice Green had surrendered as readily, he would be alive and I would be a respected former police officer. Darin Chase told the Free Press that considering my health, this third trip to prison amounted to "cruel and unusual punishment."

As the most notorious inmate at a 750-bed maximum prison, and as someone who had been responsible for countless felons winding up in such places, I'd have to say it would have amounted to "cruel and unusual" even if I were young and in perfect health. Michigan in winter is not Miami, and my one hour a day of "freedom" from my cell was outdoors – as was my only telephone access. A big chunk of time I should have spent walking I instead spent hunkered down at an outdoor pay phone. In my cell I read. I wrote letters. I wrote notes about my appeal. I worked on this book. I counted days. I read a book by a guy who spent months traveling Nevada and playing my favorite game, blackjack. I suppose I occasionally pondered the fact that just a couple miles outside Oaks's razor wire, free citizens at a tribal casino were making decisions about whether to stay with the hand they were dealt or double up their bets. I reinstituted my "no visitors" policy, but a few friends from outside the family broke the rule and drove up to Manistee. I appreciated the visits, but I really couldn't handle having to talk by phone with someone sitting two feet away. The yard pay phone was my real contact with the outside world, and Nancy once again went back to her cheerleading role. I kept my mind in shape, if not my body, and weathered a winter. Everybody survives life by looking ahead to good things. I focused on parole.

I didn't stay at Oaks as long as the pundits expected, or as long as I expected for that matter. Darin and Nancy and others kept the pressure on Lansing. Governor Engler did not pardon me, but I suspect the executive branch played a role in the Corrections Department deciding that nine months in solitary was enough for their model prisoner with less than half his breathing capacity. Word filtered back to me that during one lobbying session at Corrections headquarters a bureaucrat said someone at Oaks had reported seeing me playing cards every day in the recreation room. Aside from that not being true, the fact is Oaks does not even have a recreation room. In May 2001, the Corrections Department released me on an electronic tether. The news media didn't pick up on that until several days after the fact, and didn't care much anyway. The Free Press ran a small item on an inside page. Michael Duggan, the new Wayne County prosecutor (to be replaced three years later by Kym Worthy) said the Corrections Department had made a big mistake, and that I should remain incarcerated for Boykin's full sentence. In all, my three trips to prison added up to five years and eighty days. Considering I view that as five years and eighty days too many, and Mike Duggan wasn't even working as a lawyer at the time of the Malice Green trial, I have to say he had no idea what he was talking about. No doubt the same staff that had pressed for a murder charge kept him informed.

Nancy had accepted a buyout from her job after thirty-six years. The cash allowed us to move out of the "mansion" where we had overstayed our time. We bought a place in Macomb County, about twenty miles from the city limits and a few miles farther from the precinct I knew as well as I knew the few paces in my prison cell. I was released under literal "house" arrest, not allowed to leave home except for doctor appointments and haircuts. A new phone line was installed, a direct connection to my parole officer. The phone was to be used for no purpose except for my case officer to check up on me. On my second or third day at home, the special phone rang and I answered. It was a telemarketer. I forget what he was selling.

Parole came that summer and would last two years after my six months on tether. As a parolee, I was free to leave the house but forbidden to keep company with anyone possessing a gun – which included most of my friends, who as police officers were required to carry a gun even off-duty. I couldn't leave Michigan. Gradually, the system was giving me back my freedom. I could lead the rest of my life without threat of being led away again in handcuffs. I would never really have my life back, of course, unless I cleared my name and made the world see the difference between murder and a legitimate arrest gone bad. So the appeals process marched on. Even so late in the game the criminal justice system, especially the Michigan Supreme Court, still had some yo-yo surprises in store for me.

Some of you understand entirely, and some probably do not, that when you go before an appellate court it is nothing like rehearing the trial. It strictly has to do with mistakes made by the court and the prosecutor. If you attend your own appellate hearing after going through a major trial and incarceration as I did, it is one weird experience. There is no defense table. You find a seat in the audience, like anyone else. The arguments by prosecution and your appeals lawyer have nothing to do with the facts of the case. It's not about you or the events in question; it's about the law and whether the legal system made "reversible" mistakes. It's like an out-of-body experience. You are sitting there, but it's as if you're not present. The whole proceeding is about you, but at the same time it's not about you at all. In March 2003, I sat in an auditorium at Wayne State University and listened as an Appeals Court panel wrestled with the Supreme Court's smoke signals about lesser cognate offenses, and Boykin's refusal to limit his jury instructions to the charge of second-degree murder. In my entire march through the criminal justice system, it was probably my happiest day in court. The judges understood. In fact, they didn't bother with any of our other appeals issues. A couple of them were even sarcastic in their questioning of the prosecutor's appellate lawyer, and in their sense that the Michigan Supreme Court itself had told judges like Boykin to avoid setting the stage for compromise verdicts. Result? Trial Two was overturned, just as Judge Zatkoff had overturned Trial One. The bad news was the fact that many would regard this as a mere "technicality." The still-worse news was that the Prosecutor's Office still had avenues to pursue against me.

Pete Waldmeier, senior columnist at the Detroit News, wrote a piece about my newest status in legal limbo. Here's a sample: "Retrying Nevers for a third time in the 1992 beating death of drug addict Malice Green just doesn't make any sense for Duggan, even politically. If he was running for election this year, maybe it would earn him some brownie points in the Detroit community. But realistically, you can only kick a guy so many times when he's down just because you're convinced he's guilty, but his trials keep getting screwed up. After a while, Nevers, who has lung cancer and has spent five of the last 10 years in jail, becomes exactly what you're trying to avoid: a victim and an apparent target of personal frustration . . . Now, the ball's back in the prosecutor's court. Duggan's the new headman, and Doug Baker's a key aide. So, what's next? Go through another emotional, divisive trial and have Nevers end up getting time-served, too? Enough, already."

Trial *Three*? Was that possible? Well, yes. After all, Duggan told the Free Press the Corrections Department screwed up when it released me before Boykin's sentence was complete. Walter was a guilty man appealing his manslaughter conviction from his own Trial Two. Meanwhile, I now stood as an innocent man, despite having been to prison more than a year longer than Walter. Nothing this Prosecutor's Office might do in pursuing its version of the Malice Green incident could possibly surprise me. But before even considering a Trial Three, there was the matter of whether the Michigan Supreme Court saw this one particular Boykin screw-up as clearly as the Court of Appeals did. The prosecution wasted no time taking the Appeals Court decision straight to Michigan's highest court. My scoreboard there stood at Supremes 2, Nevers 0 – the justices had refused to overturn my Trial One (they were obliterated on that one by a federal judge, and the prosecution failed to reverse that decision despite pursuing it all the way to the U.S. Supreme Court), and the state justices had overturned the Court of Appeals in revoking my appeal bond and sending me back to prison the third time. So while I had a lot of faith in the merit of our appeal, I had no faith in the elected members of the Michigan Supreme Court. Still, I remained in my usual stance of eternal optimist.

My record before the Supreme Court went to 0-3 in September 2003. The news media barely took notice. It would take a lawyer to explain why the elected justices, in their alleged wisdom, ruled that the issue of lesser- included offenses did not apply to my case – even though both Neil Fink and my appeals lawyer, to say nothing of the Court of Appeals – were confident that the state's highest court had said it did. So we went back to the Court of Appeals, which hadn't even bothered to address our other appellate issues, including prosecutorial misconduct. The appeals judges refused even to take those matters to a hearing. We appealed that refusal back to the Supreme Court and were shut out again – ending the string there at 0-for-4. If a lawyer did explain all this for you, the bottom line would be that I had due-process claims that could be appealed to the federal courts. It would be good to take it all to some judges who don't have to run for re-election and are far removed from Detroit politics. But sorry, no. Time and cash both have their limits. After two trial courts, four appellate courts, and three trips to prison, the official record appears to be sealed. The criminal justice system has determined that I am a felon.

It is a very hard thing for a dedicated police officer to accept designation as a felon when he believes, passionately, that he is not a felon. As you are well aware by now, I do *not* accept. I believe I was doing my job and wound up in a bad situation that for many reasons – pre-ordained by the chemistry of cocaine – resulted in Malice Green's death. My refusal to accept being a felon drives the legal establishment, and the pundits and racial politicians, nuts. I am convinced this had a lot to do with what happened on two different sentencing days in two different courts. Stoic Walter got points for keeping his mouth shut. The legal system wanted me to declare myself guilty, and then piled it on when I refused. The commentators branded me as a "whiner" for speaking my mind. Do you suppose if a jury refused to convict me, then Doug Baker and John O'Hair and Ulysses Boykin would have stood on a soapbox and proclaimed how much they believed my innocence? I don't think so. We know what the mob was chanting in that regard. The buzz said that if the first verdict had gone the other way there would have been not whining, but rioting. There was a second trial and another verdict, but I think I've made it pretty clear that a "new trial" in this case was a pipe dream. I think I've made it equally clear that come sentencing day Judge Boykin piled it on with enthusiasm. I can't reverse any of that. But I can write down my story, and now I have.

Walter lost the appeal of his own Trial Two. The Michigan Supreme Court refused to review a negative ruling by the Court of Appeals. Walter, always quiet, always a workaholic, had a job at the time as manager of a VFW club. How vindictive could the prosecutors be with Walter? His time served in Texas added up to just a couple days less, literally, than the minimum sentence. There was lots of talk about putting him back in the slam even if only for a few days. Instead they put him on an electronic tether. Meanwhile, despite the exemplary life Walter had led since leaving Texas, his parole officer made him give up his job because the VFW he managed served alcoholic beverages.

There's an old saying that offers one way of trying to figure things out when you are confronted by a complex story and you aren't entirely sure where to turn. It says: "Follow the money." If you follow the money in the Malice Green incident, you will find a police chief and a mayor and a city council and a medical examiner's office that screwed up in more ways than you can count. At the very least, the money trail puts an exclamation point on the hysteria that rolled over the Green case at every step. The bottom line is that almost everybody involved, except Walter and me, collected a lot of money from the City of Detroit or the County of Wayne. In my deer-in-the-headlights frame of mind, I can't help but think any appeals judge understood that if Walter and I had prevailed in the end, all these other settlements and judgments would look like nothing by comparison. Whether this entered into the wisdom of the appellate bench or not, the other half of the equation is a fact. Consider the money trail and you'll see what I mean.

The big number, of course, was the $5.2 million awarded to the Green family in world-record time. I've told you about that. The other shoe dropped while Walter and I were in prison. U.S. District Judge Gerald Rosen said various lawyers who piggybacked onto that lawsuit were "maximizing attorneys' fees for an ever-growing number of attorneys who have done little, if any, real legal work in this case." It figures they had little work to do, seeing as someone in the police department obviously handed them key information and greased the skids for a settlement while I was in court for Trial One's preliminary examination. In a rare move, Judge Rosen not only chided the lawyers for their greed but slashed the $1.7 million in fees they had deducted for their "efforts." Meanwhile, the Green family was still bickering about what was left of the money in the summer of 2001. Malice Green's daughter, Jacqueline Dennison, an Illinois resident, went to court in an effort to remove her stepmother, Green's estranged wife Rose Mary, as administrator of the estate. The court paperwork said Rose Mary Green, who had never held a job paying more than $6 an hour, had squandered money and billed the estate $125 an hour for her duties in administering the estate – including attendance at "justice" rallies.

Bobby Lessnau, in a rush to go back to the job he loved

as I told you, quickly settled for more than $400,000 soon after he was acquitted. That payout was discussed at the city council meeting where Darin Chase was kicked and jeered as he returned to his seat after speaking. The other suspended officers took longer to be compensated for the injustice inflicted on them, and it cost the city dearly. The Detroit News reported in 1997 that my old friends in the City Law Department had advised the city council to accept various additional settlements or awards involving Jim Kijek, Karl Gunther, Paul Gotelaere and Sergeant Freddie Douglas. The meter at that point stood at $4.5 million and counting, with interest payments mounting by the day. Ever so reluctantly, the amounts were approved. I'm not sure in the end whether the total went above $4.5 million, rivaling the amount paid to the Green family. Karl Gunther, like Bobby Lessnau, stayed on the force. I'm told that every year – and to this day for all I know – he would ask for a trial board. One result of a trial board could be his firing. Another result could be departmental embarrassment for having – I can't think of a better word – over-reacted in his suspension and dismissal. Last I heard, Karl was never given a trial board.

Remember Charles Henry, the black commander who was appointed to chair our board of review but was never able to get Stanley Knox to let the board do its work? A jury awarded Henry more than $1 million for his wrongful dismissal lawsuit. The irony is that Henry's revelations about the board of review emerged as Bobby Lessnau launched his own suit for wrongful dismissal. Henry got double the amount Bobby got. It pays to be a commander.

And let us not forget Kalil ("cocaine meant no more than the color of his eyes") Jiraki. The one fired person who in my opinion deserved firing was compensated very well for picking up a pink slip. A Wayne County jury awarded him $2.3 million after being convinced that Jiraki was fired because he refused to bend to coercion from Bader Cassin regarding cocaine on the autopsy report. Considering that cocaine *should* have been on that autopsy report, and considering that Bader Cassin

BORDERS®

signing

Larry Nevers

Good Cops, Bad Verdict

Thursday, July 26th   7:00 PM
Utica
45290 Utica Park Blvd. • 586.726.8555

The journal of Larry Never's nightmare that occurred after the very public arrest of Malice Green. He writes of testimonials, forensics and the battle he and his fellow officers fought to try to clear themselves.

Contact the store for details and event guidelines.

FL.053.172763

was never publicly willing to give the role of cocaine its due, Jiraki's court victory was doubly ironic. Mike Duggan was the chief mouthpiece for county government at the time, and an original respondent to Jiraki's suit. Maybe that's why he was so annoyed when, while he was prosecutor, I was released from prison for the final time. Remember, he was one of those Jiraki said was conspiring to get Walt and me acquitted. Only in Detroit.

I may be overlooking a settlement or an award that went to someone. Oh yeah – Lee Hardy's. But I come up with a rough calculation of at least $14 million in various awards and settlements, all resulting from administrative incompetence or stomping on due process or both. The people responsible for these awards are the same people who "brought Starsky and Hutch to justice." That is where you wind up if you follow the money trail in this case. No one who collected any of this money spent one day in jail. I can't imagine what the settlement total might have looked like if the criminal justice system had reached a verdict that Walter and I were just doing our jobs. Those who refuse to believe me and the other six suspended officers are fond of describing police conduct that night as "bizarre." I would suggest that all this money flying around resulted from bizarre conduct elsewhere. I'll even concede it points to a department that failed to do at least a minimal job of training and equipping those of us who were out there obeying one Stanley Knox directive no one ever heard much about – the one that ordered street officers to investigate all suspicious activity around dope houses.

So here I sit, apparently at the end of my legal avenues, with a large number of people thinking I am a murderer and a large number of people – at least among those who know Detroit – thinking I was a good cop who got tossed to the sharks. I suppose that will never change among those who are now alive. It bothers me that most of what made its way into print about the Malice Green incident for future generations follows the prosecution script right down the line. That's a serious wrong, and that's the main reason I put my story down on paper. I suppose that's selfish. But I also did it for all officers everywhere who do real police work. I know the vast majority of them will understand, and will say so even if they don't know me. Every street cop rolls the dice each time he winds up in a confrontational situation. You never know how the dice will fall. Sometimes what you find defies your experience and training – even if you have been out there many years and have made thousands of arrests.

Events in the arrest of Malice Green were unlike anything else I ever encountered. It's that simple. I regret with all my heart that he and I were brought together as police officer and arrest subject, and that twenty-four years of working the streets with no tools but my wits and my revolver ended with him a dead man and me a devastated man. There are police officers who have fired more rounds in one minute than I fired in more than two decades. And you won't find many who spent as many years on the street as I did, let alone in a highly productive booster car. You will find no Malice Greens in any of my other 6,000 or so days and nights as a police officer. I didn't brutalize street people who were known to me *for years* as felons. The prosecution's imaginary video, in which I brutalized someone I didn't even know, simply does not add up. That's why they had to use their imaginations and make it something it wasn't. The "drop gun" and supposed run-book forgery alone were enough to make me a bitter man. I hope I've helped you understand why.

The racial stuff and the hysteria? What more can I say? No one who knows Walter and me – and for that matter anyone who does a close examination of our career records – will believe for a moment that the events of November 5, 1992, happened because Malice Green was a black man. Like they say, you could look it up. On the other hand, I defy anyone to argue with a straight face that the way the criminal justice system came after us was about anything except race. Just read the Malice Green funeral sermon. Just examine the facts about the NAACP's role in it all. If the white cops in this story weren't stereotyped and racially profiled, nobody ever was. Like I said back at the beginning, I'm not a sociologist. So I don't know what to make of all that. I'm not qualified. But those who supposedly are qualified got that part of it all wrong.

Back at the beginning, I also said Walter and I were just two cops doing their jobs. I said that was a cliché, but that it is absolutely true. In the end, after filling in the blanks for you, that's really all there is to say. It should have been enough.

ACKNOWLEDGEMENTS

My family has been my rock and my inspiration since the fateful night of November 5, 1992. But countless people – most of them strangers – stepped forward with spiritual, emotional, and financial support that touched my heart deeply, helped me immeasurably, and will never be forgotten. There is not enough space to mention you all here, and frankly I am more worried about unintentionally leaving someone off my gratitude list. You know who you are, and you know how much I thank you.

Just a few special words, however, are required for:

Darin, the one I called the "kid that came out of nowhere." Darin was a young, up-and-coming businessman who recognized immediately that I was facing a political lynching. Without his clear-thinking, political savvy, and all-around good-sense I would probably still be in prison. He was absolutely the driving force in gaining release and retrial. Thank you, Dink!

Mark Scott, not just a radio personality but a true warrior, did not live to see this book in print. Early on, Mark was the only media personality in town who stood up for the truth while most called for my head. Mark's platform was always "Let's hear both sides of this case before we pass judgment." I was proud to call you my friend. May you rest in peace.

Friendship, dedication and hard work from key members of the support group - Diane and Sue, Len and Barb, Nick, Rita, and Vickie - will always be remembered.

My good friend Paul Fitzgerald fought the good fight against his debilitating illness even as he fought to enlighten those who did not understand what happened. A real police officer, and a real man. I miss him.

Without Lynne, this book would have never been written. Although I mapped out my story a thousand times in my mind, it was Lynne who encouraged and guided me as I set out to write it longhand in a prison cell. Lynne is a wonderful woman who is raising ten beautiful children but still found a way to devote immeasurable amounts of time to my cause. Thank you.

Into the despair of prison confinement came a letter from a fine gentleman named Grove – then another letter, and another. This stranger made sure I received at least a letter a week, more often two or three. Because of his generosity I was able to purchase food and other items from the prison commissary. Thank you, Grove, from the bottom of my heart for your tireless support.

All of my old sergeants and lieutenants will tell you that I could not have written these chapters in the way you have read them – but that they hear me and my story in every paragraph. That is a tribute to the professional assistance I had with some interviews, and the writing, editing and designing of this volume. Thank you for helping me get my story down on paper.